Fodor's 18th Edition

Bahamas

The Guide
for All Budgets

Completely
Updated

Where to Stay, Eat,
and Explore

On and Off
the Beaten Path

When to Go,
What to Pack

Maps, Travel Tips,
and Web Sites

Fodor's Travel Publications • New York, Toronto, London, Sydney, Auckland
www.fodors.com

Fodor's Bahamas

EDITOR: Paul Eisenberg

Editorial Contributors: Kathy Borsuk, Michael de Zayas, JoAnn Milivo-jevic, Daniel J. Taras, Chelle Koster Walton
Editorial Production: Tom Holton
Maps: David Lindroth, *cartographer*; Rebecca Baer and Robert Blake, *map editors*
Design: Fabrizio La Rocca, *creative director*; Guido Caroti, *art director*; Jolie Novak, *senior picture editor*; Melanie Marin, *photo editor*
Cover Design: Pentagram
Production/Manufacturing: Yexenia (Jessie) Markland
Cover Photograph: Stephen Frink/Tony Stone Images

Copyright

Eighteenth Edition

ISBN 1–4000–1027–6

ISSN 1524–7945

Important Tip

Although all prices, opening times, and other details in this book are based on information supplied to us at press time, changes occur all the time in the travel world, and Fodor's cannot accept responsibility for facts that become outdated or for inadvertent errors or omissions. So **always confirm information when it matters,** especially if you're making a detour to visit a specific place.

Special Sales

Fodor's Travel Publications are available at special discounts for bulk purchases for sales promotions or premiums. Special editions, including personalized covers, excerpts of existing guides, and corporate imprints, can be created in large quantities for special needs. For more information, contact your local bookseller or write to Special Markets, Fodor's Travel Publications, 280 Park Avenue, New York, NY 10017. Inquiries from Canada should be directed to your local Canadian bookseller or sent to Random House of Canada, Ltd., Marketing Department, 2775 Matheson Boulevard East, Mississauga, Ontario L4W 4P7. Inquiries from the United Kingdom should be sent to Fodor's Travel Publications, 20 Vauxhall Bridge Road, London SW1V 2SA, England.

PRINTED IN THE UNITED STATES OF AMERICA

10 9 8 7 6 5 4 3 2 1

CONTENTS

5 Turks and Caicos Islands   *179*

6 Portraits of the Bahamas   *204*

Index   *219*

Maps and Plans

ON THE ROAD WITH FODOR'S

THE MORE YOU KNOW before you go, the better your trip will be. The Bahamas's most fascinating small museum (or its most enticing beachfront grill) could be just around the corner from your hotel, but if you don't know it's there, it might as well be on the other side of the globe. That's where this book comes in. It's a great step toward making sure your next trip lives up to your expectations. As you plan, check out the Web as well. Guidebooks have been helping smart travelers for years; the Web is one more tool. Whatever reference you consult, always consider the source. Images and language can be massaged to make places appear better than they are. And one traveler's quaint is another's grimy.

Here at Fodor's, and at our on-line arm, Fodors.com, our goal is to provide you with useful, accurate information. Our editors put enormous effort into getting things right, beginning with the search for the best contributors. There's no substitute for advice from a like-minded friend who has just come back from where you're going, but our writers, having seen all the corners of the Bahamas, are the next best thing. If you knew them, you'd poll for tips yourself.

Although a native of the Windy City, **Kathy Borsuk** now enjoys the much warmer trade winds of the Turks and Caicos Islands. She is managing editor of *Times of the Islands,* a quarterly publication covering the stunning natural resources, fascinating history, interesting personalities, and varied hotel and restaurant choices in the Turks and Caicos. Kathy wouldn't trade her job for anything.

Michael de Zayas, a twentysomething Cuban-American poet and writer from Miami, snorkeled and explored caves in the Bahamas during childhood vacations. Visiting Nassau and five Out Islands on a four-seater plane for this assignment inspired him to begin flying lessons for his next trip. Besides the Bahamas, he has covered Anguilla, Argentina, Chile, Cuba, El Salvador, Florida, Mexico, New York

City, St. Martin, Spain, and Uruguay for Fodor's. He rests in New York City when not traveling.

JoAnn Milivojevic is a Chicago-based free-lance writer whose Caribbean stories have appeared in magazines and newspapers nationwide. Her CD, "Confessions of a Caribbean Addict," includes collected stories of her island adventures.

Geographer, photographer, writer, and chef **Daniel J. Taras** has spent the last 10 years criss-crossing the globe, with extended layovers in Africa, New York, Mexico, Oregon, and Hawai'i, where he owned and operated a sushi bar and café. Feeling overworked, he retired from the restaurant business, took up writing and photography, and now rarely works at all. Daniel is a frequent contributor to Fodor's, and updated Smart Travel Tips A to Z for this book. He was last spotted shoveling snow in the mountains of British Columbia.

Chelle Koster Walton admits she's a "fair-weather writer." She specializes in travel to Florida and the Caribbean for such publications as *FamilyFun, Caribbean Travel & Life, Endless Vacation,* and the *Miami Herald.* A resident of Sanibel Island, Florida, for 20 years, she is author of several guidebooks, including the *Sarasota, Sanibel Island & Naples Book, Fun with the Family in Florida, Insight Orlando,* and *Adventure Guide to Tampa Bay & Florida's West Coast.*

Don't Forget to Write

Your experiences—positive and negative—matter to us. If we have missed or misstated something, we want to hear about it. We follow up on all suggestions. Contact the Bahamas editor at editors@fodors.com or c/o Fodor's, 280 Park Avenue, New York, New York 10017. And have a fabulous trip!

Karen Cure
Editorial Director

The Bahamas

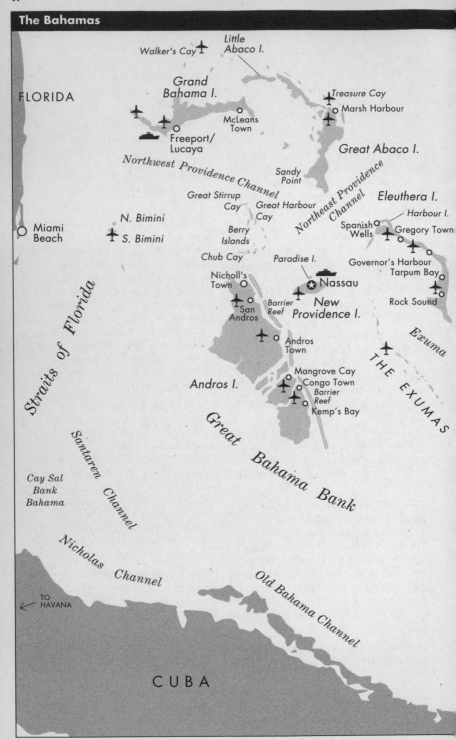

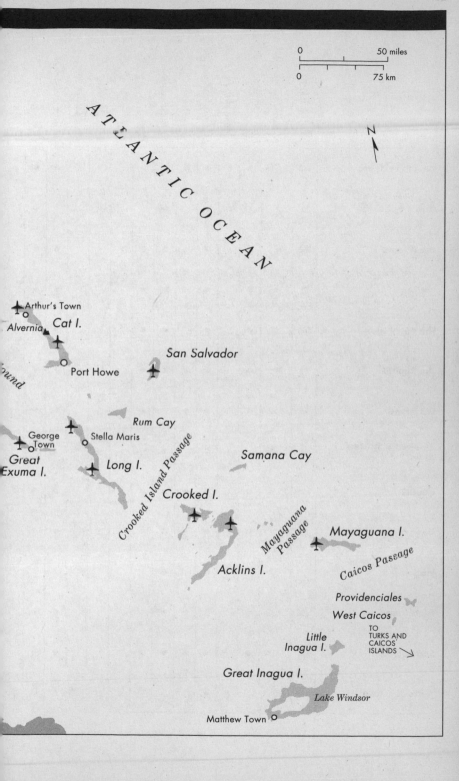

A T L A N T I C   O C E A N

N

Arthur's Town

Alvernia **Cat I.**

Port Howe

San Salvador

Rum Cay

George
Town   Stella Maris

**Great
Exuma I.**   **Long I.**

Samana Cay

Crooked Island Passage

Crooked I.

*Mayaguana
Passage*

Mayaguana I.

Caicos Passage

Acklins I.

Providenciales

West Caicos

TO
TURKS AND
CAICOS
ISLANDS

*Little
Inagua I.*

Great Inagua I.

Lake Windsor

Matthew Town

ound

Island Finder

	Cost of Island	Number of rooms	Nonstop flights (from the U.S.)	Cruise ship port	U.S. dollars accepted	Historic sites	Natural beauty	Lush	Arid	Mountainous	Rain forest	Beautiful beaches	Good roads
New Providence	$$$	8,645	•	•	•	•	•					•	•
Grand Bahama	$$	3,598		•	•		•					•	•
The Abacos	$$$	835	•		•		•	•				•	•
Andros	$$	315	•		•		•	•				•	•
The Berry Islands	$$$	91	•		•		•	•				•	•
The Biminis	$$	229	•		•	•	•	•				•	•
Cat Island	$$	132	•		•	•	•	•				•	•
Crooked & Acklins Islands	$$	53			•		•					•	
Eleuthera	$$$	537	•		•	•	•	•				•	•
The Exumas	$$	189	•		•	•	•	•				•	•
Inagua	$	17			•		•						
Long Island	$$$	106	•		•	•	•	•				•	•
San Salvador	$$$	328	•		•	•	•	•				•	•
Turks & Caicos	$$$	2,059		•	•				•			•	

	Public transportation	Fine dining	Local cuisine	Shopping	Music	Casinos	Nightlife	Diving and Snorkeling	Sailing	Golfing	Hiking	Ecotourism	Villa rentals	All-inclusives	Luxury resorts	Secluded getaway	Good for families	Romantic hideaway
	●	●	●	●	●	●	●	●	●			●	●	●	●		●	
	●	●	●	●	●	●	●	●	●			●	●	●	●		●	
		●	●	●	●		●	●				●			●	●	●	●
			●					●	●			●	●	●	●	●	●	●
		●	●					●	●	●		●	●		●	●	●	●
		●	●	●	●		●	●	●			●			●	●	●	●
			●					●	●		●	●	●			●	●	●
			●					●						●		●		
		●	●	●	●		●	●	●			●	●	●	●	●	●	●
		●	●		●			●				●	●	●	●	●	●	●
			●					●				●	●			●		●
		●	●		●			●				●	●		●	●	●	●
		●	●					●	●				●	●	●	●	●	●
			●			●		●	●	●			●	●	●	●		●

ESSENTIAL INFORMATION

ADDRESSES

"Whimsical" might best describe Bahamas addresses. Streets change name for no apparent reason, and many buildings have no numbers. In more remote locations, such as the Out Islands, street addresses often aren't used. To find your destination, you might have to ask a local. Postal codes aren't used throughout the Bahamas.

AIR TRAVEL

Most international flights to the Bahamas—to Nassau, Freeport, and the Out Islands alike—connect through cities in Florida, New York, or Atlanta, depending on the airline. Most domestic flights make a quick stop in Miami. If you are flying to the Out Islands, you may have to make a connection in both Florida and Nassau. British Airways flies direct from London to Nassau; Alitalia has a direct route from Milan to Freeport during summer months only.

BOOKING

When you book **look for nonstop flights** and **remember that "direct" flights stop at least once.** Try to avoid connecting flights, which require a change of plane. For more booking tips and to check prices and make on-line flight reservations, log on to www.fodors.com.

CARRIERS

A few major U.S. carriers fly into the Bahamas. British Airways is the only European carrier with flights into Nassau—about 3 per week. Other European carriers get you as close as Miami.

Continental codeshare partner Gulfstream International Airways has nearly 200 flights per day in Florida and the Bahamas—Fort Lauderdale, Miami and West Palm Beach to Nassau, Freeport, Treasure Cay, Paradise Island, Marsh Harbour, and North Eleuthera. Delta flies direct to Nassau from New York, Orlando, and Atlanta. Trans World Airlines flies nonstop from New York's JFK to Nassau. US Airways flies direct from Philadelphia and Charlotte, North Carolina, to Nassau; from Miami to North Eleuthera and Governor's Harbour; from Orlando to Treasure Cay; and from West Palm Beach to Treasure Cay and Marsh Harbour. From Canada, Air Canada flies from Montréal and Toronto to Nassau and Freeport (seasonally).

There are also smaller airlines with service to the Bahamas. Air Sunshine flies out of Fort Lauderdale to Marsh Harbour, Treasure Cay, New Bight on Cat Island, Governor's Harbour, and George Town. American Eagle flies to Nassau, Freeport, Governor's Harbour, Marsh Harbour, George Town, and Treasure Cay from Miami. Bahamasair, the national carrier of the Bahamas, flies from Miami, Orlando, and Fort Lauderdale to Nassau, with connections to George Town, Stella Maris, Marsh Harbour, Treasure Cay, Acklins, Andros, Cat Island, Eleuthera (North Eleuthera, Governor's Harbour, and Rock Sound), George Town, Inagua, Stella Maris, and San Salvador. There's a direct flight from West Palm Beach to Marsh Harbour. Chalks Ocean Airways flies to Paradise Island, Bimini, and Walkers Cay from Fort Lauderdale and Miami. Comair flies to Nassau from Cincinnati and Orlando. Island Express flies from Fort Lauderdale to Marsh Harbour, Treasure Cay, and North Eleuthera, as well as to Turks and Caicos. Lynx Air International connects Fort Lauderdale to Marsh Harbour, Freeport, Cat Island, and George Town, Great Exuma. Twin Air flies out of Fort Lauderdale to Abaco, Eleuthera, Treasure Cay, and Governor's Harbour.

To reach the more remote islands, fly Bahamasair or charter a plane at Nassau International Airport through Sky Unlimited. Cherokee Air runs charters from Marsh Harbour. Major Air flies out of Freeport. Some Grand Bahama and Out Islands lodgings charter planes for guests, so *see* Chapters 3 and 4 as well. For service throughout the Bahamas and Caribbean, including Jamaica and Puerto Rico, check with LeAir—they, like many charters, offer an air ambulance service as well as normal charters.

To travel interisland within the Turks and Caicos, contact Sky King or other local charters.

➤ MAJOR AIRLINES FROM THE U.S. AND CANADA: **Air Canada** (☏ 888/ 247–2262, WEB www.aircanada.ca). **Gulfstream International Airways** (☏ 800/525–0280, WEB www. gulfstreamair.com). **Delta** (☏ 800/ 221–1212 or 800/241–4141, WEB www.delta.com). **Trans World Airlines** (☏ 800/221–2000 or 800/ 231–0856, WEB www.twa.com). **US Airways** (☏ 800/428–4322, WEB www.usair.com).

➤ SMALLER AIRLINES: **Air Sunshine** (☏ 800/327–8900 or 954/434–8900, WEB www.airsunshine.com). **American Eagle** (☏ 800/433–7300, WEB www. aa.com). **Bahamasair** (☏ 800/222– 4262, WEB www.bahamasair.com). **Bel Air Transport** (☏ 954/524–9814, WEB www.flybelair.com). **Chalks Ocean Airways** (☏ 800/424–2557, WEB www. chalksoceanairways.com). **Cherokee Air** (☏ 242/367–2089, WEB www. cherokeeair.com). **Comair** (☏ 800/ 354–9822, WEB www.comair.com). **Island Express** (☏ 954/359–0380). **Lynx Air International** (☏ 888/596– 9247, WEB www.lynxair.com). **Twin Air** (☏ 954/359–8266, WEB www. flytwinair.com).

➤ WITHIN THE BAHAMAS: **Bahamasair** (☏ 242/352–8341, WEB www. bahamasair.com). **LeAir** (☏ 242/ 377–2356, WEB www.bahamas.net/ leair). **Major Air** (☏ 242/352–5778). **Sky Unlimited** (☏ 242/377–8993, WEB www.bahamas.mall.bs).

➤ WITHIN THE TURKS AND CAICOS: **Sky King** (☏ 649/941–5464, WEB www.skyking.tc).

CHECK-IN AND BOARDING

Always **ask your carrier about its check-in policy.** Plan to arrive at the airport about two hours before your scheduled departure time for domestic flights and 2½ to 3 hours before international flights.

Airlines routinely overbook planes, assuming that not everyone with a ticket will show up, but sometimes everyone does. When that happens, airlines ask for volunteers to give up their seats. (This is a common occurrence in Miami.) In return, volunteers usually get a certificate for a free flight and are rebooked on the next flight out. If there are not enough volunteers, the airline must choose who will be denied boarding. The first to get bumped are passengers who checked in late and those flying on discounted tickets, so **get to the gate and check in as early as possible,** especially during peak periods. If you're not in a hurry to get to your destination and would like a couple hundred dollars' worth of free air travel, **volunteer at check-in so your name goes at the top of the list.** Always **bring a government-issued photo I.D. to the airport.** You may be asked to show it before you are allowed to check in.

CUTTING COSTS

The least expensive airfares to the Bahamas must usually be purchased in advance and are nonrefundable. It's smart to **call a number of airlines, and when you are quoted a good price, book it on the spot**—the same fare may not be available the next day. Always **check different routings** and look into using different airports. Travel agents, especially low-fare specialists, are helpful.

Consolidators are another good source. They buy tickets for scheduled international flights at reduced rates from the airlines, then sell them at prices that beat the best fare available directly from the airlines, usually without restrictions. Sometimes you can even get your money back if you need to return the ticket. Carefully read the fine print detailing penalties for changes and cancellations, and **confirm your consolidator reservation with the airline.**

➤ CONSOLIDATORS: **Cheap Tickets** (☎ 800/377–1000, WEB www. cheaptickets.com). **Up & Away Travel** (☎ 212/889–2345, WEB www.upandaway.com). **World Travel Network** (☎ 800/409–6753, WEB www.bestfares.com).

ENJOYING THE FLIGHT

For more legroom, **request an emergency-aisle seat.** Don't sit in the row in front of the emergency aisle or in front of a bulkhead, where seats may not recline. Ask the airline whether a snack or meal is served on the flight. If you have dietary concerns, **request special meals when booking.** These can be vegetarian, low-cholesterol, or kosher, for example. On long flights, try to maintain a normal routine, to help fight jet lag. At night, **get some sleep.** By day, **eat light meals, drink water** (not alcohol), and **move around the cabin** to stretch your legs. For additional jet-lag tips consult *Fodor's FYI: Travel Fit & Healthy* (available at bookstores everywhere).

FLYING TIMES

A direct flight from New York City to Nassau takes approximately three hours. The flight from Charlotte, North Carolina, to Nassau is two hours, and the flight from Miami to Governor's Harbour takes about an hour with a prop plane.

HOW TO COMPLAIN

If your baggage goes astray or your flight goes awry, complain right away. Most carriers require that you **file a claim immediately.**

➤ AIRLINE COMPLAINTS: U.S. Department of Transportation **Aviation Consumer Protection Division** (✉ C-75, Room 4107, Washington, DC 20590, ☎ 202/366–2220, WEB www. dot.gov/airconsumer). **Federal Aviation Administration Consumer Hotline** (☎ 800/322–7873, WEB www. faa.gov/apa).

AIRPORTS

The major gateways to the Bahamas include Freeport, on Grand Bahama Island, and Nassau, on New Providence Island. There are also some direct flights from Florida to Out Islands airports such as Marsh Har-

bour and Treasure Cay in the Abacos. *See* the A to Z sections *in* Chapter 4 for more airports.

➤ AIRPORT INFORMATION: **Freeport** (☎ 242/352–4504). **Nassau** (☎ 242/ 377–7281).

BIKE TRAVEL

Biking in the Bahamas is fairly easy due to the flat island terrain. Some hotels offer bikes as amenities to their guests, or rent them out—so do general stores. In the Out Islands and Turks and Caicos, bikes are often the most logical way to get around on land and match the laid-back pace of life. For the location of bike rental outlets, ☞ *see* the Biking sections of individual chapters.

BIKES IN FLIGHT

Most airlines accommodate bikes as luggage, provided they are dismantled and boxed. Airlines sell bike boxes for about $5 (it's at least $100 for bike bags). Your local bike shop probably has a free box, and they can pack it up for you. International travelers can sometimes substitute a bike for a piece of checked luggage at no charge; otherwise, the cost is about $100. Domestic and Canadian airlines charge $25–$50.

➤ BICYCLING RESOURCES: **Bahamas Amateur Cycling Federation** has information on upcoming races, and a listing of bike shops and local contacts (✉ Box CB–12352, Nassau, WEB www. xtremesp.tripod.com/bacf.html). **Wolf's Extreme Cycling** has information on triathlons in the Bahamas, as well as cycling (WEB www.xtremesp. tripod.com/wolf.html).

BOAT AND FERRY TRAVEL

If you're of an adventurous frame of mind, and have time to spare, you can revert to the mode of transportation that islanders used before the advent of air travel: ferries and the traditional mailboats, which regularly leave Nassau from Potter's Cay, under the Paradise Island bridge. You may find yourself sharing company with goats and chickens, and making your way on deck through piles of lumber. Fares vary from $20 to $70 each way, depending on the destination. **Don't plan to arrive or depart punctually;** the flexible schedules can be thrown off by bad weather. Remember, too, that they operate on Bahamian time, which is a casual, unpredictable measure. You cannot book ahead, and services are extremely limited. In Nassau, check details with the dockmaster's office at Potter's Cay. You can purchase tickets from the dockmaster or from the captain or mate just before departure.

Within the Bahamas, ferries connect Nassau to Harbour Island and North Eleuthera twice daily. Round-trip fares cost $90, and more expensive excursion rates are available. The trip from Nassau's Harbour Club to Harbour Island takes less than two hours; you can take advantage of the bar and food service on board.

Bahamas Fast Ferry connects Nassau to Harbour Island and Spanish Wells once daily departing at 8 AM, but leaves twice daily on Fridays only, at 8 AM and 1:30 PM. Boats from Nassau to Governor's Harbour (Eleuthera) sail twice weekly, on Friday at 7:30 AM and Sunday at 4:45 PM. Boats sail from Harbour Island to Nassau Monday–Thursday and Saturday at 3:55 PM, Friday at 10:25 AM and 3:55 PM, and Sunday at 2. From Governor's Harbour, boats depart Friday at 9:45 PM and Sunday at 7 PM. Travel times from Nassau to Harbour Island are 2¼ hours; from Nassau to Governor's Harbour, 2 hours. For information about mailboat service, contact the Potter's Cay dockmaster.

From Nassau, ferries are also available to North and South Cat Island (Arthur's Town, Bennett's Harbor, Bew Bight), San Salvador, Exuma (George Town), North Andros (Nicholl's Town, Mastic Point, Morgan Bluff), Harbour Island, Abaco (Sandy Point, Moore's Island, Bullock's Harbor, Berry Island), Eleuthera (Rock Sound, Davis Harbor, South Eleuthera), Mangrove Cay, Freeport, Ragged Island (Exuma Cays, Barraterre, Staniel Cay, Black Point, Farmer's Cay, Highbourne's Cay), and Central Andros (Fresh Creek, Stafford Creek, Blanket Sound, Staniard Creek, Behring Point.)

If you're setting sail yourself, note that cruising boats must clear customs at the nearest port of entry before begin-

ning any diving or fishing (you must have a permit for sports fishing, which costs $20 per trip; $150 per year).

➤ BOAT AND FERRY INFORMATION: **Bahamas Fast Ferry** (☎ 242/323–2166, FAX 242/322–8185, WEB www.bahamasferries.com). **Potter's Cay dockmaster** (☎ 242/393–1064).

BUS TRAVEL

Buses on New Providence Island and Grand Bahama are called jitneys, and are actually vans. Route numbers are clearly marked. Exact change of $1 is required, and while there are established stops, you can sometimes hail a jitney. Let the driver know where you would like to get off.

BUSINESS HOURS

BANKS AND OFFICES

Banks are open Monday–Thursday 9:30–3 and Friday 9:30–5. Commonwealth Bank opens at 8:30. Principal banks are Bank of the Bahamas, Bank of Nova Scotia, Barclays Bank, Canadian Imperial Bank of Commerce, Chase Manhattan Bank, Citibank, Commonwealth Bank, and Royal Bank of Canada. Most Bahamian offices observe bank hours.

MUSEUMS AND SIGHTS

Hours for attractions vary. Most open between 9 and 10 and close around 5.

PHARMACIES

Though some drugstores typically abide by normal store hours, some stay open 24 hours.

SHOPS

Shops in downtown Nassau are open Monday–Saturday 9–5. Grand Bahama's International Bazaar and Port Lucaya Marketplace are open 10–6. Most stores, with the exception of straw markets and malls, close on Sunday. **Shop in the morning,** when streets are less crowded. Remember that when you're shopping in Nassau, Freeport, and Port Lucaya, you may be competing with the hordes of passengers that pour off cruise ships daily.

CAMERAS AND
PHOTOGRAPHY

Frothy waves in a turquoise sea and palm-lined crescents of beach are relatively easy to capture on film if you **don't let the brightness of the sun on sand and water fool your light meter.** You'll need to compensate or else work early or late in the day when the light isn't as brilliant and contrast isn't such a problem. Try to **capture expansive views** of waterfront, beach, or village scenes; consider shooting down onto the shore from a clearing on a hillside or from a rock on the beach. Or **zoom in on something colorful,** such as a delicate tropical flower or a craftsman at work. Always **ask permission to take pictures of locals or their property** and **offer a gratuity.** The *Kodak Guide to Shooting Great Travel Pictures* (available at bookstores everywhere) is loaded with tips.

➤ PHOTO HELP: **Kodak Information Center** (☎ 800/242–2424).

EQUIPMENT PRECAUTIONS

Don't pack film and equipment in checked luggage, where it is much more susceptible to damage. X-ray machines used to view checked luggage are becoming much more powerful and therefore are much more likely to ruin your film. Always **keep film and tape out of the sun.** Carry an extra supply of batteries, and **be prepared to turn on your camera or camcorder** to prove to security personnel that the device is real. Always **ask for hand inspection of film,** which becomes clouded after repeated exposure to airport X-ray machines, and **keep videotapes away from metal detectors.**

FILM AND DEVELOPING

Film is expensive in the Bahamas, so it's best to buy it back home. Popular brands of film are available in Nassau and Freeport, with a more limited selection in the Out Islands. Likewise, you'll find film developing stores (some with one-hour service) in shopping centers in Nassau and Freeport, but developing likely will be pricier and more difficult to find in the Out Islands.

CAR RENTAL

To rent a car, you must be 21 years of age or older in both the Bahamas and the Turks and Caicos.

➤ MAJOR AGENCIES: **Alamo** (☎ 800/522–9696). **Avis** (☎ 800/331–1084; 800/879–2847 in Canada; 02/837–4428–47 in Australia; 09/275–7239 in New Zealand; 9/8899–1000 in the U.K. **Budget** (☎ 800/527–0700; 0870/607–5000 in the U.K., through affiliate Europcar). **Dollar** (☎ 800/800–6000; 612–92–23–1444 in Australia). **Hertz** (☎ 800/654–3001; 800/263–0600 in Canada; 020/8897–2072 in the U.K.; 02/9669–2444 in Australia; 09/256–8690 in New Zealand). **National Car Rental** (☎ 800/227–7368; 208/750–2800 in the U.K., where it is known as National Europe).

➤ LOCAL AGENCIES: **Wallace's Car Rental** (✉ Marathon and Wulff Rds., Nassau, ☎ 242/393–0650). **Zulu's Discount Rentals** (✉ Freeport International Airport, Freeport, ☎ 242/351–5232).

INSURANCE

When driving a rented car you are generally responsible for any damage to or loss of the vehicle as well as for any property damage or personal injury that you may cause. Before you rent, see what coverage your personal auto-insurance policy and credit cards provide.

REQUIREMENTS AND RESTRICTIONS

In the Bahamas your own driver's license is acceptable for up to three months. An International Driver's Permit is a good idea; it's available from the American or Canadian automobile association, and, in the United Kingdom, from the Automobile Association or Royal Automobile Club. These international permits are universally recognized, and having one in your wallet may save you a problem with the local authorities.

SURCHARGES

Before you pick up a car in one city and leave it in another, **ask about drop-off charges or one-way service fees,** which can be substantial. Note, too, that some rental agencies charge extra if you return the car *before* the time specified in your contract. To avoid a hefty refueling fee, **fill the tank prior to turning in the car,** but be aware that gas stations near the rental outlet may overcharge.

CAR TRAVEL

EMERGENCY SERVICES

In case of road emergency, **stay in your vehicle with emergency flashers engaged and wait for help,** especially after dark. If someone stops to help, relay information through a small opening in the window. If it's daylight and help does not arrive, walk to the nearest phone and call for help. In the Bahamas, motorists readily stop to help drivers in distress.

ROAD CONDITIONS

In and around Nassau, roads are good, although a bit crowded in high peak season. From 7–10 AM and 3–6 PM, downtown Nassau and most major arteries are congested with cars and pedestrians. When cruise ships are in, pedestrian traffic further stifles the flow. On Grand Bahama Island and the Out Islands, conditions vary from the perfectly paved and manicured boulevards in Freeport to severely potholed and winding roads of the countryside. **Make sure you have a spare tire in good condition and necessary tools.**

ROAD MAPS

Bahamas Trailblazer Maps and AT&T Road Maps, which are fairly dependable (some small streets and roads are not included), are distributed for free throughout the islands.

RULES OF THE ROAD

Remember, like the British, islanders **drive on the left side of the road,** which can be confusing because most cars are American with the steering wheel on the left. It is illegal, however, to make a left-hand turn on a red light. Many streets in downtown Nassau are one-way. Roundabouts pose further confusion to Americans. Remember to keep left and yield to oncoming traffic as you enter the roundabout and at GIVE WAY signs.

CHILDREN IN THE BAHAMAS

Be sure to plan ahead and **involve your youngsters** as you outline your trip. Take them to the library and **find children's books about life in the islands** to prepare them for the new culture they will be experiencing. Check out *The Bahamas* from the Enchantment of the World Book Series, by Martin and Stephen Hinta, to get your kids up to speed. When packing, include things to keep them busy en route. On sightseeing days, try to schedule activities of special interest to your children. If you are renting a car don't forget to **arrange for a car seat** when you reserve. Besides beaches, the Bahamas offers a variety of kid-friendly parks, museums, and natural attractions and plenty of chances to learn how to make local crafts. Many large resorts supervise children's programs. The Out Islands are less accommodating, but even the most remote, with their rich culture and family-centric lifestyles, are intriguing to children. **Make your visit a learning experience for the children** whenever possible. For general advice about traveling with children, check out *Fodor's FYI: Travel with Your Baby* (available in bookstores everywhere).

FLYING TO THE BAHAMAS

If your children are two or older, **ask about children's airfares.** As a general rule, infants under two not occupying a seat fly at greatly reduced fares or even for free. When booking, **confirm carry-on allowances** if you're traveling with infants. In general, for babies charged 10% of the adult fare you are allowed one carry-on bag and a collapsible stroller; if the flight is full, the stroller may have to be checked or you may be limited to less.

Experts agree that it's a good idea to use safety seats aloft for children weighing less than 40 pounds. Airlines set their own policies: U.S. carriers usually require that the child be ticketed, even if he or she is young enough to ride free, since the seats must be strapped into regular seats. Do **check your airline's policy about using safety seats during takeoff and landing.** And since safety seats are not allowed everywhere in the plane— typically they must be placed on window seats—get your seat assignments early.

When reserving, **request children's meals or a freestanding bassinet** if you need them. But note that bulkhead seats, where you must sit to use the bassinet, may lack an overhead bin or storage space on the floor.

FOOD

Nassau and Freeport have all the fast-food chains children love. Try to **introduce them to local cuisine,** which is entirely palatable to children. Peas 'n' rice, macaroni and cheese, and chicken are common specialties. Adventurous little ones will think it's fun eating conch fritters and johnnycake.

LODGING

Most hotels in the Bahamas allow children under a certain age to stay in their parents' room at no extra charge, but others charge for them as extra adults; be sure to **find out the cutoff age for children's discounts.** Club Med, Breezes, Sandals, and some small inns discourage or don't permit children. Be sure to ask. Other large resorts are designed around families. Resorts with fine kids' facilities and programs include Atlantis in Paradise Island, Radisson Cable Beach Resort, Nassau Marriott Resort, Royal Oasis Resort, Our Lucaya in Grand Bahama Island, Small Hope Bay in Andros, and Beaches in Providenciales.

PRECAUTIONS

Babies' and children's skin is highly susceptible to the strength of the tropical sun. Child-grade sun protection is available in Nassau, Freeport, and other large towns. If you're staying on an Out Island, **bring your own child-grade sun protection.**

It's also a good idea to check with locals before you head for a swim at a deserted beach—currents can sometimes be too rough for kids, and for many adults.

SIGHTS AND ATTRACTIONS

Places that are especially appealing to children are indicated by a rubber-duckie icon (🦆) in the margin.

SUPPLIES AND EQUIPMENT

Disposable diapers, baby formula, and other necessities are widely available throughout the Bahamas, though at a higher price than you would pay at home. **Take your own disposable diapers** so you will have the extra space for souvenirs on the trip home. For older children, you can find toys and games at stores throughout the islands, again at up to double what they would cost in the States. Straw markets sell inexpensive maracas and folk dolls.

COMPUTERS ON THE ROAD

If you are carrying a laptop into the Bahamas, you must **fill out a Declaration of Value form** upon arrival, noting make, model, and serial number. **Bring an extra battery.** They're not always readily available in out-of-the-city locations. Bahamian electrical current is compatible with U.S. computers. If you are traveling from abroad, **pack a standard adaptor.**

CONSUMER PROTECTION

Whenever shopping or buying travel services in the Bahamas, **pay with a major credit card,** if possible, so you can cancel payment or get reimbursed if there's a problem. If you're doing business with a particular company for the first time, **contact your local Better Business Bureau and the attorney general's offices** in your state and (for U.S. businesses) the company's home state as well. Have any complaints been filed? Finally, if you're buying a package or tour, always **consider travel insurance** that includes default coverage (☞ Insurance, *below*).

➤ BBBs: **Council of Better Business Bureaus** (✉ 4200 Wilson Blvd., Suite 800, Arlington, VA 22203, ☎ 703/276–0100, 𝔽𝔸𝕏 703/525–8277, 𝚆𝙴𝙱 www.bbb.org).

CRUISE TRAVEL

A cruise can be one of the most pleasurable ways to see the islands. A multi-island excursion allows for plenty of land-time because of the short travel times between destinations. Be sure to shop around before booking. To learn how to plan, choose, and book a cruise-ship voyage, check out Cruise How-to's at www.fodors.com.

➤ CRUISE LINES: **Carnival Cruise Lines** (✉ 3655 N.W. 87th Ave., Miami, FL 33178, ☎ 800/327–9501, 𝚆𝙴𝙱 www.carnival.com). **Celebrity Cruises** (✉ 5201 Blue Lagoon Dr., Miami, FL 33126, ☎ 800/437–3111, 𝚆𝙴𝙱 www.celebrity-cruises.com). **Costa Cruise Lines** (✉ 80 S.W. 8th St., Miami, FL 33130, ☎ 800/462–6782, 𝚆𝙴𝙱 www.costacruises.com).

Crystal Cruises (⊠ 55 5th Ave., New York, NY 10017, ☎ 800/528–6273, WEB www.cruisecrystal.com). Discovery Cruises (⊠ Box 527-544, Miami, FL 33152-7544, ☎ 800/937–4477, WEB www.discoverycruiseline.com). Norwegian Cruise Line (⊠ 7665 Corporate Center Dr., Miami, FL 33126, ☎ 800/327–7030, WEB www.ncl.com). Royal Caribbean International (⊠ 1050 Caribbean Way, Miami, FL 33132, ☎ 800/327–6700, WEB www.rccl.com). Seabourn Cruise Line (⊠ 6100 Blue Lagoon Dr. Suite 400, Miami, FL 33126, ☎ 800/929–9595, WEB www.seabourn.com). Silversea Cruises (⊠ 110 E. Broward Blvd., 26th floor, Fort Lauderdale, FL 33301, ☎ 800/722–6655, WEB www.silversea-cruises.com).

CUSTOMS AND DUTIES

When shopping, **keep receipts** for all purchases. Upon reentering the country, **be ready to show customs officials what you've bought.** If you feel a duty is incorrect or object to the way your clearance was handled, note the inspector's badge number and ask to see a supervisor. If the problem isn't resolved, write to the appropriate authorities, beginning with the port director at your point of entry.

IN AUSTRALIA

Australian residents who are 18 or older may bring home $A400 worth of souvenirs and gifts (including jewelry), 250 cigarettes or 250 grams of tobacco, and 1,125 ml of alcohol (including wine, beer, and spirits). Residents under 18 may bring back $A200 worth of goods. Prohibited items include meat products. Seeds, plants, and fruits need to be declared upon arrival.

➤ INFORMATION: **Australian Customs Service** (Regional Director, ⊠ Box 8, Sydney, NSW 2001, Australia, ☎ 02/9213–2000 or 1300/363263, FAX 02/9213–4043, WEB www.customs.gov.au).

IN THE BAHAMAS AND TURKS AND CAICOS

Customs allows you to bring in 50 cigars or 200 cigarettes or 1 lb of tobacco and a quart of liquor and 1 quart of wine in addition to personal effects, purchases up to $100, and all the money you wish. But **don't even think of smuggling** in marijuana or any kind of narcotic. Justice is swift and severe in the Bahamas.

You would be well advised to **leave pets at home,** unless you're considering a prolonged stay in the islands. An import permit is required from the Ministry of Agriculture and Fisheries for all animals brought into the Bahamas. The animal must be more than 6 months old. You'll also need a veterinary health certificate issued by a licensed vet. The permit is good for 90 days from the date of issue, costs $15, and the process must be completed immediately before departure.

➤ INFORMATION: **Ministry of Agriculture and Fisheries** (⊠ Levy Bldg., East Bay St., Nassau, ☎ 242/325–7502).

IN CANADA

Canadian residents who have been out of Canada for at least seven days may bring home C$750 worth of goods duty-free. If you've been away fewer than seven days but more than 48 hours, the duty-free allowance drops to C$200; if your trip lasts 24–48 hours, the allowance is C$50. You may not pool allowances with family members. Goods claimed under the C$500 exemption may follow you by mail; those claimed under the lesser exemptions must accompany you. Alcohol and tobacco products may be included in the seven-day and 48-hour exemptions but not in the 24-hour exemption. If you meet the age requirements of the province or territory through which you reenter Canada, you may bring in, duty-free, 1.14 liters (40 imperial ounces) of liquor, 1.5 liters of wine, *or* 24 12-ounce cans or bottles of beer or ale. If you are 16 or older you may bring in, duty-free, 200 cigarettes and 50 cigars. Check ahead of time with Revenue Canada or the Department of Agriculture for policies regarding meat products, seeds, plants, and fruits.

You may send an unlimited number of gifts worth up to C$60 each duty-free to Canada. Label the package UNSOLICITED GIFT—VALUE UNDER $60. Alcohol and tobacco are excluded.

➤ INFORMATION: **Canada Customs and Revenue Agency** (⊠ 2265 St.

Laurent Blvd. S, Ottawa, Ontario K1G 4K3, ☎ 204/983–3500; 506/ 636–5064; 800/461–9999 in Canada, WEB www.ccra-adrc.gc.ca).

IN NEW ZEALAND

Homeward-bound residents 17 or older may bring back $700NZ worth of souvenirs and gifts. Your duty-free allowance also includes 4.5 liters of wine or beer; one 1,125-ml bottle of spirits; and either 200 cigarettes, 250 grams of tobacco, 50 cigars, or a combination of the three up to 250 grams. Prohibited items include meat products, seeds, plants, and fruits. Gift parcels with a value under $110NZ can be sent without penalty.

➤ INFORMATION: **New Zealand Customs** (✉ Head Office, The Customhouse, 17–21 Whitmore St., Box 2218, Wellington, ☎ 09/300–5399, WEB www.customs.govt.nz.

IN THE U.K.

From countries outside the European Union (EU), including the Bahamas, you may bring home, duty-free, 200 cigarettes or 50 cigars; 1 liter of spirits or 2 liters of fortified or sparkling wine or liqueurs; 2 liters of still table wine; 60 ml of perfume; 250 ml of toilet water; plus £145 worth of other goods, including gifts and souvenirs. If returning from outside the EU, prohibited items include meat products, seeds, plants, and fruits.

➤ INFORMATION: **HM Customs and Excise** (✉ Portcullis House, 21 Cowbridge Rd. E, Cardiff CF11 9SS, ☎ 029/2038–6423 or 0845/010–9000, WEB www.hmce.gov.uk).

IN THE U.S.

U.S. residents who have been out of the country for at least 48 hours and who have not used the $600 allowance or any part of it in the past 30 days may bring home $600 worth of foreign goods duty-free. This allowance, higher than the standard $400 exemption, applies to the 24 countries in the Caribbean Basin Initiative (CBI)—including the Bahamas. If you visit a CBI country and a non-CBI country, such as Martinique, you may still bring in

$600 worth of goods duty-free, but no more than $400 may be from the non-CBI country. If you're returning from the U.S. Virgin Islands (USVI), the duty-free allowance is $1,200. If your travel included the USVI and another country—say, the Dominican Republic—the $1,200 allowance still applies, but at least $600 worth of goods must be from the USVI.

U.S. residents 21 and older may bring back 2 liters of alcohol duty-free, as long as one of the liters was produced in a CBI country. In addition, regardless of your age, you are allowed 200 cigarettes and 100 non-Cuban cigars. Antiques, which the U.S. Customs Service defines as objects more than 100 years old, enter duty-free, as do original works of art done entirely by hand, including paintings, drawings, and sculptures. You may also send packages home duty-free, with a limit of one parcel per addressee per day (except alcohol or tobacco products or perfume worth more than $5). You can mail up to $200 worth of goods for personal use; label the package PERSONAL USE and attach a list of its contents and their retail value. If the package contains your used personal belongings, mark it PERSONAL GOODS RETURNED to avoid paying duties. You may send up to $100 worth of goods ($200 from the U.S. Virgin Islands) as a gift; mark the package UNSOLICITED GIFT. Mailed items do not affect your duty-free allowance on your return.

➤ INFORMATION: **U.S. Customs Service** (✉ 1300 Pennsylvania Ave. NW, Washington, DC 20229, WEB www. customs.gov; inquiries ☎ 202/354– 1000; complaints c/o ✉ 1300 Pennsylvania Ave. NW, Room 5.4D, Washington, DC 20229; registration of equipment c/o ✉ Resource Management, ☎ 202/927–0540).

DINING

The restaurants we list are the cream of the crop in each price category. You'll find all types, from cosmopolitan to the most casual restaurants, serving all types of cuisine. The fine restaurants have an affinity for tableside-prepared dishes.

Price categories are as follows:

CATEGORY	COST*
$$$$	over $40
$$$	$30–$40
$$	$20–$30
$	$10–$20
¢	under $10

per person for a main course at dinner

MEALS AND SPECIALTIES

Dining in the Bahamas is a mirror of its island location and mixed cultures. While there, check out fresh seafood and home-grown vegetables in pan-Caribbean styles like fish stew, and *souse* (a soup of onion, lime, celery, peppers, and meat). Touches of the American South show up in the popular brunch dish boiled fish and grits. Almost every main course will be accompanied by peas 'n' rice, and you'll also find johnnycakes (baked biscuits) on many a local menu (and table). Much of Caribbean cooking owes its flair to the Indian subcontinent, such as in dishes like curried fish stew, and coconut rice.

No menu in the Bahamas is complete without conch. Pronounced "konk," this ubiquitous "Queen of the Shellfish" (gastropod mollusk) is at the heart of Caribbean cuisine and has had a place in local life for centuries, having been used for jewelry, fishhooks, and religious ornaments. Edible conch, actually the foot of the sea snail, weighs around 4–12 oz. You'll have the chance to try it deep fried (cracked conch) or prepared raw with lime and spices, similar to ceviche. It's also used in stews, salads, and fritters.

MEALTIMES

Unless otherwise noted, the restaurants listed in this guide are open daily for lunch and dinner.

RESERVATIONS AND DRESS

Reservations are always a good idea: we mention them only when they're essential or not accepted. Book as far ahead as you can, and reconfirm as soon as you arrive. We mention dress only when men are required to wear a jacket or a jacket and tie, otherwise you can assume that dining out is a casual affair.

DISABILITIES AND ACCESSIBILITY

Downtown Nassau took into account wheelchair accessibility when it underwent redevelopment in 1995. The Bahamas Association for the Physically Disabled has a van for hire that can pick up people with disabilities from the airport or provide other transportation. Reservations must be made well in advance. The association can also provide temporary ramps and other portable facilities.

➤ LOCAL RESOURCES: **Bahamas Association for the Physically Disabled** (☎ 242/322–2393).

LODGING

Most major hotels throughout the Bahamas have special facilities for people with disabilities, in the way of elevators, ramps, and easy access to rooms and public areas. Here are some suggestions based on a survey conducted by the Bahamas Association for the Physically Disabled:

➤ NASSAU: **British Colonial Hilton Nassau** (✉ 1 Bay St., Box N-7148, ☎ 242/322–3301, WEB www.hilton.com). **Nassau Beach Hotel** (✉ Cable Beach, Box N-7756, ☎ 242/327–7711, WEB www.nassaubeachhotel.com). **Nassau Marriott Resort & Crystal Palace Casino** (✉ Box N-8806, ☎ 242/327–6200, WEB www.marriott.com). **Radisson Cable Beach Casino & Golf Resort** (✉ West Bay St., Box N-4914, ☎ 242/327–6000, WEB www.radisson.com).

➤ PARADISE ISLAND: **Atlantis Resort and Casino, Paradise Island** (✉ Box N-4777, ☎ 242/363–3000, WEB www.atlantis.com). **Bay View Village** (✉ Box SS-6308, ☎ 242/363–2555, WEB www.bayviewvillage.com).

➤ GRAND BAHAMA: **Country Club Resort at Bahamia** (✉ Box F-40207, ☎ 242/352–9661, WEB www.bahamia.com).

➤ LONG ISLAND: **Stella Maris Resort Club** (✉ Box LI-30105, ☎ 242/338–2050 or 800/426–046, WEB www.stellamarisresort.com).

RESERVATIONS

When discussing accessibility with an operator or reservations agent, **ask hard questions.** Are there any stairs, inside *or* out? Are there grab bars next to the toilet *and* in the shower/tub? How wide is the doorway to the room? To the bathroom? For the most extensive facilities meeting the latest legal specifications, **opt for newer accommodations.**

SIGHTS AND ATTRACTIONS

The beaches of the Bahamas and the Turks and Caicos are generally accessible. In Grand Bahama Island, the two largest shopping malls—International Bazaar and Port Lucaya—have some second-story restaurants not accessible by wheelchair. The Dolphin Experience can make special arrangements for travelers with disabilities. In Nassau, Ardastra Gardens is accessible in most areas, Government House has limited access, and Parliament Square is fully accessible.

➤ COMPLAINTS: **Aviation Consumer Protection Division** (☞ Air Travel, *above*) for airline-related problems. **Departmental Office of Civil Rights** (for general inquiries, ✉ U.S. Department of Transportation, S-30, 400 7th St. SW, Room 10215, Washington, DC 20590, ☎ 202/366–4648, FAX 202/366–3571, WEB www.dot.gov/ost/docr/index.htm). **Disability Rights Section** (✉ NYAV, U.S. Department of Justice, Civil Rights Division, 950 Pennsylvania Ave. NW, Washington, DC 20530; ☎ ADA information line 202/514–0301, 800/514–0301, 202/514–0383 TTY, 800/514–0383 TTY, WEB www.usdoj.gov/crt/ada/adahom1.htm).

TRAVEL AGENCIES

In the United States, the Americans with Disabilities Act requires that travel firms serve the needs of all travelers. Some agencies specialize in working with people with disabilities.

➤ TRAVELERS WITH MOBILITY PROBLEMS: **Access Adventures** (✉ 206 Chestnut Ridge Rd., Scottsville, NY 14624, ☎ 716/889–9096, dltravel@prodigy.net), run by a former physical-rehabilitation counselor. **CareVacations** (✉ 5-5110 50th Ave., Leduc, Alberta T9E 6V4, Canada, ☎ 780/986–6404 or 877/478–7827, FAX 780/986–8332, WEB www.carevacations.com), for group tours and cruise vacations. **Flying Wheels Travel** (✉ 143 W. Bridge St., Box 382, Owatonna, MN 55060, ☎ 507/451–5005, FAX 507/451–1685, WEB www.flyingwheelstravel.com). **Tomorrow's Level of Care** (✉ Box 470299, Brooklyn, NY 11247, ☎ 718/756–0794 or 800/932–2012), for nursing services and medical equipment.

➤ TRAVELERS WITH DEVELOPMENTAL DISABILITIES: **New Directions** (✉ 5276 Hollister Ave., Suite 207, Santa Barbara, CA 93111, ☎ 805/967–2841 or 888/967–2841, FAX 805/964–7344, WEB www.newdirectionstravel.com). **Sprout** (✉ 893 Amsterdam Ave., New York, NY 10025, ☎ 212/222–9575 or 888/222–9575, FAX 212/222–9768, WEB www.gosprout.org).

DISCOUNTS AND DEALS

Be a smart shopper and **compare all your options** before making decisions. A plane ticket bought with a promotional coupon from travel clubs, coupon books, and direct-mail offers or on the Internet may not be cheaper than the least expensive fare from a discount ticket agency. And always bear in mind that what you get is just as important as what you save.

DISCOUNT RESERVATIONS

To save money, **look into discount reservations services** with toll-free numbers, which use their buying power to get a better price on hotels, airline tickets, even car rentals. When booking a room, always **call the hotel's local toll-free number** (if one is available) rather than the central reservations number—you'll often get a better price. Always ask about special packages or corporate rates.

When shopping for the best deal on hotels and car rentals, **look for guaranteed exchange rates,** which protect you against a falling dollar. With your rate locked in, you won't pay more, even if the price goes up in the local currency.

➤ AIRLINE TICKETS: ☎ **800/FLY–ASAP.**

➤ HOTEL ROOMS: **Hotel Reservations Network** (☎ 800/964–6835, WEB www.hoteldiscount.com). **Turbotrip.com** (☎ 800/473–7829, WEB www.turbotrip.com).

PACKAGE DEALS

Don't confuse packages and guided tours. When you buy a package, you travel on your own, just as though you had planned the trip yourself. Fly/drive packages, which combine airfare and car rental, are often a good deal.

ECOTOURISM

There are 12 National Parks in the Bahamas, and 58 more areas are slated to join the natural reserve network, all of which are managed by the Bahamas Natural Trust. Included in those areas is the Andros Barrier Reef, the third largest living coral reef in the world, and the 287 square mile Inagua National Park, home to world's largest flock (more than 60,000) of brilliant pink West Indian Flamingos. Environmental consciousness has been heightened in the Bahamas, as it has been elsewhere. Tour operators have begun focusing on kayaking, hiking, and biking as well as on the islands' traditional sports of fishing, diving, and boating. Local guides have become more in tune with their environment. The Bahamas offers a full array of adventures in places untainted by civilization. Right outside Freeport are designated wildlife preserves. In the Out Islands, especially Abaco, Andros, and Great Inagua, you'll find rare and endangered animals, pristine "bush," and vital reefs. Near Providenciales (Turks and Caicos), Little Water Cay Nature Trail takes you into the habitat of the rare West Indian rock iguana. You can do your part to keep the Bahamas beautiful—don't purchase products made from endangered species, use care when diving to avoid damage to reefs, don't leave any of your belongings or trash behind (or, in outdoor parlance, pack out what you pack in), and properly dispose of anything you can't remove. Also, be sure your eco-tour really is, in fact, eco-friendly.

ECOTOURISM RESOURCES

Bahamas Naturalist Expeditions (⊠ Box AB-20714, Marsh Harbour, Abaco, ☎ 242/367–4504). **Eco–Bahamas** (⊠ WEB www.bahamasnet. com/w.ecohome). **UNEXSO** (⊠ Box F-42433, Marsh Harbour, Abaco, ☎ 242/373–1244, WEB www.unexso.com).

ELECTRICITY

Electricity is 120 volts/60 cycles AC, which is compatible with all U.S. appliances.

EMERGENCIES

The emergency telephone number in the Bahamas is **911.**

EMERGENCY AIR SERVICES

Emergency airlifts can be arranged by **Med Evac** (⊠ 4th Terrace, Centerville, Box N–3018, Nassau, ☎ 242/322–2881).

EMBASSIES

When you're on the road, its a good idea to get in touch with your country's consulate or embassy to let them know you're in the area. This is especially true if you plan to get way off the beaten path (or lost), or think that you might be in harm's way where you're traveling. They are also key in replacing lost passports, or with assistance in emergencies.

➤ EMBASSY CONTACTS: **United States** (⊠ Mosmar Bldg., Queen St., Nassau, ☎ 242/322–1181). **United Kingdom** (⊠ 8197 East St., Ansbacher House, 3rd floor, Nassau, ☎ 242/325–7471 or 242/325–7472).

ETIQUETTE AND BEHAVIOR

Bahamians greet people with a proper British "good morning," "good afternoon," or "good evening." When approaching an islander to ask directions or information, **preface your request with such a greeting,** and ask "how are you?" **Smile, and don't rush into a conversation,** even if you're running late.

Humor is a wonderful way to relate to the islanders, but don't force it. Don't try to talk their dialect unless you are adept at it. This takes long exposure to the culture. Church is central in the lives of the Bahamians. They dress up in their fanciest finery; it's a sight to behold on Saturday evening and Sunday morning. To show respect, dress accordingly if you plan to attend religious ceremonies. No doubt, you'll be outdone, but do dress up regardless.

BUSINESS ETIQUETTE

Business in the Bahamas is conducted very much like it is in the United States. Handshakes, business card swapping, and other protocols are the same. Meetings are usually held in office conference rooms, and occasionally at a local restaurant for lunch, in which case either the person who invites pays, or all pay their own tab. Islanders wear suits and typical business attire for work and meetings, so **don't be tempted to wear resort dress** in an office atmosphere.

GAY AND LESBIAN TRAVEL

➤ GAY- AND LESBIAN-FRIENDLY TRAVEL AGENCIES: **Different Roads Travel** (✉ 8383 Wilshire Blvd., Suite 902, Beverly Hills, CA 90211, ☎ 323/651–5557 or 800/429–8747, FAX 323/651–3678, lgernert@tzell. com). **Kennedy Travel** (✉ 314 Jericho Turnpike, Floral Park, NY 11001, ☎ 516/352–4888 or 800/237–7433, FAX 516/354–8849, WEB www.kennedytravel.com). **Now Voyager** (✉ 4406 18th St., San Francisco, CA 94114, ☎ 415/626–1169 or 800/255–6951, FAX 415/626–8626, WEB www.nowvoyager.com).

HEALTH

Hospitals and other health care facilities are readily available in Nassau, Freeport, and Grand Turk. In the Out Islands, facilities range from clinics to private practitioners. You will, however, always be able to find a local bush medicine practitioner. If you're comfortable with alternative treatments, many Bahamians have had herbal remedies passed down to them. For more serious emergencies, an airlift can be arranged from any location.

DIVERS' ALERT

Do not fly within 24 hours of scuba diving.

Always know where your nearest decompression chamber is *before* you embark on a dive expedition, and how you would get there in an emergency.

➤ DECOMPRESSION CHAMBERS: **Doctors Hospital** (✉ Shirley St. and Collins Ave., Box N-3018, Nassau, ☎ 242/322–8411).

FOOD AND DRINK

In the Bahamas the major health risk is traveler's diarrhea, caused by ingesting fruits, shellfish, and drinks to which your body is unaccustomed. **Go easy at first on new foods such as mangoes, conch, and rum punch.**

There are rare cases of contaminated fruit, vegetables, or drinking water. If you are susceptible to digestive problems, **avoid ice, uncooked food, and unpasteurized milk and milk products,** and **drink bottled water.** Mild digestive treatments might include Immodium (known generically as loperamide) or Pepto-Bismol, both of which can be purchased over the counter. Travelers prone to travel-related stomach disorders—and, as noted above, are comfortable with alternative medicine—might pick up some *po chai* tablets from a doctor of Oriental medicine or Asian pharmacy—it's a great stomach cure-all. Drink plenty of purified water or tea—chamomile is a good folk remedy. In severe cases, rehydrate yourself with a salt-sugar solution (½ teaspoon salt and 4 tablespoons sugar per quart of water).

Consult a doctor—preferably your own physician, and prior to your trip—before ingesting any medication that's new to you. And not only pack familiar digestive remedies with your belongings, **but also have them on you** if you're out traveling for the day.

HOSPITALS

Most medical situations can be handled by local area hospitals.

➤ LOCAL HOSPITALS: **Princess Margaret Hospital** (✉ Shirley St., Nassau, ☎ 242/352–2861). **Rand Memorial Hospital** (✉ East Atlantic Dr., Freeport, ☎ 242/352–6735).

MEDICAL PLANS

No one plans to get sick while traveling, but it happens, so **consider signing up with a medical-assistance company.** Members get doctor referrals, emergency evacuation or repatriation, hot lines for medical consultation, cash for emergencies, and other assistance.

➤ MEDICAL-ASSISTANCE COMPANIES: **International SOS Assistance** (✉ 8 Neshaminy Interplex, Suite 207, Trevose, PA 19053, ☎ 215/245–4707 or 800/523–6586, FAX 215/244–9617, WEB www.internationalsos.com; ✉ 12 Chemin Riantbosson, 1217 Meyrin 1, Geneva, Switzerland, ☎ 22/785–6464, FAX 22/785–6424; ✉ 331 N. Bridge Rd., 17-00, Odeon Towers, Singapore 188720, ☎ 338–7800, FAX 338–7611).

OVER-THE-COUNTER REMEDIES

Pharmacies carry most of the same pain relief products you find in the United States, but often at a higher price, so **pack any over-the-counter medications you regularly use.** They also sell a product called 2-2-2, which is equal parts aspirin, caffeine, and codeine. It's an effective pain killer but can cause stomach upset.

PESTS AND OTHER HAZARDS

No-see-ums (sand fleas) and mosquitoes pose the worst bother. Some travelers have allergies to sand-flea bites, and the itching can be extremely bothersome. To prevent the bites, **use a recommended bug repellent.** To ease the itching, **rub alcohol on the bites.** Some Out Island hotels provide sprays or repellents in the room, but it's a good idea to bring your own.

SHOTS AND MEDICATIONS

A vaccination against yellow fever is required if you're arriving from an infected area. Otherwise, no special shots are required before visiting the Bahamas.

SUNBATHING

Basking in the sun is one of the great pleasures of a Bahamian vacation, but because the sun is closer to Earth the farther south you go, it will burn your skin more quickly, so take precautions against sunburn and sunstroke. On a sunny day, even people who are not normally bothered by strong sun should **cover up with a long-sleeve shirt, a hat, and pants or a beach wrap** while on a boat or midday at the beach. **Carry UVA/UVB sunblock** (with a sun protection factor, or SPF, of at least 15) for nose, ears, and other sensitive areas. If you're engaging in water sports, be sure the sunscreen is waterproof. Wear sunglasses because eyes are particularly vulnerable to direct sun and reflected rays. Be sure to **drink enough liquids—water or fruit juice preferably**—and avoid coffee, tea, and alcohol. Above all, limit your sun time for the first few days until you become accustomed to the rays. Do not be fooled by an overcast day. Quite often you will get the worst sunburns when you least expect them. The safest hours for sunbathing are 4–6 PM, but even then it is wise to limit initial exposure.

► HEALTH WARNINGS: **National Centers for Disease Control and Prevention** (CDC; National Center for Infectious Diseases, Division of Quarantine, Traveler's Health Section, ✉ 1600 Clifton Rd. NE, M/S E-03, Atlanta, GA 30333, ☎ 888/232–3228 general information, 877/394–8747 travelers' health line, 800/311–3435 public inquiries, FAX 888/232–3299, WEB www.cdc.gov).

HOLIDAYS

The grandest holiday of all is Junkanoo, a carnival that embraces the Christmas season. **Don't expect to conduct any business during the week of festivities.** During other legal holidays, most offices close. In the Bahamas, they include New Year's Day, Good Friday, Easter, Whit Monday (last Monday in May), Labour Day (first Monday in June), Independence Day (July 10), Emancipation Day (first Monday in August), Discovery Day (Oct. 12), Christmas Day, and Boxing Day (Dec. 26). In Turks and Caicos, islanders also celebrate Commonwealth Day (March), Easter Monday, National Heroes Day (May), The Queen's Birthday (June), National Youth Day (September), and International Human Rights Day (October). They do not celebrate Whit Monday, Labour Day, or Independence Day.

INSURANCE

The most useful travel-insurance plan is a comprehensive policy that includes coverage for trip cancellation and interruption, default, trip delay, and medical expenses (with a waiver for preexisting conditions).

Without insurance you will lose all or most of your money if you cancel your trip, regardless of the reason. Default insurance covers you if your tour operator, airline, or cruise line goes out of business. Trip-delay covers expenses that arise because of bad weather or mechanical delays. Study the fine print when comparing policies.

If you're traveling internationally, a key component of travel insurance is coverage for medical bills incurred if you get sick on the road. Such expenses are not generally covered by Medicare or private policies. U.K. residents can buy a travel-insurance policy valid for most vacations taken during the year in which it's purchased (but check preexisting-condition coverage). British and Australian citizens need extra medical coverage when traveling overseas.

Always **buy travel policies directly from the insurance company**; if you buy them from a cruise line, airline, or tour operator that goes out of business you probably will not be covered for the agency or operator's default, a major risk. Before making any purchase, **review your existing health and home-owner's policies** to find what they cover away from home.

➤ TRAVEL INSURERS: **Travel Guard International** (✉ 1145 Clark St., Stevens Point, WI 54481, ☎ 715/345–0505 or 800/826–1300, FAX 800/955–8785, WEB www.travelguard.com). **Wallach and Company** (✉ 107 W. Federal St., Middleburg, VA 20118–480, ☎ 800/237–6615 or 540/687–3166, FAX 540/687–3172, WEB www.wallach.com).

➤ INSURANCE INFORMATION: In the U.K.: **Association of British Insurers** (✉ 51–55 Gresham St., London EC2V 7HQ, U.K., ☎ 020/7600–3333, FAX 020/7696–8999, WEB www.abi.org.uk). In Canada: **Voyager Insurance** (✉ 44 Peel Center Dr., Brampton, Ontario L6T 4M8, Canada, ☎ 905/791–8700, 800/668–4342 in Canada, WEB www.ask-voyager.com). In Australia: **Insurance Council of Australia** (✉ Level 3, 56 Pitt St., Sydney NSW 2000, ☎ 03/9614–1077, FAX 03/9614–7924, WEB www.ica.com.au). In New Zealand: **Insurance Council of New Zealand** (✉ Box 474, Wellington, New Zealand, ☎ 04/472–5230, FAX 04/473–3011, WEB www.icnz.org.nz).

LANGUAGE

Islanders speak English with a lilt influenced by their Scottish, Irish, and/or African ancestry. When locals talk among themselves in local dialect, it is virtually impossible for the unaccustomed to understand them. They take all sorts of short cuts and pepper the language with words all their own. When islanders speak to visitors, they will use standard English.

LODGING

The lodgings we list are the cream of the crop in each price category. We always list the facilities that are available—but we don't specify whether they cost extra: when pricing accommodations, always ask what's included and what costs extra. Properties marked ✕🏠 are lodging establishments whose restaurants warrant a special trip.

Assume that hotels operate on the **European Plan** (EP, with no meals), unless we specify that they use either the **Continental Plan** (CP, with a Continental breakfast), **Breakfast Plan** (BP, with a full breakfast), or the **Modified American Plan** (MAP, with breakfast and dinner), **Full-American Plan** (all meals are included), or are **all-inclusive** (including all meals and most activities).

CATEGORY	COST*
$$$$	over $400
$$$	$300–$400
$$	$200–$300
$	$100–$200
¢	under $100

*All prices are for a standard double room in high season, excluding 9% tax and 10%–15% service charge. Note that the government hotel tax doesn't apply to guest houses with fewer than four rooms.

APARTMENT AND VILLA RENTALS

➤ INTERNATIONAL AGENTS: **At Home Abroad** (✉ 405 E. 56th St., Suite 6H, New York, NY 10022, ☎ 212/421–9165, FAX 212/752–1591, WEB www.athomeabroadinc.com). **Hideaways International** (✉ 767 Islington St., Portsmouth, NH 03801, ☎ 603/430–4433 or 800/843–4433, FAX 603/430–4444, WEB www.hideaways.com; membership $129). **Hometours International** (✉ Box 11503, Knoxville, TN 37939, ☎ 865/690–8484 or 800/367–4668, WEB http://thor.he.net/~hometour/). **Vacation Home Rentals Worldwide** (✉ 235 Kensington Ave., Norwood, NJ 07648, ☎ 201/767–9393 or 800/633–3284, FAX 201/767–5510,

WEB www.vhrww.com). **Villas and Apartments Abroad** (✉ 1270 Avenue of the Americas, 15th floor, New York, NY 10020, ☎ 212/897–5045 or 800/433–3020, FAX 212/897–5039, WEB www.vaanyc.com). **Villas International** (✉ 4340 Redwood Highway, Suite D 309, San Rafael, CA 94903, ☎ 415/499–9490 or 800/221–2260, FAX 415/499–9491, WEB www.villasintl.com).

➤ LOCAL AGENTS: **Bahamas Home Rentals** (✉ 2722 Riverview Dr., Melbourne, FL 32901, ☎ 888/881–2867 or 321/725–9790, FAX 321/676–1452, WEB www.bahamasweb.com). **Bahamas Vacation Homes** (✉ Box EL-27528, Spanish Wells, Bahamas, ☎ FAX 242/333–4080). **Hope Town Hideaways** (✉ 1 Purple Porpoise Pl., Hope Town, Abacos, ☎ 242/366–0224, FAX 242/366–0434, inquiries@ hopetown.com).

HOME EXCHANGES

If you would like to exchange your home for someone else's, **join a home-exchange organization,** which will send you its updated listings of available exchanges for a year and will include your own listing in at least one of them. It's up to you to make specific arrangements.

➤ EXCHANGE CLUBS: **HomeLink International** (✉ Box 47747, Tampa, FL 33647, ☎ 813/975–9825 or 800/638–3841, FAX 813/910–8144, WEB www.homelink.org; $98 per year). **Intervac U.S.** (✉ 30 Corte San Fernando, Tiburon, CA 94920, ☎ 800/756–4663, FAX 415/435–7440, WEB www.intervacus.com; $93 yearly fee includes one catalogue and on-line access).

HOSTELS

No matter what your age, you can **save on lodging costs by staying at hostels.** In some 4,500 locations in more than 70 countries around the world, Hostelling International (HI), the umbrella group for a number of national youth-hostel associations, offers single-sex, dorm-style beds and, at many hostels, rooms for couples and family accommodations. Membership in any HI national hostel association, open to travelers of all ages, allows you to stay in HI-affiliated hostels at member rates; one-

year membership is about $25 for adults (C$35 for a two-year minimum membership in Canada, £13 in the United Kingdom, A$52 in Australia, and NZ$40 in New Zealand); hostels run about $10–$30 per night. Members have priority if the hostel is full; they're also eligible for discounts around the world, even on rail and bus travel in some countries.

➤ ORGANIZATIONS: **Australian Youth Hostel Association** (✉ 10 Mallett St., Camperdown, NSW 2050, Australia, ☎ 02/9565–1699, FAX 02/9565–1325, WEB www.yha.com.au). **Hostelling International—American Youth Hostels** (✉ 733 15th St. NW, Suite 840, Washington, DC 20005, ☎ 202/783–6161, FAX 202/783–6171, WEB www.hiayh.org). **Hostelling International—Canada** (✉ 400–205 Catherine St., Ottawa, Ontario K2P 1C3, Canada, ☎ 613/237–7884 or 800/663–5777, FAX 613/237–7868, WEB www.hostellingintl.ca). **Youth Hostel Association of England and Wales** (✉ Trevelyan House, Dimple Rd., Matlock, Derbyshire DE4 3YH, U.K., ☎ 0870/870–8808, FAX 0169/592–702, WEB www.yha.org.uk). **Youth Hostel Association Australia** (✉ 10 Mallett St., Camperdown, NSW 2050, ☎ 02/9565–1699, FAX 02/9565–1325, WEB www.yha.com.au). **Youth Hostels Association of New Zealand** (✉ Level 3, 193 Cashel St., Box 436, Christchurch, ☎ 03/379–9970, FAX 03/365–4476, WEB www.yha.org.nz).

HOTELS

Many American, European, and Caribbean chains operate in the Bahamas, including Marriott, Sheraton, Comfort Suites, Radisson, Sandals, SuperClubs, and Club Med. Their full-service resorts, along with other individual properties, are destinations in themselves. Smaller lodges and resorts offer easier access to local life and are attractive to travelers who want a cultural experience or a sequestered getaway focused on fishing, diving, and other watery pastimes. Many small, family-run hotels throughout the Bahamas, including the occasional B&B, offer low-key, warm accommodations. All hotels listed have private bath unless otherwise noted.

➤ TOLL-FREE NUMBERS: **Best Western** (☎ 800/528–1234, WEB www.bestwestern.com). **Choice** (☎ 800/424–6423, WEB www.choicehotels.com). **Clarion** (☎ 800/424–6423, WEB www.choicehotels.com). **Colony Hotels & Resorts** (☎ 800/777–1700, WEB www.colony.com). **Comfort Inn** (☎ 800/424–6423, WEB www.choicehotels.com). **Hilton** (☎ 800/445–8667, WEB www.hilton.com). **Holiday Inn** (☎ 800/465–4329, WEB www.sixcontinentshotels.com/holiday-inn). **Le Meridien** (☎ 800/543–4300, WEB www.lemeridien-hotels.com). **Marriott** (☎ 800/228–9290, WEB www.marriott.com). **Quality Inn** (☎ 800/424–6423, WEB www.choicehotels.com). **Renaissance Hotels & Resorts** (☎ 800/468–3571, WEB www.renaissancehotels.com). **Sheraton** (☎ 800/325–3535, WEB www.starwood.com/sheraton). **Sleep Inn** (☎ 800/424–6423, WEB www.choicehotels.com). **Wyndham Hotels & Resorts** (☎ 800/822–4200, WEB www.wyndham.com).

MAIL AND SHIPPING

Regardless of whether the term "snail mail" was coined in the Bahamas, you're likely to find that you arrive home long before your postcards do. No postal (zip) codes are used in the Bahamas—all mail is collected from local area PO boxes.

OVERNIGHT SERVICES

FedEx delivers to Nassau, Freeport, Andros, Eleuthera, Provo, and Grand Turk. UPS has service to numerous Bahamas locales and provides incoming delivery only in Turks and Caicos.

➤ MAJOR SERVICES: **FedEx** (Freeport: ☎ 242/352–3402 or 242/352–3403; Nassau: ☎ 242/322–5656 or 242/322–5657; U.S. international customer service: ☎ 800/247–4747). **UPS** (Abaco: ☎ 242/367–2722; Eleuthera: ☎ 242/332–2454; Exuma: ☎ 242/336–2148; Freeport: ☎ 242/352–3434; Nassau: ☎ 242/325–8227 or 242/325–8228).

POSTAL RATES

First-class mail to the United States is 65¢, 70¢ to Europe, and 80¢ to Australia and New Zealand per half-ounce. Airmail postcards to the United States, Canada, the United Kingdom, Europe, Australia, and South America require a 55¢ stamp in the Bahamas; the stamps must be Bahamian. In Turks and Caicos, prices are comparable, about 50¢–80¢.

RECEIVING MAIL

Mailing time to the United States from the Bahamas is five to 10 days, 10–18 days to Canada, and 20 days to the United Kingdom, Australia, and New Zealand.

SHIPPING PARCELS

U.S. citizens may increase their duty-free by mailing home up to $200 worth of goods for personal use, with a limit of one parcel per addressee per day (and no alcohol or tobacco products or perfume worth more than $5). Label the package PERSONAL USE and attach a list of its contents and their retail value. Don't label the package UNSOLICITED GIFT, or your duty-free exemption will drop to $100.

MEDIA

NEWSPAPERS AND MAGAZINES

You'll get all the Bahamian news and a good idea of what's going on internationally in the *Tribune, Bahamas Observer,* and *Nassau Guardian* on New Providence and in the *Freeport News* on Grand Bahama. Local newspapers are available in most Out Islands one day after publication. If you want up-to-date news on what's happening around the world, you can also get the *Miami Herald,* the *Wall Street Journal, USA Today,* and the *New York Times* daily at newsstands.

TELEVISION

Cable brings American television to the Bahamas. The local TV station is ZNS.

MONEY MATTERS

Generally, prices in the Bahamas reflect the exchange rate: they are about the same as in the United States, less expensive than in the United Kingdom. A hotel can cost anywhere from $35 a night (for cottages and apartments in downtown Nassau and in the Out Islands) to $185 and up (at the ritzier resorts on Cable Beach and Paradise Island and in Freeport and Lucaya), depending on the season. Add $35–$50 per person per day for meals. Four-day/three-night and eight-day/seven-night package stays offered by most hotels can cut costs considerably. In the Out Islands, you'll notice that meals and simple goods can be expensive; prices are high due to the remoteness of the islands and the costs of importing. Prices throughout this guide are given for adults. Substantially reduced fees are almost always available for children, students, and senior citizens. For information on taxes, *see* Taxes, *below.*

ATMS

There are ATMs at banks and malls throughout the major islands. You'll find an ATM at Nassau International Airport and at 29 other locations on New Providence and Paradise Island. There are two at the Princess Casino, two others at banks in Freeport on Grand Bahama Island, and seven throughout the Out Islands.

➤ ATM LOCATIONS: Cirrus (☎ 800/424–7787). Plus (☎ 800/843–7587) for locations in the United States and Canada, or visit your local bank.

CREDIT CARDS

Both credit and debit cards offer excellent, wholesale exchange rates. And both protect you against unauthorized use if the card is lost or stolen. Your liability is limited to $50, as long as you report the card missing. If your American Express card is lost, call the local number to report it. Some smaller hotels in the islands do not accept credit cards.

Throughout this guide, the following abbreviations are used: AE, American Express; D, Discover; DC, Diners Club; MC, MasterCard; and V, Visa.

➤ REPORTING LOST CARDS: American Express (☎ 242/322–2931).

CURRENCY

The U.S. dollar is on par with the Bahamian dollar and is accepted all over the Bahamas. The U.K. pound sterling will get you 1.46 Bahamian dollars, and the Canadian dollar about .63 pence. Bahamian money runs in bills of $1, $5, $10, $20, $50, and $100. The rare 50¢ and $3 bills make unusual souvenirs. The U.S. dollar is the currency of the Turks and Caicos.

CURRENCY EXCHANGE

In the Bahamas, only U.S. cash will be exchanged freely in hotels, stores, or restaurants, and since the U.S. currency is accepted throughout, there really is no need to change to Bahamian. Also, you won't incur any transaction fees for currency exchange, or worry about getting stuck with unspent Bahamian dollars. Carry small bills when bargaining at straw markets. For the most favorable rates, change money through banks. Although ATM transaction fees may be higher abroad than at home, ATM rates are excellent because they are based on wholesale rates offered only by major banks. You won't do as well at exchange booths in airports or rail and bus stations, in hotels, in restaurants, or in stores. To avoid lines at airport exchange booths, get a bit of local currency before you leave home.

➤ EXCHANGE SERVICES: International Currency Express (☎ 888/278–6628 orders). Thomas Cook Currency Services (☎ 800/287–7362 for telephone orders and retail locations, WEB www.us.thomascook.com).

TRAVELER'S CHECKS

Do you need traveler's checks? It depends on where you're headed. If you're going to rural areas and small towns, go with cash; traveler's checks are best used in cities. Lost or stolen checks can usually be replaced within 24 hours. To ensure a speedy refund, buy your own traveler's checks—don't let someone else pay for them: irregularities like this can cause delays. The person who bought the checks should make the call to request a refund. American Express has locations worldwide.

OUTDOORS AND SPORTS

BICYCLING

Companies in Nassau and Freeport offer nature bike tours although biking is most popular on the more remote, less-trafficked islands, especially Abaco, Andros, Eleuthera, and Providenciales. Many resorts in these locations provide bikes for guests. In

Grand Bahama, long-distance road and trail biking is a growing sport outside of the Freeport-Lucaya area.

BOATING

The Bahamas and its 700 islands provide 100,000 square mi of seas ideal for sailing, motor-boating, and island-hopping. Every major island has marinas. For inexperienced sailors, charter companies take the helm for sea exploration. Custom and immigration clearance are available on Abaco, Andros, Berry Islands, Bimini, Cat Cay, Cat Island, Eleuthera, Exuma, and Grand Bahama.

DIVING AND SNORKELING

World-class diving has built a reputation for the Bahamas and the Turks and Caicos. The variety is astounding—caves, walls, ledges, shipwrecks, reefs, and blue holes set the stage for incredible marine life. Diving facilities and tours are available on most of the islands. In Grand Bahama Island, UNEXSO (Underwater Explorers Society) has carved a niche for shark, dolphin, and cave diving. Many resorts rent snorkeling equipment, and tour boats offer snorkeling excursions.

➤ DIVING INFORMATION: Get information on certified dive shops and courses before you leave home. **PADI International** (✉ Unit 7, St. Philips Central, Albert Rd., St. Philips, Bristol BS2 OPD, UK, ☎ 117/300–7234) or **PADI USA** (✉ 30151 Tomas St., Rancho Santa Margarita, CA 9268, ☎ 800/729–7234, WEB www.padi.com).

FISHING

Most celebrated for their bonefishing flats, the islands of Bahamas and Turks and Caicos have thrilled sports lovers with marlin, tuna, mahimahi, and other deep-sea catches.

GOLF

Golf aficionados steer their vacations in the direction of Grand Bahama Island or Nassau/Paradise Island. Grand Bahama Island has four 18-hole courses; the Nassau area, two. Other resort courses are found on Treasure Cay in the Abacos, Eleuthera, the Berry Islands, and Exuma. In the Turks and Caicos, Providenciales has one course and Grand Turk another.

HIKING

As ecotourism grows in the islands, so do the opportunities for hiking in the wilds. Grand Bahama Island is supreme in its hiking and nature trails. In the other islands, beach-walking is the favored form of by-foot travel.

KAYAKING AND CANOEING

Both sea and inland water kayaking have grown as a popular and intimate means of exploring nature and seeking thrills. Canoe outfitters are found to a lesser extent throughout the islands.

PACKING

The reason you're going to the Bahamas is to get away from all of that suit-shirt-and-tie turmoil, so your wardrobe should reflect the informality of the experience. Aside from your bathing suit, which will be your favorite uniform, take lightweight clothing (short-sleeve shirts, T-shirts, cotton slacks, lightweight jackets for evening wear for men; light dresses, shorts, and T-shirts for women). If you're going during the high season, between mid-December and April, toss in a sweater for the occasional cool evening. Cover up in public places for downtown shopping expeditions, and save that skimpy bathing suit for the beach at your hotel.

Some of the more sophisticated hotels require jackets for men and dresses for women at dinner. There is no dress code in any of the Bahamas' casinos.

In your carry-on luggage, **pack an extra pair of eyeglasses or contact lenses** and **enough of any medication you take** to last a few days longer than the entire trip. You may also ask your doctor to write a spare prescription using the drug's generic name, since brand names may vary from country to country. In luggage to be checked, **never pack prescription drugs or valuables.** To avoid customs delays, carry medications in their original packaging. And don't forget to carry with you the addresses of offices that handle refunds of lost traveler's checks. Check *Fodor's How to Pack* (available in bookstores everywhere) for more tips.

CHECKING LUGGAGE

You are allowed one carry-on bag and one personal article, such as a purse or a laptop computer. Make sure that everything you carry aboard will fit under your seat or in the overhead bin. Get to the gate early, so you can board as soon as possible, before the overhead bins fill up.

If you are flying internationally, note that baggage allowances may be determined not by piece but by weight—generally 88 pounds (40 kilograms) in first class, 66 pounds (30 kilograms) in business class, and 44 pounds (20 kilograms) in economy.

Airline liability for baggage is limited to $1,250 per person on flights within the United States. On international flights it amounts to $9.07 per pound or $20 per kilogram for checked baggage (roughly $640 per 70-pound bag) and $400 per passenger for unchecked baggage. You can buy additional coverage at check-in for about $10 per $1,000 of coverage, but it excludes a rather extensive list of items, shown on your airline ticket.

Before departure, **itemize your bags' contents** and their worth, and label the bags with your name, address, and phone number. (If you use your home address, cover it so potential thieves can't see it readily.) Inside each bag, **pack a copy of your itinerary.** At check-in, **make sure that each bag is correctly tagged** with the destination airport's three-letter code. If your bags arrive damaged or fail to arrive at all, file a written report with the airline before leaving the airport.

PASSPORTS AND VISAS

When traveling internationally, **carry your passport** even if you don't need one (it's always the best form of I.D.) and **make two photocopies of the data page** (one for someone at home and another for you, carried separately from your passport). If you lose your passport, promptly call the nearest embassy or consulate and the local police.

ENTERING THE BAHAMAS

Residents of the United States or British Commonwealth countries can stay in the Bahamas for up to 8 months. Countries whose citizens require a visa include China, Colombia, Egypt, India, Nigeria, Pakistan, Poland, Russia, and Saudi Arabia. For specific entry questions, contact the Bahamas Immigration Department or the nearest consulate.

➤ CONTACT: **Bahamas Department of Immigration** (⌂ Hawkins Hill, Nassau, Box N–831, ☎ 242/322–7530).

ENTERING TURKS AND CAICOS

U.S. citizens need some proof of citizenship, such as a birth certificate with a raised seal, plus a photo ID or a current passport. British subjects are required to have a current passport. All visitors must have an ongoing or return ticket.

PASSPORT OFFICES

The best time to apply for a passport or to renew is in fall and winter. Before any trip, check your passport's expiration date, and, if necessary, renew it as soon as possible.

➤ AUSTRALIAN CITIZENS: **Australian Passport Office** (☎ 131–232, WEB www.passports.gov.au).

➤ CANADIAN CITIZENS: **Passport Office** (☎ 819/994–3500; 800/567–6868 in Canada, WEB www.dfait-maeci.gc.ca/passport).

➤ NEW ZEALAND CITIZENS: **New Zealand Passport Office** (☎ 0800/22–5050 or 04/474–8100, WEB www.passports.govt.nz).

➤ U.K. CITIZENS: **London Passport Office** (☎ 0870/521–0410, WEB www.ukpa.gov.uk) for fees and documentation requirements and to request an emergency passport.

➤ U.S. CITIZENS: **National Passport Information Center** (☎ 900/225–5674; calls are 35¢ per minute for automated service, $1.05 per minute for operator service, WEB www.travel.state.gov).

REST ROOMS

Most attractions, restaurants, and shopping areas have reasonably clean, and sometimes attended, public rest rooms. Beaches away from the resorts often have no facilities. **Headquarter your beach escape near a bar or restaurant** for rest-room access.

SAFETY

Crime against tourists is rare, and, unlike some of the Caribbean countries, the Bahamas has little panhandling. But take the precautions you would in any foreign country: be aware of your wallet or handbag at all times, and keep your jewelry in the hotel safe. **Be especially wary in remote areas, always lock your rental vehicle, and don't keep any valuables in the car, even in the locked trunk.**

WOMEN IN THE BAHAMAS AND TURKS AND CAICOS

Women traveling alone should not go out walking unescorted at night in Nassau or in remote areas. Crime is low, but there's no need to take unnecessary risks. In most other cases, women are safe and treated with respect. To avoid unwanted attention, **dress conservatively and cover up swimsuits off the beach.**

SENIOR-CITIZEN TRAVEL

To qualify for age-related discounts, **mention your senior-citizen status up front** when booking hotel reservations (not when checking out) and before you're seated in restaurants (not when paying the bill). When renting a car, ask about promotional car-rental discounts, which can be cheaper than senior-citizen rates.

➤ EDUCATIONAL PROGRAMS: **Elderhostel** (✉ 11 Ave. de Lafayette, Boston, MA 02111-1746, ☎ 877/426-8056, FAX 877/426-2166, WEB www.elderhostel.org).

SHOPPING

There's enough of a savings over U.S. prices (30%–50%, in many cases) to make duty-free shopping profitable on New Providence and Grand Bahama. On all the islands, be sure to visit the straw markets, where you can bargain for low-priced hats, baskets, place mats, T-shirts, and other items. But be aware that most of the straw goods you find in a straw market are actually imported from Taiwan or other places.

KEY DESTINATIONS

In Nassau, Bay Street is the center for duty-free shopping, souvenirs, straw market goods, and art galleries.

Grand Bahama Island has two popular shopping arenas. International Bazaar in Freeport carries items from around the world and is a good place to look for duty-free jewelry, cigars, perfume, and crystal. Newer Port Lucaya carries many of the same goods in charming Bahamian-style stores.

In Providenciales (Turks and Caicos), small shopping malls near the resorts at Ports of Call, and near the airport at the Market Place and Central Square, sell limited duty-free items and a variety of souvenirs.

SMART SOUVENIRS

For authentic souvenirs, check out the art and crafts galleries you will find throughout the Bahamas, but most are concentrated in Nassau. Bahamian artists hold their own in the burgeoning marketplace for Caribbean art.

Trademark products include Junkanoo-inspired art, wood sculpture, painted straw masks, handmade batik, model ships, and hand-plaited straw work. Brent Malone is the master of Junkanoo art. His Marlborough Gallery in Nassau sells his work and that of other innovative artists.

Long Island is known for its handplaiting, which has survived the onslaught of cheap imported goods. The island of Andros is home to the Androsia Batik factory, which produces island-style batik cloth and clothing that is available throughout the islands.

On the island of Green Turtle Cay, the Lowe brothers are famous. Albert Lowe is the official Bahamian artist, whose masterpieces dwell in the four- and five-figure price range. Vertram Lowe assembles realistic models of sailing ships, which start around $700.

In Providenciales in the Turks and Caicos, Bamboo Gallery carries fine local, Haitian, and other Caribbean sculpture and paintings. You can contribute to the well-being of the islands' environment by taking home handmade crafts that don't include such natural items as coral, feathers, and rare shells.

WATCH OUT

U.S. Customs does not allow any product made from black coral or tortoise shell into the country. **Smoke your Cuban cigars in the Bahamas.** They're illegal in the United States, and the fine is stiff.

STUDENTS IN THE BAHAMAS

TRAVEL AGENCIES

Students of marine ecology and biology flock to the Bahamas like West Indian Flamingos. If you're a student visitor, there are resources to help save money—**look into deals available through student-oriented travel agencies.** To qualify you'll need a bona fide student I.D. card. Members of international student groups are also eligible.

➤ I.D.s AND SERVICES: **Council Travel** (✉ 205 E. 42nd St., ground floor, New York, NY 10017, ☎ 212/822–2700 or 888/266–8624, FAX 212/822–2719, WEB www.councilexchanges.org) for mail orders only, in the United States). **Travel Cuts** (✉ 187 College St., Toronto, Ontario M5T 1P7, Canada, ☎ 416/979–2406 or 888/838–2887, FAX 416/979–8167, WEB www.travelcuts.com).

TAXES

There's no sales tax in the Bahamas. There is a $15 departure tax ($18 from Grand Bahama Island) for all travelers older than 6 years of age (age 12 in the Turks and Caicos). Tax on your hotel room is 8%, a small service charge on your room for maid service and bellman may be about 4%. U.S. visitors can take home $600 worth of duty-free goods. The next $1,000 is taxed at 10% (☞ Customs and Duties, *above*).

TAXIS

There are taxis waiting at every airport, and in Nassau along Bay Street and outside all of the main hotels and cruise ship docks. Beware of "hackers"—drivers who don't display their license (and may not have one). You can negotiate a fare, but you must do so before you enter the taxi. On Grand Bahama and New Providence, taxi rates are $2.20 for two passengers for ¼ mi, 30¢ for each additional ¼ mi. Third passengers can

incur a fee of $3. Cabs can also be hired by the hour for $20, and $10 for every additional half hour. In the Out Islands, rates are negotiated, and you might find that renting a car is more economical. Upon arriving, you're likely to find that Bahamian taxi drivers are more loquacious than their U.S. counterparts, so by the time you've reached your hotel, you will be already familiar with points of interest. Taxi rates from the Nassau airport to Cable Beach are $12; from Paradise Island airport to Cable Beach, $18.

TELEPHONES

BATELCO (Bahamas Telecommunications Corporation) is the phone company in the Bahamas. Most public phones require BATELCO phone cards (available at outlets throughout the islands) and also use AT&T calling cards. Check on the surcharge from your calling card provider prior to making calls, and always ask at your hotel desk if there is a charge for making card calls from your room.

AREA AND COUNTRY CODES

The area code for the Bahamas is 242. The area code for the Turks and Caicos is 649. You can dial either number from the United States as you would make an interstate call. The country code is 1 for the United States and Canada, 61 for Australia, 64 for New Zealand, and 44 for the United Kingdom.

DIRECTORY AND OPERATOR ASSISTANCE

Dial 916 for directory information and 0 for operator assistance.

INTERNATIONAL CALLS

From outside the United States and Canada, the country code for the Bahamas is 1. After dialing the appropriate international access code (00 in the U.K.), dial 1 followed by the 242 Bahamas area code.

LOCAL CALLS

Within the Bahamas, to make a local call from your hotel room, dial 9, then the number. If your party doesn't answer before the fifth ring, hang up or you'll be charged for the call. Some 800 and 888 numbers—particularly airline and credit card numbers—can be called from the Bahamas. Others can be reached by substituting an 880 prefix and paying for the call.

LONG-DISTANCE SERVICES

AT&T, MCI, and Sprint access codes make calling long distance relatively convenient, but you may find the local access number blocked in many hotel rooms. First ask the hotel operator to connect you. If the hotel operator balks, ask for an international operator, or dial the international operator yourself. One way to improve your odds of getting connected to your long-distance carrier is to travel with more than one company's calling card (a hotel may block Sprint, for example, but not MCI). If all else fails, call from a pay phone.

➤ ACCESS CODES: Access codes are as numerous as the number of calling plans offered by the major phone carriers. Be sure to write your access number, and your phone and PIN numbers in more than one location before you leave home.

PHONE CARDS

To place a call from a public phone using your own calling card, dial 0 for the operator, who will then place the call using your card number.

PUBLIC PHONES

Pay phones cost 25¢ per call; Bahamian and U.S. quarters are accepted as are BATELCO phone cards.

➤ CONTACT: **BATELCO** (☎ 242/ 302–7000).

TIME

The Bahamas and the Turks and Caicos lie within the Eastern Standard Time (EST) Zone, which means that it's 7 AM in the Bahamas (or New York) when it's noon in London and 10 PM in Sydney. During the summer, the islands switch to Eastern Daylight Time (EDT).

TIPPING

The usual tip for service from a taxi driver or waiter is 15% and $1 a bag for porters. Many hotels and restaurants automatically add a 15% gratuity to your bill.

TOURS AND PACKAGES

Because everything is prearranged on a prepackaged tour or independent vacation, you'll spend less time planning—and often get it all at a good price. Many prearranged tours aren't for those who like to spread their wings. If you get a good enough deal, however, book the tour, but skip the excursions. Many cost extra anyway.

BOOKING WITH AN AGENT

Travel agents are excellent resources. But it's a good idea to collect brochures from several agencies as some agents' suggestions may be influenced by relationships with tour and package firms that reward them for volume sales. If you have a special interest, **find an agent with expertise in that area**; ASTA (☞ Travel Agencies, *below*) has a database of specialists worldwide.

Make sure your travel agent knows the accommodations and other services of the place they're recommending. Ask about the hotel's location, room size, beds, and whether it has a pool, room service, or programs for children, if you care about these. Has your agent been there in person or sent others whom you can contact?

Do some homework on your own, too: local tourism boards can provide information about lesser-known and small-niche operators, some of which may only sell direct.

BUYER BEWARE

Each year consumers are stranded or lose their money when tour operators—even large ones with excellent reputations—go out of business. So **check out the operator.** Ask several travel agents about its reputation, and try to **book with a company that has a consumer-protection program.** (Look for information in the company's brochure.) In the United States, members of the National Tour Association and the United States Tour Operators Association are required to set aside funds to cover your payments and travel arrangements in the event that the company defaults. It's also a good idea to choose a company that participates in the American Society of Travel Agents' Tour Operator Program (TOP); ASTA will act as mediator in any disputes between you and your tour operator. Trip-cancellation insurance can sometimes be purchased from an agency other than the trip provider.

Remember that the more your package or tour includes the better you can predict the ultimate cost of your vacation. Make sure you know exactly what is covered, and **beware of hidden costs.** Are taxes, tips, and transfers included? Entertainment and excursions? These can add up.

➤ TOUR-OPERATOR RECOMMENDATIONS: **American Society of Travel Agents** (☞ Travel Agencies, *below*). **National Tour Association** (NTA; ✉ 546 E. Main St., Lexington, KY 40508, ☎ 859/226–4444 or 800/682–8886, WEB www.ntaonline.com). **United States Tour Operators Association** (USTOA; ✉ 275 Madison Ave., Suite 2014, New York, NY 10016, ☎ 212/599–6599 or 800/468–7862, FAX 212/599–6744, WEB www.ustoa.com).

TRAVEL AGENCIES

A good travel agent puts your needs first. Look for an agency that has been in business at least five years, emphasizes customer service, and has someone on staff who specializes in your destination. In addition, **make sure the agency belongs to a professional trade organization.** The American Society of Travel Agents (ASTA)—the largest and most influential in the field with more than 26,000 members in some 170 countries—maintains and enforces a strict code of ethics and will step in to help mediate any agent-client disputes if necessary. ASTA (whose motto is "Without a travel agent, you're on your own") also maintains a Web site that includes a directory of agents. (If a travel agency is also acting as your tour operator, *see* Buyer Beware *in* Tours & Packages, *above*.)

➤ LOCAL AGENT REFERRALS: **American Society of Travel Agents** (ASTA; ☎ 800/965–2782 24-hr hot line, FAX 703/739–7642, WEB www.astanet.com). **Association of British Travel Agents** (✉ 68–71 Newman St., London W1T 3AH, U.K., ☎ 020/7637–2444, FAX 020/7637–0713, WEB www.abtanet.com). **Association of Canadian Travel Agents** (✉ 130 Albert St., Suite 1705, Ottawa, Ontario K1P 5G4, Canada, ☎ 613/237–3657, FAX 613/237–7502, WEB www.acta.ca). **Australian Federation of Travel Agents** (✉ Level 3, 309 Pitt St., Sydney NSW 2000, Australia, ☎ 02/9264–3299, FAX 02/9264–1085, WEB www.afta.com.au). **Travel Agents' Association of New Zealand** (✉ Box 1888, Wellington 6001, New Zealand, ☎ 04/499–0104, FAX 04/499–0827, WEB www.taanz.org.nz).

VISITOR INFORMATION

➤ TOURIST INFORMATION: **Bahamas Tourist Office,** WEB www.gobahamas.com (☎ 800/422–4262; ✉ 8600 W. Bryn Mawr Ave., Suite 820, Chicago, IL 60631, ☎ 773/693–1500, FAX 773/693–1114; ✉ Bahama Out Islands Promotion Board, 19495 Biscayne Blvd., Suite 809, Aventura, FL 33180, ☎ 800/688–4752, FAX 305/359–8098; ✉ 3450 Wilshire Blvd., Suite 1204, Los Angeles, CA 90010, ☎ 213/385–0033, FAX 213/383–3966; ✉ 121 Bloor St. E, Suite 1101, Toronto M4W 3M5, ☎ 416/968–2999, FAX 416/968–6711; ✉ 3, The Billings, Walnut Tree Close, Guildford, Surrey G1 4UL, U.K., ☎ 01483/448–900, FAX 01483/571–846).

Bahamas Tourism Center (✉ 150 E. 52nd St., 28th floor N, New York, NY 10022, ☎ 800/823–3136 or 212/758–2777, FAX 212/753–6531). **Caribbean Tourism Organization** (✉ 80 Broad St., 32nd floor, New York, NY 10017, ☎ 212/635–9530, FAX 212/697–4258, WEB www.doitbahamas.com). **Morris-Kevan International Ltd.** (✉ International House, 47 Chase Side, Enfield, Middlesex EN2 6NB, ☎ 0181/364–5188, FAX 0181/367–9949). **Nassau/Paradise Island Promotion Board** (✉ 19495 Biscayne Blvd., Suite 804, Aventura, FL 33180, ☎ 305/931–1555, FAX 305/931–3005).

Turks and Caicos Islands Tourist Board (✉ Box 128, Front St., Grand Turk, Turks and Caicos Islands, ☎ 800/241–0824 or 649/946–2321, FAX 649/946–2733, WEB www.turksandcaicostourism.com).

➤ U.S. GOVERNMENT ADVISORIES: **U.S. Department of State** (✉ Overseas Citizens Services Office, Room 4811 N.S., 2201 C St. NW, Washington,

DC 20520, ☏ 202/647–5225 interactive hot line or 888/407–4747, WEB www.travel.state.gov); enclose a business-size SASE.

WEB SITES

Do check out the World Wide Web when you're planning your trip. You'll find everything from weather forecasts to virtual tours of famous cities. Be sure to **visit Fodors.com** (www.fodors.com), a complete travel-planning site. You can research prices and book plane tickets, hotel rooms, rental cars, vacation packages, and more. In addition, you can post your pressing questions in the Travel Talk section. Other planning tools include a currency converter and weather reports, and there are loads of links to other travel resources.

WHEN TO GO

The Bahamas is affected by the refreshing trade-wind flow generated by an area of high atmospheric pressure covering a large part of the subtropical North Atlantic, so the climate varies little during the year. The most pleasant time is from December through May, when the temperature averages 70°F–75°F. It stands to reason that hotel prices during this period are at their highest—around 30% higher than during the less popular times. The rest of the year is hot and humid and prone to tropical storms; the temperature hovers around 80°F–85°F. Hurricane season is from about June 1st through November 30th, with greatest risk for a storm from August through October.

Whether you want to join it or avoid it, be advised that Spring Break takes place between the end of February and mid-April. This means a lot of vacationing college students, beach parties, sports events, and entertainment.

CLIMATE

What follows are average daily maximum and minimum temperatures for Nassau. Freeport's temperatures are nearly the same: a degree or two cooler in the spring and fall, and a degree or two warmer in the summer.

➤ FORECASTS: **Weather Channel Connection** (☏ 900/932–8437, 95¢ per minute from a Touch-Tone phone).

NASSAU

Jan.	77F	25C	May	85F	29C	Sept.	88F	31C
	62	17		70	21		74	23
Feb.	78F	26C	June	87F	31C	Oct.	85F	29C
	63	17		73	23		72	22
Mar.	80F	27C	July	89F	32C	Nov.	82F	28C
	64	18		75	24		68	20
Apr.	82F	28C	Aug.	89F	32C	Dec.	79F	26C
	66	19		75	24		64	18

FESTIVALS AND SEASONAL EVENTS

➤ DEC.: The **Sun International Bahamas Open,** an event attracting some of the world's highest-ranked tennis players, is held at the Ocean Club on Paradise Island.

➤ DEC.: The **Authentically Bahamian Christmas Trade Show** showcases crafts, pottery, jewelry, and batiks.

➤ DEC.: The **National Junkanoo Competition Finals,** the "Olympics of Junkanoo," is held on Paradise Island.

➤ DEC.: **Christmas Day** and **Boxing Day,** December 26, are both public holidays. Boxing Day coincides with the first of the **Junkanoo** parades.

➤ DEC.: The **Breitling Crystal Our Lucaya Lucayan Course Pro-Am Golf Tournament** is a week of meets at Grand Bahama's Our Lucaya Lucayan Course that draws a roster of professional and amateur golfers almost as long as the tourney's name.

➤ DEC.: Other annual December doings in Nassau include the **Christ-**

mas at Government House festivities, **Police Band Annual Christmas and Classical Concert, Junior Junkanoo Parade, Parliament Square Tree Lighting,** and **Renaissance Singers Concert.**

➤ JAN.: **Junkanoo** continues its uniquely Bahamian (Mardi Gras–style) festivities welcoming the New Year, with the **New Year's Day Junkanoo Parade,** in downtown Nassau. Less extensive celebrations take place in the Out Islands—also on January 1, a public holiday.

➤ JAN.: The **New Year's Day Sailing Regatta** at Montagu Bay, Nassau, includes competition among Bahamian-built sloops, whereas the annual **Staniel Cay Annual New Year's Day Cruising Regatta** is celebrated in the Exumas.

➤ JAN.: Pomp and pageantry take over when the **Supreme Court** opens in Nassau with the Chief Justice inspecting the Royal Bahamas Police Force Guard-of-Honor, accompanied by the acclaimed Bahamas Police Force Band.

➤ JAN.: For cultural types, the repertory season begins at Nassau's **Dundas Centre for the Performing Arts.**

➤ JAN.: The **Bahamas Wahoo Tournament** draws great numbers of anglers to the waters around several Out Islands for a series of competitions beginning in November and running through February.

➤ JAN.: The **Royal Oasis Golf Resort & Casino Crystal Pro-Am Golf Tournament,** on Grand Bahama Island, is one of the area's most prestigious, bringing amateurs and professionals (who play together on teams) to the Bahamia's Ruby and Emerald golf courses.

➤ JAN.: The **Grand Bahama Island Carnival** comes to town the last two weeks of January. Held in Goombay Park, with games, food, music, and rides.

➤ FEB.: The **Farmer's Cay Festival** is held the first Friday on this tiny cay in the Exumas. Boat races, treasure hunts, music, and food are highlights.

➤ FEB.: The **Bacardi Cup Challenge** has native 17 ft–28 ft sloops that compete off Montagu Bay.

➤ FEB.: The **Bahamas Wahoo Tournament** has its final installment on several Out Islands.

➤ MAR.: The annual **Red Cross Fair** at the Queen Elizabeth Sports Centre rounds off Nassau's winter social season.

➤ MAR.: The annual **George Town (All Exuma) Cruising Regatta** is a popular sailing event attracting more than 500 visiting yachts for a week of fun and festivities.

➤ MAR.: Hope Town, Elbow Cay, comes alive with a **Heritage Day** with games, a raffle, a treasure hunt, and plenty of food.

➤ MAR.: The weeklong **Bacardi Rum Billfish Tournament** on Bimini is one of the most prestigious events of the year for deep-sea sportfishers.

➤ MAR.: The **Andros Annual International Square Celebration** is a celebration of Andros residents of all heritages, with flag raising, music, and international cuisines.

➤ MAR.: A one-man show by one of the islands' foremost painters, the **Annual Alton Lowe Art Exhibition** is held at the Nassau Beach hotel.

➤ APR.: Held at Long Bay Cays Park, the **Andros Going Back to the Island Festival** is a week of contests, native food and music, games, and fun.

➤ APR.: **Good Friday, Easter,** and the following **Easter Monday** are public holidays.

➤ APR.: George Town, Exuma, hosts the **Family Island Regatta,** the Bahamas's most important yachting event of the year.

➤ APR.: It's a big month for anglers, with the **Bimini Break Blue Marlin Rendezvous; billfish tournaments** at Treasure Cay and Marsh Harbour, Abacos; the **Eleuthera Fishing Tournament;** and the Berry Islands' **Bahamas Billfish Chub Cay Championship.**

➤ APR.: The **South Eleuthera Homecoming Festival,** a four-day splash, livens up the Rock Sound area with celebrations, and the tiny Eleuthera settlement of James Cistern comes alive with food, drink, parties, and cultural events during the **James Cistern Heritage Affair Gala Fair.**

➤ MAY: The **Long Island Sailing Regatta,** Salt Pond, Long Island, has sloop races, a yacht parade, and a lot of activity both on and off the water.

➤ MAY: The **Barreterre Festival** livens up this settlement on the north end of Great Exuma.

➤ MAY: The **Rolex Classic** is played at the Ocean Club Golf Course.

➤ MAY: The **South Caicos Regatta** is held at Cockburn Harbour, South Caicos.

➤ JUNE: **Labour Day,** the first Friday of the month, and **Whit Monday** are public holidays.

➤ JUNE: Yes, more **fishing tournaments:** The Bimini Big Five and Junior tournaments, the Fly Fishing Tournament on Andros, and the Bahamas Billfish Tournament (Abaco) are major ones this month.

➤ JUNE: The **Cat Island Rake and Scrape Festival** is a two-day fest of performances of the Bahamas's indigenous rake and scrape music.

➤ JUNE: Three days of crab races, cook-offs, live rake and scrape music, and a performance by the Bahamas Police Band comprise the **All Andros Crabfest.**

➤ JUNE: Nassau's Arawak Cay is transformed into a heritage village every weekend for the cultural festival **Junkanoo in June;** live performances, crafts, kids' programs, fabulous native dishes, and a costumed Junkanoo Rushout (dancing in the streets) occur each night.

➤ JUNE: Gregory Town is the scene of the **Eleuthera Pineapple Festival,** with a Junkanoo parade, crafts displays, tours of pineapple farms, games, contests, and sports events—as well as an opportunity to sample what Eleuthera natives proclaim to be the sweetest pineapple in the world.

➤ JUNE: Sailing sloops from throughout the country meet in the **Grand Bahama Sailing Regatta,** in the exciting "Championship of the Seas."

➤ JULY: The Bahamas's most important public holiday falls on July 10—**Independence Day,** which was established in 1973 and marks the end of 300 years of British rule. **Independence Week** is celebrated

throughout the Bahamas with regattas, boat races, fishing tournaments, and a plethora of parties.

➤ JULY: Eleuthera offers two **Homecoming Festivals,** in Savannah Sound and Bluff; both are great ways to mingle with locals over food, drink, games, and general partying.

➤ JULY: The annual **Cat Island Regatta** includes parties, fashion shows, and other entertainment.

➤ JULY: The **Annual Racing Time in Abaco** is an eight-day event with five races and tons of on-shore festivities.

➤ AUG.: **Emancipation Day,** which marks when the English freed Bahamian slaves in 1834, is a public holiday celebrated on the first Monday in August.

➤ AUG.: The annual 10-day **Fox Hill Festival** in Nassau pays tribute to Emancipation with an early morning Junkanoo Rushout, music, cookouts, games, and other festivities.

➤ AUG.: The **Finco Open** is played at the South Ocean Golf Course, whereas a very different sort of competition can be seen at the annual **Miss Bahamas Beauty Pageant,** held in Nassau.

➤ AUG.: Annual **regattas** take place at two Exuma locations (Rolleville and Black Point).

➤ AUG.: The Turks and Caicos islands hold their **carnival** during the last days of the month.

➤ AUG.: Guess what, Bimini has another fishing competition, the **Bimini Native Fishing Tournament.**

➤ SEPT.: More than 200 contestants participate in the grueling **Great Abaco Triathlon,** which includes swimming, running, and biking.

➤ SEPT.: The **Grand Bahama Junkanoo Carnival** includes three days of gospel and Junkanoo concerts, and cross-cultural events like the Bahamian and Trinidadian Carnival parade.

➤ SEPT.: The **Pepsi Open** takes place at the South Ocean Golf Course.

➤ SEPT.: Three legs of the small **B.O.A.T. Tournament,** a (try to hide your surprise) Bimini fishing contest for boats less than 27 ft, take place this month.

➤ OCT.: The **Annual McLean's Town Conch Cracking Contest,** which includes games and entertainment along with good eating, takes place on Grand Bahama Island as it has for more than 25 years.

➤ OCT.: **Discovery Day,** commemorating the landing of Columbus in the islands in 1492, is observed on October 12, a public holiday.

➤ OCT.: The **Nicholl's Town (Andros) Regatta and Homecoming** perks up this island, whereas the **North Eleuthera Sailing Regatta** and the **San Salvador Sailing Regatta** each occupy five days of busy sailing.

➤ OCT.: The **World Invitational Bonefishing Championship** includes fishing competitions, cocktail parties, and a gala dinner on Exuma, renowned for the sport.

➤ OCT.: Nassau comes alive with culture this month, with the Ministry of Tourism's **Seafood and Heritage Festival** on Arawak Cay, the Ministry of Foreign Affairs–sponsored **International Cultural Weekend** at the Botanic Gardens, and the **Wine and Art Festival,** sponsored by the Bahamas National Trust at its headquarters, The Retreat.

➤ NOV.: At the **Annual One Bahamas Music and Heritage Festival** you'll enjoy three days of concerts, food, and games celebrating national unity.

➤ NOV.: **Christmas Jollification** is a two-day arts-and-crafts fair with Bahamian Christmas crafts, food, and music held at the Bahamas National Trust, Nassau.

➤ NOV.: The **Bimini Big Game Fishing Club All Wahoo Tournament** is held in the Biminis, and the **Bahamas Wahoo Tournament** has its first leg of a four-month series that traverses the Out Islands.

➤ NOV.: The monthlong **European Invitational Golf Weeks** occurs all over Grand Bahama Island. Also on Grand Bahama is the annual **Conchman Triathlon,** a swimming/running/bicycling competition for amateurs that raises funds for local charities.

➤ NOV.: Nassau society holds two annual charity events, the **Bahamas Humane Society's Annual Animals Thanksgiving Ball,** a black-tie event on tony Lyford Cay, and the **Red Ribbon Ball,** a fund-raiser for the Bahamas AIDS Foundation.

1 DESTINATION: THE BAHAMAS

A Country Built on Water

New and Noteworthy

What's Where

Pleasures and Pastimes

Great Itineraries

Fodor's Choice

A COUNTRY BUILT ON WATER: THE ALLURING WORLD OF THE BAHAMAS

BAHAMIANS LIKE TO tell the story—whether true or apocryphal—that American astronauts returning from orbit declared that they could recognize only two sights from space: the Great Wall of China and the waters of the Bahamas. It wouldn't be surprising, for the sea is the prevailing feature of this country of more than 700 islands—approximately 75% of the country lies underwater, and its shores are rimmed by some of the world's great barrier reefs. The sea is geography, attraction, livelihood, and inspiration all in one. Talk to a painter, diver, boatbuilder, fisherman, or chef, and they'll all likely agree: Without the sea, the Bahamas would lose its raison d'être.

The nation's existence is based largely on tourism. Even though you can reach it in less than an hour's flight from the Florida coast, the Bahamas's singular natural beauty and exotic appeal make it seem more like a far-flung outpost. Picture a tiny cay (pronounced "key") ringed by lacy casuarina pines, stately palms, and silken sands that meet the startling hue of the sea. The water ranges from pale aqua to deep sapphire, the spectrum changing hourly as the relentless Bahamian sun sweeps across the island sky. As you lie on the beach, a distant boat plies the calm waters. A lonely gull swoops by overhead, surprised to see that he has company. A single set of footprints—yours—crosses the strand. In many ways, you realize, things have changed very little since Christopher Columbus arrived here in 1492.

Venture inland to a lush world of tropical foliage: hibiscus of watery apricot, brilliant scarlet, and jaunty yellow; bougainvillea of shocking pink or fluorescent lavender; poinciana trees inflaming the sky with their bright orange flowers. Pineapples and guavas grow in profusion here, as do mangoes, breadfruit, papayas, sugar apples, and sapodillas. Surprisingly, all of these were imports. No fruit-bearing plant is indigenous to the Bahamas.

Tiny villages known as "settlements," often consisting of New England–style cottages dressed up in vibrant tropical hues, dot the verdant landscape. Underwater, more delights await. Beneath the 100,000 square mi of Atlantic Ocean across which the Bahamas are scattered (the country is not, as many believe, in the Caribbean) lies a wonderland waiting to delight experienced divers and novice snorkelers. Drift on the crystal sea's surface, noticing how the colors so striking from a distance fade to transparency when you're out in the water. Gaze through fantasies of frilly fan coral and phantasmagoric sponges to the sea floor below as a smiling blue tang and a phosphorescent parrot fish float past your eyes. A school of tiny silversides darts by, engulfing you in a glittering wall of motion.

Should you prefer to park yourself on a hammock strung between pines overlooking the deserted shores for a daylong nap, no one would think it odd—many tourists' favorite activity is no activity at all. There's something about the atmosphere here—the steamy sun, the picture-perfect vistas, the alluringly slow–paced local life—that beckons even the most active types to a shocking indolence. It's a magic that works subtly but effectively. Harried executives suddenly find that their most pressing business is watching the waves beat against the shore, and bankers with type-A personalities discover their commerce dwindling to the collection of sand dollars from a deserted beach.

You may even find, to your surprise, that you ventured out of your resort without wearing your watch. Congratulations! You've discovered "Bahamian time," where 20 minutes could mean an hour and a half, and days could stretch endlessly in patterns of fabulous idleness, rendering the concept of time flexible, if not downright meaningless. Ask five Bahamians how long it takes to get to a certain place; you're guaranteed to get five different answers. Tell someone self-importantly that you need something done "yesterday," and you'll unfailingly be met with an all-knowing and sympathetic smile. You can try to fight it if you like, but there's really no point. Things just don't move too quickly down here. Get used to that fact, and you'll have come a long way toward appreciating these laid-back and leisurely isles.

Life in the Bahamas is not *all* about glorious laziness. Nassau, the country's capital, is a bustling town on New Providence Island with shops, nightclubs, and an enviable array of restaurants, glitzy casinos, and posh hotels. Even in Nassau, though, there are quiet byways and shady lanes where you can escape the main tourist drags' tumult. Shop 'til you drop or wander past colonial buildings that reveal the capital's fascinating history. Dine on delicate French cuisine in an elegant restaurant or rub shoulders with Bahamians in a down-home friendly eatery. Drop your dollars in a clangorous casino or escape to Paradise Island's secluded Versailles Gardens. Boogie the night away in a rowdy club or take a nighttime stroll along now-quiet Cable Beach, the daytime hubbub just a memory.

O**F COURSE, YOU CAN FLEE** the hurly-burly altogether and head straight for one of the Out Islands (the term refers to everything except New Providence Island and Grand Bahama Island). The most exciting development in the Out Islands is usually the outcome of last night's domino game, the most pressing news the size of the wave that crashed onto the shore that afternoon. In contrast to the modernity of Nassau and Freeport resorts, you'll find intimate inns here where you can escape from the world entirely.

But it would be a shame to escape too completely, for the Bahamians are about as wonderful a group of people as you're likely to meet. This is a country where children stop on their bicycles to say hello and to ask, in a distinctive, not-quite-Caribbean lilt, "Everyt'ing OK?" A country where the drugstore cashier is the mother of your hotel manager, where a stranger you meet on the Nassau–to–Paradise Island bridge turns out to be the brother of a straw-weaver you encountered on Exuma. Where your waitress, discovering she's run out of iced tea, heads to the back of the bar for her thermos and pours you a glass of her private supply. In response to your effusive thanks, she looks at you, a smile on her face but surprise in her eyes that you'd

consider this at all unusual. "Well, it's no problem," she declares, "no problem at all. That's what friends are for."

Everyone's a friend in the Bahamas. Strike up a conversation with the person sitting next to you at the bar or strolling along the harbor wall. If there's one thing Bahamians enjoy, it's talking. Take advantage of this garrulousness. You might find that you come away with new and fascinating insights.

You may, for instance, find out about bush medicine, a time-honored use of the plants that grow in such profusion throughout the islands. On some islands, you can even take a bush-medicine tour. Your guide will point out the swelling bush (good for back problems) or love vine (not surprisingly used in many romance-involved concoctions). Have a headache? Try some breadfruit leaves, beaten with warm water. You may be surprised at the results.

Strike up another conversation. It's getting easier, isn't it? Is that because you've finally opened up to the amicable Bahamian style, or could it be the potent rum drinks you've been downing while listening to your newfound friends? Whichever, you've done well, for there's a wealth of information waiting in this many-layered culture. Perhaps you'll hear about the renaissance of Bahamian painting and vow to discover for yourself the works of Eddie Minnis, Walter Bethel, Amos Ferguson, or Alton Lowe, or listen to local music, which ranges from old-time gospel and calypso to Bahamian rake 'n' scrape, played on cowbells and other uncommon instruments. You might be regaled with stories of local church activities. These establishments are so important to Bahamian society that one Paradise Island resort offers a church visit at its activities desk, and tiny Man-O-War Cay, in the Abacos, boasts three churches in as many blocks. If you're lucky, you'll be invited to a church supper or afternoon fish fry.

Maybe you'll discover some of the engrossing history that gives the country its multicultural heritage, which in turn makes for enviably easy relations among races. The islands are full of historians, both amateur and professional, and if you can sort out the facts from the embroidery you'll come away truly enlightened. At the very least, you'll hear a long, complicated, and undeniably vivid saga. Pull up a bar stool as the story begins. Order another Goombay Smash from the smiling bartender. You'll undoubtedly need it before the tale is over.

It's a colorful story, beginning with the Lucayan Indians—the first residents of the islands—who gave our language such words as "iguana," "potato," "guava," and (interesting for such a peace-loving people) "cannibal." It continues with Spanish invaders led by the likes of Columbus and Ponce de León. The Spanish virtually wiped out the indigenous population by 1520 and gave their own name to these islands surrounded by a "Baja Mar," or shallow sea—a term that later became corrupted into "Bahama." It tells of English settlers escaping religious repression (the islands were claimed by England in 1629 and remained under its control, except for brief periods, for almost three and a half centuries), of British Loyalists fleeing the Carolinas and New England after the Revolutionary War. It's a tale of marauding pirates, from Edward Teach (better known as Blackbeard) and Henry Morgan to Calico Jack Rackham and his notorious female cohorts, Anne Bonney and Mary Read. The story tells of slaves and former slaves, some freed at sea and transported to Bahamian shores to form their own settlements, some emancipated only with the ending of slavery here in the 1830s. You can still see the effects of slavery in the names of many residents, who often took on the surnames of their former owners; this is why, for instance, every other resident of Exuma seems to be named Rolle.

Above all, it's a story of intriguing characters. There's Captain Woodes Rogers, the first royal governor of the Bahamas, a former privateer himself, who's widely credited with ending the reign of piracy by, among other things, hanging eight offenders on the site of what was to become Nassau's British Colonial Hotel. There's Sir Harry Oakes, a rough-and-ready Canadian who made his fortune in gold during the 1940s. He built the Bahamas Country Club and developed the Cable Beach Golf Course. On July 8, 1943, his battered and badly charred body was found in his bed. The mystery remains unsolved to this day.

There's that famous pair of lovebirds, the Duke and Duchess of Windsor, who arrived in the Bahamas in 1939 for the duke's stint as governor. The Bahamians were impressed. A calypso ballad, "Love Alone," was composed in honor of the couple's fairy-tale romance. Sentimental? Perhaps. Unfailingly romantic? Of course. But then there's always been a romantic streak here. Live your life among such beauty and see if you don't develop a bit of a tender touch yourself. An evening on a quiet Out Island bluff is enough to bring out the soft-hearted underside of even the most confirmed cynic.

IN THE END it comes back to the sea, as it always has in this country surrounded by, and built upon, the water. Independent from Britain since 1973, the Bahamas has come a long way toward restoring prosperity and stability. The country is progressing faster than ever: Its tourism is booming, and new construction is relentless, at least in the major resort areas. Head to the Out Islands, though, or even to many corners of the bigger towns, and you'll still discover a feeling of being lost in time, transported to a different, more relaxed era.

Like the sea, the changes ebb and flow, but also like the sea, the things that make the Bahamas what they are—and have been—are little changed: the overwhelming natural beauty, the extraordinary progression of cultures, and above all the steadfastly congenial Bahamian people themselves. With a warmth that seems to flow directly from the unceasing tropical sun, with the constancy of the inexorable sea itself, they welcome the ever-increasing numbers of visitors who come to spend a few days, or weeks, or perhaps (stranger things have happened) the rest of their lives in this little corner of paradise.

— Rich Rubin

NEW AND NOTEWORTHY

Those who remember the Bahamas from college spring-break trips might be surprised on a return visit. Both the Bahamian government and the private sector have been investing time and money to enhance the tourism infrastructure, and the islands' advertising slogan ("It just keeps getting better") is that rare publicity motto that actually has a ring of truth to it. Service standards have been raised through training programs for those who interact with visitors, including police and immigration officers, taxi drivers, tour operators, and hotel workers.

Nassau continues to be a popular cruise-ship destination, but there's a resurgence of visits by a more upscale crowd, and a sophistication that belies the city's rowdy and dowdy reputation, with hotels upgrading, dining possibilities expanding, and new vacation homes popping up everywhere, particularly on Cable Beach's western edge. Construction of a second bridge linking Nassau and Paradise Island has helped ease traffic between the two, but the one-way system installed on downtown Nassau's two main streets has done little to ease congestion. In fact, many locals think it's made matters worse. Parking remains a problem as well. The dock area has been spruced up, but progress in the new phase of renovation has been infuriatingly slow. Nassau visitors wanting an escape from the town's bustle can now head to Eleuthera and Harbour Island for the day on high-speed ferries, which whisk travelers to these Out Islands in about three hours. With daily trips back and forth, it's a welcome addition to Nassau's ever-expanding day-tour possibilities.

Of course, even life in paradise has its setbacks: Dejection set in when residents, including hundreds of vendors, watched the Straw Market, along with the Bahamas Ministry of Tourism offices, burn to the ground in September 2001. A temporary site for the displaced vendors was set up a few weeks later on nearby Bay Street, and you can spar with the sellers as always. The Ministry is considering how and when to rebuild the market.

In the hotel sector, construction and refurbishment proceed at an astounding rate. Sun International now owns more than 70% of Paradise Island. It continues to expand the Atlantis resort—which is more than double its original size—with the upscale Ocean Club, a 63-slip marina, the addition of harborside shops designed by noted local architect Jackson Burnside, and a redesign of the Ocean Club Golf Course (formerly the Paradise Island Golf Club). One victim of the expansions is the Paradise Island Airport. Nassau International Airport is now the only option for those arriving by air.

In downtown Nassau, the British Colonial Hilton Nassau (formerly the British Colonial Hotel) has completed its banking and business wing, which is also the new home of the Nassau Stock Exchange. Graycliff, Nassau's venerable mansion hotel, was already maintaining a formidable cigar motif with its six tobacco-themed guest rooms and cigar-themed Humidor Restaurant; the property has taken its stogie passion to the next level by acquiring an entire cigar factory, open to the public for tours and purchases. If pampering yourself doesn't involve lighting up, you'll also want to note that the ultra-modern spa Windermere has opened a branch at Graycliff.

The 18-hole Cable Beach Golf Club, the oldest course in the Bahamas, is undergoing a major renovation, but golfers take heart: you can still play nine holes until the new course opens.

And it's not only in Nassau and on Paradise Island that change is taking place. On Grand Bahama Island, a major facelift has been completed over the past seven years. It began with a makeover of several resorts into the grand Our Lucaya resort, opened in 2000. It includes three new luxury hotels, two 18-hole golf courses, convention facilities, a shopping village, three separate theme pools, and a sprawling casino whose opening has yet to be scheduled. Not to be outdone, Royal Oasis Golf Resort & Casino (formerly the Resort at Bahamia) underwent a $42 million renovation with a whole new Mediterranean image and a beach pool as its centerpiece. At the West End, elegant new Old Bahama Bay revives a town of past glories.

Major hotel development projects are *not* the news in all of the serene Out Islands, with the exception of the Abaco Beach Resort & Boat Harbour in Marsh Harbour, and a mega-room, mega-acre Emerald Bay Resort & Co. property underway on Great Exuma, which will include a casino and 18-hole Greg Norman golf course. Most of the Out Islands lodging landscape is focused on the renovation of many existing hotels and rental homes. Adding freshwater pools and equipping rooms with whirlpool bathtubs, telephone, cable TV, and air-conditioning are current priorities. The ubiquitous Web has arrived in a big way. Many hotels now maintain Web pages that include reservation forms.

WHAT'S WHERE

The Bahamian Islands—with their exquisite gold- and pink-sand beaches, lush tropical landscapes, unsullied waters, and year-round sunshine—couldn't have sprung from the sea in more perfect shape for 21st-century vacationers. The archipelago begins 55 mi off the Florida coast and contains more than 700 islands, approximately 30 of them inhabited, scattered over 100,000 square mi of the Atlantic.

New Providence Island

Many travelers make New Providence Island—more specifically Nassau, the nation's capital and something of a tourist mecca—their principal stop in the Bahamas. Discover the nation's past in the island's historic buildings, forts, gardens, and monuments. Cable Beach and Paradise Island are chockablock with luxurious resorts, upscale restaurants, groomed beaches, water sports aplenty, and a busy nightclub scene.

Grand Bahama Island

Grand Bahama, the fourth-largest island in the Bahamas after Andros, Eleuthera, and Great Abaco, lies only 52 mi off Palm Beach, Florida. The Gulf Stream's ever-warm waters lap its western tip, and the Little Bahama Bank protects it from the northeast.

Grand Bahama's twin cities, Freeport and Lucaya, may not have Nassau's colonial charm, but if you want to shop, gamble, or just hang out at the beach—at a slightly lower cost than in the capital—there's no need to go elsewhere. Freeport, which was built in the '60s, has a much-visited International Bazaar, where you'll find imported goods at duty-free prices. In Lucaya, adjacent to Freeport, you can swim with dolphins or learn to dive at a world-renowned scuba school. Resorts are split between the cities, and both have access to shopping, gambling, and golf. Lucaya's resorts sit directly on the beach and marina. Outside the resort area lie pristine beaches, ecotourism attractions, and old-island fishing settlements.

The Out Islands

To escape New Providence's and Grand Bahama's crowds and glittering modernity, hop a plane, boat, or even a helicopter to one of the Out Islands, where life progresses at a slower pace, and the landscape is still largely unaffected by major development. In fact, many seasoned Bahamas travelers skip the more populated islands altogether and head straight for these unspoiled isles, usually called the Family Islands by locals (it's the rare Bahamian who doesn't have roots here). Wander uncluttered beaches and narrow, sand-strewn streets, or lunch in a village where fishermen's tidy homes are painted in soft pastel shades and shrouded in brilliantly colored vegetation. The Out Islands' common traits— an abundance of natural beauty and small-town atmosphere—should not disguise their differences, however. You may be surprised by the variety of sites and activities the islands have to offer.

The Abacos

The Abacos, a center for boatbuilding, have attracted sailing and yachting fans over the years with their translucent waters and excellent marina facilities. If you come without a yacht, you can still enjoy a look at Elbow Cay's famous striped lighthouse and strap on your fins to explore Pelican Cay, an underwater national park. Marsh Harbour, the third-largest city in the country, is well stocked with restaurants and shops (as well as the only stoplight in the Abacos, a source of great local pride).

Andros

Andros, the largest Bahamian island, is flanked by the world's third-largest coral reef—a spectacular, 140-mi-long haunt for underwater creatures, making it a favorite for diving enthusiasts. On land, the appeal is equally wild, with the little-explored island of forests and swamps having none of the buildup of the more heavily visited spots. This is also where Androsia fabric, a Bahamian version of batik, is made, as well as some of the country's finest straw work.

The Berry Islands

The tiny cays of the Berry Islands are virtually uninhabited but for seabirds and big-game fishers, who appreciate the proximity to the Tongue of the Ocean and the excellent marinas on Chub and Great Harbour cays.

The Biminis

Deep-sea anglers find bliss in Bimini, for in its waters roam great warriors such as marlin, swordfish, giant tuna, wahoo, sailfish, dolphin, and bonefish. Literary aficionados can follow in the footsteps of Papa himself. In the '30s, Ernest Hemingway chose the Biminis as his favorite getaway. Both the bar he frequented and one of his homes are accessible to visitors.

Cat Island

Lush, hilly, and unspoiled, shrouded in an air of mysticism, this is a tranquil isle of small farms and fishing villages. Father Jerome's crumbling hilltop hermitage dominates the landscape. Its isolation makes it a perfect getaway for honeymooners, modern-day Robinson Crusoes, or anyone in search of natural beauty. A few resorts have sprung up to take advantage of a coast ringed with stunning—and usually deserted—beaches.

Crooked and Acklins Islands

Divers, snorkelers, and bonefishers find plenty to do on these adjoining, undeveloped islands. Miles of virgin barrier reef seem to be a well-kept secret, far off the beaten path.

Eleuthera

Eleuthera, notable for beaches, surfing, and excellent diving, is also an agricultural center producing crops from mangoes to okra and peas. This 100-mi-long island is sparsely populated, with just a handful of small, friendly settlements scattered across its bounteous landscape. Just off Eleuthera's north coast lies tiny Harbour Island. With its renowned 3-mi pink-sand beach, some of the Bahamas's most distinctive small hotels, and the New England–style village of Dunmore Town, it's one of the best-known Out Islands, but tourist activity hasn't ruined its low-key appeal. Also off Eleuthera is Spanish Wells, which thrives on fishing. Although residents can seem a little closed to outsiders, particularly in contrast to Harbour Island's tourism-based existence, it nonetheless makes an interesting expedition.

The Exumas

These hundreds of little cays are prime cruising ground for yachters, but you might also come to enjoy the charms of several attractive towns, welcoming small hotels, Exuma Land and Sea Park (a favorite with snorkelers and bird-watchers), and a 7-mi beach fabled for its seashells. Tourist activity is centered in the capital of George Town, on Great Exuma, whose residents are known for friendliness, and whose lovely Elizabeth Harbour fills with boats during regatta time.

Inagua

Bird-watchers marvel at the flock of more than 60,000 resident flamingos in a national park on Inagua, the southernmost of the Bahamian islands. Hundreds of other bird species also make their home in the island's salt flats, which provide much of the raw material for the Morton Salt Company, whose processing plant is located here.

Long Island

Two contrasting coastlines make Long Island one of the most scenic Out Island destinations. Although the western coast has soft, sandy beaches, the eastern side (never more than 4 mi away on this stretched, skinny strip) falls down to the ocean in dramatic rocky cliffs.

San Salvador

History may have been made on this little island, the legendary landfall of Christopher Columbus—although the claim is open to dispute. You can visit the marker commemorating the event or dive, snorkel, and fish in the surrounding waters.

The Turks and Caicos Islands

The Turks and Caicos, two groups of islands that lie to the southeast of the Bahamas, are nearly unknown to all but avid divers and seekers of untrod beaches. Although there's talk of developing the islands along the lines of some Bahamian destinations, for now you'll find all of the beauty but very little glitz.

PLEASURES AND PASTIMES

Beaches

You're standing in water so clear you can see straight down to your toes; in the distance, the sea becomes the patchwork of emerald, aqua, and sapphire that you thought existed only in postcards. The torrid Bahamian sun beats inexorably down, and golden sands stretch toward infinity. As you look around, you realize there's only one thing you don't see: other people. And that—sun, sea, sand—is the appeal of the Bahamas in a nutshell. Best of all, the concept of private beaches doesn't apply here; all beaches in the Bahamas are public up to the high-water mark. Of course, land access can be restricted, so you may need to boat into that unspoiled Eden. But if you can get there, it's yours— for the afternoon, anyway.

In Nassau, the major Cable Beach and Paradise Island hotels sit right on the water, whereas hotels on the outskirts are always near beaches such as Love Beach and Saunders Beach on New Providence's north shore and Adelaide Beach on the south. On Grand Bahama, only Our Lucaya, Xanadu, Viva Fortuna, and a few other properties are beachside, but if you're staying in Freeport you'll have access to public beaches such as Xanadu Beach, Taino Beach, and the long strip at Williams Town, all local favorites. The Out Islands are similarly brimming with beautiful beaches. One of the most intriguing is the pink-sand beach at Harbour Island, off Eleuthera.

Most islands' calm, leeward, western sides have the safest and most popular swimming beaches. There are no big waves, little undertow, and the buoyant salt water makes staying afloat almost effortless. The islands' windward, or Atlantic, sides are a different story, and even strong, experienced swimmers should exercise caution here. For novices, ocean waves are powerful and can be dangerous, and unseen currents, strong undertows, and uneven, rocky bottoms only make things more perilous. Some beaches post signs or flags to alert swimmers to water conditions, but few—even those at the best hotels—are protected by lifeguards. Swim at your own risk.

Casinos

There are three glitzy casinos in the Bahamas: two on New Providence Island— the Crystal Palace Casino at the Nassau Marriott Resort on Cable Beach and the Paradise Island Casino at Paradise Island's Atlantis resort; and one on Grand Bahama—Freeport's Royal Oasis Casino (formerly the Casino at Bahamia). All have above-average restaurants and lounges, and some have colorfully costumed revues. Although a couple of Out Island resorts have apparently received casino licenses, there are no immediate plans to bring gambling to these low-key locales.

Dining

Restaurants on New Providence (Nassau, Paradise Island, and Cable Beach) and Grand Bahama (Freeport and Lucaya) range from Indian and Chinese to upscale French and Italian. Ironically, Bahamian cuisine used to be hard to find in the tourist centers. Yet nowadays the Ministry of Tourism's "Real Taste of the Bahamas" program, which encourages the use of local ingredients, is thankfully changing the culinary landscape. One night you might be munching conch fritters and panfried grouper at an out-of-the-way local spot, and the next you might be savoring a Grand Marnier soufflé in a fancy French bistro. On the Out Islands, Bahamian food predominates, but international fare is gaining ground, particularly at resorts.

Most Bahamian cuisine looks to the sea, which provides a cornucopia of fresh products. Meat, on the other hand, is often imported and consequently expensive. The islands' signature seafood is the conch. This slow-moving creature abounds in the Bahamas's shallow waters, and thus finds its way onto many a menu. Its widely touted aphrodisiacal qualities don't hurt its popularity either. (Its shell's shiny pink interior appears in pendants, bracelets, earrings, brooches, and other ornaments, and you can even find the occasional conch pearl.) Conch meat turns up in a variety of incarnations, including cracked conch (pounded until tender and fried in seasoned batter), conch salad (raw, marinated in lime juice, with onions and peppers), conch chowder, conch fritters, even conch burgers. You can find stands selling fresh conch salad throughout the islands, and you might see fishermen on docks preparing scorched conch, which is eaten straight from the shell after being spiced with hot peppers—said to cure hangovers—salt, and lime.

Grouper is the headline fish, and you can feast on it and other fish from dawn to dusk if you so desire. For breakfast, you might try "boil fish," cooked with salt pork, onions, peppers, and spices, or "stew fish," in a rich brown gravy—both are usually served with grits or mildly sweet johnnycake. For lunch you might move on to steamed fish, cooked with a fragrant tomato base, then sample panfried grouper for dinner. Bahamian lobster, clawless and somewhat toothier than its cousins from Maine, is another delicious option. Order minced lobster and the meat will come shredded and cooked with tomatoes, green peppers, and onions.

At lunch and dinner, your entrée will likely be flanked by a generous mound of peas 'n' rice, potato salad, coleslaw, baked macaroni and cheese, or fried plantains. Some other local specialties, easier to find in the Out Islands, include turtle steak, wild boar, mutton, okra soup, "peas soup" and dough (dumplings), and the morning eye-opener known as souse—pigs' feet, chicken parts, sheep's tongue, or other bits of meat simmered with onions and potatoes in a spicy broth. Salads and other greens are scanty on most local menus, but fruit is abundant. Walk by a neighborhood fruit stand and you're likely to see such alluring offerings as mangoes, pineapples, breadfruit, sugarplums, hog plums, sapodillas, sea grapes, coco plums, soursops, avocados, tangerines, tamarinds, and papayas.

For many, beer is the thirst quencher of choice. Be sure to try locally brewed Kalik, a beer named for the sound of the cowbells played in indigenous Junkanoo music. When you're in the mood for a fruity, rum-based concoction, sip a Goombay Smash, a Bahama Mama, or a Yellowbird.

Bring your meal to a sweet close with guava duff, made by slathering guava jelly on a strip of dough, rolling and boiling it, then pouring a cream, rum, and egg–based sauce onto warm slices. Bahamians also love benny cake (created by cooking sesame seeds with sugar) and coconut jimmy (chewy dumplings in coconut sauce).

For the most inexpensive local treats, stop in on one of the fund-raising cookouts or parties periodically hosted on beaches and in Nassau and Freeport churches. The staff at your hotel or local newspapers can provide details.

Fishing

The Bahamas is an angler's dream. Light tackle, heavy tackle, fly-fishing, deep-sea fishing, reef fishing, fishing for blue marlin, bonefishing—you name it. Fishing in the Bahamas starts in the waters of Bimini off the Florida coast and ends at the southernmost island, Inagua, on the Caribbean's northern edge. Tournaments pop up all over the Out Islands during the year. Bimini alone has a dozen.

Golf

Golfers will find some enticing courses, most of them with refreshing sea views. The 18-hole, par-72 championship courses on New Providence and Paradise islands are all spectacularly beautiful and will put your swing to the test. Cable Beach Golf Club is on West Bay Street in Nassau, across the boulevard from Breezes Bahamas. The South Ocean Golf Club, on the island's south coast, is secluded and scenic. A third course, the Ocean Club Golf Course, covers most of the east end of Paradise Island. All three courses are open to the public (although this may be in the process of changing on Paradise Island), and instruction is available. A fourth course, at the Lyford Cay Golf Club, is available only to members and their guests. There are also four courses on Grand Bahama. Paradise Island, Freeport, and Grand Bahama Island host tournaments annually. PGA championship golf returned to the Bahamas in November 1995, with the initiation of the annual Paradise Island Invitational Pro-Am Tournament. Our Lucaya's Reef Course on Grand Bahama Island hosts the Senior PGA's Senior Slam in December.

Although your choices for teeing off on the Out Islands are more limited, you'll still find some appealing courses: one in Treasure Cay, Great Abaco; another at the Cotton Bay Club in Rock Sound, Eleuthera (the once-upscale hotel is closed, but the golf course is open to the public); and a nine-holer on Great Harbour Cay, Berry Islands.

Junkanoo

Nowhere is the Bahamians' zest for life more exuberantly expressed than in the Junkanoo celebrations held yearly on Boxing Day (the day after Christmas) and New Year's Day. Junkanoo can be likened in its uninhibited and frenzied activities to Carnival in Rio de Janeiro and Mardi Gras in New Orleans. Although festivals occur throughout the islands, the biggest celebrations are in Nassau. Raucous revelers dressed in costumes representing everything from kaleidoscopic dragons to eye-poppingly bright fish carry elaborately adorned floats fashioned from cardboard fastened to aluminum rods and decorated with glitter and crepe paper. The music, too, is distinctly Bahamian and indisputably clamorous, filling the breezy night with the sounds of goatskin drums, clanging cowbells, and shrieking whistles.

Lodging

Beachfront resort hotels—on Cable Beach and Paradise Island on New Providence Island, and in Lucaya on Grand Bahama Island—are among the most expensive. They also have the widest range of sports facilities, including tennis courts and sailboats. High room rates in many hotels in winter season (slightly less on Grand Bahama than on New Providence) are cut by as much as 30% during the slower May–December period, when managements try to outdo one another with attractive three-day or one-week packages. Prices at hotels away from the beach tend to be considerably lower and are often a better deal because accessible beaches are never far away.

In addition to cottages that come with fully equipped kitchens, Out Islands lodging includes numerous furnished apartment rentals.

People-to-People Programme

The free People-to-People Programme, a popular social event in the islands, gives visitors a more intimate glimpse of Bahamian life. The most extensive programs are on New Providence and Grand Bahama islands, where coordinators match visitors with Bahamians who have similar interests. Your hosts may show you around their town, invite you to attend a church service or community event, or even ask you into their home for a meal. People-to-People also sponsors an afternoon tea at Government House on the last Friday of each month (January–August). People-to-People events in the Out Islands consist mainly of monthly teas, fashion shows, barbecues, dances, and other gatherings; check with the local tourist office to see whether anything's been scheduled during your stay.

Coordinators ask that potential participants contact the **People-to-People Programme** (☏ 242/326–0435) or a Bahamas tourist office in the United States two to three weeks before their visit. Arrangements can sometimes be made with short notice, however, so if you're already in the islands, go to a Nassau or Freeport Tourist Information Centre or ask at your hotel's events desk.

Sailing and Seafaring

Crystal seas tinted every color from deep sapphire to pale aqua are dotted with tiny, palm-fringed cays that beckon the weary sailor to step ashore for a brief respite. With more than 700 to visit, the best and only way to reach many of the isles is by ship. And with such pleasures as prime-quality diving and snorkeling, it would be a shame not to get off the islands for some exploration. Boat rentals are scattered through the islands, making it easy to procure your own craft for a seafaring adventure (most also offer crews for the sailing-challenged). Sheltered waters, protected by offshore cays and undersea coral reefs, make navigating relatively easy, and plentiful marinas (many Out Island hotels offer facilities to boaters) means you're never far from a spot to tie up for the night.

Scuba

Few places in the world offer a wider variety of diving opportunities than the Bahamas. Wrecks and reefs, blue holes and drop-offs, sea gardens and shallow shoals can all be found here. In fact, one of the most famous scuba schools and NAUI (National Association of Underwater Instructors) centers in the world is UN-EXSO (Underwater Explorers Society), in Lucaya, Grand Bahama. For the most stunning peek at the watery underworld, head to the less crowded Out Islands, where many hotels offer economical dive packages.

With hundreds of islands, the Bahamas has literally thousands of dive sites in its crystal-clear waters. Local dive shops can offer regularly scheduled dives or personalized custom diving and are generous in offering correct and precise directions to many dive sites. In some cases, they will even give you the coordinates of a location. Unless you and your navigational equipment are extremely sharp, however, you could miss a site by 100 yards or so, which would still give you a lot of seabed to search. Some sites, of course, are obvious; you won't need a local guide to show you a sunken ship that stands 25 ft out of the water, and drop-offs aren't that hard to spot. Local experts, however, will know the best places to dive, the drop-offs, the safest places to drop an anchor, and even the best time of day to dive.

Tennis

New Providence has more than 80 courts, Grand Bahama has about 40, and many of the Out Islands, including Eleuthera, Exuma, and the Abacos, are also in on the racket. Each year, Paradise Island sponsors the Bahamas International Tennis Open, and the Freeport Tennis Open is held on Grand Bahama.

Weddings

Although perhaps not a "Pleasure and Pastime" for everyone, getting married in the Bahamas is very popular. In fact, there are so many visitors who say "I do" in the Bahamas that the Ministry of Tourism has established a separate Weddings Division, which takes care of all the paperwork necessary to marry in the Bahamas. It can arrange everything from a shipboard service to nuptials in the stunning Versailles Gardens—and it even finds the minister and photographer.

GREAT ITINERARIES

The most important thing to decide is what kind of vacation you want: a quiet getaway or an action-packed excursion. If you want shopping, dining, and nightlife, head straight for Nassau on New Providence, where's there's plenty to do and lots to see. If it's a tranquil trip you're seek-

ing, go to the Out Islands. Below are suggested itineraries for both areas. See the Exploring sections in each chapter for more information about individual sights.

If You Have 3 Days

If you've opted for a lively three days on New Providence, spend your first morning in **downtown Nassau** visiting historic sights. Have a leisurely lunch and spend the afternoon shopping. Be sure to check out the shopping on Bay Street and its environs. Day or night, you can test your luck in the two **casinos** (one on Cable Beach, one on Paradise Island). On day two, begin by exploring the sights on the island's eastern side, including **The Retreat** and **St. Augustine's Monastery.** Continue west around the island, perhaps taking time to visit the **Bacardi Distillery** or the **Commonwealth Brewery.** Head back toward Nassau and stop by **Arawak Cay,** a nice spot for a quick, local-style lunch. Or, alternatively, visit three nearby sites: **Fort Charlotte,** the **Nassau Botanic Gardens,** and **Ardastra Gardens and Conservation Centre,** home to the famous marching flamingos. If you have any energy left after this, dance the night away in a club or see one of the glittery extravaganzas offered by the resorts. Spend your last day on Paradise Island wandering through the **Atlantis, Paradise Island resort,** visiting **Cabbage Beach** or **Paradise Beach,** and spending a few minutes in the lovely **Versailles Gardens.** If you're still in search of more activity, water sports abound, and, of course, lounging on the beach can occupy the rest of your time.

If you've decided to head for the Out Islands, **Exuma** is a good choice if your time is limited. You can fly straight into George Town airport, outside Great Exuma's main town. On your first day, wander through the village of **George Town,** stopping to chat with the ladies in the tiny straw market. On day two, pick up some goodies at Mom's Bakery, a roadside van right in the town's center, before catching the ferry to picture-perfect **Stocking Island,** just a few minutes away and good for a half-day's worth of shelling and tanning. If you're feeling adventurous, rent a car and see some of this enticing island, from the tiny settlements of **Barreterre** and **Rolleville** in the north all the way down to **Williams Town** at Little Exuma's southern tip, connected to Great

Exuma by a bridge. On your last day, you may want to try bonefishing, diving, or snorkeling. There are operators in town (check with the local tourist office) who will gladly set you up. Another half-day possibility: a bush-medicine tour with a local flora expert, who will show you how various island plants are used medicinally.

Of course, your interests will determine what will be the right destination for you. If you're a dedicated angler, Bimini or the Berry Islands are where you should head. Bird-watchers should choose Inagua; devotees of island architecture should try Green Turtle Cay in the Abacos (or, for that matter, Nassau). Those enamored of a more modern look should consider Freeport and Lucaya on Grand Bahama Island. And if you're interested in doing nothing at all, consider Cat Island.

If You Have 5 Days

If you're traveling to Nassau, follow the first three-day itinerary above and spend your fourth day on an excursion to the **Exuma Cays,** reached by powerboat or seaplane. You can also take a day trip via boat or helicopter to quaint **Harbour Island.** In either case you can make it back to Nassau in time for dinner. Spend your last day in the water—swim for a few hours or sign up for a guided tour. With Dolphin Encounters, you can actually swim with dolphins. More experienced underwater types might consider the shark dive available in south New Providence.

If traveling to the Out Islands, follow the Exuma three-day itinerary above, and on the fourth day, fly to **Marsh Harbour** in the Abacos. Start your explorations in **Elbow Cay**—be sure to visit charming Hope Town with its vibrant Cape Cod–style houses and peppermint-stripe lighthouse. If you can arrange to rent a boat for the rest of your stay, you'll discover endless possibilities for exploring the cays. But even on the infrequent ferry service, you can manage a day trip to **Man-O-War Cay,** home of the Abacos's boat-building industry. Visit **Albury's Sail Shop,** where several generations of women fashion luggage and other products from brightly colored sail canvas, or wander some of the most isolated beaches in the country. Spend your final day on **Green Turtle**

Cay (it's a ferry, cab, and ferry ride from Elbow Cay, but doable), relaxing on tranquil **Coco Beach** or the wilder ocean shores, visiting the charming village of **New Plymouth,** or arranging a snorkeling expedition through **Brendal's Dive Shop** on the Green Turtle Club grounds. Then, it's time to head home. The best place to fly out of from here is Treasure Cay.

If You Have 10 Days or More

See the best of both worlds, spending half your time in Nassau and the rest on one of the Out Islands, just a short flight away. If you're determined, you could manage to see three destinations. Spend four days in Nassau, and split the rest of your days between, for instance, Exuma and Cat Island. You could fly directly to George Town, Exuma, catch a flight back to Nassau from there, and head out a few days later to Cat, returning home on a flight out of Cat Island International Airport by way of Nassau. But that gets a little complicated. Maybe you're best plunking yourself down on a quiet patch of Exuma, Eleuthera, Cat, Long, Andros, or any of the scores of other islands in the archipelago, and learning to live (for 10 days, at least) on Bahamian time.

FODOR'S CHOICE

Best Beaches
Great Guana Cay. The 7-mi-long western coast of this cay in the Abacos is a deserted stretch of white sand bordered by palms.

Harbour Island. Perhaps the most famous beach in the Bahamas, this 3-mi Eleutheran beach is covered in pink sand, colored by pulverized coral and shells.

Long Island. Extremely fine, bright white sand edges brilliantly blue water on Cape Santa Maria Beach, on the island's northwestern shore.

Stocking Island. Known for its shelling, this delightful little cay is off Great Exuma.

Treasure Cay. A large peninsula connected to Great Abaco by a narrow spit of land offers a magnificent 3½-mi pristine white-sand beach, crystal-clear water, and no crowds.

Fun for Kids

Glass-bottom boat trips. Even children who don't swim can take a peek at the underwater world on these boats that depart from Nassau's Prince George Wharf.

Horseback riding. Ride along Grand Bahama's coast on mounts from the Pinetree Stables in Freeport.

Snorkeling. Many facilities offer instruction and expeditions for all levels. At some Out Islands spots, children can discover the underwater wonderlands just a few feet off the beach, in less than 2 ft of water.

Swimming with dolphins. The Dolphin Experience, in Lucaya, Grand Bahama, and on Blue Lagoon Island near Nassau, can put kids (even the adult variety) in close contact with the sensitive marine mammals.

Great Golf

Cable Beach Golf Club. The highly regarded par-72, 7,040-yard course on Cable Beach, in New Providence, is the oldest course in the Bahamas. It has ponds and small lakes among the back nine. At press time, it was undergoing renovations that limited its play to just nine holes.

Emerald Golf Course. One of two courses at the Royal Oasis Golf Resort on Grand Bahama (the other is called the Ruby), the par-72, 6,679-yard Emerald was originally designed by Dick Wilson and renovated by the Fazio Group in 2001.

Lucayan Course. The 6,824-yarder is one of the oldest on Grand Bahama and requires more precision than power. It is part of Lucaya's Our Lucaya resort and was designed by Dick Wilson.

Ocean Club Golf Course. Formerly the Paradise Island Golf Club, it was first designed by Dick Wilson (the new design is by the renowned Tom Weiskopf) and clocks in at 6,085 yards and par 72.

South Ocean Golf Club. The rolling hills of this 6,707-yard Joe Lee course, considered the best on New Providence Island, are unusual for the Bahamas.

Treasure Cay Hotel Resort and Marina. Designed by Dick Wilson, this course is the centerpiece of the Treasure Cay Resort and Marina. Measuring 6,985 yards from the blue tees, and with 60 strategically placed sand bunkers, it challenges even the best players.

Flavors

Runaway Hill Club. Local chefs whip up culinary masterpieces at this homey inn on beautiful Harbour Island, off Eleuthera. $$$$

Buena Vista. This Nassau institution is housed in one of the city's gracious colonial mansions. $$$–$$$$

Arawak Dining Room. Fine nouvelle Continental cuisine capitalizes on local seafood and a view of Our Lucaya Lucayan Golf & Country Club. $–$$

Café Matisse. A Continental menu with local Nassau flair is immaculately prepared in this century-old house with a quiet, shady garden. $–$$

Luciano's. Enjoy Italian and French specialties at this spot overlooking the water in Lucaya. $–$$

Chat & Chill. Kenneth Bowe's very hip, upscale, casual eatery on the point at Stocking Island offers incredible edibles grilled over an open fire. ¢–$

Jean's Dog House. Great Exuma history and fabulous meals-on-the-go are served up from a bright yellow, former mini school bus that has been converted into a tiny, spotless kitchen on wheels. ¢

Queen Conch. A quarter mile from Government dock in tony Harbour Island, this bright green open-air stand serves the most succulent conch salad on the island. Orders are placed for take-home to all corners of the globe. ¢

Hideaways in the Out Islands

Deep Water Cay Club. If you want to get away from it all and angle for bonefish, consider this private island east of Grand Bahama. $$$$

Dunmore Beach Club. An elegant collection of ultraprivate New England–style cottages on Harbour Island with all amenities imaginable, including marble whirlpool tubs large enough for two. $$$$

Abaco Beach Resort & Boat Harbour. If you love to lounge, this oceanfront Marsh Harbour resort provides plenty of amenities and comforts. Adventurous types can explore small, uninhabited Abaco Cays, strategically located across the Sea of Abaco. $–$$$$

Bluff House Beach Hotel. The vistas are spectacular, the welcome effusive, and the oceanfront suites a delight at this laid-back Green Turtle Cay (Abacos) Resort. *$–$$$$*

Hotel Higgins Landing. The only resort on luscious, undeveloped Stocking Island, this refined hotel has immaculate interiors with antique furnishings, and superb gourmet dinners served by candlelight. *$$$*

Green Turtle Club. The Abaco hotel is among the most handsomely appointed in the Out Islands. Behold the mahogany Queen Anne– and plantation-style furniture in the guest rooms. *$–$$$*

Cape Santa Maria Beach Resort. Luxury probably doesn't come more remote than this: a resort on an exquisite 4-mi arc of white sand on Long Island. *$$*

The Landing. Fewer spots are more accommodating than this historic Dunmore Town inn, whose restaurant is not to be missed. *$$*

Dolphin Beach Resort. Pine cottages painted in exuberant Junkanoo colors dot the bluff overlooking gorgeous, uninhabited Guana Cay Beach at this upscale, pocket-size haven. *$–$$*

Fernandez Bay Village. Oceanfront villas hewn from native stone front one of Cat Island's prettiest crescents of sand at this friendly resort, indisputably Cat's finest and a perfect spot in which to escape the daily bustle. *$–$$*

Bahama House Inn. The charming, pastel-pink, 18th-century inn is Harbour Island's only upscale B&B. *$*

Comforts

Ocean Club Golf & Tennis Resort. Experience the good life at this upscale resort, where you'll have a drink in your hand before you finish check-in, and your room, overlooking Paradise Island's prettiest stretch of beach, gets thrice-daily maid service. *$$$$*

Viva Fortuna. This European-owned resort east of Lucaya on Grand Bahama is one of the island's few all-inclusives. *$$–$$$$*

Compass Point. Junkanoo-color cottages and great dining make this small hotel the hippest getaway on New Providence. *$$–$$$*

Our Lucaya. Grand Bahama's most ambitious resort has 36 holes of golf, a shopping center, 12 restaurants, and a children's camp and water-play areas. *$–$$*

Radisson Cable Beach Casino & Golf Resort. At the center of Cable Beach action, and connected to the Crystal Palace casino by a shopping arcade, this resort has a wide variety of water sports and a well-designed golf course. *$–$$*

Royal Oasis Golf Resort & Casino. Two golf courses, a giant casino, a beach-entry pool, and proximity to the International Bazaar shopping arcade make the twin resorts on this property among the most popular in Freeport. *$–$$*

2 NEW PROVIDENCE ISLAND

The exquisite beaches, lush tropical landscapes, unsullied waters, and year-round sunshine make this island the perfect vacation haven. Although Nassau and Paradise Island are the big hitters in the Bahamian lineup, there's plenty more to do than doze in the sun: You're invited to shop and snorkel, explore forts, and sample conch—and don't forget the casinos, which are always open (or so it seems). And after dark, Nassau's nightlife hops.

Updated by
Michael de
Zayas

NEW PROVIDENCE ISLAND, home to two-thirds of all Bahamians, is a study in contrasts: glitzy casinos and quiet, shady lanes; trendy, up-to-date resorts and tiny settlements that recall a distant, simpler age; land development unrivaled elsewhere in the Bahamas; and vast stretches of untrod territory. In the course of its history, the island has weathered the comings and goings of lawless pirates, Spanish invaders, slave-holding British Loyalists who fled the United States after the Revolutionary War, Civil War–era Confederate blockade runners, and Prohibition rumrunners. Nevertheless, New Providence remains most influenced by England, which sent its first royal governor to the island in 1718. Although Bahamians won government control in 1967 and independence six years later, British influence is felt to this day.

Nassau is the nation's capital and transportation hub, as well as the banking and commercial center. Although businesspeople take advantage of bank secrecy laws that rival Switzerland's and enjoy the absence of inheritance, income, and sales taxes, most visitors need look no farther than Nassau's many duty-free shops for proof of the island's commercial vitality. The fortuitous combination of tourist-friendly enterprise, tropical weather, and island atmosphere with a European overlay has not gone unnoticed: Each year more than a million cruise-ship passengers arrive at Nassau's Prince George Wharf, on short trips from Florida or as a stop on Caribbean cruises.

Exploring Nassau's Bay Street shops is a vivid experience—and a joy for hard-bargaining shoppers.

As reported in Chapter 1 of this book, a 2001 fire destroyed the **Straw Market,** a premier Nassau shopping attraction. The Ministry of Tourism is considering how and when to rebuild it; in the meantime, you can spar with many of the same vendors at a **temporary straw market site** on nearby Bay Street.

A mile or so east of town, under the bridge from Paradise Island, Potter's Cay Dock is another colorful scene: Sloops bring catches of fish and conch, and open-air stalls carry fresh fruit, vegetables, and local foods—freshly made conch salad predominates. If the daytime bustle isn't enough, the nighttime action at the island's nightclubs and casinos can take you into the wee hours of the morning.

Be sure to leave some time for outdoor activities, one of the area's major draws. From shark diving and snorkeling to bicycle tours, horseback riding, tennis, and golf, active pursuits abound in Nassau. Avid watersports fans will find a range of possibilities, including waterskiing, sailing, windsurfing, and deep-sea fishing. Or simply cruise the clear Bahamian waters for an exciting day trip or a pleasurable evening. Although the resorts have a great deal to offer, it would be a shame not to venture into the incredible alfresco world that is the Bahamas's calling card.

You'll find most hotels either on Cable Beach or Paradise Island; just outside downtown Nassau, these tourist areas offer unfettered beach access and proximity to casinos. Cable Beach, so named because the Bahamas's first transatlantic telephone cable was laid here, is a crescent-shape stretch of sand west of Nassau, rimmed by resorts and the Crystal Palace Casino. Although by no means secluded—a string of high-profile resorts rub up against each other on the shore—Cable Beach is one of New Providence Island's prettiest stretches.

Paradise Island is connected to downtown Nassau's east end by a pair of bridges, one leading to P.I. (as locals call the island), and the original, just east, heading back to Nassau. Its status as an unspoiled alternative to the glitz of Cable Beach is already history; Paradise Island has been irrevocably changed by the mega-resort Atlantis. The tallest building in the Bahamas is home to a beachfront resort complete with a gamut of dining options, the largest casino in the Caribbean, and some of its fanciest shops. Most memorable however are the variety of water-based aquariums, slides, and activities. Love it or despise it (and most fall into the former category), it's today's face of Paradise.

EXPLORING NEW PROVIDENCE ISLAND

Tourist action is concentrated on New Providence's northeastern side. If you have time, you can make your way around the rest of this 7- by 21-mi island in a day, including occasional stops. The terrain is flat, and getting around is easy. Renting a car is your best bet—or pick up a scooter for a more adventurous ride. Either way, drive on the left-hand side of the road. Remember to pick up a copy of a New Providence map at your hotel desk. Wear comfortable shoes, and try to do most of your walking before the sweltering Bahamian sun reaches its full midday force.

Numbers in the text correspond to numbers in the margin and on the Nassau and Paradise Island and New Providence Island maps.

A Good Tour

In a day, you can take in most of the markets, gardens, and historic sites of **Nassau** ①–⑮ and **Paradise Island** ⑯–⑳. Most of the historic sites can be reached on foot or by bicycle, scooter, or horse-drawn carriage. Set aside a half day or more for an excursion to Lake Nancy for a few hours of canoeing, a trip to the **Commonwealth Brewery** ㉜ or the **Bacardi Distillery** ㉞, or a spin through the largely residential east end of the island, stopping at the gardens of **The Retreat** ㉒.

A good starting point is **Rawson Square** ①, which opens off Bay Street's north side in the heart of downtown Nassau. Pick up brochures and maps at the Ministry of Tourism information booth on the square's northern side, then head west along the north side of famous Bay Street. Although there are stores galore on this broad, palm-lined boulevard, save your shopping for later, as your newfound treasures will prove cumbersome during your explorations. Continue west to the **Pompey Museum** ④ for an educational excursion into the slave days of old Nassau and a glimpse of contemporary Bahamian art. Follow the bend at Navy Lion Road past the historic British Colonial Hilton Nassau (formerly the British Colonial Hotel), at the entrance to Bay Street, which curves around the hotel to become West Bay Street.

Continue along West Bay, up along the Western Esplanade beach, for a spectacular view of the ocean and the harbor.

If you've packed a sense of adventure, stray west for lunch and a bit of local flavor at **Arawak Cay** ㉘, which lies farther along West Bay Street on the north side. It's quite a long walk, about 30 minutes. You can also save Arawak Cay for another day, perhaps combining it with a visit to **Fort Charlotte** ㉕, **Ardastra Gardens and Conservation Centre** ㉖, and the **Nassau Botanic Gardens** ㉗, all about a 10-minute walk south of Arawak Cay.

Head back east along West Bay Street to West Street, then turn right and take in the typical Bahamian houses lining the street. Turn left onto West Hill Street. Walk across Blue Hill Road as West Hill Street angles around to turn into Duke Street. Here you can snap a picture with

18

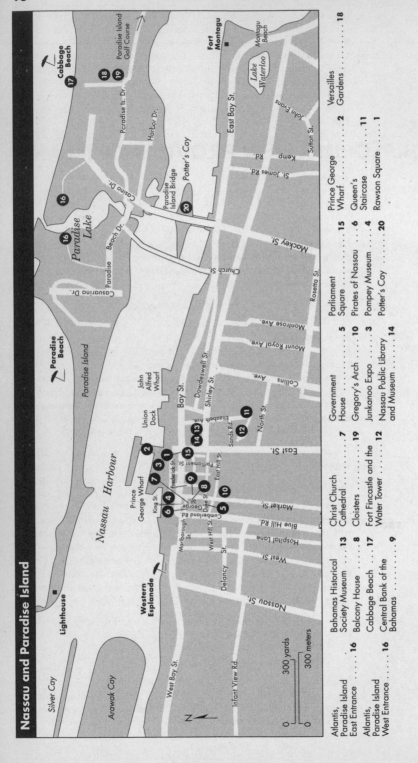

Nassau and Paradise Island

Christopher Columbus, whose likeness graces the entrance to the stately **Government House** ⑤.

Head north onto George Street (it begins at Government House). On the left, at the corner of King Street, is the fun museum **Pirates of Nassau** ⑥. Across the street is the regal **Christ Church Cathedral** ⑦. From the cathedral, turn east on King Street, then south along Market Street, where you'll see the pink **Balcony House** ⑧, typical of late-18th-century Bahamian architecture. Check whether local artists' work is on display at the **Central Bank of the Bahamas** ⑨ across the street and then continue east until you reach Frederick Street. Trinity Methodist Church is on the corner.

Head east on Shirley Street until you reach Elizabeth Avenue. Turn right, going south, and you'll find the **Queen's Staircase** ⑪—hand-cut out of limestone—and **Fort Fincastle and the Water Tower** ⑫, the highest point on the island.

When you're finished at the fort, backtrack along Elizabeth Avenue to Shirley Street. At the corner you'll find the **Bahamas Historical Society Museum** ⑬. Turn left, walking west on Shirley Street. Between Parliament Street and Bank Lane is the **Nassau Public Library and Museum** ⑭. Walk north on Bank Lane to Bay Street. Stop to take in the buildings at **Parliament Square** ⑮ and then return to Rawson Square and Woodes Rogers Walk, which bisects the square, to get a close look at the cruise ships, horse-drawn surreys, and the stylists at work in the hair-braiding pavilion.

From here you can catch a cab to Paradise Island, where you can take in **Atlantis, Paradise Island** ⑯, **Versailles Gardens** ⑱, and the **Cloisters** ⑲. Then spend some time relaxing on the beach.

TIMING
This tour will take up the better part of a day. If Arawak Cay seems too far, or you seek more commodious surroundings for lunch, consider the countless good restaurants along the route. To keep your bearings, remember that Bay Street runs one way west to east and Shirley Street east to west; streets linking them run north–south. Heading in the direction of Cable Beach means traveling west. The harbor (or should we say "harbour") is on the northern edge of downtown.

Nassau

Nassau's sheltered harbor bustles with cruise-ship hubbub, while a block away, broad, palm-lined Bay Street is alive with commercial activity. Shops angle for tourist dollars with fine imported goods at duty-free prices, yet you will find a handful of shops overflowing with authentic Bahamian crafts, food supplies, and other delights. Most of Nassau's historic sites are centered around downtown.

With its thoroughly revitalized downtown, and the revamped British Colonial Hilton leading the way, Nassau is recapturing some of its past glamour. Nevertheless, modern influence is very apparent: Fancy restaurants, suave clubs, and trendy coffeehouses have popped up everywhere. This trend comes partly in response to the growing number of upper-crust crowds that now supplement the spring-breakers and cruise passengers who have traditionally flocked to Nassau.

Today the seedy air of the town's not-so-distant past is almost unrecognizable. Petty crime is no greater than in other towns of this size, and the streets not only look cleaner but feel safer. Of course, you can still find a wild club or a rowdy bar, but you can also sip cappuccino while viewing contemporary Bahamian art or dine by candlelight beneath prints of old Nassau, serenaded by the soft, island-inspired calypso music. Culture and glamour abound: Coffeehouses advertise art exhibitions and bistro nights, and along the streets you'll find elegant stores that many bigger towns would be lucky to have.

Sights to See

⑬ **Bahamas Historical Society Museum.** For those interested in the country's origins and life before European settlement, this small collection contains a wealth of archaeological, historical, and anthropological artifacts. ⊠ *Shirley St. and Elizabeth Ave.,* ☎ *242/322–4231.* ⊡ *$1.* ⊙ *Mon. 10–1, Tues.–Fri. 10–4, Sat. 10–noon.*

★ ⑧ **Balcony House.** A charming 18th-century landmark—a pink two-story house named aptly for its overhanging balcony—this is the oldest wooden residential structure in Nassau, and its furnishings and design recapture the elegance of a bygone era. The house was originally built of American cedar. A mahogany staircase, believed to have been salvaged from a ship during the 19th century, is a highlight of the interior. A guided tour through this fascinating building is an hour well spent. ⊠ *Market St. and Trinity Pl.,* ☎ *242/302–2621.* ⊡ *Donation recommended.* ⊙ *Mon.–Wed., Fri. 10–4:30, Thurs., Sat. 10–1.*

⑨ **Central Bank of the Bahamas.** The Central Bank of the Bahamas monitors and regulates the country's financial institutions. The building's cornerstone was laid by Prince Charles on July 9, 1973, during the country's Independence celebrations, and the bank was opened by Queen Elizabeth II in February 1975 (you can find commemorations of these events at the back of the building). Throughout the year, exhibits on two floors of the lobby display emerging Bahamian artists' work. ⊠ *Market St. and Trinity Pl.,* ☎ *242/322–2193.* ⊙ *Weekdays 9:30–4:30.*

★ ⑦ **Christ Church Cathedral.** It's worth the short walk off the main thoroughfare to see the stained-glass windows of this cathedral, built in 1837. The white pillars of the church's spacious, airy interior support ceilings beamed with dark wood. The crucifixion depicted in the east window's center panel is flanked by depictions of the Empty Tomb and the Ascension. Be sure to spend a few minutes in the small, flower-filled Garden of Remembrance, where stone plaques adorn the walls. ⊠ *George and King Sts.,* ☎ *242/322–4186.* ⊙ *Daily 8:30–6.*

⑫ **Fort Fincastle and the Water Tower.** Shaped like a paddle-wheel steamer and perched near the top of the **Queen's Staircase,** Fort Fincastle—named for Royal Governor Lord Dunmore (Viscount Fincastle)—was completed in 1793 to serve as a lookout post for marauders trying to sneak into the harbor. It served as a lighthouse in the early 19th century. The fort's 126-ft-tall water tower, which is more than 200 ft above sea level, is the island's highest point. From here, the panorama of Nassau and its harbor is spectacular. ⊠ *Top of Elizabeth Ave. hill, south of Shirley St.* ⊡ *Water Tower 50¢.* ⊙ *Daily 8–5.*

★ ⑤ **Government House.** The official residence of the governor-general of the Bahamas since 1801, this imposing pink-and-white building on Duke Street is an excellent example of the mingling of Bahamian-British and American Colonial architecture. Its graceful columns and broad, circular drive recall the styles of Virginia or the Carolinas. But its pink color, distinctive white quoins (cross-laid cornerstones), and louvered wooden shutters (to keep out the tropical sun) are typically Bahamian. Halfway up the white steps that lead to the entrance is an 1830 statue of Christopher Columbus. Here you can also catch the crisply disciplined but beautifully flamboyant changing of the guard ceremony, which takes place every other Saturday morning at 10. The stars of the pomp and pageantry are members of the Royal Bahamas Police Force Band, who are decked out in white tunics, red-striped navy trousers, and spiked, white pith helmets with red bands. The drummers sport leopard skins. ✉ *Duke and George Sts.,* ☎ *242/322–7500 for changes in ceremony schedule.*

⑩ **Gregory's Arch.** Named for John Gregory (royal governor from 1849 to 1854), this arch, at the intersection of Market and Duke streets, separates downtown from the "over-the-hill" neighborhood of **Grant's Town**, where much of Nassau's population lives. Grant's Town was laid out in the 1820s by Governor Lewis Grant as a settlement for freed slaves. Visitors once enjoyed late-night mingling with the locals in the small, dimly lighted bars of Grant's Town. Nowadays, tourists should exhibit the same caution they would if they were visiting impoverished areas of a large city; nevertheless, it's a vibrant section of town. Here you can rub shoulders with Bahamians at a funky take-out food stand or down-home restaurant while catching a glimpse of local life.

③ **Junkanoo Expo.** Handmade floats and costumes used by revelers during the annual Bahamian Junkanoo celebration are exhibited in an old customs warehouse at the wharf's entrance. Junkanoo celebrations are held yearly on Boxing Day (the day after Christmas) and New Year's Day and can be likened in its uninhibited and frenzied activities to Carnival in Rio de Janeiro and Mardi Gras in New Orleans. Visiting the Expo is the next best thing to seeing the festivities in person. The accommodating staff will tell you everything you want to know about Junkanoo, and the colorful displays speak for themselves. ✉ *Prince George Wharf.* ▤ *$1.* ۞ *Daily 9–5:30.*

⑭ **Nassau Public Library and Museum.** The octagonal building near Parliament Square was the Nassau Gaol (the old British spelling for *jail*), circa 1797. You're welcome to pop in and browse. The small prison cells are now lined with books. The museum has an interesting collection of historic prints and old colonial documents. ✉ *Shirley St. between Parliament St. and Bank La.,* ☎ *242/322–4907.* ▤ *Free.* ۞ *Mon.–Thurs. 10–8, Fri. 10–5, Sat. 10–4.*

⑮ **Parliament Square.** Nassau is the seat of national government. The Bahamian Parliament comprises two houses—a 16-member Senate (Upper House) and a 40-member House of Assembly (Lower House)—and a ministerial cabinet headed by a prime minister. Parliament Square's pink, colonnaded government buildings were constructed in the early 1800s by Loyalists who came to the Bahamas from North Carolina. The square is dominated by a statue of a slim young Queen Victoria that was erected on her birthday, May 24, in 1905. In the immediate area are a half dozen magistrates' courts (open to the public; obtain a pass at the door to view a session). Behind the House of Assembly is the **Supreme Court.** Its four-times-a-year opening ceremonies (held the first weeks of January, April, July, and October) recall the wigs and mace-bearing pageantry of the Houses of Parliament in London. The Royal Bahamas Police Force Band is usually on hand for the event. ✉ *Bay St.,* ☎ *242/322–7500 for information on Supreme Court ceremonies.* ▤ *Free.* ۞ *Weekdays 10–4.*

🖑 ⑥ **Pirates of Nassau.** Take a journey through Nassau's pirate days in this interactive museum devoted to such notorious members of the city's past as Blackbeard, Mary Read, and Anne Bonney. Costumed guides greet you at every turn, some of them offering dialogue straight from a period adventure novel. Board a pirate ship, see dioramas of intrigue on the high seas, hear historical narration, and experience sound effects re-creating some of the gruesome highlights. Two children under 12 get in free with an adult admission, and after that kids pay half price,

JUNKANOO

IT'S AFTER MIDNIGHT, and the streets of Nassau are crowded but hushed; the only sound is a steady buzz of anticipation. Everyone is waiting. Suddenly the streets erupt in a kaleidoscope of sight and sound—the Junkanoo groups are rushing down Bay Street. Their vibrant costumes sparkle in the light of the street lamps, and the crowd shouts with delight. Best of all is the music. The revelers bang on goatskin drums, clang cowbells, and blow on conch-shell horns, hammering out a steady beat of celebration. It's Junkanoo time again.

Junkanoo holds an important place in the history of the Bahamas, but the origin of the word Junkanoo remains a mystery. Many believe it comes from John Canoe, an African tribal chief who was brought to the West Indies in the slave trade and then fought for the right to celebrate with his people. Others believe the word stems from the French gens inconnus, which means "the unknown people"—significant because Junkanoo revelers wear costumes that make them unrecognizable.

The origin of the festival itself is more certain. Though its roots can be traced back to West Africa, it began in the Bahamas during the 16th or 17th century when Bahamian slaves were given a few days off around Christmas to celebrate with their families. They left the plantations and had elaborate costume parties where they danced and played homemade musical instruments. They wore large, often scary-looking masks, which gave them the freedom of anonymity, so they could let loose without fear of being recognized. After slavery was abolished, Junkanoo almost vanished, but a few former slaves kept the tradition alive, and over time it grew into the massively popular celebration you'll see today.

Junkanoo is an important part of the Christmas season in the Bahamas. Parades are held in the wee hours of the morning (1 or 2 AM until dawn) on Boxing Day (December 26) and again on New Year's Day. Surprisingly, what appears to be a random, wild expression of joy is actually a very well organized and planned event. Family and friends gather in large groups (often as many as 500–1,000) and perform together in the parade.

Competition is heated among the groups, who choose a different theme each year and keep it a closely guarded secret until Junkanoo day, when their efforts are revealed. And what an effort each group makes: Most spend months preparing for the big day at what they call their "base camp" or "shack." They choreograph dance steps, choose music, and design intricate costumes. Then it's time to practice, practice, practice. Among the regular groups are the "Saxons," "Valley Boys," "Roots," and "One Family." Judges watch the event closely and award prizes for best music, best costumes, and best overall group presentation. With thousands of dollars of prize money up for grabs, groups go to extremes to please the crowd and put on the best show.

If you're lucky enough to be in the Bahamas around Christmas, don't miss this spectacular sight. The grandest Junkanoo celebration is in Nassau, where the best views are upstairs on Bay Street, or on the benches that line the streets. Plan ahead and arrive early to secure a good spot. You can also experience Junkanoo on Grand Bahama Island, Eleuthera, Bimini, and Abaco. If you miss the festivities, be sure to stop by the **Junkanoo Expo** in downtown Nassau to see some of the most memorable costumes and floats from years past.

making it a fun (if slightly scary) family outing. Be sure to check out the offbeat souvenirs in the Pirate Shop, and the lively Pirate Pub and Courtyard Grill, next door. ⊠ *George and King Sts.,* ☎ *242/356–3759,* WEB *www.pirates-of-nassau.com.* 🎫 *$12.* ⊙ *Mon.–Sat. 9–5.*

❹ **Pompey Museum.** In a building where slave auctions were held in the 1700s, this museum is named for a rebel slave who lived on the Out Island of Exuma in 1830. Exhibits focus on the issues of slavery and emancipation and highlight the works of local artists, such as Amos Ferguson, one of the country's best-loved artists; his folk-art canvases depict a wide variety of subject matter, from religious imagery to nature study. ⊠ *Bay and George Sts.,* ☎ *242/326–2566.* 🎫 *$1.* ⊙ *Weekdays 10–4:30, Sat. 10–1.*

❷ **Prince George Wharf.** The wharf that leads into Rawson Square is the first view that cruise passengers encounter after they tumble off their ships. Up to a dozen gigantic cruise ships call on Nassau at any one time, and passengers spill out onto downtown, giving Nassau an instant, and constantly replenished, surge of life. ⊠ *Waterfront at Rawson Sq.*

⓫ **Queen's Staircase.** These 65 steps are thought to have been carved out of a solid limestone cliff by slaves in the 1790s. The staircase was later named to honor Queen Victoria's 65-year reign. Recent innovations include a waterfall cascading from the top, and an ad hoc straw market along the narrow road that leads to the site. ⊠ *Top of Elizabeth Ave. hill, south of Shirley St.*

❶ **Rawson Square.** Many locals congregate at this square, which connects Bay Street to Prince George Wharf. As you enter off Bay Street, note the statue of Sir Milo Butler, the first post-independence (and first native Bahamian) governor-general. Horse-drawn surreys wait for passengers in Woodes Rogers Walk, which runs down the middle of the square (expect to pay about $10 for a half-hour ride through Nassau's streets). On the Walk's other side, you can look into (or perhaps stop inside) the **hair-braiding pavilion,** where women work their magic at prices ranging from $2 for a single strand to $100 for an elaborate do. An often-overlooked pleasure near the pavilion: Randolph W. Johnston's lovely bronze statue, *Tribute to Bahamian Women.* ⊠ *Bay St.*

Paradise Island

The graceful, arched Paradise Island bridges ($1 toll for cars and motorbikes from Nassau to P.I.; free for bicyclists and pedestrians), 1 mi east of Nassau's Rawson Square, lead to and from the extravagant world of Paradise Island.

Until 1962, Paradise Island was largely undeveloped and known as Hog Island. A&P heir Huntington Hartford changed the name when he built the island's first resort complex. Although several huge high-rise resorts have been erected since then—as have many million-dollar houses—you can still find several quiet getaway spots. The north shore is lined with white-sand beaches, and the protected south shore, directly across the harbor from Nassau, is a haven for yachts. Aptly renamed, the island *is* a paradise for beach lovers, boaters, and fun lovers.

Sights to See

★ ⓒ ⓰ **Atlantis, Paradise Island.** The unmistakable sight of this peach fantasia— bold enough to still surprise and delight Nassau residents—comes into view just as you cross the Paradise Island Bridge. The towering sunstruck visage is actually Royal Towers, the largest and newest wing of the Atlantis resort. With glitzy shopping malls, a cabaret theater, and seemingly unlimited choices for dining and drinks, Atlantis is as much a tourist attraction as a resort hotel. Many of its facilities, such as restaurants and the casino, are open to nonguests. For a peak at the rest, take the self-guided "Discover Atlantis" tour, which begins near the main lobby at an exhibition called "The Dig." This wonderful series of walk-through aquariums, themed around the lost continent and its re-created ruins, brings you face to face with sharks, manta rays, and innumerable exotic sea life. The rest of the tour tempts you with a walk through the many water slides and pools not accessible to nonguests. ⊠ *Casino Dr.,* ☎ *242/363–3000.* ☞ *Discover Atlantis tour $25, casino admission free.* ⊙ *Tours daily 9–5, casino daily 24 hrs.*

⑰ Cabbage Beach. The stretch of white sand along the north side is one of the prettiest on New Providence. Although resorts line much of its length, several minutes' stroll to the east will take you to a nearly uninhabited span of beach overlooking emerald waters and tiny offshore cays.

★ **⑲ Cloisters.** At the top of the **Versailles Gardens** stand the remains of a 14th-century French stone monastery that were imported to the United States in the 1920s by newspaper baron William Randolph Hearst. (The cloister is one of four that have ever been removed from French soil.) Forty years later, grocery-chain heir Hartford bought the Cloisters and had them rebuilt on their present commanding site. At the center is a graceful, contemporary white marble statue called *Silence,* by U.S. sculptor Dick Reid. Nearly every day tourists take or renew wedding vows under the delicately wrought gazebo overlooking Nassau Harbour. The Cloisters are owned by the Ocean Club, but visitors are welcome to look around. ⊠ *Paradise Island Dr.*

★ **⑳ Potter's Cay.** From Nassau, walk the road beneath the Paradise Island Bridge to watch sloops bring in and sell loads of fish and conch. Along the road to the cay are dozens of stands where you can watch the conch, straight from the sea, being extracted from its glistening pink shell. It makes a delicious, and affordable, dish. If you don't have the know-how to handle the tasty conch's preparation—getting the diffident creature out of its shell requires boring a hole at the right spot to sever the muscle that keeps it entrenched—you can enjoy a conch salad on the spot, as fresh as it comes, and take notes for future attempts. Empty shells are sold as souvenirs. Many locals and hotel chefs come here to purchase the fresh catches; you can also find vegetables, herbs, and such condiments as fiery Bahamian peppers preserved in lime juice, and locally grown pineapples, papayas, and bananas.

⑱ Versailles Gardens. Fountains and statues of luminaries and legends (such as Napoleon and Josephine, Franklin Delano Roosevelt, David Livingstone, Hercules, and Mephistopheles) adorn Versailles Gardens, the terraced lawn at the Ocean Club Golf & Tennis Resort, which was once the private hideaway of Huntington Hartford. The Cloisters grace the top of the gardens. Although the property is owned by the Ocean Club, visitors are welcome. ⊠ *Ocean Club, Paradise Island Dr.,* ☎ *242/363–2501.*

Eastern New Providence

New Providence Island's eastern end is residential, although there are some interesting historic sites and fortifications here. From East Bay Street, just beyond the Paradise Island bridges, it's a short, scenic drive along Eastern Road, which is lined with gracious homes, to Eastern Point (also known as East End Point)—about 20 minutes, depending on traffic.

Sights to See

㉑ Fort Montagu. The oldest of the island's three forts, Montagu was built of local limestone in 1741 to repel Spanish invaders. The only action it saw was when it was occupied for two weeks by rebel American troops—among them a lieutenant named John Paul Jones—seeking arms and ammunition during the Revolutionary War. The small fortification is in disrepair, though you are welcome to go inside. The second level has a number of rusted cannons. A narrow public beach stretching for more than a mile beyond the fort looks out upon Montagu Bay, where many international yacht regattas and Bahamian sloop races are held annually. ⊠ *East of Bay St. on Eastern Rd.* ✍ *Free.*

㉓ Fox Hill. Settled by freed slaves who were given land grants, which they paid for either in cash or labor, this residential area was originally four smaller settlements. Today there's not much here of tourist interest—except on the second Tuesday of August, when the community holds its annual Fox Hill Day celebration. It falls a week after the rest of the island celebrates Emancipation Day (some say that's because back in 1834 it took a week for the news of the emancipation to reach the community here). Festivities include music, home-cooked food, and arts-and-crafts booths. Call the Ministry of Tourism (☎ 242/322–7500) for more information.

★ **㉒ The Retreat.** Nearly 200 species of exotic palm trees grace the 11 verdant acres appropriately known as The Retreat, which serves as the headquarters of the Bahamas National Trust. Stroll in blessed silence through the lush grounds, past smiling Buddhas, and under stone arbors overhung with vines. It's a perfect break on a steamy Nassau day. Guided tours are available, or walk through this sanctuary on your own. ⊠ *Village Rd.,* ☎ *242/393–1317.* ✍ *$2.* ☉ *Weekdays 9–5.*

㉔ St. Augustine's Monastery. The Romanesque home of the Bahamas's Benedictine brothers was built in 1946 by a monk named Father Jerome, also famed for his carvings of the Stations of the Cross on Cat Island's Mt. Alvernia. The St. Augustine buildings, home to a college as well as the religious complex, overlook beautiful gardens. A truly off-the-beaten-track sight. Call first to see if the monks will give you a tour. ⊠ *Bernard Rd., west of Fox Hill Rd.,* ☎ *242/364–1331.*

Western New Providence and South Coast

Starting from downtown Nassau, West Bay Street follows the coast west past the resorts, posh residential neighborhoods, and ever-increasing new developments of Cable Beach, then past popular Love Beach to Northwest Point. Just beyond is Lyford Cay, the island's most exclusive residential area. Old-money pioneers started settling the cay four decades ago, and along with its 200-odd houses there is a private golf course for residents. Your experience of Lyford Cay is likely to be voyeuristic at best—an entrance gate wards off all but residents and friends.

Much of the interior and southwestern coast of New Providence is undeveloped, and the coastal scenery and long, low stretches of palmetto and pine forest are picturesque. The loop around the island's west and south coasts can be done in a couple of hours by car or scooter; however, you may wish to take time out for lunch and a swim along the way.

Sights to See

㉝ Adelaide Village. The small community on New Providence's southwestern coast sits placidly, like a remnant of another era, between busy Adelaide Road and the ocean. It was first settled during the early 1830s by Africans who had been captured and loaded aboard slave ships bound for the New World. They were rescued on the high seas

New Providence Island

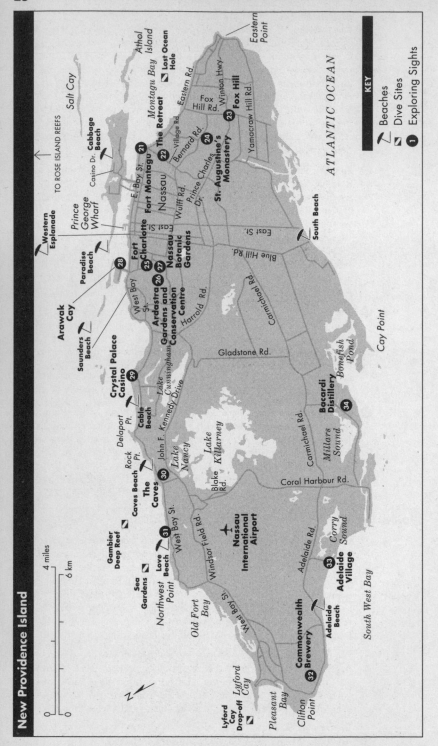

ATLANTIC OCEAN

Eastern Point

Athol Island
Montagu Bay Island
◪ Lost Ocean Hole

Salt Cay

TO ROSE ISLAND REEFS

Cabbage Beach

Casino Dr.

21 Fort Montagu
22 The Retreat

Eastern Rd.

Fox Hill Rd.
24
23 Fox Hill

Winton Hwy.

Village Rd.

Bernard Rd.

Nassau

Prince Charles Dr.

St. Augustine's Monastery

Yamacraw Hill Rd.

E. Bay St.

Wulff Rd.

Western Esplanade

Prince George Wharf

Paradise Beach

Fort Charlotte
25
27
26 Nassau Botanic Gardens

Ardastra Gardens and Conservation Centre

East St.

Harrold Rd.

Blue Hill Rd.

South Beach

East St.

Arawak Cay

Saunders Beach

West Bay St.

28

Carmichael Rd.

Gladstone Rd.

Cay Point

Crystal Palace Casino
29

Lake Cunningham

Lake Nancy

Lake Killarney

Blake Rd.

Bonefish Pond

Bacardi Distillery
34

Millars Sound

Delaport Pt.

Cable Beach

John F. Kennedy Drive

Coral Harbour Rd.

Rock Pt.

Caves Beach
The Caves
30

Carmichael Rd.

Corry Sound

Gambier Deep Reef ◪

West Bay St.

Nassau International Airport

Adelaide Rd.

Adelaide Village
33

Sea Gardens ◪

Love Beach
31

Windsor Field Rd.

Northwest Point

Old Fort Bay

Adelaide Beach

South West Bay

West Bay St.

Commonwealth Brewery
32

Lyford Cay Drop-off ◪

Pleasant Bay

Lyford Cay

Clifton Point

4 miles

6 km

0

0

by the British Royal Navy, and the first group of liberated slaves reached Nassau in 1832. Today, only a few dozen families live in Adelaide. They grow vegetables, raise chickens, and inhabit well-worn, pastel-painted wooden houses, sheltered by bougainvillea and other vegetation. The village has a primary school, some little grocery stores, and locally popular **Avery's Restaurant and Bar** (⊠ Adelaide Rd., ☎ 242/362–1547).

㉘ Arawak Cay. Known to Nassau residents as "The Fish Fry," Arawak Cay is one of the best places to knock back a Kalik beer (brewed right on New Providence Island), chat with the locals, or sample traditional Bahamian fare. You can get small noshes or full meals at one of the pastel-color shacks that line the large fairgrounds' perimeter. Order some fried fish or fresh conch salad, a spicy mixture of chopped conch (just watching the expert chopping is a show as good as any in town) mixed with diced onions, cucumbers, tomatoes, and hot peppers in a lime marinade. Goldie's Enterprises, on the cay's western side, is one of the most popular stalls. Try their "crack conch" and Goldie's famous Sky Juice (a potent gin and coconut-water concoction).

To reach Arawak Cay, head west along Bay Street, follow the main road around the British Colonial Hilton hotel, and continue west past Western Esplanade beach. The cay is on the north side of the T-junction of West Bay and Chippingham Road. It's approximately a five-minute drive or 30-minute walk.

㉖ Ardastra Gardens and Conservation Centre. Marching flamingos? These national birds of the Bahamas give a parading performance at Ardastra daily at 11, 2, and 4. The zoo, with more than 5 acres of tropical greenery and flowering shrubs, also has an aviary of rare tropical birds, native Bahamian creatures such as rock iguanas, and a global collection of small animals. ⊠ *Chippingham Rd., south of W. Bay St.,* ☎ *242/323–5806.* ⊡ *$12.* ⊙ *Daily 9–5.*

㉞ Bacardi Distillery. The factory, established in 1962, is open to the public for tours. You can sample a range of its well-known rum products (and, needless to say, purchase some) at the Visitors Pavilion. ⊠ *Bacardi and Carmichael Rds.,* ☎ *242/362–1412.* ⊡ *Free.* ⊙ *Mon.–Thurs. 10–3.*

㉚ The Caves. These large limestone caverns that the waves have sculpted over the aeons are said to have sheltered the early Arawak Indians. An oddity perched right beside the road, they're worth a glance—although in truth, there's not much to see, as the dark interior doesn't lend itself to exploration. Just a short drive beyond the caves, on an island between traffic lanes, is **Conference Corner,** where U.S. president John F. Kennedy, Canadian prime minister John Diefenbaker, and British prime minister Harold Macmillan planted trees on the occasion of their 1962 summit in Nassau. ⊠ *W. Bay St. and Blake Rd.*

㉜ Commonwealth Brewery. Kalik, Nassau's very own beer, pale in color but with a full-bodied taste, is brewed here. The local beverage—by far the most popular among Bahamians—is named for the sound of the cowbells used in the Junkanoo Parade. Free tours are given by appointment only. ⊠ *Clifton Pier and Southwest Rd.,* ☎ *242/362–4789.*

㉙ Crystal Palace Casino. You can try your luck at baccarat, blackjack, roulette, craps, and Caribbean stud poker or simply settle for the slots. There's plenty to keep you entertained, including a sports book for betting on your favorite teams, and games from "pai gow poker" to "let it ride" and "war" tables. ⊠ *Nassau Marriott Resort, Cable Beach, Nassau,* ☎ *242/327–6200.* ⊙ *Tables 10 AM–4 AM weekdays, 24 hrs weekends; slots 24 hrs daily.*

★ ㉕ **Fort Charlotte.** Built in the late 18th century, this imposing fort comes complete with a waterless moat, drawbridge, ramparts, and dungeons. Lord Dunmore, who built it, named the massive structure in honor of George III's wife. At the time, some called it Dunmore's Folly because of the staggering expense of its construction. It cost eight times more than was originally planned. (Dunmore's superiors in London were less than ecstatic with the high costs, but he managed to survive unscathed.) Ironically, no shots were ever fired in battle from the fort. It is about 1 mi west of central Nassau. ⊠ *W. Bay St. at Chippingham Rd.* ⊠ *Free.* ⊙ *Local guides conduct tours daily 8–4.*

㉛ **Love Beach.** One of the island's loveliest little beaches is near New Providence's northwestern corner. About 1 mi off Love Beach are 40 acres of coral and sea fan, with forests of fern, known as the Sea Gardens. The clear waters are a favorite with snorkelers.

㉗ **Nassau Botanic Gardens.** Six hundred species of flowering trees and shrubs, a small cactus garden, and two freshwater ponds with lilies, water plants, and tropical fish cover 18 acres. The many trails that wind through the gardens are perfect for leisurely strolls. The Botanic Gardens are across the street from the **Ardastra Gardens and Conservation Centre**, home of Nassau's zoo. ⊠ *Chippingham Rd., south of W. Bay St.,* ☎ *242/323–5975.* ⊠ *$1.* ⊙ *Weekdays 8–4, weekends 9–4.*

BEACHES

New Providence is blessed with stretches of white sand studded with palm and sea-grape trees. Some of the beaches are small and crescent shape, whereas others stretch for miles. Right in downtown Nassau, you'll find the **Western Esplanade.** It sweeps west from the British Colonial Hilton on Bay Street and offers public rest rooms. On Paradise Island, **Paradise Beach,** at the island's far western tip, is a nice stretch of sand, but Paradise Island's real showpiece is 3-mi-long **Cabbage Beach,** which rims the north coast from the Atlantis lagoon to Snorkeler's Cove. At the north end you can rent jet skis and nonmotorized pedal boats, and go parasailing.

Cable Beach is on New Providence's north shore, about 3 mi west of downtown Nassau. Resorts line much of this beautiful, broad swath of white sand, but there is public access. Jet-skiers and beach vendors abound, so don't expect quiet isolation. Just west of Cable Beach is a rambling pink house on the Rock Point promontory, where much of the 1965 Bond film *Thunderball* was filmed. Tiny, crescent-shape **Caves Beach** is beyond Cable Beach on the north shore, about 7 mi from downtown just before the turnoff on Blake Road that leads to the airport. **Love Beach** is a snorkeler's favorite, on the north shore beyond Caves Beach, about 9 mi from town (about a 20-minute drive). Access technically lies within the domain of Love Beach residents, but they aren't inclined to shoo anyone away. On the south shore, drive down to **Adelaide Beach,** at the end of Adelaide Village, for sand that stretches down to Coral Harbour. The people who live at the island's east end flock to **South Beach,** at the foot of Blue Hill Road on the south shore.

DINING

With the escalation of Bahamian tourism, meal preparation at the better dining spots has become as sophisticated as that in any leading U.S. city. European chefs brought in by the top restaurants have trained young Bahamians in the skills of fine cuisine. Chinese, Indian, Mexican, Creole, and Japanese fare have also become available.

However, don't neglect the very appealing Bahamian fare. Several relatively inexpensive spots serve traditional dishes, which are now also appearing on the ritzier menus: peas 'n' rice, conch (chowder, fritters, and cracked), Bahamian lobster, "stew" or "boil" fish, grouper fingers, fresh local bread, and, for dessert, guava duff, a warm marriage of boiled Guava dough and sweet sauce. Because meats and some seafood often have to be imported, local fish is usually the most economical entrée.

Coffeehouses have sprung up everywhere. Most serve light fare and desserts plus a variety of specialty coffees and teas.

Many all-inclusives also offer meal plans for nonguests.

For general information, *see* Dining *in* Smart Travel Tips A to Z at the front of the book.

CATEGORY	COST*
$$$$	over $40
$$$	$30–$40
$$	$20–$30
$	$10–$20
¢	under $10

per person for a main course at dinner

Nassau

Bahamian

¢–$$$ ✕ **Conch Fritters Bar & Grill.** A favorite in downtown Nassau, this lively, tropically themed restaurant is best known for conch. You can sample this Bahamian specialty in chowders, salads, and, of course, fritters. That said, conch-phobes need not worry. You'll find a diverse menu brimming with burgers, sandwiches, and pasta; the selection of steaks includes a serious 24-ounce porterhouse. There's a live band 7 to midnight nightly except Monday and a festive Junkanoo celebration on Saturday from 8 to 11 PM. ✉ *Marlborough St., across from the British Colonial Hilton,* ☎ 242/323–8778. *AE, MC, V.* ☺ *Breakfast also served.*

$–$$ ✕ **The Poop Deck.** Just east of the bridge from Paradise Island and a quick cab ride from the center of town is this favorite haunt of locals. Breezy tables on the large waterfront deck scan the vista of the Bahamas's largest marina. Its popularity has resulted in a second Poop Deck on Cable Beach's west end, but for residents, this is still the place. Expect spicy dishes with such names as Mama Mary's steamed fish and Rosie's chicken; there's also an extensive wine list. Save room for guava duff and a calypso coffee spiked with secret ingredients. ✉ *E. Bay St., at Nassau Yacht Haven Marina, east of bridge from Paradise Island,* ☎ *242/393–8175,* ⓦⓔⓑ *www.thepoopdeck.com. AE, D, MC, V.*

¢–$$ ✕ **Shoal Restaurant and Lounge.** Saturday morning at 9 you'll find hordes of hungry Bahamians digging into boil fish and johnnycake, the restaurant's specialty. A bowl of this peppery local dish, filled with chunks of boiled potatoes, onions, and grouper, may keep you coming back to this dimly lighted, basic, out-of-the-way "Ma's kitchen," where Bahamian dishes, including peas 'n' rice and cracked conch, are staples. ✉ *Nassau St., between Meadow St. and Poinciana Dr.,* ☎ *242/323–4400. AE, D, MC, V. Closed Wed.*

¢–$ ✕ **Mama Lyddy's Place.** Just off the beaten tourist track, this old house
★ is the place for true Bahamian cooking. Start with a local-style breakfast of souse or "boil fish" and watch Nassau residents stream in for take-out or sit-down meals. For lunch and dinner try fried snapper, cracked conch, minced or broiled crawfish, pork chops, and chicken. All are served with peas 'n' rice or peas 'n' grits and other typical Ba-

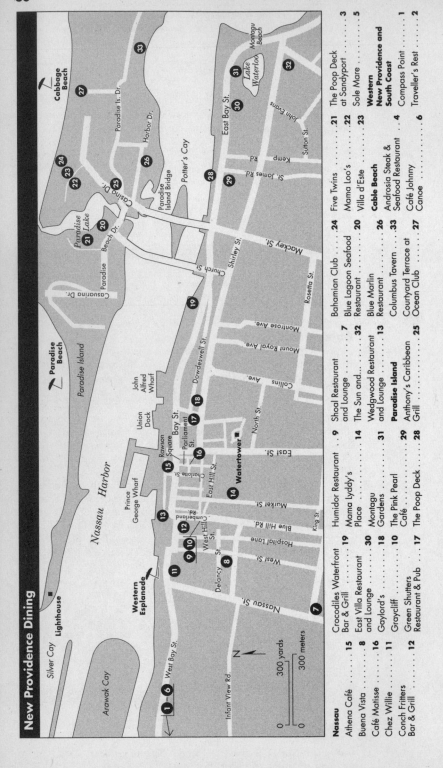

New Providence Dining

New Providence Dining

Nassau

Athena Café **15**
Buena Vista **8**
Café Matisse **16**
Chez Willie **11**
Conch Fritters
Bar & Grill **12**
Crocodiles Waterfront
Bar & Grill **19**
East Villa Restaurant
and Lounge **30**
Gaylord's **18**
Graycliff **10**
Green Shutters
Restaurant & Pub **17**

Humidor Restaurant . . **9**
Mama Lyddy's
Place **14**
Montagu
Gardens **31**
The Pink Pearl
Café **29**
The Poop Deck **28**

Shoal Restaurant
and Lounge **9**
The Sun and **32**
Wedgwood Restaurant
and Lounge **13**

Paradise Island

Anthony's Caribbean
Grill **28**

Bahamian Club **24**
Blue Lagoon Seafood
Restaurant **20**
Blue Marlin
Restaurant **26**
Columbus Tavern . . . **33**
Courtyard Terrace at
Ocean Club **25**

Five Twins **21**
Mama Loo's **22**
Villa d'Este **23**

Cable Beach

Androsia Steak &
Seafood Restaurant . **4**
Café Johnny
Canoe **27**

The Poop Deck
at Sandyport **3**
Sole Mare **5**

**Western
New Providence and
South Coast**

Compass Point **1**
Traveller's Rest **2**

hamian side dishes. ⊠ *Market St. at Cockburn St.,* ☎ *242/328–6849. No credit cards.*

Chinese

$–$$ ✕ **East Villa Restaurant and Lounge.** Nassau residents declare that this dimly lighted restaurant, set back from the busy street, serves the best Chinese food in town. The Chinese-Continental menu includes such entrées as conch with black bean sauce, *hung shew* (walnut chicken), and steak *kew* (cubed prime fillet served with baby corn, snow peas, water chestnuts, and vegetables). The New York strip steak is nirvana. A short taxi ride from Paradise Island or downtown Nassau, this is the perfect spot if you're seeking something a little different from the typical area restaurants. ⊠ *E. Bay St., near Nassau Yacht Club,* ☎ *242/393–3377. AE, MC, V. No lunch Sat.*

Contemporary

$$ ✕ **The Pink Pearl Café.** The Pink Pearl continues to delight with its in-
★ ventive menu, impeccable service, and lovely ambience in a 1943 mansion made of limestone and local pine. Weekend diners on the breezy side porch have front-row seats for live jazz; the main rooms have vibrant contemporary art. From the moment you arrive, you know you're in for a treat—aromatic bread arrives in a large calabash shell. Entrées might include an elaborate roasted grouper with a ragout of onion, tomato, thyme, mushrooms, and potatoes, or a simple grilled conch drizzled with tamarind barbecue sauce. ⊠ *E. Bay St., east of bridge from Paradise Island,* ☎ *242/394–6413. AE, D, DC, MC, V. Closed Sun.*

Continental

$$$–$$$$ ✕ **Buena Vista.** High on a hill above Nassau Harbour, this serene
★ restaurant sits secure in its reputation as one of the city's dining institutions; it draws a loyal local clientele. Established in 1946, it occupies what was once a rambling private home built in the early 1800s. Tuxedoed waiters whisk about the dining room, where tables are set with china, crystal, and silver. Although jackets aren't absolutely required, you'll find most gentlemen wearing them. Exemplary entrées include grouper and rack of spring lamb. Leave room for Mrs. Hauck's Orange Pancakes, baked in a Grand Marnier sauce—a house specialty for decades. ⊠ *W. Hill and Delancy Sts.,* ☎ *242/322–2811. AE, DC, MC, V. Closed Sun. No lunch.*

$$$–$$$$ ✕ **Graycliff.** A meal at Graycliff—an experience that lingers in the memory—begins in the elegant parlor, where, over live piano music, drinks are served and orders taken; when your appetizer is ready, you're escorted into one of several dining rooms. Graycliff's signature dishes include roast rack of lamb and the thermidor-style Lobster Graycliff. The clientele includes presidents and celebrities, but the prices are, surprisingly, no higher than other top-notch Nassau restaurants. Except for wine: The cellar contains more than 175,000 bottles, some running into the tens of thousands of dollars, handpicked by owner Enrico Garzaroli, a connoisseur *par excellence.* Finish with a hand-rolled cigar produced in Graycliff's own factory. ⊠ *W. Hill St. at Cumberland Rd., across from Government House,* ☎ *242/322–2796,* WEB *www.graycliff.com. AE, DC, MC, V. No lunch weekends.*

$$$–$$$$ ✕ **The Sun and . . .** If you're hoping to catch sight of international su-
★ perstars, this is a good place to look (assuming, that is, that they—or you—make it past the hostess). Dine in a series of rooms surrounding an enclosed garden area with a rock pool and fountain—as magical a dining setting as Nassau offers. Feast on such creations as salmon mousseline and crayfish tails rolled in grouper fillets, topped with Chardonnay-lobster sauce, or veal with porcini mushrooms and white truffle oil. End your meal divinely with one of Belgian owner-chef Ronny

Deryckere's six soufflés, which range from almond amaretto to guava. ⊠ *Lakeview Rd. and E. Shirley St.,* ☎ *242/393–1205. Jacket required. AE, D, MC, V. Closed Mon. and Aug.–Sept. No lunch.*

$$–$$$ ✕ **Humidor Restaurant.** Carved-wood statues of pipe smokers, imported
★   from Cuba, set the tone at this relaxed restaurant in the Graycliff hotel's Graycliff Cigar Company wing. This spot is a stogie-lover's delight. Here you can get a set meal including a selection of cigars. The tasty bistro fare includes tuna tartare, lobster cakes, and risotto with porcini mushrooms and lamb. For postprandial indulgence, retire to the lounge for a seat on the leather sofa and a selection from the wall-length display of cigars, or stroll along the hotel's garden terraces and fountains. Look closely at that car on the central counter: It's actually a humidor. ⊠ *W. Hill St., off Cumberland Rd.,* ☎ *242/328–7050. AE, DC, MC, V. Closed Sun.*

$$–$$$ ✕ **Wedgwood Restaurant and Lounge.** A major addition to the downtown dining scene, this comfortably elegant spot at the British Colonial Hilton Nassau lives up to its name: Pale blue walls lined with intricate molding make you think you're inside a piece of the signature porcelain (which is used, of course, for table settings). Start with a drink in the cozy English-style lounge; rich wood floors and etched-glass booths with blue leather love seats set a sumptuous tone. In the dining room, feast on the sea view and elegant setting as well as such British-Continental standards as cockie-leekie soup, Dover sole, an extensive grill selection, and the house specialty, a seafood pepper pot. ⊠ *British Colonial Hilton Nassau, 1 Bay St.,* ☎ *242/322–3301. Jacket required. AE, D, DC, MC, V.*

$–$$$ ✕ **Montagu Gardens.** Angus beef and fresh native seafood—flame grilled and seasoned with home-mixed spices—are the specialties at this romantic restaurant in an old Bahamian mansion on Lake Waterloo. The dining room opens to a walled courtyard niched with Roman-style statues and gardens that lead to a waterside balustrade. Besides seafood and steak (carnivores love the filet mignon smothered in mushrooms), menu selections include chicken, lamb, pasta, ribs, and several Bahamian-inspired dishes such as conch fritters and minced crawfish with taco chips. A favorite dessert is Fort Montagu Mud Pie. ⊠ *E. Bay St.,* ☎ *242/394–6347. AE, MC, V. Closed Sun.*

Eclectic

$–$$$ ✕ **Crocodiles Waterfront Bar & Grill.** The informal outdoor grill, with deck tables shaded by palms and adorned with signs from a plethora of Nassau establishments, is a good spot to linger under thatched umbrellas and take in harbor views. You can opt for a light bite—conch salad, burgers (standard and conch varieties), calamari, nachos, and sandwiches—or try one of the heartier choices such as the mammoth T-bone steak. The sea breezes, relaxing music, and friendly staff make happy hour at Crocodiles (daily 5 to 7:30) a Nassau classic. ⊠ *E. Bay St., west of bridge to Paradise Island,* ☎ *242/323–3341. MC, V.*

$–$$ ✕ **Café Matisse.** Low-slung settees, stucco arches, and, of course, re-
★   productions of the eponymous artist's works set a casually refined tone at this restaurant, owned by a husband-and-wife team—he's Bahamian, she's northern Italian. In a century-old house, it's a favorite with those who want an unforgettable dining experience. Consider starting with salmon carpaccio or crispy fried calamari, then dive into perennially popular curried shrimp on jasmine rice, freshly made pasta such as duck-filled ravioli and lobster cannelloni, or such delights as pizza *frutti di mare* (topped with fresh local seafood). You can dine at candlelit tables inside or alfresco in the ground-floor garden under large white canvas umbrellas. ⊠ *Bank La. and Bay St., behind Parliament Sq.,* ☎ *242/ 356–7012. AE, D, MC, V. Closed Sun.*

English

$–$$$ ✕ **Green Shutters Restaurant & Pub.** In a 190-year-old building, this popular watering hole looks and feels like it's tucked away in jolly old England (except for the sight of palm trees through the windows). And it's no wonder: The entire pub area, as well as the restaurant's tables and chairs, were shipped over from Britain and reassembled. Sip a pint of Guinness or Boddingtons while you wait for your steak and kidney pie. If you prefer, the restaurant also offers Bahamian gourmet dinners like Grouper Marsha (grouper stuffed with minced lobster) and coconut-crusted snapper. ⊠ *48 Parliament St.*, ☏ *242/322–3701. AE, MC, V.*

French

$$$ ✕ **Chez Willie.** Elegant and romantic, this restaurant specializes in French cuisine with a Bahamian twist. Dine by candlelight in the intimate dining room or alfresco on the patio overlooking the lush gardens. Start with caviar or goose liver pâté, then try the signature grouper served in a puff pastry with crabmeat and coconut cream sauce. Or go with someone you love and share the chateaubriand for two. ⊠ *W. Bay St.*, ☏ *242/322–5364. Reservations essential. AE, MC, V. Dinner only.*

Greek

$–$$ ✕ **Athena Café.** A pleasant Greek restaurant in a central Bay Street locale, Athena offers diners the choice of the second-floor interior, filled with Grecian statuary, or a balcony overlooking the main drag (most people's choice). Enjoy souvlaki, moussaka, and spanakopita, among other specialties, along with Greek beer in a relaxed and friendly atmosphere. Gregarious owner Peter Mousis and his family create a nice break in the Nassau culinary routine. Enter the restaurant through the downstairs gift shop. ⊠ *Bay St. at Charlotte St.*, ☏ *242/322–8833. AE, D, MC, V. Closed Sun.*

Indian

$–$$ ✕ **Gaylord's.** A handsome historic building that dates from the 1870s is home to this restaurant. Plates, plaques, and other Indian works of art decorate the walls of the two dining areas. Draped silk adorns the ceilings. Begin with a *samosa* (a savory vegetable or meat filling enveloped in pastry and then deep fried). Next try one of the tandoori dishes cooked in a special clay oven, including nan bread (plain, or stuffed with chicken, cheese, garlic, or lamb) and mild *korma* (lamb or chicken in a rich cream sauce) to fiery vindaloo. ⊠ *Dowdeswell St. near Victoria Ave.*, ☏ *242/356–3004. AE, MC, V. No lunch weekends.*

Paradise Island

Caribbean

$–$$$ ✕ **Anthony's Caribbean Grill.** The first thing you'll notice at Anthony's are the colors: bright red, yellow, and blue tablecloths spiked with multihued squiggles; yellow-and-green walls with jaunty cloths hanging from the ceilings; booths printed with bright sea themes; and buoyant striped curtains. The lively spirit is reflected in the bouncy, often live music, and cheery service. The food is standard Caribbean fare: jerk chicken, rib eye seasoned with "Rasta" spices, or ribs served a multitude of ways—jerk, barbecue, or coconut-mango style. There's also a good selection of burgers, pasta, and salads. ⊠ *Paradise Village Shopping Centre*, ☏ *242/363–3152. AE, D, MC, V.*

Chinese

$$–$$$ ✕ **Mama Loo's.** Chinese delights are the order of the evening at this dinner-only restaurant in Atlantis. The tropical-Chinese atmosphere is enhanced with huge porcelain urns, carved wood ceilings, lush floral

arrangements, and black-lacquer chairs. Pick grouper stir-fry, braised duck, cashew chicken, or beef with oyster sauce. ⊠ *Atlantis, Paradise Island*, ☎ *242/363–3000. AE, D, DC, MC, V. Closed Mon. No lunch.*

Continental

$$$$ ✕ **Courtyard Terrace at Ocean Club.** An elite clientele congregates here
★ to indulge in refined dining under the stars, accompanied by the music of a calypso combo. With its Wedgwood china, Irish-linen napery, lighted fountains, and towering palms, this garden setting is one of the most romantic in the Bahamas. The carefully orchestrated menu emphasizes the lighter side of Continental cuisine, with a distinct island touch. Sample the duck breast with brandied cherry sauce, lobster tail with crab fried rice, or sweet and tart grouper. Alfresco dining begins at twilight. Service is superb. ⊠ *Ocean Club Dr.*, ☎ *242/363–2501. Reservations essential. Jacket required. AE, D, DC, MC, V. No lunch.*

$$$–$$$$ ✕ **Bahamian Club.** A clubby British atmosphere prevails in this handsome restaurant, where walls are lined with dark oak and overstuffed chairs and banquettes are upholstered in leather. Meat is the specialty of the house—grilled T-bone steak, veal chop, roast prime rib, and chateaubriand for two—but grilled swordfish steak, Bahamian lobster, salmon fillet, and other fresh seafood dishes are all prepared with finesse. Dinner is accompanied by soft piano music; between courses, couples can waltz on the small dance floor. ⊠ *Atlantis, Paradise Island*, ☎ *242/363–3000. AE, D, DC, MC, V. No lunch.*

Eclectic

$$$–$$$$ ✕ **Five Twins.** The only one of Atlantis's fine-dining restaurants that's right in the casino dining complex, Five Twins, offers a menu with Asian flair: sushi, sashimi, and Indonesian *sates* (marinated pieces of chicken or beef on skewers) complement dishes such as Indian-spiced squab and Szechuan duck breast. Imbibers may want to visit the Rum Bar at the restaurant's entrance. ⊠ *Atlantis, Paradise Island*, ☎ *242/363–3000. Jacket required. AE, D, DC, MC, V. No lunch.*

Italian

$$$–$$$$ ✕ **Villa d'Este.** Upscale Northern Italian cuisine is served in an Italianate room with dark wood, upholstered chairs, statuary, and an impressive fresco on the ceiling. The antipasti display is effective in whetting the appetite for such dishes as veal in Madeira and asparagus sauce or spaghetti alla carbonara. The dessert pastries are delectable. ⊠ *Atlantis, Paradise Island*, ☎ *242/363–3000. AE, D, DC, MC, V. No lunch.*

Seafood

$$–$$$ ✕ **Blue Lagoon Seafood Restaurant.** The decor tends to the nautical, with hurricane lamps and brass rails, in this narrow third-floor dining room looking out to Nassau on one side and Atlantis to the other. Choose from simply prepared choices like broiled Bahamian lobster tail or grouper, or such fancy selections as almond-fried shrimp and stuffed grouper au gratin. ⊠ *Club Land'Or*, ☎ *242/363–2400. AE, DC, MC, V. No lunch.*

$$–$$$ ✕ **Columbus Tavern.** Overlooking Nassau Harbour, this casual restaurant has a nautical feel—from the enormous open windows and decklike floors to the blue and white accents throughout. Watch the boats sail by as you dine on lobster, grouper, and conch. Or set aside your seafaring ways and try the steak Diane Flambé—it's served flaming, as the name implies. The tavern serves three meals a day, every day. ⊠ *Paradise Island Dr.*, ☎ *242/363–2534. MC, V.*

$–$$ ✕ **Blue Marlin Restaurant.** A longtime favorite in the Hurricane Hole Plaza, Blue Marlin is (no surprise) known for seafood—try seafood linguine, lobster thermidor, or the ever-popular cracked conch—although such dishes as Eleuthera Coconut Chicken and Guava Ribs will also please. Limbo and steel-pan band shows, as well as reasonably priced lunch and dinner specials, keep the place hopping. The restaurant upstairs, Bahama Mama's, uses the same kitchen but adds some Italian dishes. ⊠ *Hurricane Hole Plaza,* ☎ *242/363–2660. AE, D, MC, V.*

Cable Beach

Bahamian

$ $$ ✗ **Café Johnny Canoe.** Johnny Canoe is said to have been a wild-living African chieftain from whose name, most believe, the word *Junkanoo* is derived. A mini-Junkanoo show winds among this crowded restaurant's tables on Friday night. With a spacious outdoor seating area and a menu of traditional Bahamian fare—cracked conch and grouper fillet—as well as burgers, chicken, ribs, and tropical drinks, this has become a favorite casual tourist hangout. Desserts include such specialties as guava duff and Bacardi rum cake. ⊠ *W. Bay St., next to the Nassau Beach Hotel,* ☎ *242/327–3373.* ☉ *Breakfast also served. AE, MC, V.*

Continental

$$$–$$$$ ✗ **Androsia Steak & Seafood Restaurant.** The specialty here is Peppersteak au Paris, a New York sirloin served with Dijon mustard, cracked peppercorns, cream, and brandy. But you'll find a wide seafood selection as well at this comfortably upscale restaurant, where rich striped curtains create an elegant ambience, and starfish and lanterns on the wall add a nautical flavor. ⊠ *W. Bay St., in the Shoppers Haven Plaza,* ☎ *242/327–7805 or 242/327–6430. AE, MC, V. Closed Sun. No lunch.*

Italian

$$–$$$ ✗ **Sole Mare.** The elegant ocean-view setting, excellent service, and ex-
★ pertly prepared entrées make this one of the best Italian restaurants on the island. Start off with imported meats and cheeses from the antipasti cart before plunging into any of a range of pastas or entrées, including chicken with white wine and artichokes, lobster fra diavolo, and several other delicious possibilities. The best way to end? A Marsala-strawberry or chocolate-ricotta soufflé. ⊠ *Nassau Marriott Resort & Crystal Palace Casino,* ☎ *242/327–6200 Ext. 6861. AE, D, DC, MC, V. Closed Mon. No lunch.*

Seafood

$$–$$$$ ✗ **The Poop Deck at Sandyport.** A more upscale version of the other Poop Deck, this waterside restaurant has soaring ceilings, a cool pink and aqua color scheme, and a dazzling view of Cable Beach. You might start with sweet-potato fish cakes or grilled shrimp and Brie before proceeding to a variety of seafood, accompanied by a selection from the extensive wine list. There's even a smattering of choices for the seafood-phobic. ⊠ *W. Bay St.,* ☎ *242/327–3325,* ᵂᴱᴮ *www.thepoopdeck.com. AE, D, DC, MC, V. Closed Mon.*

Western New Providence and South Coast

Bahamian

$–$$ ✗ **Traveller's Rest.** Across the street from Compass Point, this relaxed family restaurant with a great ocean view opened in the early 1970s. A fresh seafood dinner served just steps from the beach is a real treat—conch, grouper, and crawfish are the big hitters. Try the "smudder fish"—a tasty local fish literally smothered in onions, peppers, and other vegetables. Dine outside or in, and toast the sunset with a fresh-fruit banana daiquiri—a house specialty. ⊠ *W. Bay St., Gambier,* ☎ *242/327–7633. AE, MC, V.*

Contemporary

$$–$$$ ✗ **Compass Point.** Like the hotel in which it's housed, the Compass
 ★   Point restaurant is New Providence's hippest spot. The indoor section
         is a mix of cracked tile and colorful wall decor, a look that's carried
         outside to the ocean-view terrace and the small but comfy bar. As if
         the setting weren't glorious enough, Bahamian, European, and Asian
         cuisines collide in a dynamic, changing menu, featuring standbys such
         as Bahamian conch sushi rolls with bits of cucumber and mango, and
         local lobster. Is that a fashion model or recording star next to you? No
         matter—everyone's treated like a celebrity at this customer-friendly spot.
         ✉ *Compass Point Resort, W. Bay St., Gambier,* ☎ *242/327–4500. AE,
         MC, V.*

LODGING

New Providence Island is fortunate to have an extensive range of hotels, from quaint, family-owned guest houses to the megaresorts at Cable
Beach and on Paradise Island. Downtown Nassau's beaches are not
beautiful; if you want to be beachfront on a gorgeous white strand,
stay on Cable Beach or Paradise Island's Cabbage Beach. Reasons to
stay in Nassau include proximity to shopping, and affordability (although the cost of taxis to and from the better beaches can add up).
Nassau's British Colonial Hilton, for instance, is a world-class hotel;
but its man-made beach, while nice, can't compare to Cabbage Beach
or Cable Beach.

The homey, friendly little spots will probably not be on the beach—
and you'll have to go out to eat unless you have access to a kitchen
(although some inns will prepare meals for you on request). On the
flip side, your stay is likely to be relaxing, low-key, and less removed
from everyday Bahamian life. The plush resorts are big and beautiful,
glittering and splashy, but they can be overwhelming. In any case, these
big, top-dollar properties generally have more amenities than you
could possibly make use of, a selection of dining options, and a full
roster of sports and entertainment. The battle for the tourist dollar rages
ceaselessly between Cable Beach and Paradise Island. The competition,
of course, encourages a wide variety of vacation packages, with en-
ticements such as free snorkeling gear, free scuba lessons, and free admission to Las Vegas–style revues.

Paradise Island was once the quieter alternative to more active resorts
on Cable Beach. With the spread of the Atlantis Resort, however,
that's changed. You'll still find a few peaceful retreats on P.I., but the
boisterous megaresort has eliminated most of the quiet strolling lanes
and brought its own brand of flash to the island. However, Cable Beach
probably still tilts younger in its orientation. Some prefer the lineup
of resorts along the Cable Beach strip, some like the look of P.I., which
has the hotels scattered around every corner (and which is, unlike Cable
Beach, walkable from downtown).

A tax ranging from 8% to 10%, representing resort and government
levies, is added to your hotel bill. Some hotels also add a gratuity charge
of between $2.50 and $4 (or higher) per person, per day, for the house-
keeping or pool staff.

The prices below are based on high-season (winter) rates, generally in
effect from December through March. Expect to pay between 15% and
30% less off-season at most resorts. In general, the best rates are available through packages, which almost every hotel offers. Call the hotel
directly or ask your travel agent.

CATEGORY	COST*
$$$$	over $400
$$$	$300–$400
$$	$200–$300
$	$100–$200
¢	under $100

*All prices are for a standard double room in high season, excluding 9% tax and 10%–15% service charge. Note that the government hotel tax doesn't apply to guest houses with fewer than four rooms.

Nassau

$$–$$$ ★ ⊞ **Graycliff.** The old-world flavor of this Georgian Colonial landmark has made it a perennial favorite with an upscale crowd. Over the years, the house has seen such guests as the Duke and Duchess of Windsor, Winston Churchill, Aristotle Onassis, and the Beatles—not to mention its original owner, pirate Captain John Howard Graysmith. Still, the elegance here is tropical, not stuffy. A series of garden villas and cottages, amid limestone courtyards with ponds and fountains, is enveloped in thick foliage, allowing you to forget you're just steps from downtown Nassau. The hotel's original restaurant, Graycliff, is one of the island's premier places to dine. The adjoining property incorporates a cigar factory and restaurant, appropriately named Humidor. ⊠ *W. Hill St. (Box N-10246),* ☎ *242/322–2796 or 800/688–0076,* FAX *242/326–6110,* WEB *www.graycliff.com. 7 rooms, 13 suites. 2 restaurants, in-room hot tubs, 3 pools, 3 bars, hair salon, massage, sauna, health club, business services. AE, DC, MC, V. CP.*

$$ ★ ⊞ **British Colonial Hilton Nassau.** From a lustrous saffron facade to gleaming marble floors and arched, skylighted ceiling, this landmark building, first opened in 1900 as the Hotel Colonial, is the sharpest and most elegant in all of Nassau. Its rooms have sleek wood furniture and good views. A small man-made beach overlooks the cruise ships among lushly landscaped grounds, the Wedgwood Restaurant and Lounge offers elegant dining, and afternoon tea in the Palm Court Lounge is perfect for those with a taste for graciousness. With first-rate conference facilities, free direct Internet connection in your room, and an executive lounge, the hotel is the best business choice in the Bahamas; the Nassau Stock Exchange is in an adjacent wing. ⊠ *1 Bay St. (Box N-7148),* ☎ *242/322–3301,* FAX *242/302–9035,* WEB *www.bchilton.com. 270 rooms, 21 suites. 2 restaurants, 3 lounges, room service, in-room data ports, in-room safes, cable TV, pool, health club, hair salon, massage, spa, beach, dive shop, snorkeling, volleyball, shops, baby-sitting, laundry service, concierge floor, Internet, business services, convention center, meeting rooms, car rental. AE, D, DC, MC, V.*

$ ⊞ **Buena Vista Hotel.** Surrounded by a beautiful 3-acre garden, this 19th-century plantation house is ½ mi from downtown Nassau. The two-story building is better known for its restaurant, but the spacious, simple, and rather imposingly dark rooms, surprisingly affordable in this elegant setting, are individually decorated with solid-wood furniture. Climb the aqua-hued staircase from the low-key, tasteful lobby, which is filled with tropical greenery, to a long hallway where the rooms are all but invisible to the restaurant guests. The public beach is just a 10-minute walk away. ⊠ *Delancy St. (Box N-564),* ☎ *242/322–2811,* FAX *242/322–5881. 5 rooms. Restaurant, bar, refrigerators, cable TV. AE, DC, MC, V. FAP.*

$ ★ ⊞ **Dillet's Guest House.** You know you're in for something special the minute you enter the lounge of this family-run guest house—the arched entry, ceiling fans, wicker furniture, caged birds, and massive flower arrangements exude old Nassau charm. Although not fancy, the place is

Nassau and Paradise Island Lodging

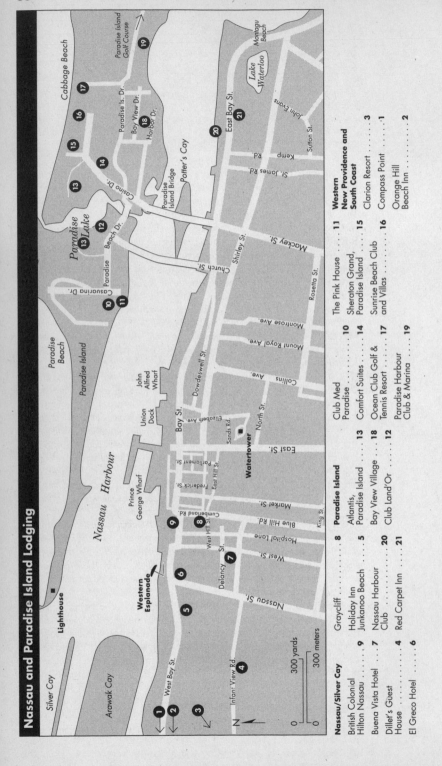

spotless and furnished with true island flair. The large guest rooms are named after island fruits, indicated by hand-painted pieces of driftwood on the doors. A few miles removed from downtown Nassau, this home is for those seeking to experience Bahamian life first-hand; there are no better models of graciousness than Iris—recently named Bahamas Hotelier of the Year—and her daughter Danielle. ⊠ *Dunmore Ave. and Strachan St. (Box N-204),* ☎ *242/325–1133,* ℻ *242/325–7183,* 🕸 *www. islandeaze.com/dillets. 7 rooms. Dining room, minibars, some kitchenettes, microwaves, pool, bicycles, library, Internet. AE, MC, V. CP.*

$ 🏨 **El Greco Hotel.** Pleasant Greek owners and friendly staff create an ambience more in keeping with a cozy guest house than a hotel. Although not fancy, rooms are quite large; decorated in soothing, old-fashioned earth tones, they surround a small pool tucked within a bougainvillea-filled courtyard. The resulting atmosphere is quiet and appeals primarily to a European crowd. The El Greco is a few minutes walk from Bay Street and downtown and is directly across the street from the public Western Esplanade beach. For those on a budget who want to be in Nassau, El Greco is a pleasant find. ⊠ *W. Bay St. (Box N-4187),* ☎ *242/325–1121,* ℻ *242/325–1124,* 🕸 *www. bahamasnet.com/elgrecohotel. 26 rooms. Restaurant, bar, cable TV, pool, bar, baby-sitting. AE, MC, V.*

$ 🏨 **Holiday Inn Junkanoo Beach.** The salmon-colored, five-story chain hotel is a moderately priced option a few minutes west of downtown, across the street from little Western Esplanade beach. The hotel is modern and well managed: An activities desk in the lobby will help coordinate your island activities. Some suites come with hot tubs and/or bunk beds. ⊠ *W. Bay St. (Box SS-19055),* ☎ *242/356–0000 or 800/ 465–4329,* ℻ *242/323–1408. 168 rooms, 6 suites. Restaurant, room service, in-room safes, in-room data ports, cable TV, 2 pools, hot tub, gym, bar, shop, laundry service, meeting rooms, convention center. AE, D, DC, MC, V.*

$ 🏨 **Red Carpet Inn.** Cleanliness and quiet are stressed here—it's one of the few area hotels in its price category not geared toward springbreakers. The owners live on premises, which explains the devotion to spotlessness and the agreeable atmosphere, and the hotel is far enough off the beaten path to provide a sense of island solitude. Rooms are simple, but come with microwaves and full-size refrigerators. The Barn serves Bahamian and American fare daily at breakfast and lunch. Downtown Nassau is a 15- to 20-minute walk away. ⊠ *E. Bay St. (Box SS-6233),* ☎ *242/393–7981,* ℻ *242/393–9055,* 🕸 *www.bahamasvg.com/ redcarpetinn. 40 rooms. Restaurant, bar, in-room safes, microwaves, refrigerators, pool, laundry facilities. AE, D, MC, V.*

$–$ 🏨 **Nassau Harbour Club.** The Harbour Club is popular with international sailing aficionados and hordes of spring-breaking students, which, along with its location a mile down the main road into town, does not make it an oasis of peace and quiet. Locals and tourists gather at the downstairs Dockside Bar and Grill to watch televised sports or sit outside on the deck overlooking the harbor. On the hotel's main floor, up a spiral wooden staircase from the bar, is Chiban Sushi restaurant. ⊠ *E. Bay St. (Box SS-5755),* ☎ *242/393–0771,* ℻ *242/393–5393. 50 rooms. Restaurant, bar, pool, dock. AE, MC, V.*

Paradise Island

$$$$ 🏨 **Ocean Club Golf & Tennis Resort.** Once the private hideaway of A&P
★   heir Huntington Hartford, this ultra-expensive resort on magnificent Cabbage Beach's quietest stretch provides the ultimate in understated elegance. The atmosphere is decidedly posh, and the staff is friendly and accommodating: just place a flag by your chaise and a waiter will

be on the beach in seconds. The resort's centerpiece, Versailles Gardens, is 35 acres of terraced serenity topped by an imported French cloister. Spacious colonial-style rooms have private garden settings, intricately carved furniture, and marble bathrooms. The open-air restaurant perched over the beach is excellent. ⊠ *Ocean Club Dr. (Box N-4777, Nassau),* ☎ *242/363–2501 or 800/321–3000,* ℻ *242/363–2424,* WEB *www.sunint.com. 99 rooms, 8 villas, 10 suites. 2 restaurants, 2 bars, room service, cable TV, pool, spa, golf privileges, 9 tennis courts, health club, beach, snorkeling, windsurfing, boating, waterskiing, bicycles, baby-sitting, laundry service. AE, D, DC, MC, V.*

$$$–$$$$ 🏨 **Club Med Paradise.** Club Med was permitted to develop this stunning setting on the condition that the original private estate gardens be preserved; thus the meandering paths bordered by swaying casuarina trees and graceful palms, an Olympic-size swimming pool surrounded by a garden of more than 100 species of plants, and long stretches of green lawn. Guests are likely to be parents traveling without their kids, honeymooners (especially in the secluded "House in the Woods"), and other romantic sorts. The closely guarded gate ensures privacy and security but tends to keep the guests in a world far removed from Bahamian culture and its people. ⊠ *Casuarina Dr. (Box N-7137, Nassau),* ☎ *242/363–2640 or 800/258–2633,* ℻ *242/363–5855. 314 rooms. 2 restaurants, 3 bars, minigolf, 2 saltwater pools, 18 tennis courts, archery, boccie, gym, beach, snorkeling, windsurfing, billiards, nightclub. AE, MC, V. All-inclusive.*

$$–$$$$ 🏨 **Atlantis, Paradise Island.** A bustling fantasy world—part water
★ ☺   park, entertainment complex, megaresort, and beach oasis—this is by far the biggest and boldest resort in the country. The overriding theme here is water—for swimming, snorkeling, and observing marine life, as well as for mood and effect, in lagoons, caves, waterfalls, several walk-through aquariums (touted as the largest marine habitat in the world). The public areas are lavish, with fountains, glass sculptures, and gleaming shopping arcades. Numerous sporting activities are available, and there is plenty of nightlife on the premises; the casino, ringed by restaurants, is the largest in the Bahamas and the Caribbean. ⊠ *Casino Dr. (Box N-4777, Nassau),* ☎ *242/363–3000 or 800/321–3000,* ℻ *242/363–3524,* WEB *www.atlantis.com. 2,097 rooms, 230 suites. 20 restaurants, 13 bars, room service, in-room data ports, in-room safes, cable TV, 11 pools, hair salon, spa, golf privileges, 10 tennis courts, basketball, health club, jogging, volleyball, beach, dock, snorkeling, windsurfing, boating, deli, casino, comedy club, nightclub, shops, baby-sitting, children's programs (ages 4–12), concierge floor, Internet, business services, convention center, meeting rooms, travel services, car rental. AE, D, DC, MC, V. MAP.*

$$$ 🏨 **Sunrise Beach Club and Villas.** Lushly landscaped with crotons, co-
★   conut palms, bougainvillea, and hibiscus, this low-rise, family-run resort on Cabbage Beach has a tropical wonderland feel. Two pools sustain the ambience with statuary and tropical plantings, and the beach is accessible via a long flight of wooden stairs built right into the cliff. Paths wind through the floral arcadia, past trickling fountains, archways, and terra-cotta tiles with color insets. Lodgings are an eclectic architectural mix—take your pick from one-bedroom town houses with spiral staircases that lead to an upstairs bedroom, two-bedroom apartments, or three-bedroom villas. All have fully equipped kitchens, king-size beds, and patios. ⊠ *Casino Dr. (Box SS-6519, Nassau),* ☎ *242/363–2234,* ℻ *242/363–2308,* WEB *www.sunrisebeachvillas.com. 18 1-, 2-, and 3-bedroom units. Snack bar, bar, cable TV, kitchens, microwaves, 2 pools, beach, baby-sitting, laundry facilities, Internet. AE, D, MC, V.*

$$–$$$ 🏨 **Paradise Harbour Club & Marina.** With a marina and an enviable location, this collection of oversize, comfortable apartments is a great

choice for those who want the freedom of a private residence with the facilities of a large resort. Full kitchens (complete with refrigerator, mini-bar, and dishwasher) lend a homey feeling to these somewhat characterless but very cushy lodgings. Commodious closet and sink space are among the extras. If you prefer a view, opt for the top-floor digs. ⊠ *Paradise Island Dr. (Box SS-5804, Nassau),* ☎ *242/363–2992; 800/ 742–4276 reservation service,* FAX *242/363–2840,* WEB *www.phclub.com. 22 units. Restaurant, bar, kitchenettes, pool, hot tub, tennis court, boating, bicycles. AE, MC, V.*

\$\$–\$\$\$ ⊞ **Sheraton Grand, Paradise Island.** A soaring lobby and pleasant rooms containing Sheraton's usual amenities make this one of the island's top hotels. Although not as grand as Atlantis next door, the Sheraton is not far from its neighbor's casino, and shares a quieter bit of the same lovely beach. Every room overlooks the water from at least a small side balcony. The activities desk is among the busiest in town. Note the fine print: Some guests are displeased at checkout by daily per person energy and housekeeping surcharges; and, odd for a hotel of its caliber, there's no Internet access. ⊠ *Casino Dr. (Box SS-6307, Nassau),* ☎ *242/363–3500 or 800/325–3535,* FAX *242/363–3900,* WEB *www.sheratongrand.com. 340 rooms. 4 restaurants, 3 bars, room service, in-room safes, cable TV, minibars, pool, tennis court, health club, volleyball, beach, dive shop, snorkeling, windsurfing, boating, parasailing, waterskiing, bicycles, nightclub, baby-sitting, meeting rooms, travel services. AE, D, DC, MC, V.*

\$\$ ⊞ **Club Land'Or.** In Atlantis's shadow just over the bridge from Nassau, this friendly time-share property has one-bedroom villas with full kitchens, bathrooms, living rooms, desks, and patios or balconies that overlook the lagoon, the gardens, or the pool. The units are described as accommodating four people, but they seem better suited to couples. The Blue Lagoon Seafood Restaurant is a favorite of locals and guests. Many activities are planned throughout the week. ⊠ *Paradise Beach Dr. (Box SS-6429, Nassau),* ☎ *242/363–2400,* FAX *242/363–3403,* WEB *www.clublandor.com. 72 villas. Restaurant, 2 bars, in-room data ports, microwaves, kitchens, cable TV, pool, bicycles, shops, baby-sitting, laundry facilities, Internet. AE, D, MC, V. EP, MAP.*

\$\$ ⊞ **Comfort Suites.** The all-suites, three-story pink-and-white hotel has an arrangement with Atlantis that allows guests to use that resort's facilities. Kids can also enroll at the Atlantis's Discovery Channel Camp. For many, that's reason enough to stay here, in the middle of the Paradise Island action. Rooms share a cozy feel and have sitting areas with sofa beds. There's free Continental breakfast, a swim-up bar, and poolside lunch for those who want to stay on the nicely landscaped grounds. Cabbage Beach is just a hop, skip, and a jump away. ⊠ *Casino Dr. (Box SS-6202, Nassau),* ☎ *242/363–3680 or 800/228–5150,* FAX *242/363–2588. 228 junior suites. Restaurant, bar, in-room safes, minibars, cable TV, pool, baby-sitting. AE, D, MC, V. CP.*

\$–\$\$ ⊞ **Bay View Village.** At this 4-acre condominium resort, guests socialize around three pools (two for general use, one reserved for the villas). The atmosphere is intimate, and the lush tropical landscaping includes several hibiscus and bougainvillea varieties. Choose between one- and two-bedroom apartments and two- and three-bedroom villas, all of which are spacious, clean, comfortable, and decorated in bright island style. All rooms have private balconies or garden terraces. Cabbage Beach is a 10-minute walk away. ⊠ *Bay View Dr. (Box SS-6308, Nassau),* ☎ *242/363–2555 or 800/757–1357,* FAX *242/363–2370,* WEB *www. bayviewvillage.com. 72 units and villas. Bar, snack bar, cable TV, fans, kitchens, microwaves, 3 pools, tennis court, baby-sitting, laundry facilities. AE, MC, V.*

$ ⊡ **The Pink House.** A former Sears family estate, this charming guest
★   house appears through a thicket of bamboo and palm trees in the middle of a wonderful tropical garden. A throwback to colonial times, it
sits placidly on its own plot of land within Club Med's gates, and guests
can take advantage of that resort's private beach and gardens. You're
also just steps from Atlantis: the combination of location and price are
unbeatable on New Providence. Owner Minnie Winn's personal attention will make you feel like a resident or treasured family member.
Not for those craving luxury or anonymity, but for old-time Nassau
hospitality, you won't go wrong here. ⊠ *Casuarina Dr. (Box SS-19157,
Nassau),* ☏ *242/363–3363,* FAX *242/377–3383,* WEB *www.bahamasnet.
com/pinkhouse. 4 rooms. Cable TV, pond. No credit cards. CP.*

Cable Beach

$$$$ ⊡ **Guanahani Village.** The substantial, well-furnished accommodations
at this resort are perfect for young families or groups of friends traveling together. Stucco units are spread across landscaped grounds. The
tiled three-bedroom luxury villas, oceanfront or garden side, sleep six
comfortably, up to eight using roll-aways (so the price, although in the
top category, is really quite reasonable when shared by several people). Each unit has oversize rooms, a delightful secluded patio, a fully
equipped kitchen, a washer and dryer, and a dishwasher. The pool overlooks the ocean, although beaches are a bit of a walk. ⊠ *W. Bay St.
(Box CB-13317, Nassau),* ☏ *242/327–5236 or 242/327–7568,* FAX
242/327–8311, WEB *www.guanahanivillage.com. 35 units. Snack bar,
cable TV, kitchens, pool. AE, MC, V.*

$$$$ ⊡ **Sandals Royal Bahamian Resort & Spa.** Cable Beach's most expensive
spot presents an elegant environment and spa facilities with nicely furnished rooms with views of the ocean, pool, or grounds replete with
pillars and faux Roman statuary. There's a state-of-the-art fitness
club, and a multilingual concierge service assists foreign guests. Eight
restaurants offer cuisines ranging from Caribbean to Japanese (make
reservations well in advance wherever they're required), and nightly
entertainment takes place in the resort's amphitheater. Sandals' "couples only" policy, it should be noted, means "heterosexual couples
only"—it will turn away gay and lesbian couples who try to reserve.
⊠ *W. Bay St. (Box CB-13005, Nassau),* ☏ *242/327–6400 or 800/
726–3257,* FAX *242/327–6961,* WEB *www.sandals.com. 166 rooms, 240
suites. 8 restaurants, 7 bars, room service, cable TV, 5 pools, spa, 2
tennis courts, basketball, croquet, health club, shuffleboard, volleyball, gym, beach, dive shop, snorkeling, windsurfing, boating, waterskiing, dance club, recreation room, Internet, meeting rooms. AE,
MC, V. All-inclusive.*

$$$–$$$$ ⊡ **Breezes Bahamas.** Right on Cable Beach, this SuperClubs property
offers couples and singles (age 16 or older) an attractive package; the
all-inclusive rate includes lodging, entertainment, unlimited food and
beverages, land and water sports, airport transfers, taxes, and gratu-
ities. Take advantage of the fitness center, five freshwater pools, swim-
up bar, and nightly entertainment, including local bands, toga or
pajama parties, karaoke, and the like. The open-air lobby is bright and
cheery, with a huge fish chandelier and multicolor tile floor. Large, mod-
ern rooms are pleasant although not striking, and food is available in
several locales 24 hours a day. ⊠ *W. Bay St., (Box CB-13049, Nas-
sau),* ☏ *242/327–5356 or 800/859–7873,* FAX *242/327–5155,* WEB *www.
breezesbahamas.com. 392 rooms. 2 restaurants, 4 bars, room service,
snack bar, cable TV, 5 pools, 3 tennis courts, basketball, health club,
volleyball, beach, windsurfing, boating, bicycles, billiards, dance club,
Internet. AE, MC, V. All-inclusive.*

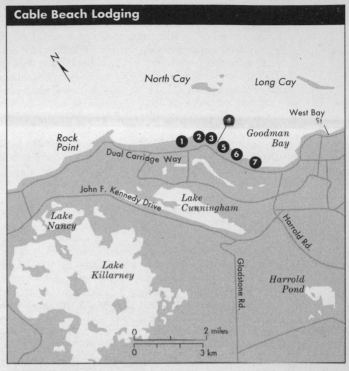

Cable Beach Lodging

North Cay

Long Cay

West Bay St.

Goodman Bay

Rock Point

Dual Carriage Way

John F. Kennedy Drive

Lake Cunningham

Lake Nancy

Lake Killarney

Harrold Rd.

Gladstone Rd.

Harrold Pond

0   2 miles

0   3 km

$$ ⌂ **Nassau Marriott Resort & Crystal Palace Casino.** It's not hard to find your way back to the Marriott at night: The five towers are illuminated with bands of varying colors, making the hotel look like a giant rainbow reflecting off the ocean. High-rollers love the Crystal Club, three concierge floors at the top of the Casino Tower with 30 spectacularly decorated executive suites. The resort has its own palm-fringed beach and lagoon for swimming, sunbathing, and water sports; a health club with top-notch equipment and daily aerobics classes; a Marriotter Kids Klub program for youngsters; and the 35,000-square-ft Crystal Palace Casino. ⊠ *W. Bay St. (Box N-8306, Nassau),* ☎ *242/327–6200 or 800/ 222–7466,* FAX *242/327–6459,* WEB *www.marriotthotels.com/nasbs. 743 rooms, 124 suites. 6 restaurants, 5 bars, room service, cable TV, pool, hair salon, aerobics, health club, beach, snorkeling, water slide, windsurfing, boating, shops, casino, recreation room, theater, baby-sitting, children's programs (ages 4 and up), concierge floors, Internet, meeting room. AE, D, DC, MC, V. FAP, MAP.*

$$ ⌂ **West Wind II.** Privacy is the lure of these cozy villas on Cable Beach's west end, 6 mi from downtown. Two-bedroom, two-bath condominiums have fully stocked kitchens and balconies or patios overlook the gardens or pools. The reasonable prices and relaxed atmosphere are ideal for families or groups on a budget, and the pleasant, quiet location— off the road amid manicured lawns and pruned gardens—gives children the freedom to play outdoors. The spectacular sea view somewhat compensates for the tiny and very windy beach. A bus stop and taxi stand are right outside. ⊠ *W. Bay St. (Box CB-11006, Nassau),* ☎ *242/327– 7211 or 242/327–7019,* FAX *242/327–7529. 54 villas. Snack bar, cable TV, fans, kitchenettes, 2 pools, 2 tennis courts, beach, snorkeling, boating, baby-sitting, laundry service, travel services. MC, V.*

$–$$ ⌂ **Nassau Beach Hotel.** Built in the 1940s, this Cable Beach mainstay still has the prettiest lobby on Cable Beach and has brightened up its hallways, but room upgrades proceed slowly. All rooms have balconies, but views vary: Some face the ½-mi sandy beach, and others overlook neighboring buildings. Guests have use of all non-motorized water-sports equipment. Tennis on the six courts (three lighted) is free before 5 PM, $7 per person hourly during "prime time" (5–9). The hotel has indoor and outdoor restaurants on-site, as well as a shopping arcade. The Crystal Palace Casino is next door, and the Cable Beach Golf Club is across the street. ⊠ *W. Bay St. (Box N-7756, Nassau),* ☎ *242/327–7711 or 888/627–7282,* FAX *242/327–8829,* WEB *www.nassaubeachhotel.com. 403 rooms. 5 restaurants, 3 bars, room service, cable TV, 2 pools, 6 tennis courts, gym, beach, snorkeling, windsurfing, boating, shops, baby-sitting, convention center, meeting room. AE, DC, MC, V. CP, EP, FAP, MAP.*

$–$$ ⊡ **Radisson Cable Beach Casino & Golf Resort.** One of the area's top
★ resorts, this high-rise property is smack in the middle of Cable Beach action. Connected by a shopping arcade to Crystal Palace Casino, the hotel fairly buzzes with activity. Daytime options include dance lessons by the pool, beach volleyball, free scuba lessons, and plenty of children's activities. Guests get special rates at the hotel's challenging 18-hole Cable Beach Golf Club. At night, choices range from a slew of dining possibilities to beach parties, revues, and—of course—gambling at the adjoining casino. All rooms have balconies and face either the beach and pool or gardens. ⊠ *W. Bay St. (Box N-4914, Nassau),* ☎ *242/327–6000,* FAX *242/327–6907,* WEB *www.cablebeachbahamas.com. 669 rooms, 31 suites. 6 restaurants, 2 bars, room service, cable TV, 3 pools, hair salon, 18-hole golf course, 5 tennis courts, health club, racquetball, squash, volleyball, beach, snorkeling, boating, bicycles, shops, casino, baby-sitting, children's programs (ages 4–11), Internet, meeting room. AE, DC, MC, V. All-inclusive, EP.*

Western New Providence and South Coast

$$–$$$ ⊡ **Compass Point.** Hotelier and recording-studio mogul Chris Black-
★ well has scored a hit with this cheerful beachfront property 20 minutes west of downtown Nassau. Designer Barbara Hulanicki's brilliant Junkanoo colors are a feast for the eyes. The hotel attracts a trendy crowd of celebrities and wanna-bes, but the staff treats everyone with the same down-to-earth, welcoming helpfulness. Cottages, huts, and cabanas appear through dense foliage like vibrant parrots. Some are duplexes on stilts, some are octagonal, some directly face the ocean. Compass Point has a small beach, and Love Beach—which is great for snorkelers—is next door. ⊠ *W. Bay St., Gambier (Box CB-13842, Nassau),* ☎ *242/327–4500 or 800/688–7678,* FAX *242/327–3299,* WEB *www.islandoutpost.com/compasspoint. 16 1-bedroom units, 2 2-bedroom units, 1 3-bedroom penthouse. Restaurant, bar, fans, in-room fax, kitchenettes, in-room VCRs, pool, tennis court, beach, snorkeling, fishing. AE, MC, V.*

$–$$ ⊡ **Clarion Resort.** Imposing oceanfront villas with cool Mexican tile floors, four-poster beds, whirlpool baths, 25-inch TVs, and sea-view balconies make Clarion's Great Houses a great choice. Lower-priced accommodations in the main house of this Clarion property have a tropical feel, with wicker chairs and bright prints. Facilities on-site or nearby include an 18-hole golf course at which Clarion guests receive reduced rates, and Stuart Cove's Dive South Ocean facility, one of the town's best dive operations. ⊠ *S. Ocean Dr. (Box N-8191, Nassau),* ☎ *242/362–4391 or 800/252–7466,* FAX *242/362–4810,* WEB *www.clarionnassau.com. 238 rooms. 3 restaurants, 3 bars, snack bar, cable TV, 2 pools, 18-hole golf course, 4 tennis courts, beach, dive shop, snorkeling, boating, baby-sitting. AE, DC, MC, V.*

$ ◫ **Orange Hill Beach Inn.** If you prefer down-home coziness over slick glamour, then this charming inn—on the site of a former orange plantation perched on a hilltop overlooking the ocean—is the place to stay. Guests are treated like family, and the homey feel extends to the comfortably eclectic living room and daytime honor bar. Orange Hill has a reputation as an inexpensive alternative for honeymooners and scuba divers. It's a half-hour drive from town, 15 minutes from the casino, and 300 ft from a pleasant roadside beach. Rooms and apartments vary considerably in size. ⊠ *W. Bay St. (Box N-8583, Nassau),* ☎ *242/327–7157,* FAX *242/327–5186,* WEB *www.orangehill.com. 32 rooms. Restaurant, bar, cable TV, no room phones, some kitchenettes, pool, basketball, laundry facilities. AE, MC, V.*

NIGHTLIFE AND THE ARTS

Nightlife

Cable Beach and Paradise Island resorts have their own flashy clubs where residents and visitors alike come to enjoy a variety of late-night entertainment. The attire for attending these soirees is typically as casual as the atmosphere, although some clubs require dressier duds. The casinos also are casual, so leave your black tie at home. You have to be at least 18 years old to gamble; Bahamians and permanent residents are not permitted to indulge. Most coffeehouses are open late into the evening, but note that a few listed close at about 6.

Cable Beach

CASINOS

Crystal Palace Casino. Slots, craps, baccarat, blackjack, roulette, Big Six, and face-up 21 are among the games in this 35,000-square-ft space. There's a Sports Book facility for sports betting, equipped with big-screen TVs, which air live sporting events. Both VIPs and low-limit bettors have their own areas. Casino gaming lessons are available for beginners. Tables and slots are open 24 hours daily. ⊠ *Nassau Marriott Resort, Cable Beach,* ☎ *242/327–6200.*

NIGHTCLUBS

Zoo Nightclub. Nassau's largest indoor nightclub, Zoo has five regular bars, a sports bar, and a VIP lounge where the drinks keep coming while party animals dance the night away to top chart hits. Its café is open from noon until the wee hours. ⊠ *W. Bay St., across from Saunders Beach,* ☎ *242/322–7195.*

Nassau

COFFEEHOUSES

Café Paradiso. On Bay Street's eastern end, this pleasant coffeehouse serves up sandwiches and salads—try the chicken Caesar or spicy shrimp mango. Tasty desserts include Grandma's homemade brownies and a chocolate-apricot torte. ⊠ *E. Bay St., between Elizabeth St. and Victoria Ave.,* ☎ *242/356–5282. Closed Sun.*

Caffè Caribe. In the Logos Bookstore, this tiny spot has a simple, modern look with high tables and stools. Salads, quiches, and sandwiches supplement the coffee selection; there's a long list of fruity- and nutty-flavored espressos. It closes at 6 PM. ⊠ *Harbour Bay Shopping Centre, E. Bay St.,* ☎ *242/394–7040. Closed Sun.*

Cappuccino Café and Specialty Shop. Although a bit out of the way, and only open until 6 PM, this little upscale deli and coffeehouse has a bright, appealing look. There's an extensive gourmet food selection as well as coffeehouse standards. ⊠ *Royal Palm Mall, Mackey St.,* ☎ *242/394–6332. Closed Sun.*

Flamingo Cigars and Gourmet Café. Select from a range of coffees and teas at this simple shop, a refuge from Bay Street's shopping frenzy. The smoker's lounge upstairs is a hidden wood-paneled nook in which to savor the Cohibas and Montecristos for sale. ⊠ *1 Bay St., east side of Colonial Hilton Hotel,* ☎ *242/325–8510. Closed Sun.*

Le Bistro. A two-story European-style bistro in the heart of downtown Nassau, Le Bistro serves coffee, wine, bar drinks, and pastries, as well as Edy's ice cream. Early birds and late-nighters love the long hours, 9 AM–midnight (2 AM on Saturday). ⊠ *Charlotte St., north of Bay St.,* ☎ *242/326–0206. Closed Sun.*

NIGHTCLUBS

Club Waterloo. Claiming to be Nassau's largest indoor-outdoor nightclub, the club has five bars and nonstop dancing Monday through Saturday until 4 AM (live bands weekends). Try the spring break special Waterloo Hurricane, a tropical mixture of rums and punches. ⊠ *E. Bay St.,* ☎ *242/393–7324.*

The Drop Off. In the heart of downtown's Bay Street, this downstairs pub has a variety of live entertainment in a sporty, noisy atmosphere. ⊠ *Bay St.,* ☎ *242/322–3444.*

Mangoes. On the second floor of the 18th-century Seamen's Chapel, this perch above Bay Street is perhaps the most centrally located Nassau nightspot. A live DJ spins on the wooden dance floor beneath a high peaked roof. The restaurant here serves food 11 AM–10 PM. It's a fine place to have a drink on a terrace overlooking Bay Street. ⊠ *Bay St., just east of British Colonial Hilton Hotel.* 🖭 *$10 men, $5 women for nightclub.*

601 Nightclub. The most upscale club in town, 601 recaptures the feel of old Nassau in elegant environs with a doorman and dress code—the latter, considerably relaxed from former days, now forbids shorts and tennis shoes. Bands Visage and Spank keep things hopping. This club is open Friday through Sunday nights only; happy hour is 6 to 9. ⊠ *E. Bay St.,* ☎ *242/322–3041.*

Paradise Island

CASINOS

Paradise Island Casino. At 50,000 square ft (100,000 if you include the dining and drinking areas), this is the Caribbean/Bahamian area's largest facility. Ringed with restaurants, it offers more than 1,100 slot machines, baccarat, blackjack, roulette, craps tables, and such local specialties as Caribbean stud poker. There's a high-limit table area, additional games available at most of the eateries within its walls, and a spectacularly open and airy design. Tables are open from 10 AM to 4 AM daily; slots, 24 hours. ⊠ *Atlantis, Paradise Island,* ☎ *242/363–3000.*

COFFEEHOUSES

News Café. In Paradise Island's Hurricane Hole Plaza, this is the perfect place to refuel with a light, inexpensive lunch or just a delicious milk shake before heading into town or indulging in some P.I. shopping. Enjoy coffee, muffins, and excellent $5–$6 sandwiches served on your choice of fresh breads. Use the Internet, or choose from a wide range of foreign magazines and newspapers. ⊠ *Hurricane Hole Plaza, Paradise Island,* ☎ *242/363–4684,* ☯ *7:30 AM–10 PM.*

NIGHTCLUBS

Dragons Lounge and Dance Club. Part of Atlantis's casino dining/entertainment complex, Dragons offers music and dancing just steps away from the high-rolling action. ⊠ *Atlantis Resort,* ☎ *242/363–3000.*

Oasis Lounge. There's live piano or vocal music here nightly from 7:30 to midnight. ⊠ *Club Land'Or,* ☎ *242/363–2400.*

The Arts

Cable Beach

THEATER

Rainforest Theatre. The redesigned theater, which now has an atmosphere true to its name, presents lavish shows. Check with the resort for the latest offerings. ⊠ *Nassau Marriott Resort, Cable Beach,* ☎ *242/327–6200 Ext. 6861.*

Nassau

THEATER

Dundas Centre for the Performing Arts. Plays and musicals by local and out-of-town artists are staged throughout the year. ⊠ *Mackey St.,* ☎ *242/393–3728.*

OUTDOOR ACTIVITIES AND SPORTS

For all the dining, shopping, and nightlife possibilities, Nassau's draw—as with all of the Bahamas—remains its outdoor life; with flawless weather nearly year-round, it's a rare visitor to New Providence who doesn't experience some of the natural delights that remain even among the frenzied construction. Many of these pleasures revolve around—or beckon from underneath—the water, and everyone from experienced boaters and divers to novice snorkelers can enjoy seeing (in the words of one local promotion) "how the other two-thirds live." You can participate in sports activities or lie back and enjoy a cruise, often with snorkeling or other water-based fun involved.

Boating

From Chub Cay—one of the Berry Islands 35 mi north of New Providence—to Nassau, the sailing route goes across the mile-deep Tongue of the Ocean. The Paradise Island Lighthouse welcomes yachters to Nassau Harbour, which is open at both ends. The harbor can handle the world's largest cruise liners; sometimes as many as eight tie up at one time. Two looming bridges bisect the harbor connecting Paradise Island to Nassau. Sailboats with masts taller than the high-water clearance of 72 ft must enter the harbor from the east end to reach marinas east of the bridges. On the Nassau side of the harbor, you'll find **Nassau Yacht Haven** (☎ 242/393–8173, WEB www.nassauyachthaven.com), a 150-berth marina—the largest in the Bahamas—that also arranges fishing charters. **Brown's Boat Basin** (☎ 242/393–3331), on the Nassau side, offers a place to tie up your boat, as well as on-site engine repairs. **Nassau Harbour Club** (☎ 242/393–0771) is a hotel and marina on the Nassau side with 50 slips. Sixty-five-slip **Hurricane Hole Marina** (☎ 242/363–3600) is on the Paradise Island side. The marina at **Atlantis, Paradise Island** (☎ 242/363–3000) has 63 "mega-yacht slips." At the western end of New Providence, **Lyford Cay** (☎ 242/362–4131), a posh development for the rich and famous, has an excellent marina, but there is limited availability for the humble masses.

Children might love sitting in a row on a rubber banana and bouncing along behind a motorboat. Ride the big banana at **Premier Watersports** at the beach at the Sheraton Grand and Atlantis (☎ 242/324–1475 or cellular 242/427–0939).

Fishing

The waters here are generally smooth and alive with many species of game fish, which is one of the reasons why the Bahamas has more than 20 fishing tournaments open to visitors every year. A favorite spot just west of Nassau is the Tongue of the Ocean, so called because it looks like that part of the body when viewed from the air. The channel stretches for 100 mi. For boat rental, parties of two to six will pay $300 or so for a half day, $600 for a full day.

The **Charter Boat Association** (☎ 242/393–3739) has 15 boats available for fishing charters. **Born Free Charters** (☎ 242/393–4144) has three boats and guarantees a catch on full-day charters—if you don't get a fish, you don't pay. **Brown's Charters** (☎ 242/324–1215) specializes in 24-hour shark fishing trips, as well as reef and deep-sea fishing. **Chubasco Charters** (☎ 242/324–3474, WEB www.chubascocharters.com) has two boats for sportfishing and shark fishing charters. **Nassau Yacht Haven** (☎ 242/393–8173, WEB www.nassauyachthaven.com) runs fishing charters out of its 150-slip marina.

Fitness Clubs and Spas

Nassau has a number of health clubs and gyms for those in the mood for an indoor workout or some spa pampering—an energizing alternative to shopping on an overcast day. Most are stocked with the latest high-tech machinery, including stair climbers, treadmills, and exercise bikes, and offer aerobics and step classes. If you plan to stay in the area for a stretch, check into the package rates available at many clubs.

Azure Spa (✉ British Colonial Hilton, Bay St., ☎ 242/325–8497), offers quality à la carte services including facials (50-min steam, massage and mask is $70), body scrubs and wraps, hydrotherapy ($45 for 25 min), and various massages (hourlong aromatherapy is $80).
Gold's Gym (✉ Bridge Plaza, just over the eastern Paradise Island bridge, ☎ 242/394–4653) offers aerobics, step, and cardio-funk classes and has top-of-the-line fitness equipment, a juice bar, and a nursery. A full-access day pass is $8.
Palace Spa (☎ 242/327–6200), in the Marriott Crystal Palace complex and adjoining the Radisson Cable Beach, is a full-service gym with all the amenities and aerobics classes. Exercise bikes face the water, and the spa has stair machines and excellent showers. Pamper yourself at the relaxing hot tub and sauna. Fees are $10 daily and $35 weekly (discounts for Nassau Marriott Resort and Nassau Beach Hotel guests).
Windermere (✉ E. Bay St., ☎ 242/393–0033 or 242/393–8788) offers a variety of ultramodern spa treatments such as hydrotherapy and salt glows as well as top-quality facials, massages, manicures, and pedicures. There is also a small, exclusive training center. Daily rates for training equipment and steam, sauna, and shower facilities are $10 ($40/month); spa treatments start at $30 (1-hr massage $40). A new branch is in the Graycliff hotel, also in downtown Nassau.

Golf

Guests at affiliated hotels receive discounts at the following courses; prices quoted are for nonguests.

Cable Beach Golf Club (7,040 yards, par 72), the oldest golf course in the Bahamas, is undergoing a major renovation, though you can play 9 holes until the new course opens. The links are owned by the Radisson Cable Beach Casino & Golf Resort, whose guests get discount rates. ✉ *Box N-4914, Nassau,* ☎ *242/327–6000 Ext. 6189.* ⏩ *18 holes $95, 9 holes $70; carts included. Clubs $25.* ☉ *Daily 7–5:30, last tee-off at 5:15.*
Ocean Club Golf Course (6,805 yards, par 72), formerly the Paradise Island Golf Club, has undergone a major redesign by Tom Weiskopf. The championship course is surrounded by the ocean on three sides,

which means that winds can get stiff. Call to check on current availability and up-to-date prices (those not staying at Atlantis or the Ocean Club may find themselves shut out completely). ⊠ *Paradise Island Dr., next to airport (Box N-4777, Nassau),* ☎ *242/363–3925; 800/321–3000 in the U.S.* ⊜ *18 holes $225. Clubs $35.* ⊘ *Daily 7–6.*

South Ocean Golf Club (6,707 yards, par 72), on New Providence's secluded southern part, is the newest course to surrender its divots to visiting players. Narrow fairways are a notable feature. The course was designed by Joe Lee and built in 1969. ⊠ *Box N-8191,* ☎ *242/362–4391 Ext. 23.* ⊜ *18 holes $90, 9 holes $50; carts included. Clubs $20. Reductions for Clarion guests.* ⊘ *Daily 7–6.*

Horseback Riding

Happy Trails Stables gives guided 90-minute trail rides, including basic riding instruction, through remote wooded areas and beaches on New Providence's southwestern coast. Courtesy round-trip bus transportation from hotels is provided (about an hour each way). Tours are limited to eight persons, there is a 200-pound weight limit, and children must be at least nine years old. Reservations are required. ⊠ *Coral Harbour,* ☎ *242/362–1820 or 242/323–5613.* ⊜ *$85 per person. MC, V.* ⊘ *Mon.–Sat.*

Jet Skiing

Different outfitters rent jet skis in front of Atlantis and the Sheraton Grand on Cabbage Beach. **Premier Watersports** (☎ 242/324–1475 or cellular 242/427–0939) is the most reliable, and charges $55 for 30 minutes.

Parasailing

Premier Watersports (☎ 242/324–1475 or cellular 242/427–0939) lets you be lifted off a platform and into the skies for five to eight minutes for $45. Ask for Captain Tim or his crew on Cabbage Beach in front of the large hotels.

Sailing

Nassau Beach Hotel (☎ 242/327–7711 Ext. 6590) rents Sunfish sailboats for $35 per hour and 16-ft catamarans for $50 per hour.

Scuba Diving and Snorkeling

Diving operations are plentiful in Nassau. Most hotels have diving instructors who teach short courses, followed the next day by a reef trip. Many small operations have sprung up in which experienced divers with their own boats run custom dives for one to five people. A lot of these are one-person efforts. In many cases, the custom dive will include a picnic lunch with freshly speared lobster or fish cooked over an open fire on a private island beach.

Dive Sites

New Providence Island has several popular dive sites and a number of dive operators who offer regular trips. The elusive (and thus exclusive) hole, **Lost Ocean Hole** (east of Nassau, 40–195 ft), is aptly named because it is difficult to find. The rim of the 80-ft opening in 40 ft of water is dotted with coral heads and teeming with small fish—grunts, margate, and jacks—as well as larger pompano, amberjack, and sometimes nurse sharks. Divers will find a thermocline at 80 ft, a large cave at 100 ft, and a sand ledge at 185 ft that slopes down to 195 ft. The series of shallow reefs along the 14 mi of Rose Island is known as **Rose**

Island Reefs (Nassau, 5–35 ft). The coral is varied, although the reefs are showing the effects of the heavy traffic. Plenty of tropical fish make these reefs home. The wreck of the steel-hulled ship *Mahoney* is just outside the harbor.

Gambier Deep Reef, off Gambier Village about 15 minutes west of Cable Beach, goes to a depth of 80 ft. **Sea Gardens** is off Love Beach on the northwestern shore beyond Gambier. **Lyford Cay Drop-Off** (west of Nassau, 40–200+ ft) is a cliff that plummets from a 40-ft plateau almost straight into the inky blue mile-deep Tongue of the Ocean. The wall has endless varieties of sponges, black coral, and wire coral. Along the wall, grunts, grouper, hogfish, snapper, and rockfish abound. Off the wall are pelagic game fish such as tuna, bonito, wahoo, and kingfish. The south-side reefs are great for snorkelers as well as divers because of the reefs' shallowness.

Operators
All dive shops listed below are PADI facilities. Expect to pay about $65–$70 for a two-tank dive or beginner's course. Shark dives run $100–$125, and certification, $400 and up.

Bahama Divers Ltd. (☎ 242/393–1466 or 800/398–3483, WEB www.bahamdivers.com), the largest and most experienced dive operation in the country, offers twice-a-day dive safaris daily as well as half-day snorkeling trips. PADI certification courses are available, and there's a full line of scuba equipment. Destinations are drop-off sites, wrecks, coral reefs and gardens, and an ocean blue hole. For Paradise Island guests, Bahama Divers has opened a small dive operation (which also carries snorkel equipment for rent) in the Sheraton Grand.
Dive Dive Dive, Ltd. (☎ 242/362–1143, 242/362–1401, or 800/368–3480, WEB www.divedivedive.com) specializes in small groups. Dives include trips to walls and reefs, night dives, and shark dives. Transportation is provided.
Diver's Haven (☎ 242/394–8960), part of Nassau Island Cruises, offers three daily dives, state-of-the-art equipment rental, classes at several area hotels, and a four-day scuba certification course. Two-tank dives are available, or, for the more adventurous, dive trips to the Out Islands can be arranged.
Nassau Scuba Centre (☎ 242/362–1964 or 800/805–5485, WEB www.nassau-scuba-center.com) provides trips to some of Nassau's prime sites, including the James Bond Wrecks and the walls near Tongue of the Ocean. With two state-of-the-art dive boats, it's well equipped to handle beginners and experts alike.
Stuart Cove's Dive South Ocean (☎ 242/362–4171 or 800/879–9832), at the Clarion Resort on the island's south shore, runs dive trips to the south-shore reefs twice a day. Although they're well equipped to handle beginners (scuba instruction and guided snorkel tours are available), experienced thrill-seekers flock to Stuart Cove's for shark dives (Cove is one of the world's leading shark handlers), Out Island "Wilderness Safaris," and Wall Flying Adventures (3 hrs, $125), in which you ride an underwater scooter across the ocean wall. Check out the collection of celebrity photos, and you'll know you're in good company at what aficionados consider the island's leading dive shop.

Spectator Sports

Among other imperishable traditions, the British handed down to the Bahamians such sports as soccer, rugby, and cricket. The latter, somewhat confusing sport (bring an expert with you, or you'll never know what's going on) is played at Haynes Oval, baseball at Queen Elizabeth Sports Center, rugby at Winton Estates, and softball at Clifford

Park. For information on spectator sports, call the **Ministry of Tourism** (☎ 242/322–7500), or check the local papers for sports updates and calendars.

Tennis

Most people play at the hotel where they're staying. Fees below are for nonguests.

The **Nassau Beach Hotel** tennis shop (☎ 242/327–8410) charges $5 per person from 9–6 and $7 per person until 9 PM. Three of the six courts are lighted, and rackets can be rented at $6 per person hourly. Monday evenings are reserved for members.

Waterskiing

You'd be hard-pressed to find anyone waterskiing these days (most prefer jet skiing), but if the desire strikes, Captain Tim at **Premier Watersports** (☎ 242/324–1475 or cellular 242/427–0939) can make it happen.

Windsurfing

Nassau Beach Hotel (☎ 242/327–7711 Ext. 6590) rents sailboards for $20 per hour, with more advanced boards costing $30 per hour.

SHOPPING

For many, shopping is one of Nassau's greatest delights. Bargains abound between Bay Street and the waterfront, and for tonier items, don't forget to look in the hotel arcades, which have many elegant shops. You can return home with a variety of handmade Bahamian goods or splurge at duty-free shops that offer such savings you simply have to load up. You'll find duty-free prices—generally 25%–50% less than U.S. prices—on imported items such as crystal, linens, watches, cameras, sweaters, leather goods, and perfumes. Prices here rival those in other duty-free destinations.

Most of Nassau's shops are on Bay Street between Rawson Square and the British Colonial Hotel, and on the side streets leading off Bay Street. Some stores, however, are beginning to pop up on the main shopping thoroughfare's eastern end. Be aware that prices in shops are fixed, and do observe the local dress customs when you go shopping: Shorts are acceptable, but beachwear is not.

Although a few shops will be happy to mail bulky or fragile items home for you, most won't even deliver purchases to your hotel, plane, or cruise ship.

Markets and Arcades

The **International Bazaar,** a collection of shops under a huge, spreading bougainvillea, sells linens, souvenirs, and other offbeat items. This funky shopping row is on Bay Street at Charlotte Street. **Prince George Plaza,** which leads from Bay Street to Woodes Rogers Walk near the dock, just east of the International Bazaar, has about two dozen shops with varied wares. The **Nassau Arcade,** on Bay Street between East Street and Elizabeth Avenue, just east of Parliament Square, houses the Bahamas's Anglo-American bookstore (☎ 242/325–0338), a tiny storefront with a smattering of interesting reading material, as well as a few other small stores.

Specialty Shops

Antiques, Arts, and Crafts

Bahamacraft Centre (✉ Paradise Island Dr., across from Hurricane Hole Plaza, ☎ no phone) offers some top-level Bahamian crafts, including a nice selection of authentic straw work. Dozens of vendors hawk everything from baskets to shell collages inside this vibrantly colored building, designed by noted architect Jackson Burnside of Doongalik Studios. You can catch a shuttle bus from Atlantis to the center.

Balmain Antiques and Gallery (✉ Bay St., ☎ 242/323–7421) has a nice collection of Bahamian artwork and antique maps, prints, and bottles.

Doongalik Studios (✉ 18 Village Rd., ☎ 242/394–1886, WEB www.doongalikstudios.com) offers dynamic canvases inspired by Junkanoo celebrations, vibrantly painted furniture, Junkanoo masks, and kaleidoscopic sculpture. Don't miss the pleasant sculpture garden. To one side of the garden, just behind the main house, is a re-creation of a traditional Bahamian home that serves as a display room for handmade Christmas ornaments, art cards, and other inexpensive and unique gifts. You can watch a fascinating videotape of Junkanoo while you shop.

Kennedy Gallery (✉ Parliament St., ☎ 242/325–7662) sells watercolors, oils, sculpture, and other artwork by a wide variety of Bahamian artists, from the best-known to emerging young talent.

Marlborough Antiques (✉ Marlborough St., ☎ 242/328–0502) specializes in English furniture and bric-a-brac. You can also find Bahamian art, rare books, European glassware, and Victorian jewelry.

Soft Touch Productions (✉ Market St., ☎ 242/323–2128), known for its wire-sculpted dolls depicting local characters and scenes, also sells wicker and straw baskets and other souvenirs.

Baked Goods

The Bread Shop (✉ Shirley St., east of Mackey St., ☎ 242/393–7973) is, as the sign proclaims, "The home of Rosie's Raisin Bread." Cinnamon rolls, pound and banana cakes, and other sweet delights are also offered in this amiable spot in Nassau's east end.

Kelly's Bakery (✉ Market St., ☎ 242/325–0616) is a convenient place to stop for muffins, cakes, and other goodies.

Model Bakery (✉ Dowdeswell St., ☎ 242/322–2595), in Nassau's east end, is another great local bakery. Be sure to try the cinnamon twists.

China, Crystal, Linens, and Silver

Linen Shop (✉ Bay St., ☎ 242/322–4266) sells fine embroidered Irish linens and lace.

Solomon's Mines (✉ several Bay St. locations, Hurricane Hole Plaza, and Atlantis on Paradise Island, ☎ 242/322–8324) sells, among other names, Waterford, Hummel, Lladró, Wedgwood, and Lenox.

Cigars

The impressive displays of Cuban cigars, imported by Bahamian merchants, lure aficionados to the Bahamas for cigar sprees. Be aware, however, that some merchants on Bay Street and elsewhere in the islands are selling counterfeits—sometimes unwittingly. If the price seems too good to be true, chances are it is. Check the wrappers, feel to ensure that there is a consistent fill before you purchase, and chances are you won't get burned. A number of stores along the main shopping strip do stock only the best authentic Cuban stogies.

The Cigar Box (✉ Bay St., ☎ 242/326–7352), next to Planet Hollywood, offers all the well-known Cuban brands as well as a small selection of humidors.

Graycliff (✉ West Hill St., ☎ 242/322–7050, WEB www.graycliff.com) carries one of Nassau's finest selections of hand-rolled cigars, overseen by the prestigious Avelino Lara, who created some of Cuba's best-known cigars. In fact, Graycliff's operation is so popular that it has expanded the hotel to include an entire cigar factory, open to the public for tours and purchases. Rolling the cigars are a dozen Cuban men and women who live on the lovely premises, and work here through a special arrangement with the Cuban government. True cigar buffs will seek out the Graycliff's owner, Enrico Garzaroli, a world-class *bon vivant*.

Havana Humidor (⊠ Atlantis, Paradise Island, ☎ 242/363–5809) has the largest selection of authentic Cuban cigars in the Bahamas. You'll also find cigar and pipe accessories.

Pipe of Peace (⊠ Bay St., ☎ 242/322–3908) has a wide variety of cigars, pipes, and cigarettes, including all major Cuban cigars. Although the cigar counter occupies just a small portion of the eclectic souvenir shop, it's well known as a good source.

Stogies (⊠ Prince George Plaza, Bay St. between Charlotte and Parliament Sts., ☎ 242/356–5103) has a climate-controlled room full of cigars, and the perfect boxes to put them in—these beautifully inlaid holders can run up to $700. There's also a selection of lighters, cigar-theme T-shirts, and other accessories.

Tropique International Smoke Shop (⊠ Nassau Marriott Resort & Crystal Palace Casino, ☎ 242/327–7292) carries a wide choice in its atmosphere-controlled humidors; the well-trained staff provides knowledgeable guidance.

Eclectic

Far East Traders (⊠ Prince George's Plaza, Bay St., ☎ 242/325–7095) has embroidered linens from Asia, silk nighties and kimonos, and handwoven blouses and vests.

Green Lizard (⊠ Bay St., ☎ 242/323–8076) is home to a delightful cornucopia of native and imported gifts, including a specialty item you might be tempted to use during your stay: string hammocks.

House of Music (⊠ Mackey St., ☎ 242/393–0331) has the best selection of island calypso, soca, reggae, and Junkanoo music.

The Island Shop and Island Bookstore (⊠ Bay St., ☎ 242/322–4183) sells travel guides, novels, paperbacks, gift books, and international magazines, as well as clothing, swimwear, and souvenirs, on its two floors. Take a peek at the "Bahamian Books" section, where you'll find texts on everything from history to cookery.

Island Tings (⊠ Bay St., ☎ 242/326–1024) carries a variety of items, some Bahamian, some not (look carefully before assuming you're buying local work). Art includes prints by Eleutheran artist Eddie Minnis, Androsia fabric, and wood carvings. There's also a wide variety of foods.

Fashion

Clothing is no great bargain in Nassau, but many stores sell fine imports. Perhaps the best local buy is brightly batiked Androsia fabric—available by the yard or sewn into sarongs, dresses, and blouses—produced on the island of Andros.

Brass and Leather (⊠ Charlotte St., off Bay St., ☎ 242/322–3806) has a wide selection of leather goods for men and women, including bags, shoes, and belts.

Cole's of Nassau (⊠ Parliament St., ☎ 242/322–8393; ⊠ Crystal Court at Atlantis, Paradise Island, ☎ 242/363–4161; ⊠ Bay Street, next to John Bull, ☎ 242/356–2498) is a top choice for designer fashions, sportswear, bathing suits, shoes, and accessories.

Fendi (⊠ Bay St. at Charlotte St., ☎ 242/322–6300) occupies a magnificent old building and carries the Italian house's luxury line of handbags, luggage, watches, jewelry, and shoes.

Mademoiselle Ltd. (⊠ Palmdale, Nassau, ☎ 242/323–6105; ⊠ Marathon Mall, Nassau, ☎ 242/393–9037) has shops throughout the Bahamas (many in hotel arcades) and stocks a variety of women's clothing. Be sure to check out the Androsia fashions.

Tempo Paris (⊠ Bay St., ☎ 242/323–6112) offers men's fashions by major designers, including Ralph Lauren, Calvin Klein, and Gianni Versace.

Jewelry, Watches, and Clocks

Coin of the Realm (⊠ Charlotte St., ☎ 242/322–4862) has Bahamian coins and native conch pearls in various jewelry settings.

Colombian Emeralds International (⊠ Bay St., ☎ 242/326–1661; ⊠ Atlantis, Paradise Island, ☎ 242/363–3128) is the local branch of this well-known jeweler, carrying not only its signature gem but a variety of other fine jewelry.

The Jewellery Box (⊠ Bay St., ☎ 242/322–4098) specializes in tanzanite jewelry. It's the largest Bahamian supplier of this gem, mined in the foothills of Mt. Kilimanjaro, but it also sells other precious and semiprecious stones and 14-karat gold jewelry.

The Jewellery Mart (⊠ Bay St., ☎ 242/328–8869) offers Movado, Bulova, and other watches as well as gold jewelry and pieces fashioned from tanzanite, rubies, and emeralds, among other gems.

John Bull (⊠ 284 Bay St., ☎ 242/322–4252; ⊠ Crystal Court at Atlantis, Paradise Island, ☎ 242/363–3956), established in 1929 and magnificently decorated in its Bay Street incarnation behind a Georgian-style facade, fills its complex with wares from Tiffany & Co., Cartier, Mikimoto, Nina Ricci, and Yves Saint Laurent.

Solomon's Mines (⊠ Three Bay St. locations, Hurricane Hole Plaza, and Atlantis on Paradise Island, ☎ 242/322–8324 or 877/765–6463, WEB www.solomons-mines.com) is the place to buy duty-free watches by Tag-Heuer, Omega, Borel, Swiss Army, and other makers. It also carries African diamonds, as well as Spanish pieces of eight in settings.

Perfumes

The Body Shop (⊠ Bay St., ☎ 242/356–2431) sells the company's internationally acclaimed line of all-natural body lotions, shampoos and conditioners, and makeup.

John Bull (⊠ 284 Bay St., ☎ 242/322–4252; ⊠ Crystal Court at Atlantis, Paradise Island, ☎ 242/363–3956) is where you'll find fragrances by Chanel, Yves Saint Laurent, and Estée Lauder.

Perfume Bar (⊠ Bay St., ☎ 242/325–1258) carries the best-selling French fragrance Boucheron and the Clarins line of skin-care products, as well as scents by Givenchy, Fendi, and other well-known designers.

Perfume Shop (⊠ Bay and Frederick Sts., ☎ 242/322–2375) is a landmark perfumery that has the broadest selection of imported perfumes and fragrances in the Bahamas.

Solomon's Mines (⊠ Three Bay St. locations, Hurricane Hole Plaza, and Atlantis on Paradise Island, ☎ 242/322–8324 or 877/765–6463, WEB www.solomons-mines.com), one of the Caribbean's largest duty-free retailers, stocks French, Italian, and U.S. fragrances, skin-care products, and bath lines.

NEW PROVIDENCE ISLAND A TO Z

To research prices, get advice from other travelers, and book travel arrangements, visit www.fodors.com.

AIR TRAVEL

Flights listed below originate in the United States and Canada. If you are arriving from the United Kingdom, the best option is to fly to Miami and transfer to one of the numerous carriers listed below for the hour-long final leg to Nassau.

CARRIERS

Air Canada flies from Montréal and Toronto. American Eagle, an American Airlines subsidiary, flies into Nassau daily from Miami and Fort Lauderdale and also serves the Abacos, Exumas, and other destinations in the Out Islands. Bahamasair, the national carrier, has daily flights from Miami and Fort Lauderdale, as well as five flights weekly from Orlando. The airline also flies to all of the Out Islands. Continental flies in daily from Newark under service operated by Nassau–Paradise Island Express, and daily from West Palm Beach, Fort Lauderdale, and Miami on Continental's partner, Gulf Stream International. Delta is one of the busier carriers, with daily flights from Atlanta, New York City, Cincinnati, Charleston, and Orlando. Trans World Airlines flies to Nassau daily from New York's John F. Kennedy airport. US Airways flies in daily from Charlotte, NC, and offers seasonal services from Philadelphia.

➤ AIRLINES AND CONTACTS: **Air Canada** (☎ 800/776–3000). **American Eagle** (☎ 800/433–7300). **Bahamasair** (☎ 242/377–5505 or 800/222–4262). **Continental** (☎ 242/377–2050 or 800/722–4262). **Delta** (☎ 800/221–1212). **Gulf Stream International** (☎ 242/377–4314 or 800/231–0856). **Trans World Airlines** (☎ 800/221–2000). **US Airways** (☎ 242/377–8887 or 800/622–1015).

AIRPORTS AND TRANSFERS

Nassau International Airport, 8 mi west of Nassau by Lake Killarney, is served by an increasing number of airlines. With the closure of the Paradise Island Airport, it's the only game in town now.

➤ AIRPORT INFORMATION: **Nassau International Airport** (☎ 242/377–7281).

AIRPORT TRANSFERS

No bus service is available from Nassau International Airport to New Providence hotels, except for guests on package tours. (Breezes, Sandals, and Atlantis have promotional booths at the airport.) A taxi ride from the airport to Cable Beach costs $15; to Nassau, $22; and to Paradise Island, $28 (this includes the $1 causeway toll). These are fixed costs for two passengers; each additional passenger is $3. In addition, drivers expect a 15% tip. Some resorts offer airport shuttle service.

BOAT AND FERRY TRAVEL

Nassau is a port of call for a number of cruise lines, including Carnival Cruise Lines, Celebrity Cruises, Costa Cruise Line, Disney Cruise Line, Premier Cruise Lines, Regal Cruises, Royal Caribbean International, and Silversea Cruises. Ships dock at Prince George Wharf, in downtown Nassau.

Ferries operate during daylight hours (usually 9–5:30) at half-hour intervals between Prince George Wharf and Paradise Island. The one-way cost is $3 per person.

BUS TRAVEL

For the adventuresome, consider jitney (bus) service to get around Nassau and its environs. Rides in these buses, which career along with windows open and music blaring, range from smooth sailing to hair-raising. If you want to join locals on a jitney, hail one at a bus stop, hotel, public beach, or in a residential area. Most carry their owner's name in boldly painted letters, so they're easy to spot, and with downtown's main streets being one-way, it's not hard to tell where they're going. If you're not sure of the jitney's direction, ask your concierge on which side of the street to stand, or check with the friendly drivers. The fare is 75¢, exact change required. Call out to the driver as your stop approaches.

In downtown Nassau, you'll find jitneys on Frederick Street between Bay Street and Woodes Rogers Walk. Bus service runs throughout the day until 7.

BUSINESS HOURS

Banks are open on New Providence Island Monday–Thursday 9:30–3 and Friday 9:30–5. They are closed on weekends. Principal banks on the island are Bank of the Bahamas, Bank of Nova Scotia, Barclays Bank, Canadian Imperial Bank of Commerce, Citibank, and Royal Bank of Canada.

Shops are generally open Monday–Saturday 9–5 (many stay open later). Bay Street shops are legally permitted to open on Sunday, but the main thoroughfare remains all but deserted.

CAR RENTAL

Avis Rent-A-Car has branches at the Nassau International Airport, on Paradise Island in the Paradise Village Shopping Centre, and downtown, just west of the British Colonial Hotel. Budget has branches at the Nassau International Airport and on Paradise Island. Dollar Rent-a-Car, which often has the lowest rates (there are frequent $39 rentals), can be found at Nassau International Airport and downtown, at the base of the British Colonial Hotel. Hertz has branches at Nassau International Airport and on East Bay Street, a block east of the bridge from Paradise Island. Thrifty has a branch at the airport.
➤ MAJOR AGENCIES: **Avis Rent-A-Car** (☎ 242/377–7121, 242/363–2061, or 242/326–6380). **Budget** (☎ 242/377–9000 or 242/363–3095). **Dollar Rent-a-Car** (☎ 242/377–7301 or 242/325–3716). **Hertz** (☎ 242/377–6231 or 242/393–0871). **Thrifty** (☎ 242/377–0355).

CAR TRAVEL

For exploring at your leisure, you'll want to have a car. Rentals are available at Nassau International Airport, downtown, on Paradise Island, and at some resorts. Plan to pay $60–$80 a day at major firms, $400–$480 a week, depending on the type of car. Gasoline cost around $2.50 a gallon. Remember to drive on the left.

CARRIAGES

Beautifully painted horse-drawn carriages will take as many as four people around Nassau at a rate of $10 per person for a 20-minute ride; don't hesitate to bargain. Most drivers give a comprehensive tour of the Bay Street area, giving an extensive history lesson. You'll find the surreys on Woodes Rogers Walk, in the center of Rawson Square.

CONSULATES AND EMBASSIES

➤ CONTACTS: **British High Commission** (✉ Bitco Bldg., East and Shirley Sts., ☎ 242/325–7471, FAX 242/323–3871). **Canadian Consulate** (✉ Shirley Street Shopping Plaza, Shirley St., ☎ 242/393–2123, FAX 242/393–1305). **U.S. Embassy** (✉ Queen St., across from British Colonial Hilton, ☎ 242/322–1181, FAX 242/328–7838).

CRUISE TRAVEL

One of the best ways to enjoy Nassau's seafaring pleasures is to sign up with one of the many day or evening cruise operators, typically on a catamaran or similar sailboat. These offerings range from three-hour snorkeling trips to romantic sunset cruises or full-day excursions. Prices are pretty standard among the operators: A half-day snorkeling cruise will run about $30, usually including a drink and snacks; prices for a sunset sail, with drinks and hors d'oeuvres, are around the same. Full-day or dinner cruises, both with meals, cost around $50. Hotel transportation is generally included.

Barefoot Sailing Cruises transports you to a secluded Rose Island beach for snorkeling and sunbathing on a half-day sail and snorkel cruise; other options include an all-day island barbecue and champagne sunset cruise. Feeling luxurious? Arrange a private dinner cruise.

Flying Cloud runs half-day catamaran cruises at 9:30 and 2, as well as sunset "sail-and-a-dinner" cruises on which you can enjoy a candlelight meal in a secluded cove. A five-hour Sunday cruise departs at 10 AM.

Island Tours offers a half-day catamaran excursion to Rose Island beach for beach volleyball and snorkeling. Snacks and an open bar are included, as are bus transfers to and from your hotel.

Sea Island Adventures runs half- and full-day trips to Rose Island for snorkeling and a tropical lunch, as well as sunset cruises. Private charters can also be arranged.
➤ CRUISE LINES: **Barefoot Sailing Cruises** (☎ 242/393–0820 or 242/393–581). **Flying Cloud** (☎ 242/363–4430). **Island Tours** (☎ 242/327–8653). **Sea Island Adventures** (☎ 242/325–3910).

EMERGENCIES
In an emergency dial 911. Princess Margaret Hospital is government operated, and Doctors Hospital is private.
➤ CONTACTS: **Ambulance** (☎ 911 or 242/322–2221). **Police** (☎ 911 or 242/322–4444).
➤ HOSPITALS: **Doctors Hospital** (✉ Collins Ave. and Shirley St., ☎ 242/322–8411). **Princess Margaret Hospital** (✉ Shirley St., ☎ 242/322–2861).

SCOOTERS
Two people can ride around the island on a motor scooter for about $40 for a half day, $50 for a full day. Helmets for both driver and passenger and insurance are mandatory and are included in the rental price. Many hotels have scooters on the premises. You can also try Knowles, on West Bay Street, in the British Colonial Hilton parking lot, or stands in Rawson Square. Once again, remember to drive on the left.
➤ CONTACT: **Knowles** (☎ 242/356–0741).

SIGHTSEEING TOURS
More than a dozen local operators provide tours of New Providence Island's natural and commercial attractions. Some of the many possibilities include sightseeing tours of Nassau and the island, glass-bottom boat tours to Sea Gardens, and various cruises to offshore cays, all starting at $12. A full day of ocean sailing will cost around $60. In the evening, there are sunset and moonlight cruises with dinner and drinks ($35–$50) and nightlife tours to casino cabaret shows and nightclubs ($28–$45). Tours may be booked at hotel desks in Nassau, Cable Beach, and Paradise Island or directly through one of the tour operators listed below, all of which have knowledgeable guides and a selection of tours in air-conditioned cars, vans, or buses.

TAXIS
Taxis are generally the best and most convenient way to get around New Providence. Fares are fixed by the government by zones. For airport fares, *see* Airports and Transfers, *above*. The fare is $6 for trips within downtown Nassau and on Paradise Island; $9 from downtown Nassau to Paradise Island (which includes the bridge toll), $8 from Par-

adise Island to downtown Nassau; $18 from Cable Beach to Paradise Island (including toll), and $17 on the return trip. Fares are for two passengers; each additional passenger is $3, regardless of destination. It is customary to tip taxi drivers 15%. You can also hire a car or small van for sightseeing for about $50 per hour or $13 per person.

Bahamas Transport has radio-dispatched taxis. You can call the Taxi Cab Union directly for a cab. There are also stands at major hotels, or the front desk can call you a cab.
➤ Taxi Companies: **Bahamas Transport** (☎ 242/323–5111, 242/323–5112, 242/323–5113, or 242/323–5114). **Taxi Cab Union** (☎ 242/323–4555 or 242/323–5818).

TOURS AND PACKAGES
OUT ISLANDS TRIPS

Several options exist for getaways to the less-frequented Out Islands. Expect to pay from $90 for no-frills ferry service to several hundred dollars for full-day excursions with meals, snorkeling, and sightseeing.

Bahamas Fast Ferries provides a wonderful way to escape to Harbour Island—possibly the most charming island in the Bahamas—Spanish Wells, or unspoiled Eleuthera; the high-speed, colorful, and extremely safe *Bo Hengy* catamaran whisks you from Nassau to Out Island getaways in two hours. Book just transport or, better yet, a $149 package that includes historic walking tour of Harbour Island, a great lunch, and beach time at the famous pink sands—Fast Ferries has its own fully equipped cabana on the beach with complimentary refreshments. Horseback riding is usually available on the beach. You'll be back in Nassau by nightfall.

Exuma Powerboat Adventures offers full-day excursions to the Exuma Cays. After zipping over via one of three speed boats, feed iguanas at Allan's Cay, participate in a nature walk, and, of course, do some snorkeling in the Exumas' Land and Sea Park. There are also shallow-water shark feeds. It's a great way to experience some of the beauty of the less-developed islands outside Nassau. Lunch is included.

Island World Adventures offers full-day excursions to Saddleback Cay in the Exumas on a high-speed powerboat. You can take a guided trek and learn about Bahamian flora and fauna or just snorkel and sunbathe the day away. Lunch, soft drinks, beer, and rum punch are included.

Seaplane Safaris utilize low-flying craft for the Exuma Cays trip, allowing you to glide right over the water's surface. You can swim right off the seaplane into Thunderball Grotto, an eerie natural formation (scenes from the James Bond movie bearing its name were filmed here), and enjoy some snorkeling, explore nature trails, or simply loll on the beach on Warderick Wells, the headquarters of the Land and Sea Park. Lunch is included, and the trip takes a full day.
➤ Contacts: **Bahamas Fast Ferries** (☎ 242/323–2166, WEB www.bahamasferries.com). **Exuma Powerboat Adventures** (☎ 242/393–7116, WEB www.powerboatadventures.com). **Island World Adventures** (☎ 242/363–3333, WEB www.islandworldadventures.com). **Seaplane Safaris** (☎ 242/393–2522 or 242/393–1179).

SPECIAL-INTEREST TOURS

During the Close Encounter ($75 per person) arranged by Dolphin Encounters on Blue Lagoon Island (Salt Cay), just east of Paradise Island, you stand in waist-deep water while dolphins play around you. The two-hour program consists of an educational session as well as the encounter. Trainers are available to answer questions. Swim-with-the-Dol-

When you pack your MCI Calling Card, it's like packing your loved ones along too.

Your MCI Calling Card is the easy way to stay in touch when you travel. Use it to call to and from over 125 countries. Plus, every time you call, you can earn frequent flier miles. So wherever your travels take you, call home with your MCI Calling Card. It's even easy to get one. Just visit **www.mci.com/worldphone** or **www.mci.com/partners**.

EASY TO CALL WORLDWIDE

1. Just enter the WorldPhone® access number of the country you're calling from.
2. Enter or give the operator your MCI Calling Card number.
3. Enter or give the number you're calling.

Aruba ✣	800-888-8
Bahamas ✣	1-800-888-8000
Barbados ✣	1-800-888-8000
Bermuda ✣	1-800-888-8000
British Virgin Islands ✣	1-800-888-8000
Canada	1-800-888-8000
Mexico	01-800-021-8000
Puerto Rico	1-800-888-8000
United States	1-800-888-8000
U.S. Virgin Islands	1-800-888-8000

✣ Limited availability.

EARN FREQUENT FLIER MILES

Find America *with a Compass*

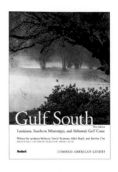

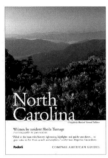

Written by local authors and illustrated throughout
with spectacular color images, Compass American
Guides reveal the character and culture of more than
40 of America's most fascinating destinations. Perfect
for residents who want to explore their own backyards
and for visitors who want an insider's perspective
on the history, heritage, and all there is to see and do.

Fodor's COMPASS AMERICAN GUIDES

At bookstores everywhere.

phins ($145 per person) actually allows you to swim with these friendly creatures for about 30 minutes. For more complete involvement, try the Assistant Trainer for a Day program ($195 per person, 16 years old minimum), where you learn about care and training by helping with feeding, cleaning, and food preparation. Programs are available daily 8–5:30, and the cost includes transfers from your hotel and the boat ride to the island. Make reservations as early as possible.

Hartley's Undersea Walk takes you for a stroll on the ocean floor. Special helmets protect hair, eyeglasses, and contacts while allowing you to see the fish and flora. Hartley's yacht, the *Pied Piper*, departs daily at 9:30 and 1:30 from the Nassau Yacht Haven on East Bay Street. Reserve in advance to guarantee a spot.

Pedal & Paddle Ecoventures is a unique, full-day ecotourism adventure that combines all-terrain bicycle rides through forests and along coastlines with kayaking tours through mangrove creeks and sheltered waters. Lunch is included in the full-day tours, which can be booked at most hotel desks. Half-day tours are also available.

Seaworld Explorer is a "semi-submarine" that cruises through the harbor as it makes its way to Sea Gardens Marine Park; you can sit above water on the deck or descend to view the ocean life firsthand through undersea windows.

Stingray City, on Blue Lagoon Island, allows you to snorkel among a variety of sea life and feed a surprisingly friendly stingray or two.
➤ CONTACTS: **Dolphin Encounters** (☎ 242/363–1003). **Hartley's Undersea Walk** (☎ 242/393–8234). **Pedal & Paddle Ecoventures** (☎ 242/362–2772). **Seaworld Explorer** (☎ 242/356–2548). **Stingray City** (☎ 242/363–3333).

WALKING TOURS

A walking tour around Historic Nassau, arranged by the Tourist Information Office at Rawson Square, is offered daily. The cost is $2. Call ahead for information and reservations.
➤ CONTACT: **Historic Nassau** (☎ 242/302–2055).

VISITOR INFORMATION

The Ministry of Tourism's Help Line is an information source that operates from 8 AM to midnight daily. The ministry also operates information booths at Nassau International Airport, open daily from 8 AM to midnight, and at Rawson Square, open weekdays from 8:30 to 5, Saturday 8:30 to 4, and Sunday 8:30 to 2. Ask about Bahamahosts, specially trained tour guides who will tell you about island history and culture and pass on their individual and imaginative knowledge of Bahamian folklore.

The Ministry of Tourism's People-to-People Programme is designed to let a Bahamian personally introduce you to the Bahamas. By prearrangement through the ministry, you can spend a day with a Bahamian family with similar interests to learn local culture firsthand or enjoy a family meal. It's best if you make arrangements—through your travel agent or by calling direct—prior to your trip. (This is not a dating service!) People-to-People also holds teas at Government House (call for details) and sponsors activities for spouses of conference attendees, student exchanges, and pen pal programs.

Fallen in love? Love the Bahamas? The Ministry of Tourism's Wedding Division arranges weddings for visiting couples. Formerly run by People-to-People, the weddings have proven so popular that the ministry has established a separate department to handle them. Ministry staff will take care of all the paperwork and set up ceremonies ranging from a simple seaside "I do" to more outrageous nuptials. Underwater vows, anyone?

➤ TOURIST INFORMATION: **Ministry of Tourism** (✉ Box N-3701, Nassau, ☎ 242/322–7500 or 242/302–2000, FAX 242/328–0945, WEB www. bahamas.com); Help Line (☎ 242/326–4357); Nassau International Airport booths (☎ 242/377–6833, 242/377–8606, or 242/377–6782); Rawson Square (☎ 242/326–9772). **People-to-People Programme** (☎ 242/326–5371 or 242/356–0435). **Wedding Division** (☎ 242/302–2034).

3 GRAND BAHAMA ISLAND

Grand Bahama's twin cities, Freeport and Lucaya, were designed for tourism—and at tourism they excel. There is much more to the 96-mi-long island than the Bahamas's second-largest metropolis, however. Merely drive east or west of the sprawling cities, where outlying fishing villages remain intriguingly remote, punctuating a vast, flat swath of casuarina, palmetto, and pine trees rimmed by long stretches of open beach. Therein lies Grand Bahama's hidden, inherent charm.

Updated by
Chelle Koster
Walton

G RAND BAHAMA, the fourth-largest island in the Bahamas after Andros, Eleuthera, and Great Abaco, lies only 52 mi off Palm Beach, Florida. The Gulf Stream's ever-warm waters lap its western tip, and the Little Bahama Bank protects it from the northeast.

In 1492, when Columbus set foot on the Bahamian island of San Salvador, Grand Bahama was already populated. Skulls found in caves here attest to the existence of the peaceable Lucayans, who were constantly fleeing the more bellicose Caribs. The skulls show that the parents flattened their babies' foreheads with boards to strengthen them, making them less vulnerable to the cudgels of the Caribs, who were reputedly cannibalistic.

Spanish conquistadors visited the island briefly in the early 16th century. They used it as a watering hole but dismissed it as having no commercial value and went on their way. In the 18th century, Loyalists settled on Grand Bahama to escape the wrath of American Revolutionaries who had just won the War of Independence. When Britain abolished the slave trade early in the 19th century, many of the Loyalists' former slaves settled here as farmers and fishermen.

Grand Bahama took on new prominence in the Roaring '20s, when the island's western end and Bimini to the south became convenient jumping-off points for rumrunners ferrying booze to Florida during Prohibition. But it was not until the 1950s, when the harvesting of Caribbean yellow pine trees (now protected by Bahamian environmental law) was the island's major industry, that American financier Wallace Groves envisioned Grand Bahama's grandiose future. Groves dreamed of establishing a tax-free port for the shipment of goods to the United States, a plan that involved building a city.

On August 5, 1955, largely due to Groves's efforts and those of British industrialist Sir Charles Hayward, the government signed an agreement that set in motion the development of a planned city and established the Grand Bahama Port Authority to administer a 200-square-mi area near the island's center. Settlers received tax concessions and other benefits. In return, the developers built a port, an airport, a power plant, roads, waterways, and utilities. They also promoted tourism and industrial development.

From that agreement, the city of Freeport and later Lucaya evolved. They are separated by a 4-mi stretch of East Sunrise Highway, although few can tell you where one community ends and the other begins. A modern industrial park has developed west of Freeport close to the harbor. Major companies were drawn here because there are no corporate, property, or income taxes and no customs duties or excise taxes on materials used for export manufacturing. In return, the companies hire local workers and have become involved in community activities and charities.

Most of Grand Bahama's commercial activity is concentrated in Freeport, the Bahamas's second-largest city. On average, about one-fourth of the roughly 4 million people who come to the Bahamas each year visit Freeport and neighboring waterfront Lucaya. They are attracted by gambling, resort hotels, golfing, duty-free shopping complexes, beaches, diving, and other water sports. Cruise-ship passengers arrive at Lucayan Harbour from the Florida ports of Fort Lauderdale and Cape Canaveral. The harbor has undergone a $10.9 million renovation and expansion with a clever Bahamian-style look, expanded

MOVING TOWARD ECOTOURISM

TO EXPAND TOURISM BEYOND the island's traditional gambling and shopping attractions, Freeport-Lucaya is now marketed as Grand Bahama Island. It makes sense. For beyond the 6-mi strip that comprises the island's metropolis lies another 90 mi of unadulterated wilderness. The balance of the island is given to natural and uncrowded beaches, old-island settlements, and untamed "bush," as the locals call the wilds.

The emphasis on the island's natural attributes began below the water line with **UNEXSO** diving and the **Dolphin Experience.** UNEXSO's preoccupation with extreme diving led to the exploration of the island's unique cave system and the opening of **Lucayan National Park,** a portal to the underground labyrinth accessible to the public. One of the caves holds a cemetery of the island's aboriginals, the Lucayans. The Smithsonian Institution dated the skeletons found there and returned them to their resting place. The park also gives intrepid visitors a taste of the beauty and seclusion of out-of-town beaches. When it opened, the park marked the end of civilization. Rutted dirt roads led to rarely visited time-stilled settlements without electricity and telephones, and long stretches of pine and palmetto forest edged in white sand. In the mid-1990s, as paved roads and telephone wires reached the remote East End, tours began to transport visitors to this other world.

Today, kayaking, biking, snorkeling, boating, jeeping, and cultural safaris help share Grand Bahama Island's most precious treasures with visitors. **East End Adventures** bumps along off-road to the island's past, to the ruins of Old Freetown, the first settlement, and its pristine beach. Along the way, safari participants peer into a blue hole, learn about bush medicine, and hear old-island tales. At McLean's Town, they jump into a boat for a conch-cracking demonstration at remote Sweeting's Cay, followed by home-cooked Bahamian lunch on an uninhabited island beach and blue-hole snorkeling. **Kayak Nature Tours** follows backwater trails to Lucayan National Park and other off-the-beaten-path destinations. Knowledgeable native guides give lessons on island ecology along the way. The company also hosts day and two-night kayak-camping trips to Water Cay, off Grand Bahama's north shore.

Parrot Jungle's Garden of the Groves was among the first to capitalize on the natural outdoor beauty of Grand Bahama Island, with lushly landscaped grounds, waterfalls, and a replica of one of the island's first churches. Right in downtown Freeport, the **Bahamas National Trust Rand Nature Centre** was also precursor to ecotourism on Grand Bahama Island. It still provides an oasis for rare birds as well as residents and visitors. At **Hydroflora Gardens,** nearby in Freeport, a native family shares its love of things that bloom, bear fruit, and smell sweet.

On the island's other extreme, close to West End, **Paradise Cove** also takes you underwater. Here you can rent snorkeling equipment, a wind glider, or a glass-bottom kayak to experience the island's best reef—Deadman's Reef—reachable from shore. Its duck pond teems with opportunities for the binoculars crowd.

Ecotourism promises to stay on Grand Bahama Island, attracting a new brand of island vacationer, one more adventurous and ready to experience the less-touted and richer offerings of Grand Bahama's great outback.

cruise-passenger terminal facilities, and two entertainment-shopping villages.

Lucaya, with the debut of the grand and sprawling Our Lucaya resort, stepped up to the role of island tourism capital. With the completion of its shopping complex, as well as a 30,000-square-ft casino that has yet to debut, it raised the bar for the island. In Freeport and the West End, Our Lucaya's challenge is met with the restructuring of Royal Oasis Golf Resort & Casino (formerly the Resort at Bahamia) and the opening of deluxe Old Bahama Bay, respectively.

Despite the bustle of business and the influx of tourists, Grand Bahama offers many opportunities to enjoy solitude and nature. For decades, tourism forces have shifted the emphasis away from Freeport to Grand Bahama Island to raise awareness of what lies beyond shopping and gambling. As far as nature-lovers are concerned, three spots in and around Freeport shouldn't be missed: Parrot Jungle's Garden of the Groves, the Bahamas National Trust's (BNT) Lucayan National Park, and the BNT Rand Nature Centre.

Eco-sensitivity has spawned stimulating ecotourism adventures, including kayak trips through the national park, adventure tours to the island's East End, bird-watching excursions to spot Grand Bahama's species not found elsewhere in North America, snorkeling tours of coral reefs, and horseback rides through pine forests and along ocean beaches. Surrounding waters lure anglers from around the world to compete in big game and bonefishing tournaments, such as the World International Invitational Bonefishing Championship held in Grand Bahama in November every third year. The island is also a mecca for scuba divers and is home of the world-famous Underwater Explorers Society (UNEXSO). For many landlubbers, the island's golf courses—known for their long fairways and water challenges—guarantee year-round entertainment and challenge.

Grand Bahama Island also affords a plenitude of opportunities for heritage tourism. The friendly local population is accessible in daily interaction and through the People-to-People Programme (call ☎ 242/352–8044 or 800/448–3386 for more information). Most restaurants serve Bahamian cuisine, and many attractions and tours explore the island's history and culture. For a potent taste of island tradition, plan your visit during Junkanoo celebrations at Christmas and in October. A throwback to slavery days, Junkanoo colorfully showcases the song, dance, and spirit of Grand Bahama Island. To get an idea of the festivities, go to Billy Joe's conch shack on the beach at Our Lucaya on Thursday and Friday nights.

EXPLORING GRAND BAHAMA ISLAND

Numbers in the text correspond to numbers in the margin and on the Freeport-Lucaya and Grand Bahama Island maps.

A Good Tour

Grand Bahama is the only planned island in the Bahamas. As such, its towns, villages, and sights are well laid out but quite a distance apart. Take one day to get to know downtown Freeport and Lucaya, both best appreciated on foot. Buses and taxis can transport you the 4-mi distance between the two. On another day, rent a car to visit the outlying attractions. You may want to spread these out over a few days.

Start the first day's tour by strolling around the **Royal Oasis Casino** ① (part of the Royal Oasis Golf Resort), adjacent to **International**

Bazaar ②. You'll find bargains on duty-free goods in this 10-acre complex of shops and restaurants.

For a fragrant souvenir, head to the **Perfume Factory** ③. After a free five-minute tour of the mixology lab you'll be ready to blend varied scents into your own concoction.

Once you've had a bite to eat and dropped off your shopping bags, make your way to the **Hydroflora Gardens** ④, a haven of blooming flora and hydroponic plant cultivation. Also be sure to fit in the **Bahamas National Trust Rand Nature Centre** ⑧. Look for pink flamingos amid the bountiful foliage from the observation deck at the end of the nature walk.

Cap the evening with shopping, dining, and dancing in Count Basie Square at **Port Lucaya Marketplace** ⑤. At **UNEXSO** ⑥, the Underwater Explorers Society, buy tickets for **The Dolphin Experience** ⑦ or reserve your spot on a dive boat. It is west of the Port Lucaya Marketplace.

Start day two with a visit to **Parrot Jungle's Garden of the Groves** ⑨, off Midshipman Road at Magellan Drive, 5 mi east of the Bahamas National Trust Rand Nature Centre. Photo opportunities greet you at each turn in this serene botanical dreamland. The native coral stone hilltop church, with a spectacular view, is a must-see.

Continue the adventure in the afternoon with a trip to **Lucayan National Park** ⑩, home of the wondrous Ben's Cave and Burial Mound Cave. To get here, turn right off Casuarina Drive onto the Grand Bahama Highway and continue about 13 mi along the pine-lined road. The park's cave and parking are on the left. Across the road, a boardwalk trail meanders about ½ mi through "the bush" to Gold Rock Beach. For lunch and a journey to an old-time island settlement, drive 9 mi east to High Rock.

TIMING
Allow about 40 minutes for the drive to High Rock, the farthest point on this tour.

Freeport

Freeport is an attractive, planned city of modern shopping centers, resorts, and other convenient tourist facilities. The airport is just a few minutes from downtown, and the harbor is about the same distance.

Sights to See

★ ⑧ **Bahamas National Trust Rand Nature Centre.** On 100 acres just minutes from downtown Freeport, ½ mi of trails show off 130 types of native plants, including many orchid species. The center is the island's birding hot spot, where you might spy a red-tailed hawk or a Cuban emerald hummingbird sipping hibiscus nectar. Don't miss the Flamingo Pond. From its observation deck you'll spot graceful pink flamingos from the Bahamian island of Inagua. The reserve is named for philanthropist James H. Rand, the former president of Remington Rand, who donated a hospital and library to the island. ⊠ *E. Settlers Way, Freeport,* ☎ *242/352–5438.* ⊡ *$5.* ☉ *Weekdays 9–4, Sat. 9–1; guided nature walk by advance reservation.*

④ **Hydroflora Gardens.** An absolute treat for plant enthusiasts and other nature lovers, Hydroflora Gardens was developed by agronomist and horticulturist Roger Victor on the concept of hydroponics, plant cultivation without soil. The Bahamas's primarily limestone soil provides the perfect natural laboratory. A member of the Victor family will always take the time to show you what's blooming and share plant lore. Wan-

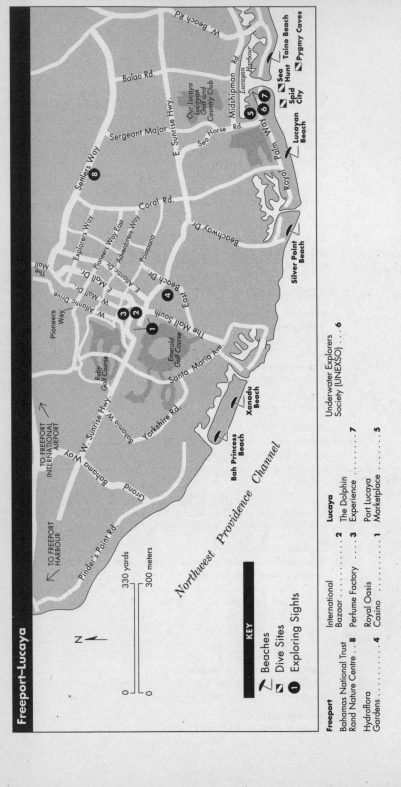

Freeport-Lucaya

KEY

⊻ Beaches
◿ Dive Sites
① Exploring Sights

Freeport

Bahamas National Trust
Rand Nature Centre . . **8**

Hydroflora
Gardens **4**

International
Bazaar **2**
Perfume Factory **3**

Royal Oasis
Casino **4**

Lucaya

The Dolphin
Experience **3**

Port Lucaya
Marketplace **5**

Underwater Explorers
Society (UNEXSO) . . . **6**

Northwest Providence Channel

330 yards
300 meters

N

TO FREEPORT INTERNATIONAL AIRPORT
TO FREEPORT HARBOUR

Pinder's Point Rd.
Grand
Bahama Way
W. Sunrise Hwy.
Bahamia W.
Yorkshire Rd.
Santa Maria Ave.
Ruby Golf Course
Pioneers Way
W. Atlantic Drive
W. Mall Dr.
E. Mall Dr.
The Mall
Explorers Way
Pioneers Way East
Adventurers Way
Poinciana
Beach Dr.
E. Atlantic Dr.
Emerald Golf Course
The Mall South
The Mall South East
Coral Rd.
Settlers Way
Sergeant Major
Balao Rd.
E. Sunrise Hwy.
Sea Horse Rd.
Midshipman Rd.
Lucayan Rd.
Our Lucaya Lucayan Golf and Country Club
W. Beach Rd.
Lucayan Harbour
Royal Palm
Beachway Dr.

Bah Princess Beach
Xanadu Beach
Silver Point Beach
Lucayan Beach
Sea Hunt
Spid City
Taino Beach
Pygmy Caves

① ② ③ ④ ⑤ ⑥ ⑦ ⑧

der through three acres on trails burgeoning with native and exotic flora to learn about medicinal and biblical plants, especially as they pertain to Bahamian history and culture. If the fruit trees are bearing their summer crop, you might get to taste a juicy mango or guava. ⊠ *E. Beach Dr. and E. Sunrise Hwy.,* ☎ *242/352–6052.* ▨ *$6 for guided tour (minimum of 4), $3 for self-guided tour.* ☉ *Weekdays 9–5, Sat. 9–4 (closed 1–2 daily); guided tours at 11 in season or by advance reservation.*

★ **②** **International Bazaar.** If the cobbled lanes and jumble of shops and restaurants in this 10-acre complex look like something from a Hollywood soundstage, that's not surprising: It was designed by special-effects artist Charles Perrin in 1967. These days, the shopping scene has a faded-glory air about it, as though it's waiting for someone to come rescue it from demise. The straw market at Port Lucaya is bigger and better, but International Bazaar still sells the widest selection of duty-free goods—jewelry, china, and perfume, along with clothing, T-shirts, and tacky souvenirs. At the entrance stands a 35-ft torii arch, a red-lacquered gate that is a traditional symbol of welcome in Japan. ⊠ *W. Sunrise Hwy. and Mall Dr.,* ☎ *no phone.* ▨ *Free.* ☉ *Mon.–Sat. 10–6.*

③ **Perfume Factory.** The quiet and elegant Perfume Factory is in a replica 19th-century Bahamian mansion—the kind built by Loyalists who settled in the Bahamas after the American Revolution. The interior resembles a tasteful drawing room. This is the home of Fragrance of the Bahamas, a company that produces perfumes, colognes, and lotions using the scents of jasmine, cinnamon, gardenia, spice, and ginger. Take a free five-minute tour of the mixology laboratory. For $30 an ounce, you can blend your own creations using any of the 35 scents. Sniff mixtures until they hit the right combination, then bottle, name, and take home the personalized perfume. ⊠ *Behind International Bazaar, on access road,* ☎ *242/352–9391.* WEB *www.perfumefactory.com.* ▨ *Free.* ☉ *Weekdays 10–5:30, Sat. noon–4.*

★ **①** **Royal Oasis Casino.** Completely renovated with new games and contemporary entertainment, this longstanding Freeport landmark (formerly the Casino at Bahamia) now has a Mediterranean look and feel. Gamblers come in droves to try their hand at about 700 slot machines, blackjack, and other gambling temptations. Place a bet on your favorite NFL, NBA, NHL, and NCAA contenders at the digitized Sports Book, surrounded by 18 sports-tuned TVs. The casino is part of the Royal Oasis Golf Resort and adjacent to the International Bazaar. ⊠ *W. Sunrise Hwy.,* ☎ *242/350–7000; 800/422–2294 in the U.S.* ☉ *Daily 8:30 AM–3 AM.*

Lucaya

Lucaya, on Grand Bahama's southern coast and just east of Freeport, was developed as the island's resort center. These days, it's booming with a megaresort complex, a fine sandy beach, championship golf courses, a first-class dive operation, and Port Lucaya's marina facilities.

Sights to See

★ **⑦** **The Dolphin Experience.** Encounter Atlantic bottle-nosed dolphins in Sanctuary Bay at one of the world's first and largest dolphin facilities, about 2 mi east of Port Lucaya. A ferry takes you from Port Lucaya to the bay to observe and photograph the animals. If you don't mind getting wet, you can sit on a partially submerged dock or stand waist deep in the water, and one of these friendly creatures will swim up and touch you. Within the sheltered waters of Sanctuary Bay, you can also engage in a swim-with-the-dolphins program. The Dolphin Experience began in 1987, when it trained five dolphins to interact with people.

Later, the animals learned to head out to sea and swim with scuba divers on the open reef. A two-hour dive program is available. If you really get hooked on these affectionate animals, you can enroll in an all-day program and work with the trainers. Buy tickets for the Dolphin Experience and the dive program at the Underwater Explorers Society (UNEXSO) in Port Lucaya. Make reservations as early as possible. ⊠ *The Dolphin Experience, Port Lucaya,* ☎ *242/373–1250 or 888/365–3483,* FAX *242/373–3948,* WEB *www.dolphinexperience.com.* ⊡ *2-hr interaction program $59, 2-hr swim program $139, full-day assistant trainer program $189.* ☉ *Daily 9–5.*

★ ⑤ **Port Lucaya Marketplace.** Lucaya's capacious and lively shopping complex—a dozen low-rise, pastel-painted colonial buildings whose style was influenced by traditional island homes—is on the waterfront 4 mi east of Freeport and across the street from a massive resort complex. The shopping center, whose walkways are lined with hibiscus, bougainvillea, and croton, has about 100 well-kept establishments, among them waterfront restaurants and bars, and shops that sell clothes, crystal and china, watches, jewelry, and perfumes. Vendors display crafts in small, brightly painted wooden stalls. A straw market embraces the complex at both ends. The marketplace's centerpiece is **Count Basie Square,** named after Freeport's own King of Jazz. Live bands, steel bands, and gospel singers often perform Bahamian music in its gazebo bandstand. ⊠ *Sea Horse Rd.,* ☎ *242/373–8446,* WEB *www.portlucaya.com.* ☉ *Mon.–Sat. 10–6.*

★ ⑥ **Underwater Explorers Society (UNEXSO).** One of the world's most respected diving facilities, UNEXSO welcomes more than 50,000 individuals each year and trains hundreds of them in scuba diving. UNEXSO's facilities include an 18-ft-deep training pool with windows that look out on the harbor, changing rooms and showers, docks, equipment rental, and an air-tank filling station. Beginners can take one-day or complete certification courses, and experienced divers can receive specialized training. Vacation packages are available. For the ultimate UNEXSO experience, pay $2,495 for a four-day, five-dive shark feeder program, use of a chain-mail diving suit included. ⊠ *On the wharf at Port Lucaya Marketplace,* ☎ *242/373–1244 or 800/992–3483,* WEB *www.unexso.com.* ⊡ *Dives from $35, shark dives $89, dolphin dives $169.* ☉ *Daily 8–5.*

Beyond Freeport-Lucaya

Grand Bahama Island narrows at picturesque West End, once Grand Bahama's capital and still home to descendants of the island's first settlers.

Little seaside villages, with concrete block houses painted in bright blue and pastel yellow, fill in the landscape between Freeport and West End. Many of these settlements are more than 100 years old. Their names derive from the original homesteaders' surnames, and most residents are descendants of these founders.

The East End is Grand Bahama's "back-to-nature" side. The road east from Lucaya is long, flat, and mostly straight. It cuts through vast pine forest to reach McLean's Town, the end of the road. Curly-tailed lizards, raccoons, pelicans, and other native creatures populate this part of the island.

Sights to See

★ ⑩ **Lucayan National Park.** In this 40-acre seaside land preserve, trails and elevated walkways wind through a natural forest of wild tamarind and gumbo-limbo trees, past an observation platform, a mangrove swamp,

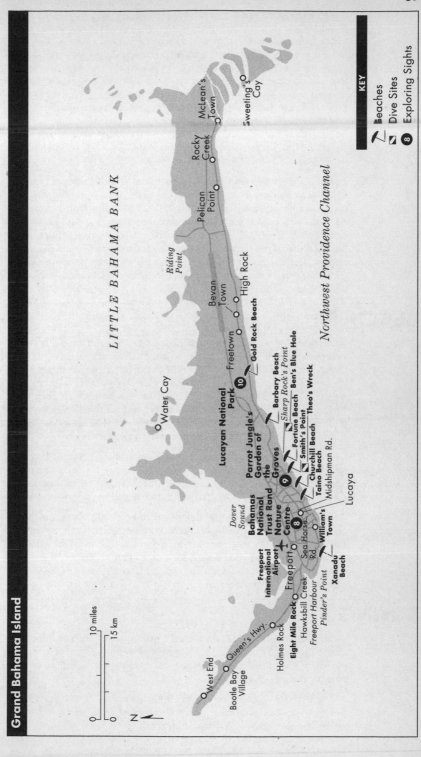

Grand Bahama Island

LITTLE BAHAMA BANK

Water Cay

Riding Point

Pelican Point

Rocky Creek

McLean's Town

Sweeting's Cay

Bevan Town

Freetown

High Rock

Gold Rock Beach

Lucayan National Park

10

Barbary Beach

Sharp Rock's Point

Ben's Blue Hole

Fortune Beach

Theo's Wreck

Smith's Point

Churchill Beach

Taino Beach

Midshipman Rd.

Lucaya

Parrot Jungle's Garden of the Groves

9

Dover Sound

Bahamas National Trust Rand Nature Centre

8

Sea Horse Rd.

William's Town

Xanadu Beach

Freeport International Airport

Freeport

Hawksbill Creek

Freeport Harbour

Pinder's Point

Eight Mile Rock

Holmes Rock

Queen's Hwy.

Bootle Bay Village

West End

Northwest Providence Channel

10 miles

15 km

N

KEY

Beaches

Dive Sites

8 Exploring Sights

sheltered pools containing rare marine species, and what is believed to be the largest explored underwater cave system in the world (7 mi long). You can enter the caves at two access points. One is closed during bat nursing season (June and July). Expert divers who wish to explore the caves should contact UNEXSO. Just 20 mi east of Lucaya, the park contains examples of the island's five ecosystems: beach, sandy or whiteland coppice (hardwood forest), mangroves, rocky coppice, and pine forest. Across the road, trails lead through pine forest and mangrove swamp to Gold Rock Beach, a beautiful, lightly populated strand of white sand, aquamarine sea, and coral reef. Signs along the trail detail the park's distinctive features. ⊠ *Grand Bahama Hwy.,* ☎ *242/352–5438.* ☜ *Free.* ☉ *Daily 9–4.*

★ ☙ ❾ **Parrot Jungle's Garden of the Groves.** Some 10,000 varieties of tropical flora, including fruit trees, ferns, bougainvillea, oleander, and chenille plant, flourish at this 12-acre botanical paradise. Birds, alligators, Bahamian raccoons, a playground, and a petting zoo add family appeal. Follow the Main Waterfall Trail to a picture-perfect church on a hill, a full-size replica of the chapel at Pine Ridge, one of Grand Bahama's earliest settlements. A small café serves breakfast and dinner daily. ⊠ *Midshipman Rd. and Magellan Dr.,* ☎ *242/373–5668,* WEB *www.gardenofthegroves.com.* ☜ *$9.95 adults, $6.95 children.* ☉ *Daily 9–4.*

BEACHES

Some 60 mi of magnificent, pristine stretches of sand extend between Freeport-Lucaya and McLean's Town, the island's isolated eastern end. Most are used only by people who live in adjacent settlements along the way. The beaches have no public facilities, so beachgoers often headquarter at one of the local beach bars. Lucaya hotels have their own beaches and water-sports activities; guests at Freeport hotels are shuttled free to beaches such as **Xanadu,** a mile of white sand, and **Taíno,** fun for families, water-sports enthusiasts, and partyers.

Local residents prefer the beach at **William's Town,** south of Freeport (off East Sunrise Highway and down Beachway Drive) and east of Xanadu Beach, where sandy solitude is broken only by the occasional passing of horseback riders from Pinetree Stables at the water's edge.

East of Port Lucaya, several delightful beaches run along the South Shore—**Churchill Beach, Smith's Point, Fortune Beach,** and lesser-known **Barbary Beach.** Farther east, at the end of the trail from the Lucayan National Park, you'll find **Gold Rock Beach,** which is only a 20-mi drive from the Lucaya hotels. On the West End, snorkeling beachgoers escape by tour to Paradise Cove.

DINING

Grand Bahama Island's restaurants, while arguably less cosmopolitan than New Providence Island's, afford better opportunities for sampling native cuisine. Also, a meal in Freeport usually costs less than a comparable one in Nassau.

You will find many options in Freeport and Lucaya, from elegant hotel dining rooms and charming waterside cafés to local hangouts and familiar fast-food chains. Menus often combine Continental, American, and Bahamian fare. A native fish fry takes place on Wednesday evening at Smith's Point, east of Lucaya (taxi drivers know the way). Here you can sample fresh fish, sweet-potato bread, conch salad, and all the fixings cooked outdoors at the beach. It's a great opportunity to meet local residents, and at about $9 per person, it's also a bargain. An automatic

15% gratuity is added to most dining tabs. For general information, *see* Dining *in* Smart Travel Tips A to Z at the front of the book.

CATEGORY	COST*
$$$$	over $40
$$$	$30–$40
$$	$20–$30
$	$10–$20
¢	under $10

*per person for a main course at dinner

Freeport

Bahamian

$–$$$ ✕ **Becky's Restaurant & Lounge.** This popular eatery opens at 7 AM and may be the best place in town to fuel up before a full day of gambling or shopping. Its diner-style booths provide a comfortable backdrop for the inexpensive menu of traditional Bahamian and American food, from conch salad and steamed mutton to steak or a BLT. Pancakes, eggs, and special Bahamian breakfasts—"boil" fish, "stew" fish, or chicken souse (lime-marinated), with johnnycake or grits—are served all day. ⊠ *E. Beach Dr. and E. Sunrise Hwy.,* ☎ *242/352–5247. MC, V.*

$–$ ✕ **Geneva's Place.** Geneva's sets the standard for home-cooked Bahamian food. The interior is nothing fancy: a former-life Italian restaurant whose brick walls have been painted light blue, a canal-scene mural, wrought-iron grating, and grape leaves. Cook and owner Geneva Munroe will prepare your grouper broiled, steamed, or fried; your pork chops fried or steamed; your conch cracked, or, for breakfast, stewed. Everything comes with a big plate of side dishes. The peas 'n' rice are fantastic. ⊠ *E. Mall Dr. and Kipling La.,* ☎ *242/352–5085. No credit cards.*

Continental

$–$$$$ ✕ **Ruby Swiss European Restaurant.** The extensive Continental menu has seafood, steak, veal, and an all-you-can-eat spaghetti bar. Specialties include steak Diana (flamed with cognac), Wiener schnitzel, fondue *bourguignonne,* and desserts flambéed tableside. The wine list's 50-odd varieties represent six countries. Dinnertime guitar music adds a romantic touch to the large dining hall and busy atmosphere. Snacks are served into the wee hours, making this a good place to come after hitting the Royal Oasis Casino, nearby. ⊠ *W. Sunrise Hwy. and Atlantic Way, across from Crowne Plaza at Royal Oasis,* ☎ *242/352–8507. AE, D, DC, MC, V.*

$$–$$$ ✕ **Rib Room.** Enjoy prime rib, juicy porterhouse, chateaubriand for two, or seafood in an elegant English hunting-lodge setting. ⊠ *Holiday Inn Sunspree at Royal Oasis Golf Resort & Casino,* ☎ *242/350–7000. Reservations essential. Jacket preferred. AE, D, DC, MC, V. No lunch.*

$–$$ ✕ **Paradiso.** Royal Oasis Resort's newest signature restaurant excels at gourmet Italian cuisine. In a setting of tasteful, dark wood and tall booths, choose from such creations as veal saltimbocca, osso buco, fettucine *pescatore* (with lobster, shrimp, conch, scallops, and fish), and filet Florentine. ⊠ *Crowne Plaza at Royal Oasis,* ☎ *242/352–7000. Reservations essential. AE, D, DC, MC, V. Closed Sun. No lunch.*

Eclectic

$–$$$ ✕ **Pub on the Mall.** You have four options at this spot across from International Bazaar called Ranfurly Circus, which is actually four restaurants clustered together. **The Prince of Wales Lounge** (☎ 242/352–2700), an authentic English-style pub, serves fish-and-chips, sandwiches, steaks, sweet-and-sour baby back ribs, and draft ale in a medieval setting. **Islander's Roost Steak House** (☎ 242/352–5110) offers an ex-

Freeport-Lucaya Dining

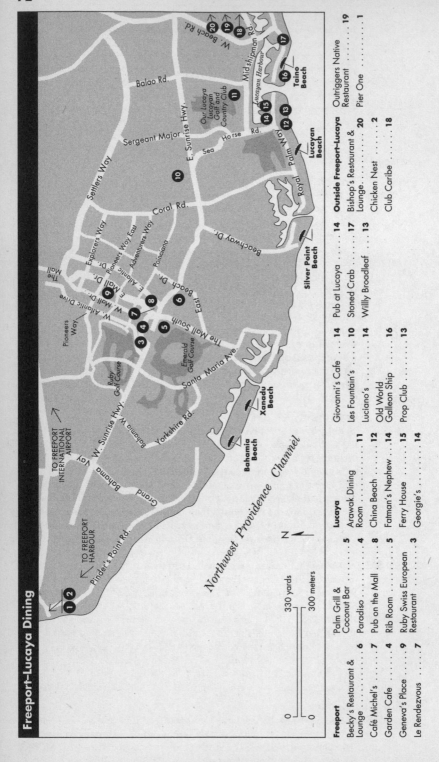

Freeport

Becky's Restaurant & Lounge	.... **6**
Café Michel's	.... **7**
Garden Cafe	.... **4**
Geneva's Place	.... **9**
Le Rendezvous	.... **7**
Palm Grill & Coconut Bar	..... **5**
Paradiso	.... **4**
Pub on the Mall	..... **8**
Rib Room	.... **5**
Ruby Swiss European Restaurant	...... **3**

Lucaya

Arawak Dining Room	...... **11**
China Beach	.... **12**
Fatman's Nephew	... **14**
Ferry House	.... **15**
Georgie's	.... **14**
Giovanni's Cafe	.... **14**
Les Fountain's	..... **10**
Luciano's	.... **14**
Old World Galleon Ship	...... **16**
Prop Club	.... **13**
Pub at Lucaya	..... **14**
Stoned Crab	...... **17**
Willly Broadleaf	... **13**

Outside Freeport-Lucaya

Bishop's Restaurant & Lounge	.... **20**
Chicken Nest	...... **2**
Club Caribe	..... **18**
Outriggers Native Restaurant	.... **19**
Pier One	.... **1**

tensive menu of Caribbean and American dishes in a relaxed atmosphere festooned with colorful Junkanoo (the local Christmas carnival) masks and costumes. Waiters sporting white jackets dish out steaks, ribs, charbroiled dolphinfish steak, and Bahamian fare in the two-level dining room and on the open-air patio. A third restaurant, **Silvano's** (☎ 242/352–5110), serves a wide selection of fine Italian-style fish, pasta, and meat in a circular sunshine-yellow dining room. The chef's special is lobster with spicy tomato and mushroom sauce. **The Red Dog Sports Bar** (☎ 242/352–2700) has a friendly if sometimes boisterous atmosphere and four TV screens, including a 96-inch monster screen. The hungry go for the pizza. ⊠ *Ranfurly Circus, opposite International Bazaar. AE, D, MC, V. Islander's Roost closes Sun.*

$$ ✕ **Garden Café.** Opening onto the Royal Oasis Resort Casino for a view of the action, it serves buffet-style meals all day. The dinner buffet includes hot, fresh-made Bahamian and international entrées, along with carved prime rib, salad and dessert bars, cold cuts, and soups. ⊠ *Casino at Royal Oasis Resort & Casino,* ☎ *242/350–7000. AE, D, DC, MC, V.*

$ ✕ **Le Rendezvous.** The epitome of the International Bazaar's cosmopolitan flair, this sidewalk café covers all of the ethnic bases—Italian, Mexican, East Indian, Caribbean, Thai, Indonesian, and Bahamian. Try curried veg-rolls or Bangkok stuffed shrimp for an appetizer; grouper piccata or Thai stir-fry for the main course. ⊠ *International Bazaar,* ☎ *242/352–9610. AE, MC, V.*

French

$–$ ✕ **Café Michel's.** Stop by this unpretentious bistro for a light meal or snack. Whereas the alfresco tables, with red umbrellas and tablecloths, place you in an ideal people-watching location just off the Bazaar's main promenade, the café's cozy interior is more intimate. The menu has French, American, and Bahamian dishes such as conch burger, hamburger, escargot, veal cordon bleu, and lobster tail. ⊠ *International Bazaar,* ☎ *242/352–2191. AE, MC, V.*

Seafood

$ ✕ **Palm Grill and Coconut Bar.** Off the lobby at Royal Oasis Golf Resort & Casino, this stylish bistro offers seating outdoors at teak tables or inside looking through floor-to-ceiling windows. Open for all meals, it concentrates on such seafood as crab cakes and grouper. Its all-day (11:30–11) menu offers everything from sandwiches and pizza to New York strip steak and seafood crepes Newburg. ⊠ *Crowne Plaza at Royal Oasis Golf Resort & Casino,* ☎ *242/350–7000. AE, MC, V.*

Lucaya

American

$–$$ ✕ **Prop Club.** Spare bits of recovered aircraft wreckage and brightly painted chairs accent this casual resort hangout, which becomes a lively dance floor by night. Giant glass-paned garage doors open to make this an indoor-outdoor place to dine and party on the beach. The menu doesn't strain beyond casual with such offerings as pizza, fajitas, "mountain of ribs," and crab cakes. ⊠ *Breakers Cay at Our Lucaya,* ☎ *242/373–1333. AE, D, DC, MC, V.*

$–$ ✕ **Old World Galleon Ship.** Eat at the ship-shaped bar or at wooden tables looking out at the beach. Fare is beach-style American, including hamburgers, conch burgers, Cajun shrimp, barbecue ribs, and pan-fried grouper. Call ahead for reservations and free transportation. On Sunday, Tuesday, and Thursday nights, a bonfire feed with chicken, ribs, and all the fixings, live music, and drinks costs $40 per adult, $30 for children. ⊠ *Pirates of the Bahamas Theme Park, 5 Jolly Roger Dr.,* ☎ *242/373–8456. AE, D, MC, V.*

Bahamian

$–$$ ✕ **Fatman's Nephew.** Owner Stanley Simmons named his restaurant for the two rotund uncles who taught him the trade. One of the better spots to dine in Port Lucaya, this place serves substantial Bahamian fare. The regular menu is somewhat limited, featuring local dishes such as Bahamian turtle, cracked conch, and curried mutton. A blackboard listing a full complement of daily seafood specials widens the offerings. The best seating is on the L-shape outdoor terrace overlooking the waterway and marina. ⊠ *Port Lucaya Marketplace,* ☎ *242/373–8520. AE, D, MC, V.*

$–$ ✕ **Georgie's.** Sit alfresco at this pleasant, casual spot on the harbor at Port Lucaya Marketplace; it's open for breakfast, happy hour and snacks, lunch, and dinner. Local favorites such as barbecue chicken, conch fritters, lobster, and grouper come with delicious cole slaw and peas 'n' rice. Georgie's cracked conch is the real thing. ⊠ *Port Lucaya Marketplace,* ☎ *242/373–8513. AE, MC, V.*

$–$ ✕ **Les Fountain's.** Open 24 hours, this longtime haunt is a bar with a tall pointed ceiling, tiled floor, and tall-back booth. Bahamian and American favorites for lunch and dinner might include jerk chicken, lobster salad, barbecue ribs, or steamed snapper. Breakfast is served all day. ⊠ *E. Sunrise Hwy.,* ☎ *242/373–9553. AE, V.*

Contemporary

$–$$ ✕ **Arawak Dining Room.** Enjoy a view of the Balancing Boulders of
★   Lucaya and an immaculate golf course as you dine on fine Continental cuisine, served lunch and dinner by an excellent staff. Indulge in such creative fare as veal chops with wild mushrooms, grouper with roasted red pepper potato puree, chateaubriand, or prawns Provençale. ⊠ *Our Lucaya Lucayan Golf & Country Club,* ☎ *242/373–1066 or 242/373–1067. Reservations essential. AE, D, DC, MC, V.*

Continental

$–$$ ✕ **Ferry House.** The windowed dining room of this bright restaurant hangs over the water just outside the Port Lucaya Marketplace. Its changing menu leans toward the experimental with such offerings as grilled grouper with black bean puree, herb-crusted rack of lamb, and rabbit casserole. Inside Bell Channel, Ferry House serves as the main restaurant for the nearby Pelican Bay at Lucaya resort. ⊠ *Port Lucaya,* ☎ *242/373–1595. AE, MC, V. No dinner Mon.*

$–$$ ✕ **Luciano's.** Halogen lamps and abstract paintings add to the mod-
★   ern decor of this sophisticated Port Lucaya restaurant overlooking the waterway. Classic Continental specialties include *filet au poivre* (fillet with peppercorn sauce), grouper almondine, chicken over fettuccine, and prime rib, served in the formal, subdued dining room or on the veranda overlooking the marina. If you want to splurge, begin your meal with beluga caviar. ⊠ *Port Lucaya Marketplace,* ☎ *242/373–9100. AE, MC, V. Closed Sun.*

Eclectic

$$$ ✕ **Willy Broadleaf.** For an adventure in dining, graze the multicultural buffet line here. Dine in the ambience of a Mediterranean marketplace, African village, maharajah's dining hall, Mexican courtyard, or Egyptian market. Sample global exotic dishes such as wild boar sausage, tandoori chicken, Greek stew, pork dumplings, and marvelous desserts. It opens for all meals. ⊠ *Breaker's Cay, Our Lucaya,* ☎ *242/373–1333. AE, DC, MC, V.*

English

$–$$ ✕ **Pub at Lucaya.** On the Port Lucaya waterfront, this amiable pub has a reputation for dependable English fare, such as shepherd's and steak-and-ale pies. You also can't go wrong with the Frenched lamb chops, Bahamian lobster tail, or strip sirloin. Lunchtime brings burgers and sandwiches. The nautical decor incorporates antiques, heavy rustic tables, and ersatz Tiffany lamps suspended from a wood-beam ceiling. Ask for a table on the outside terrace. ✉ *Port Lucaya Marketplace,* ☎ *242/373–8450. AE, DC, MC, V.*

Italian

$ ✕ **Giovanni's Cafe.** Tucked away under the bougainvillea at Port Lucaya Marketplace, this corner café evokes a bit of Italy. As you relax on the patio or study the giant mural of an Italian waterway inside the café, treat yourself to local seafood prepared Bahamian style or dressed in authentic Italian sauces. Full-flavored dishes include spaghetti carbonara and chicken marsala. ✉ *Port Lucaya Marketplace,* ☎ *242/373–9107. AE, MC, V. Closed Sun.*

Pan-Asian

$–$$$ ✕ **China Beach.** Food in this elegant dining room with its open kitchen extends far beyond Chinese, incorporating elements of Vietnamese, Korean, Thai, Indonesian, Malaysian, and other Pacific Rim styles. From the monthly changing menu, sample sushi (prepared or make-your-own), satay, seafood teppanyaki, stir-fried conch, roast duck with plum sauce, and other Far East specialties. ✉ *Breakers Cay, Our Lucaya,* ☎ *242/373–1333. AE, D, DC, MC, V.*

Seafood

$$–$$$ ✕ **Stoned Crab.** This long-standing, pyramidal-roof restaurant faces one of the island's loveliest stretches of sand, Taino Beach. Don't miss the scrumptiously sweet stone crab claws and lobsters, both locally caught. Crabs of all varieties are the specialty; try stone and snow crab, stuffed crab, and crab cake in the crab sampler. Other specialties include swordfish, wahoo, and yellowfin tuna. The calming ocean beckons you on the patio. ✉ *Taino Beach,* ☎ *242/373–1442. AE, MC, V. No lunch.*

Outside Freeport-Lucaya

Get out of town for a taste of true Bahamian cooking. Many of the island's far-flung restaurants provide courtesy shuttles from hotels.

Bahamian

$–$ ✕ **Bishop's Restaurant & Lounge.** A longtime favorite of locals and visitors who venture out into the East End's settlements, it serves all the Bahamian favorites with homemade goodness and a view of the sea. The cracked conch is light and crunchy; the peas 'n' rice full-flavored. ✉ *Box F-42029, High Rock,* ☎ *242/353–4515. No credit cards.*

$–$ ✕ **Outriggers Native Restaurant.** For Bahamian food fixed by Bahamians, head east to the generational property of an old island family. Stop at Gretchen Wilson's place for cracked conch, lobster tail, and barbecue chicken down-home style. You'll feel as though you're dining in someone's spotlessly clean home. Wednesday night the quiet little settlement comes to life when Outriggers throws its famous weekly fish fry. In winter, the Outriggers Beach Club, across the street, serves light lunch. ✉ *Smith's Point,* ☎ *242/373–4811. No credit cards. Closed Sun. and for lunch in off-season.*

¢ ✕ **Chicken Nest.** At West End, this simple, home-style spot has the no-nonsense menu of cousins Lovie and Rosie Nixon, including fish, fritters, conch salad, and homemade sweet-potato bread. You can shoot pool while you wait for your order or sit at the bar, where, if you order a hard drink, you get the bottle. ⊠ *Bayshore Rd., West End,* ☎ *242/ 346–6440. No credit cards. Closed Mon.*

Seafood

$–$$ ╳ **Pier One.** Observe Lucayan Harbour's cruise-ship activity over
★   lunch, sunset over cocktails, or the frenzied feeding of sharks over din-
      ner. Shark—prepared blackened, curried with bananas, panfried, and
      in spicy fritters—is the specialty of the house. Steak, grouper, and lob-
      ster also star on the extensive menu. In season, call ahead to reserve
      an outdoor table, or dine inside, surrounded by aquariums and nau-
      tical paraphernalia. Swarms of fish and sharks frenzy for handouts at
      7, 8, and 9 PM. ⊠ *Lucayan Harbour,* ☎ 242/352–6674. *AE, MC, V.
      No lunch Sun.*

$–$ ╳ **Club Caribe.** Small and very casual, this beachside haunt is an ideal
      place to headquarter your day at the beach. Unwind with a Bahama
      Mama, or try the local fare, such as conch fritters, grilled grouper, or
      barbecued ribs. You can also get American burgers and sandwiches.
      Free transportation is provided to and from your hotel (reservations
      are essential). Friday night brings a pig roast, volleyball, and dining at
      picnic tables on the beach. ⊠ *Mather Town, off Doubloon Rd. on Span-
      ish Main Dr.,* ☎ 242/373–6866. *AE, MC, V. Closed Mon.*

LODGING

Once a leader in exotic, glamour resort-casino complexes, Grand Bahama is rising again to set standards with complete make-overs in
Freeport, Lucaya, and West End. You can choose from among Grand
Bahama's approximately 4,000 rooms and suites, ranging from attractive
one- and two-bedroom units in sprawling resort complexes to practi-
cal apartments with kitchenettes to comfortable rooms in economy-
oriented establishments. The more extravagant hotels in Freeport and
Lucaya include the Royal Oasis Golf Resort & Casino (formerly Bahamia and Bahamas Princess); the sprawling, three-pronged Our Lucaya; Viva Fortuna, an all-inclusive east of Lucaya; and the West End's
elegant Old Bahama Bay. The latter, like many Grand Bahama resorts,
caters to the boating crowd. Small apartment complexes and time-share
rentals are economical alternatives, especially if you're planning to stay
for more than a few days. If you value proximity to the beach, stay at
Old Bahama Bay, Xanadu, Our Lucaya, Island Seas, or Viva Fortuna,
which offer beach access. The Royal Oasis Resort & Casino built its
own beach at a zero-entry pool with a sand bottom, and also appeals
to gamblers, golfers, and shoppers. UNEXSO, Grand Bahama Island's
scuba central, is within easy walking distance of Lucaya's hotels.

The larger hotels offer honeymoon, golfing, gambling, scuba, and
other packages. Families will find that many hotels offer baby-sitting
services and children's programs. Some lodgings allow children under
12 to stay in your room for free and may not charge you for a crib or
roll-away bed.

An 8% tax is added to your hotel bill, representing resort and government levies. Rates from April 15 through December 14 tend to be
25%–30% lower than during the rest of the year. For general information, *see* Lodging *in* Smart Travel Tips A to Z at the front of the
book.

The prices below are based on high-season (winter) rates, generally in
effect from December through March. Expect to pay between 15% and
30% less off-season at most resorts. In general, the best rates are avail-

able through packages, which almost every hotel offers. Call the hotel directly or ask your travel agent.

CATEGORY	COST*
$$$$	over $400
$$$	$300–$400
$$	$200–$300
$	$100–$200
¢	under $100

*All prices are for a standard double room in high season, excluding 9% tax and 10%–15% service charge. Note that the government hotel tax doesn't apply to guest houses with fewer than four rooms.

Freeport

$–$$ ⊞ **Island Seas Resort.** If you're looking for fun on the beach away from urban bustle, this time-share property accommodates nonmembers. Balconies overlook the flowery courtyard, where thatched-roofed Co-CoNuts Grog & Grub and a free-form pool with waterfalls and swim-up bar create the centerpiece. The beach, used by guests from other non-beachside resorts, is busy with watersports activity. One- and two-bedroom rooms are done in bright modern island style. The property has 117 rooms, but not all are included in the open rental plan. ✉ *Box F-44735, William's Town, Freeport,* ☎ *242/373–1271,* FAX *242/373–1275. 50 rooms. Restaurant, bar, air-conditioning, pool, basketball, horseback riding, volleyball, beach, boating, parasailing, bicycles. D, MC, V.*

$–$$ ⊞ **Royal Oasis Golf Resort & Casino.** Two sister resorts make up this
★ 1,000-acre complex with an impressive selection of amenities at midrange rates. Both share two 18-hole championship golf courses, a fitness center and spa, a children's club with a kids-only restaurant, and a massive casino. The sand beach–entry pool with sand bottom and slides brings the beach to the middle of town. If you prefer the ocean beach, hop on the free shuttle to a nearby beach club. Special packages are available for honeymooners, families, and golfers. Consider opting for the resort's Pizazz all-inclusive plan.

Crowne Plaza. Next door to the casino, this 400-room, 10-story building is the more elegant of the two properties, geared towards couples and high-rolling gamblers. A dramatic waterfall-dominated lobby and rooms dressed in fall tones and old plantation style infuse this hotel with good taste. Despite the grand architecture, it's a casual hub of activity, much of it centered around its newly beautified pool area. Proximity to shopping at International Bazaar is another plus.

Holiday Inn Sunspree. More conducive to families and golfers, this 565-room property is home to a beach-entry pool. Man-made rock formations frame the second pool and hot tub. Two- and three-story guest-room wings radiate outward like the spokes of a wheel from the circular deck around the pool area. Dressed much like the Crowne Plaza's room, but a bit smaller, they represent one of the island's greatest values. Some wings contain time-share kitchen apartments.

✉ *Box F 2623, Freeport,* ☎ *242/350–7000; 800/545–1300 in the U.S.,* FAX *242/350–7003,* WEB *www.gbvac.com. 942 rooms, 23 suites. 6 restaurants, 6 bars, air-conditioning, refrigerators, room service, 3 pools, 2 hair salons, hot tub, spa, 2 18-hole golf courses, 9 tennis courts, jogging, gym, snorkeling, boating, parasailing, waterskiing, casino, dance club, showroom, children's programs (12 and under), playground, convention center, travel services. AE, D, DC, MC, V. All-inclusive available.*

78

Freeport-Lucaya Lodging

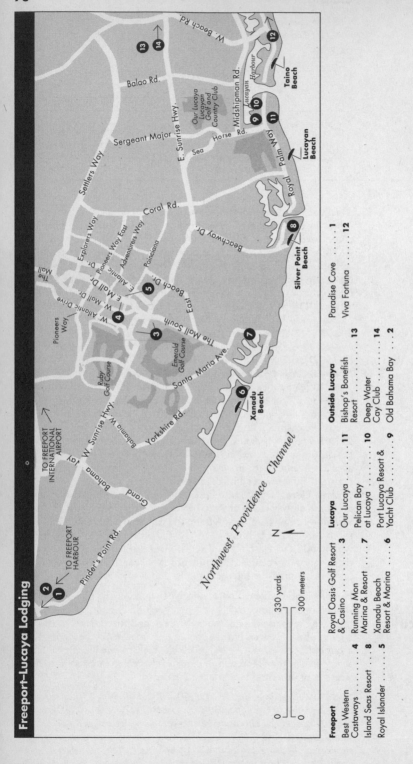

Northwest Providence Channel

Freeport
Best Western
Castaways **4**
Island Seas Resort ... **8**
Royal Islander **5**

Royal Oasis Golf Resort
& Casino **3**
Running Mon
Marina & Resort ... **7**
Xanadu Beach
Resort & Marina **6**

Lucaya
Our Lucaya **11**
Pelican Bay
at Lucaya **10**
Port Lucaya Resort &
Yacht Club **9**

Outside Lucaya
Bishop's Bonefish
Resort **13**
Deep Water
Cay Club **14**
Old Bahama Bay ... **2**

Paradise Cove **1**
Viva Fortuna **12**

$ ⊡ **Royal Islander.** All the amenities without the sticker shock: this two-story, tin-roof, motel style property is near the International Bazaar and Royal Oasis Casino and provides free scheduled shuttle service to Xanadu Beach. The rooms have light-wood and rattan furnishings, lively tropical fabrics, framed pastel prints, and tile floors on the lower level. You'll find carpeted floors upstairs, where no-smoking rooms are available. An inviting white-and-floral lobby faces the spacious pool area. ✉ *Box F 42549, East Mall Dr., Freeport,* ☎ *242/351–6000,* FAX *242/ 351–3546, 100 rooms. Bar, dining room, snack bar, air conditioning, no-smoking rooms, pool, Ping-Pong, shop, travel services. AE, MC, V.*

$ ⊡ **Running Mon Marina & Resort.** If seclusion and a boating atmosphere appeal to you, this pumpkin orange stucco hotel with natural-wood decking is ideal. Each room in this waterfront resort has a view of the 70-slip marina. Boat owners will appreciate the haul-and-launch facility, on-site mechanics, and repair services. Ask the dockmaster to arrange a deep-sea fishing charter, or take a dip in the small pool framed by oleanders and a harbor view. A white baby grand piano is the elegant centerpiece of Mainsail, the resort's restaurant and lounge. ✉ *Box F 42663, 208 Kelly Ct., Freeport,* ☎ *242/352–6834,* FAX *242/352–6835,* WEB *www.running-mon-bahamas.com. 31 rooms, 1 suite. Restaurant, bar, air-conditioning, no-smoking rooms, refrigerator, pool, boating, marina, jet skiing, fishing, bicycles, shops, video game room, playground, laundry facilities, meeting rooms, travel services. AE, D, MC, V.*

$ ⊡ **Xanadu Beach Resort & Marina.** Only a few minutes from town, the
★ property's tower, pool wing, and villas overlook the oval pool and fountain, marina, parking lot, or beach. Rooms show their age but have been spruced up with a new designer look. Coconut palms sway at the wide, gorgeous beach, a three-minute walk from the hotel. Come here for water sports and beach volleyball. An on-site water-sports concession has all the wet stuff your vacation needs. ✉ *Box F 2438, Sunken Treasure Dr., Freeport,* ☎ *242/352 6782,* FAX *242/352–6299,* WEB *www.bahamasvg. com. 137 rooms, 49 suites. 2 restaurants, 3 bars, air-conditioning, pool, massage, 3 tennis courts, Ping-Pong, volleyball, beach, dive shop, dock, snorkeling, boating, jet skiing, parasailing, fishing, baby-sitting, shop, laundry facilities, meeting rooms. AE, MC, V.*

$ ⊡ **Best Western Castaways.** Near the action in Freeport, this property
★ was gutted and re-created as a much nicer version of its former self. The prettily coral rock–accented lobby introduces four stories of rooms in bamboo and earth and floral tones. Family friendliness is underscored by a playground next to the pool, and beach shuttle is provided. The restaurant is open only for its famous breakfast. ✉ *Box F 42629, Freeport,* ☎ *242/352–6682 or 800/700–4752,* FAX *242/352–5087,* WEB *www.castaways-resort.com. 97 rooms, 21 suites. Restaurant, pool, playground, 2 bars, nightclub, baby-sitting, laundry facilities. AE, MC, V.*

Lucaya

$–$$ ⊡ **Our Lucaya.** Completed at a cost of $400 million, Grand Bahama's
★ latest grand resort spreads three hotels along 7½ acres of soft-sand beach. A colonial-style Manor House serves as the hub and lobby. The accent here is on dramatic play-area water features and 36 holes of golf. The property has completed work on a yet-to-open 30,000-square-ft casino with table and sports games and slots. Twelve restaurants—specializing in cuisines from Asian to American and Caribbean—lounges, children's camp, spa, and shopping complex make Our Lucaya the island's most ambitious full-service beach resort.

Reef Village. Geared toward family vacationers, this resort focuses on a water park with a sugar-mill ruin theme, complete with a zero-entry pool and water slide. The headquarters for children's programs is

nearby: a bright circular building with peekaboo windows for unde-
tected parental spying. Children under 12 stay free. The resort's 550
rooms and public areas have a tropical Miami Beach flair. Reef Village offers an all-inclusive plan year-round.

Breakers Cay. The 10-floor high-rise resort curves like a wavy cruise
ship between the other two, with 575 rooms and suites; a small half-
moon infinity pool encasing a swim-up bar on the beach; a long, narrow lap pool; restaurants; and bars. Popular with Americans and
business people, the centrally located resort exudes elegance, especially
at the Harbour Club on the two top floors, with personal balcony beverage service and a concierge suite.

Lighthouse Pointe. The property's 246 rooms and suites, away from
the bustle of Breakers Cays, are in two-story structures built to repli-
cate a Caribbean-style plantation manor inside and out. The 25 lanai
suites come with a steward. A half-moon infinity pool clasps the property and visually blends into the ocean beyond.

⊠ *Royal Palm Way, Lucaya,* ☎ *242/373–1333; 877/687–5822 in the
U.S.,* FAX *242/373–8804,* WEB *www.ourlucaya.com. 1,371 rooms and
suites. 12 restaurants, 8 bars, coffee shop, in-room data ports, in-
room safes, refrigerators, room service, 4 pools, spa, 2 18-hole golf
courses, 4 tennis courts, basketball, gym, horseshoes, volleyball, beach,
snorkeling, water slide, boating, waterskiing, pro shop, shops, casino,
children's programs (ages 2½ –12), concierge floor, business services,
meeting rooms, travel services. AE, D, DC, MC, V.*

$ 🏨 **Pelican Bay at Lucaya.** Experience the romance of the Caribbean
with European design. Town houses are fancifully trimmed in West Indian gingerbread and latticework. The smart reception area is furnished
with mahogany, wicker, and paintings of Bahamian scenery. Mod-
ernly furnished rooms and suites overlook the pool and whirlpool, the
channel, and the marina. Pelican Bay is next door to UNEXSO, which
makes it popular with divers. Only steps away from Port Lucaya Marketplace, the resort also has its own marina nearby. Deluxe rooms include Continental breakfast at a higher rate. ⊠ *Box F 42654, Royal
Palm Way, Freeport,* ☎ *242/373–9550 or 800/600–9192,* FAX *242/
373–9551,* WEB *www.pelicanbayhotel.com. 90 rooms, 48 suites. Restaurant, bar, air-conditioning, in-room safes, refrigerator, 3 pools, hot tub,
marina, laundry facilities. AE, MC, V.*

$ 🏨 **Port Lucaya Resort & Yacht Club.** Members can dock at the 50-slip
marina; others pull in next door at Port Lucaya Marina. Golf carts transport guests to 10 brightly painted buildings around the Olympic-size
swimming pool, hot tub, and restaurant. The rooms have garden, pool,
or marina views, punctuated sparingly with rattan furniture, tile floors,
large wall mirrors, and light tropical patterns. At night, Port Lucaya
Marketplace's celebratory sounds spill into buildings 7, 8, 9, and 10,
and guests can enjoy the festivities from their balconies. ⊠ *Box F
42452, Bell Channel Bay Rd., Freeport,* ☎ *242/373–6618 or 800/582–
2921,* FAX *242/373–6652,* WEB *www.portlucaya.com/resort. 157 rooms,
3 suites. Restaurant, 2 bars, air-conditioning, pool, hot tub, dock, marina, playground, laundry service, no-smoking floors. AE, D, MC, V.*

Outside Freeport-Lucaya

$$$$ 🏨 **Deep Water Cay Club.** Ideal if you want to get away from it all and
★   angle for bonefish, this private island has Bahamian-style one- and two-
         bedroom cottages. Activities center around a main lodge with a din-
         ing room, self-service bar, and tackle shop. Diversions include beaching,
         boating, and some of the best bonefishing in the Bahamas. Accom-

modations are available in three-, four-, or seven-night packages only, including meals, and daily guided fishing excursions. The resort can arrange a charter flight from Florida, which lands at the property's own airstrip. ⊠ *Deep Water Cay (1100 Lee Wagener Blvd., Suite 352, Fort Lauderdale, FL 33315),* ☏ *242/353–3073 or 954/359–0488,* 🆅🆇 *242/353–3095 or 954/359–9488,* 🆆🅴🅱 *www.deepwatercay.com. 9 units. Restaurant, bar, air-conditioning, pool, snorkeling, boating, fishing. No credit cards. All-inclusive.*

$$$–$$$$ 🏨 **Old Bahama Bay.** Designed principally for boating vacationers, it supplies all the amenities you need to relax and get away from it all, way away. Waterfront suites, one- and two-bedroom, treat you to luxurious heavy wood furnishings and a view of the beach through French doors. Each suite, clustered six to each pastel, island-style villa, contains a wet bar, bathrobes, cooking utensils, and a DVD-CD player. ⊠ *Box F-42546, West End,* ☏ *242/350–6500 or 800/444–9469,* 🆅🆇 *242/346–6546,* 🆆🅴🅱 *www.oldbahamabay.com. 47 suites. Restaurant, 2 bars, tennis, microwaves, refrigerators, pool, gym, massage, snorkeling, tennis, boating, marina, bicycles, fishing, shop. AE, D, MC, V.*

$$–$$$ 🏨 **Viva Fortuna.** Popular with couples and families, this secluded re-
★ sort provides a casual, low-stress, all-inclusive getaway. One price covers meals, drinks, tips, nonmotorized water sports, nightly entertainment, and other activities. A 1,200-ft private beach bustles with activity. Meals are served buffet style in the huge, gazebo-like dining pavilion or tableside at La Trattoria. Simple rooms in two-story buildings have light-wood furniture, tile floors, and balconies or porches. Kids under age 12 stay free with adults. ⊠ *Churchill Dr. and Doubloon Rd., Freeport (Box F 42398),* ☏ *242/373–4000,* 🆅🆇 *242/373–5555,* 🆆🅴🅱 *www.vivaresorts.com. 276 rooms. 2 restaurants, bar, snack bar, air-conditioning, in-room safes, pool, 2 tennis courts, aerobics, archery, boccie, Ping-Pong, gym, beach, dive shop, snorkeling, windsurfing, boating, bicycles, shops, dance club, theater, children's programs (ages 4 and up), playground, laundry service, meeting rooms, travel services. AE, D, MC, V. All-inclusive.*

$ 🏨 **Bishop's Bonefish Resort.** Stay on the beach in a small community east of Lucaya, without the hefty price tags and bustle of Lucaya. Owned by Bahamian Ruben "Bishop" Roberts, the property is comprised of eight white-tiled, spacious rooms. Bishop will arrange bonefishing excursions to the East End, feed you at his landmark native restaurant, and talk politics with you at the bar. ⊠ *Box F-42029, High Rock,* ☏ *242/353–4515,* 🆅🆇 *242/353–4417,* 🆆🅴🅱 *www.gbweekly.com. 7 rooms. Restaurant, bar, beach, refrigerators, fishing. AE, MC.*

$ 🏨 **Paradise Cove.** Owned by a local family, Paradise Cove owns a handful of two-bedroom cottages and one-bedroom apartments on the island's best reef. It's the only lodging on Deadman's Reef, quiet and far removed from the resort world. By day, activity mounts as snorkelers arrive by bus. The comfortable, unpretentious accommodations have kitchens. There's a protected stretch of beach, and snorkeling gear is available for a fee. Kayaks are available for guests' use. Staff can arrange spear fishing and other fishing excursions. ⊠ *Deadman's Reef, Freeport, (Box F 42771),* ☏ *242/349–2677,* 🆅🆇 *242/352–5471,* 🆆🅴🅱 *www.deadmansreef.com. 5 apartments and cottages. Bar, snack bar, kitchenettes, volleyball, beach, snorkeling, boating. AE, D, MC, V.*

Time-Sharing

Contact any of the following for information about rentals. For information about other time-share houses, apartments, and condominiums, check with the Grand Bahama Island Tourism Board.

Freeport Resort & Club (⊠ Box F 2514, Freeport, ☎ 242/352–5371, WEB www.freeportresort.com). The 50 suites are in a garden setting close to the International Bazaar and the Royal Oasis Casino. Owners have golf privileges at Royal Oasis courses.

Lakeview Manor Club (⊠ Box F 42699, Freeport, ☎ 242/352–9789). The club's 52 studio and one-bedroom units are adjacent to the fairway of the fifth hole of the Ruby Golf Course.

Mayfield Beach and Tennis Club (⊠ Box F 458, Freeport, ☎ 242/352–9776). The rentals here consist of apartments that share a pool, small beach, and tennis court on Port-of-Call Drive at Xanadu Beach.

Ocean Reef Resort and Yacht Club (⊠ Box F 42639, Freeport, ☎ 242/373–4661, WEB www.oryc.com). These 63 one- to three-bedroom apartments are midway between the International Bazaar and the Lucayan Beach hotels. The resort has a marina and pools.

Royal Holiday Club (⊠ Box F 44439, Freeport, ☎ 242/352–5843). A Xanadu Resort facility, it offers time-share owners the flexibility of trading off with 70 worldwide resorts.

Vacation Club at Royal Oasis (⊠ Box F 684, Freeport, ☎ 242/350–7060). On the grounds of the Holiday Inn Sunspree at Royal Oasis Golf Resort & Casino, one- and two-bedroom efficiencies and apartments allow guests resort privileges.

NIGHTLIFE AND THE ARTS

Nightlife

The casino at Royal Oasis Golf Resort is among the island's top attractions. Try your luck with state-of-the-art slot machines, craps and blackjack tables, roulette, and baccarat. Beginners can request a gaming guide, which explains each game's rules (also consult the gambling primer in this book). There's usually nightly entertainment with live music, and drinks are free to table or slots players. Tables open at 10 AM. There's no specific dress code, although bathing suits and bare feet are not permitted. You must be at least 18 years old to go into the casino, and residents of the Bahamas are not permitted to gamble. Photography is prohibited.

For noncasino evening and late-night entertainment, Grand Bahama delivers calypso music, discos, bonfire beach parties, and live bands for dancing. Nightclubs are generally open from 8 or 9 until 3. Many hotels organize their own nighttime entertainment.

Casinos

Royal Oasis Casino (⊠ Royal Oasis Golf Resort & Casino, W. Sunrise Hwy., ☎ 242/350–7000) packs its newly renovated 20,000 square ft with around 700 slot machines, 27 blackjack tables, 5 craps tables, 4 roulette wheels, 4 Caribbean poker games, and a table each for baccarat and mini-baccarat. In the 360° Tonic bar, 18 sports TVs and a digital Sports Book for betting on games charges the atmosphere. The bar also hosts tournaments and live music. An adjacent restaurant offers a view of the gambling. Slots are open daily 8:30 AM–3:30 AM; tables 10 AM–3:30 AM.

Nightclubs

Bahama Mama Cruises (⊠ Superior Watersports, ☎ 242/373–7863) offers some of the best nightlife in Grand Bahama. In addition to sunset "booze cruises," Bahama Mama serves a surf-and-turf dinner and a colorful native show for $59 adults, $39 for children ages 2–12. The Sunset Cruise and Show is $35. Reservations are essential. The dinner cruise is offered Monday, Wednesday, and Friday 6–9 (October–March) and 6:30–9:30 (April–September); Sunset Cruise and Show runs Monday, Wednesday, and Friday on the same time schedule.

Holiday Inn Sunspree at Royal Oasis Golf Resort (⊠ Royal Oasis Golf Resort, ☎ 242//350–7000) has the John B. outdoor lounge, with live music Wednesday through Monday. Lounge and disco open nightly 9–2; doors open for Goombaya show and dinner (optional) Tuesday and Saturday at 6:30; show time 7:30.

Prop Club Sports Bar & Dance Club (⊠ Our Lucaya Resort, ☎ 242/373–1333) hosts live music that propels guests out to the giant dance floor, plus karaoke on Tuesday, sumo wrestling on Wednesday, and a native show every Thursday at 9 PM. Seating is indoors as well as outdoors on the beach. Open daily for lunch and dinner and nightly entertainment.

The Arts

Theater

Freeport Players' Guild (☎ 242/373–8400), a nonprofit repertory company, produces Bahamian and traditional plays in the 450-seat Regency Theatre during its September–June season.

Grand Bahama Players (☎ 242/373–2299) perform at Regency Theatre, staging cultural productions by Bahamian, West Indian, and North American playwrights.

Port Lucaya Marketplace (⊠ Sea Horse Rd., ☎ 242/373–8446), which opens daily at 10, has a stage that becomes lively after dark, with calypso music and other performers at Count Basie Square (ringed by three popular hangouts: The Corner Bar, Pusser's Daiquiri Bar, and The Pub at Port Lucaya).

OUTDOOR ACTIVITIES AND SPORTS

Amusement Parks

Pirates of the Bahamas offers water-sport rentals, miniature golf (two 18-hole courses), live entertainment, and beach parties. There's a playground for the kids. ⊠ 5 Jolly Roger Dr., ☎ 242/373–8456. ☉ Tues., Thurs., Sun. 8:30 AM–9 PM; Mon., Wed., Fri., Sat. 9–5:30.

Water World has a scenic, well-maintained 18 holes of miniature golf set among waterfalls and water holes, plus a restaurant and ice cream parlor. Planned enhancements include a 24-lane bowling alley, rollerblading rink, batting cages, and a pool room. ⊠ E. Sunrise Hwy. and Britannia Blvd., ☎ 242/373–2197. ☉ Daily 10 AM–11 PM.

Boating and Fishing

Charters

Private boat charters for up to four people cost $250–$460 for a half day and $350 and up for all day. Bahamian law limits the catching of game fish to six dolphinfish, kingfish, or wahoo per person per day.

Capt. Phil & Mel's Bonefishing Guide Services (⊠ McLean's Town, ☎ 242/353–3023, 242/353–3960 or 877/613–2454) provides a colorful and expert foray into the specialized world of bonefishing. Cost for a whole day (8 hours) for up to 2 people is $350, transportation included; half day is $250.

Reef Tours Ltd. (⊠ Port Lucaya Marketplace, ☎ 242/373–5880) offers sportfishing for four to six people on custom boats. Equipment and bait are provided free. All vessels are licensed, inspected, and insured. Trips run from 8:30 to 12:30 and from 1 to 5, weather permitting ($80 per angler, $45 per spectator). Full-day trips are also available, as are glass-bottom boat tours, snorkeling trips, and booze cruises. Reservations are essential.

Running Mon Marina (✉ Kelly Ct., Freeport, ☎ 242/352–6834) has daily half- and full-day deep-sea fishing charters and can arrange bonefishing excursions. Equipment is included, as is free transportation to and from all Freeport hotels. Half-day deep-sea fishing charters are $70 per person. Reservations are essential. Freezer storage for bait and catches is available.

Marinas

Lucayan Marina Village (✉ Midshipman Rd., Port Lucaya, ☎ 242/373–8888) offers complimentary ferry service to Port Lucaya; the marina has 150 slips accommodating boats up to 200 ft long, a fuel dock, pool, and bar.

Old Bahama Bay (✉ West End, ☎ 242/350–6500) has 72 slips to accommodate yachts up to 120 ft long, with plans to expand to 200 slips for vessels up to 175 ft long. Facilities include a customs and immigration office, fuel, showers, laundry, and electric, cable, and water hookups.

Port Lucaya Marina (✉ Port Lucaya Marketplace, ☎ 242/373–9090) offers a broad range of water sports and has 50 slips for vessels up to 125 ft long.

Running Mon Marina (✉ Kelly Ct., Freeport, ☎ 242/352–6834) has 70 slips for boats up to 130 ft. Marina facilities include port of entry, gas and diesel fuel service, boatyard and on-site mechanics, floating and fixed docks, a 40-ton travel lift (the only one on the island), water and power hookups, a marina store, a duty-free liquor store, charters, laundry facilities, showers, and rest rooms. The boatyard operates weekdays from 7 to 6 and Saturday from 7 to noon. The marina is open daily from 7 to 7.

Xanadu Marina and Beach Resort (✉ Sunken Treasure Dr., Freeport, ☎ 242/352–6783 Ext. 1333) has 400 ft of dockage and 77 slips and is an official port of entry.

Fitness Centers

Grand Bahama Fitness Centre (✉ E. Atlantic Dr. off E. Sunrise Hwy., Freeport, ☎ 242/352–7867) offers weight and cardio machines, aerobic and yoga classes, and a free nursery. Fee is $7 per day, $20 per week.

Olympic Fitness Center (✉ Coral Beach Hotel, Lucaya, ☎ 242/373–8181) has Universal machines, weights, and aerobic classes overlooking the hotel's pool. The fee is $5 per day, $15 per week.

Royal Oasis Golf Resort & Casino (✉ W. Sunrise Hwy., Freeport, ☎ 242/350–7000) has a fitness facility at its poolside spa. Hotel guests pay a once-per-stay fee of $5; nonguests pay $5 per day, $15 per week, or $30 per month.

Senses Spa. (✉ Our Lucaya, Lucaya, ☎ 242/350–5281) has state-of-the-art cardio and exercise equipment, including free weights, a spinning studio, and fitness classes. The fee is $10 for guests and $15 for nonguests per day.

Cricket

For a taste of true Bahamian sports, visit the **Lucaya Cricket Club** (✉ Baloa Rd., Lucaya, ☎ 242/373–1460). If you feel like joining in, go to training sessions on Tues., Thurs., or Sun. The clubhouse has a bar, gym, and changing rooms.

Golf

Because Grand Bahama is such a large island, it can afford long fairways puddled with lots of water and fraught with challenge. Four championship golf courses (two are at the Royal Oasis Golf Resort, two are at Our Lucaya) and one 9-hole course constitute a major attraction on the island. The Butch Harmon School of Golf at Our Lucaya is one of three of its kind in the world. There's also talk of a new course at West End's Old Bahama Bay, once home to 27 holes. The Reef Course at Our Lucaya hosts the Senior PGA Senior Slam in November. At Our Lucaya Lucayan Course, the Breitling Crystal Pro-Am takes place also in November. The Royal Oasis Golf Resort hosts the Bogey Bash Golf Tournament and the Nat Moore Invitational Golf Tournament. Plans are underway to renovate and reopen the island's old Shannon Golf Course, originally designed by renowned golf course architects Dick Wilson and Joe Lee. Note that prices tend to be lower in the off-season (mid-May–mid-December).

Fortune Hills Golf & Country Club is a 3,453-yard, 9-hole, par-36 course—a Dick Wilson and Joe Lee design—with a restaurant, bar, and pro shop. ⊠ *E. Sunrise Hwy., Lucaya,* ☎ *242/373–2222.* ⌨ *9 holes $48, 18 holes $65 (cart included). Club rental, 9 holes $12, 18 holes $17.*

★ **Our Lucaya Lucayan Course,** designed by Dick Wilson, is a dramatic 6,824-yard, par-72, 18-hole course. The 18th hole has a double lake and a dramatic Balancing Boulders feature. Home to Butch Harmon School of Golf, it also has the Arawak Dining Room, a cocktail lounge, and a pro shop. A shared electric cart is included in the rates. ⊠ *Our Lucaya, Lucaya,* ☎ *242/373–1066; 242/373–1333; 877/687–2474 for Butch Harmon golf school.* ⌨ *$120 for resort guests in season, $60 in off-season; $140 for nonguests in season; $80 in off-season. Clubs rental is $30.*

Our Lucaya Reef Course is a par-72, 6,920-yard course designed by Robert Trent Jones, Jr., with lots of water and a tricky dog-leg left on the 18th hole. ⊠ *Our Lucaya Resort, Lucaya,* ☎ *242/373–2002,* WEB *www.thelucayan.com.* ⌨ *$120 for resort guests in season, $60 in off-season; $140 for nonguests in season; $80 in off-season. Clubs rental is $30.*

Royal Oasis Golf Resort has two 18-hole, par-72 championship courses redesigned by the Fazio Design Group: the 7,000-yard Ruby, and the 6,679-yard Emerald. A pro shop is also available. ⊠ *W. Sunrise Hwy., Freeport,* ☎ *242/350–7000.* ⌨ *$95 for 18 holes, $65 for 9 (shared cart and club rentals included).*

Horseback Riding

Pinetree Stables runs trail and beach rides Tuesday–Sunday twice a day. All 2-hour trail rides are accompanied by an experienced guide. Rides for experienced equestrians are also available. Reservations are essential. ⊠ *Beachway Dr., Freeport,* ☎ *242/373–3600.* ⌨ *2-hr beach ride $65. Closed Mon.*

Parasailing

Paradise Watersports (⊠ Xanadu Beach, Freeport, ☎ 242/352–2887) has parasailing tow boats and offers five-minute flights for $40.

Reef Tours Ltd. (⊠ Port Lucaya Marketplace, ☎ 242/373–5880) will lift parasailers up to 300 ft. It's $40 per person. You can have your flight videotaped for an extra fee.

Scuba Diving

An extensive reef system runs along Little Bahama Bank's edge; sea gardens, caves, and colorful reefs rim the bank all the way from the West End to Freeport-Lucaya and beyond. The variety of dive sites suits everyone from the novice to the advanced diver. The island is home to UNEXSO, considered one of the finest diving schools and marine research facilities in the world. It has made shark diving synonymous with Grand Bahama Island.

Grand Bahama Island offers dive sites from 10 to 100-plus ft deep. **Sea Hunt** site is a shallow dive and is named for the *Sea Hunt* television show, portions of which were filmed here. **Ben's Blue Hole** is a horseshoe-shape ledge overlooking a blue hole in 40 to 60 ft of water. **Spid City** has an aircraft wreck, dramatic coral formations, blue parrotfish, and an occasional shark. You'll dive about 40 to 60 ft down. For more experienced divers, **Theo's Wreck,** a 228-ft cement hauler, was sunk in 1982 in 100 ft of water. **Pygmy Caves,** also for the more experienced, provides a formation of overgrown ledges that cut into the reef. One of Grand Bahama Island's signature dive sites, made famous by the UNEXSO dive operation, **Shark Junction** is a 45-ft dive where four- to six-ft reef sharks hang out, along with moray eels, stingrays, nurse sharks, and grouper. UNEXSO provides orientation and a shark feeding with its dives here.

Caribbean Divers (⊠ Bell Channel Inn, opposite Port Lucaya, ☎ 242/ 373–9111) offers guided tours, NAUI instruction, and equipment rental. A resort course allows you to use equipment in a pool and then in a closely supervised open dive for $79. A one-tank dive costs $32. Shark dives are $57. You get a discount for reserving in advance.

UNEXSO (Underwater Explorers Society) (⊠ Box F 2433, Port Lucaya Marketplace, ☎ 242/373–1244 or 800/992–3483), a world-renowned scuba-diving facility, provides rental equipment, 15 guides, seven boats, and NAUI, PADI, and SSI certification. When renovations are complete, it will include a diving pool with harbor views. Underwater cameras are available for rent, or you can have your dive videotaped. It offers a wide variety of dives for beginners and experienced divers, starting at $39. UNEXSO and its sister company, the Dolphin Experience, are known for their work with Atlantic bottle-nosed dolphins.

Xanadu Undersea Adventures (⊠ Xanadu Beach Resort, ☎ 242/352– 3811 or 800/327–8150) offers a resort course for $79, single dives for $37, shark dives for $72, and night dives for $52.

Snorkeling

Aside from dive shops, a number of tour operators offer snorkeling trips to nearby reefs.

East End Adventures (⊠ Freeport, ☎ 242/373–6662) takes you on a Blue Hole Snorkeling Safari that includes a 55-mi jeep ride and a powerboat jaunt. Guests dive for conch to prepare as part of a Bahamian-style barbecue. The daylong (8–5:30) excursion is $85 for adults, $35 for children.

Old Bahama Bay (⊠ West End, ☎ 242/350–6500) rents snorkel equipment and has mapped out a series of seven snorkeling trails to reefs and wrecks in waters 5–15 ft deep.

Paradise Cove (⊠ Deadman's Reef, ☎ 242/349–2677) allows you to snorkel right offshore at Deadman's Reef, a two-system reef with water ranging from very shallow to 35 ft deep. It's considered the island's best for snorkeling off the beach. Snorkel equipment rentals are available for $10 a day, $5 an hour extra for wet suits or flotation belts.

For $28 ($30 with food), a snorkel tour includes briefing, transportation, and equipment.

Paradise Watersports (✉ Xanadu Beach, ☎ 242/352–2887) offers a 90-minute Reef 'N' Wreck snorkeling cruise ($30), during which you'll explore coral reefs and a 40-ft wreck.

Pat & Diane Fantasia Tours (✉ Our Lucaya, ☎ 242/373–8681) takes snorkelers to a shallow reef three times a day on 2¼-hour cruises aboard a fun-boat catamaran with 30-ft wall climbing and slides into the water for $30.

UNEXSO (✉ Port Lucaya Marketplace, ☎ 242/373–1244 or 800/992–3483) sells video snorkeling adventures at $29 per adult, including video and equipment.

Tennis

The island has more than 50 courts, many lighted for night play.

Our Lucaya has four lighted courts: one each grass, artificial grass, clay, and hard. Racquet rental, lessons, and clinics available. ✉ *Our Lucaya,* ☎ *242/373–1333.* ⊡ *$10–$18 per hr per person, depending upon type of court.*

Royal Oasis Golf Resort & Casino has nine hard courts between the two resorts, five of which are lighted. ✉ *W. Sunrise Hwy., Freeport,* ☎ *242/ 352–6721 Ext. 6560.* ⊡ *$10 per hr for guests, $12 per hr for nonguests.*

Xanadu Beach Resort has three clay courts. ✉ *Sunken Treasure Dr., Freeport,* ☎ *242/352–6782.* ⊡ *Guests free, nonguests $5 per hr.*

Waterskiing

Paradise Watersports (✉ Xanadu Beach, Freeport, ☎ 242/352–2887) lets you ski roughly 1½ mi of waves for $20; a half-hour lesson is $40.

SHOPPING

In the hundreds of stores, shops, and boutiques in Freeport's International Bazaar and at the Port Lucaya Marketplace, you can find duty-free goods costing up to 40% less than what you might pay back home. At the numerous perfume shops, fragrances are often sold at a sweet-smelling 25% below U.S. prices. Be sure to limit your haggling to the straw markets.

Shops in Freeport and Lucaya are open Monday–Saturday from 9 or 10 to 6. Stores may stay open later in Port Lucaya.

Markets and Arcades

International Arcade (✉ between the International Bazaar and the Royal Oasis Casino, ☎ no phone) has a varied collection of shops, primarily branches of stores found at the adjacent International Bazaar, including Colombian Emeralds International, the Leather Shop, and Parfum de Paris.

International Bazaar (✉ W. Sunrise Hwy. and E. Mall Dr., ☎ 242/ 352–2828) carries imported goods, exotic items, and the island's largest selection of duty-free merchandise. A small straw market gathers on one side.

Port Lucaya Marketplace (✉ Sea Horse Dr., ☎ 242/373–8446) has about 80 boutiques and restaurants in 12 pastel-color buildings in a harborside setting. Local musicians often perform at the bandstand in the afternoons and evenings. Artisans sell paintings, carvings, and jewelry from kiosks.

Port Lucaya Straw Market (✉ Sea Horse Dr., ☎ no phone) is a collection of wooden stalls at the Port Lucaya complex's east and west ends. Vendors will expect you to bargain for straw goods, T-shirts, and souvenirs.

Specialty Shops

Antiques

Ye Olde Pirate Bottle House (✉ Port Lucaya Marketplace, ☎ 242/373–2000) is a well-stocked souvenir shop, and the adjoining museum, dedicated to the history of bottles, is worth the $3 admission. On display are 250 bottles, some dating from the 17th century.

Art

Bahamian Tings (✉ 15B Poplar Crescent St., Freeport, ☎ 242/352–9550) carries the fine art and crafts of Bahamians.

Barefoot in the Bahamas (✉ Crowne Plaza at Royal Oasis Golf Resort Lobby, ☎ 242/351–4226) sells Bahamian and Haitian art, fine crafts, jewelry, and beach wraps.

Bits of Paradise (✉ Port Lucaya, ☎ 242/373–9487) carries African and island art, wood carvings, batik, and common souvenirs.

Flovin Gallery (✉ International Bazaar and Port Lucaya, ☎ 242/352–7564 or 242/373–8388) has art that ranges from handicrafts to island works, seascapes, and other fine art.

Leo's Art Gallery (✉ Port Lucaya, ☎ 242/373–1758) showcases the Haitian-style paintings of local artist Leo Brown.

China and Crystal

Island Galleria (✉ International Bazaar and Port Lucaya Marketplace, ☎ 242/352–8194 or 242/373–8404) carries china and crystal by Waterford, Wedgwood, Aynsley, Swarovski, and Coalport, as well as Lladró figurines.

Cigars

Note: It's illegal to bring Cuban cigars into the United States.

Smoker's World (✉ International Bazaar, ☎ 242/351–6899) is a tiny shop that carries Cuban cigars exclusively.

Fashion

Animale (✉ International Arcade, ☎ 242/351–7197) is known for the wild appeal of its fine ladies' clothing and jewelry.

Bandolera (✉ Port Lucaya Marketplace, ☎ 242/373–7691) sells European-style women's fashions, bags, and jewelry.

Caribbean Cargo (✉ International Bazaar, ☎ 242/352–2929) has swimwear, beachwear, and sea-inspired jewelry.

Today's Men (✉ Port Lucaya Marketplace, ☎ 242/373–8912) carries Tommy Hilfiger fashions, belts, bags, and shoes.

Jewelry and Watches

The Colombian (✉ Port Lucaya Marketplace, ☎ 242/373–2974) purveys a line of Colombia's famed emeralds plus other jewelry and crystal.

Colombian Emeralds International (✉ International Bazaar, International Arcade, and Port Lucaya Marketplace, ☎ 242/352–5464, 242/352–7138, 242/373–8400, or 800/666–3889) is *the* place to find emeralds, diamonds, rubies, sapphires, and gold jewelry. The best brands in watches, including Tag Heuer, Breitling, and Omega, are also available here.

Leather Goods

Leather Shop (✉ International Bazaar, ☎ 242/352–5491 or 242/373–2323; ✉ Port Lucaya Marketplace, ☎ 242/352–5491 or 242/373–2323) sells HCL, Vitello, Land, and Fendi handbags, shoes, and briefcases.

Unusual Centre (✉ International Bazaar and Port Lucaya Marketplace, ☎ 242/352–3994) carries eel-skin leather, peacock-feather goods, hand-painted leather bags, and fine fashion jewelry.

Perfumes

Les Parisiens Perfumes (✉ International Bazaar, ☎ 242/352–5080) stocks Giorgio products and the latest French perfumes.

Oasis (✉ International Arcade, International Bazaar, and Port Lucaya Marketplace, ☎ 242/352–5923) is a complete drugstore with a selection of cosmetics and French perfumes.

Parfum de Paris (✉ International Arcade, International Bazaar, and Port Lucaya Marketplace, ☎ 242/352–8164 or 242/373–8403) offers the most comprehensive range of French fragrances on the island, including Lancome, Fendi, and Tommy.

Perfume Factory (✉ International Bazaar, ☎ 242/352–9391) sells a large variety of perfumes, lotions, and colognes by Fragrance of the Bahamas. Pink Pearl cologne actually contains conch pearls, and Sand cologne for men has a little island sand in each bottle. You can also create your own scent and brand name and register it.

Miscellaneous

Intercity Records (✉ International Bazaar and Port Lucaya Marketplace, ☎ 242/352–8820) is the place to buy records, tapes, and CDs of Junkanoo, reggae, and soca music.

Photo Specialist (✉ Port Lucaya Marketplace, ☎ 242/373–7858) repairs cameras and carries photo and video equipment.

UNEXSO Dive Shop (✉ UNEXSO, Port Lucaya Marketplace, ☎ 242/373–1244) sells everything water related, from swimsuits, marine animal T-shirts, dolphin jewelry, and sarongs to state-of-the-art dive equipment and computers.

GRAND BAHAMA ISLAND A TO Z

To research prices, get advice from other travelers, and book travel arrangements, visit www.fodors.com.

AIR TRAVEL

Several United States airlines fly to the Grand Bahama International Airport from cities on the east coast, including Atlanta, Chicago, New York City, Miami, and Fort Lauderdale. Interisland flights to and from Nassau and other destinations are also available.

CARRIERS

AirTran flies from Atlanta nonstop daily, with connections to major U.S. cities, and from Chicago Midway. American Eagle serves Freeport from Miami and Fort Lauderdale, with American Airlines connections from many U.S. cities. Bahamasair serves Grand Bahama International Airport with flights from Miami, as well as via Nassau. GulfStream Continental Connection operates flights from Fort Lauderdale, West Palm Beach, and Miami. US Airways provides daily nonstop service from LaGuardia airport in New York. Lynx Air International conducts flights from Fort Lauderdale every Thursday and Saturday. TNT Vacations provides nonstop service from Boston.

From Canada, Canada 3000 offers direct service from Toronto daily.

Grand Bahama Vacations packages Lakers Airlines airfare from 10 American cities with accommodations at 11 Grand Bahama Island resorts. Add-on ground and water tours are also available.

Major's Air Services offers interisland flights.

➤ AIRLINES AND CONTACTS: **AirTran** (☎ 800/247–8726). **American Eagle** (☎ 800/433–7300). **Bahamasair** (☎ 242/352–8341 or 800/222–4262). **Canada 3000** (☎ 877/359–2263). **GulfStream Continental Connection** (☎ 305/871–1200 or 800/231–0856). **Lynx Airlines** (☎ 888/596–9247). **Major's Air Services** (✉ Box F 41282, ☎ 242/352–5778, FAX 242/352–5788). **TNT Vacations** (☎ 800/498–5586). **US Airways** (☎ 800/428–4322).

AIRPORTS AND TRANSFERS

Grand Bahama International Airport is just off Grand Bahama Highway, about six minutes from downtown Freeport and about 10 minutes from Port Lucaya.

➤ AIRPORT INFORMATION: **Grand Bahama International Airport** (☎ 242/352–6020).

TRANSFERS

No bus service is available between the airport and hotels. Metered taxis meet all incoming flights. Rides cost about $7 for two to Freeport, $9 to Lucaya (it's half of that for a single passenger).

BIKE TRAVEL

By virtue of its flat terrain, broad avenues, and long, straight stretches of highway, Grand Bahama is perfect for bicycling. Wear sunblock, carry a bottle of water, and look left. Inexpensive bicycle rentals ($10–$15 a day) are available from some resorts. Royal Oasis Golf Resort, Old Bahama Bay, and Running Mon Resort have bikes for rent. Viva Fortuna allows guests free use of bicycles. For a biking nature tour along Grand Bahama's south shore, contact Kayak Nature Tours. The 5-hr off-road rides along hard-packed mountain bike trails take you through forest, over dunes, and to the beach for $69 per person.

➤ BIKE RENTALS: **Royal Oasis Golf Resort** (✉ W. Sunrise Hwy., ☎ 242/350–7000). **Kayak Nature Tours** (✉ Queen's Cove, ☎ 242/373–2485).

BOAT AND FERRY TRAVEL

Freeport and Lucaya are the ports of call for about 60 cruise ships a month, including Carnival Cruise Line, Discovery Cruises, and Disney Cruise Lines (☞ Cruise Travel *in* Smart Travel Tips A to Z, at the beginning of the book). Discovery Cruises provides daily ferry service from Fort Lauderdale.

Taxis meet all cruise ships. Two passengers are charged $8 and $10 for trips to Freeport and Lucaya, respectively. The price per person drops with larger groups.

BUS TRAVEL

Buses are an inexpensive way to travel the 4 mi between downtown Freeport and Port Lucaya Marketplace daily until about 10 PM. The fare is $1 for adults, 50¢ for children. Some resorts provide free shuttle service to shopping and beaches.

BUSINESS HOURS

BANKS

Banks are generally open Monday–Thursday 9:30–3 and Friday 9:30–5. Some of the major banks on the island include Bank of the Bahamas, Bank of Nova Scotia, Barclays Bank, and Royal Bank of Canada.

SHOPS

Shops are usually open Monday–Saturday 9 or 10 to 5 or 6. Straw markets, grocery stores, and drugstores are open on Sunday.

CAR RENTAL

If you plan to drive around the island, it's cheaper to rent a car than to hire a taxi. Automobiles, jeeps, and vans can be rented at the Grand Bahama International Airport. Cars run $65–$80 per day; gas is about $2.50 a gallon. Avis Rent-A-Car rents vehicles starting from around $85. Bahama Buggies, at Les Fountain's restaurant in Lucaya, rents bright pink and teal open jeeps starting at $50 for a 9–5 rental, $65 per day. Dollar Rent-A-Car and Thrifty rent cars beginning at $65. Hertz rentals start at $70. Some agencies provide free pickup and delivery service to Freeport and Lucaya resorts.

➤ MAJOR AGENCIES: **Avis Rent-A-Car** (☏ 242/352–7666; 888/897–8448 in the U.S.). **Dollar Rent-A-Car** (☏ 242/352–9325 or 800/800–4000). **Hertz** (☏ 242/352–3297 or 800/654–3131). **Thrifty** (☏ 242/352–9308 or 800/367–2277).

➤ LOCAL AGENCIES: **Bahama Buggies** (☏ 242/352–8750).

EMERGENCIES

Dial 911 to reach the police in case of an emergency. Ambulance service and the fire department have separate numbers.

➤ CONTACTS: **Ambulance** (☏ 242/352–2689 or 242/352–6735). **Bahamas Air Sea Rescue** (☏ 242/325–8864). **Fire Department** (☏ 242/352–8888 or 911). **Police** (☏ 911). **Rand Memorial Hospital** (✉ E. Atlantic Dr., ☏ 242/352–6735).

SIGHTSEEING TOURS

Tours can be booked through the tour desk in your hotel lobby, at tourist information booths, or by calling one of the tour operators listed below.

A three-hour sightseeing tour of the Freeport/Lucaya area costs $25–$35. Four-hour West End trips cost about $40. A glass-bottom-boat tour to offshore reefs starts at $20. For a trip to the Garden of the Groves, expect to pay about $30. A tour of Lucayan National Park runs about $40.

For evening entertainment, a dinner cruise will cost around $50, with a show. Sunset "booze cruises" run about $30 each, transportation included ($35 with show).

You can take a day trip to New Providence Island that includes round-trip air transportation, a sightseeing tour of Nassau, a visit to Paradise Island, and shopping on Bay Street. Such a package will cost about $225.

The following tour operators on Grand Bahama offer a combination of the tours described above, and several of them have desks in major hotels. (All mailing addresses are for Freeport.) Executive Tours does sightseeing land tours. H. Forbes Charter & Tours and Sun World Travel work through the major resorts to offer a great variety of land tours, trips to Nassau, nightlife, and other adventures. For on-the-water adventures, contact Reef Tours Ltd.

➤ FEES AND SCHEDULES: **Sunworld Travel & Tours** (✉ Box F 42631, Freeport, ☏ 242/352–3717). **Executive Tours** (✉ Box F 42509, Freeport, ☏ 242/373–7863). **Grand Bahama Vacations** (1170 Lee Wagner Blvd., Suite 200, Ft. Lauderdale, FL, 33315,, ☏ 800/422–7466 or 800/545–1300, WEB www.gbvac.com). **H. Forbes Charter & Tours** (✉ Box F 41315, Freeport, ☏ 242/352–9311). **Reef Tours Ltd.** (✉ Box F 42609, Freeport, ☏ 242/373–5880).

BOAT TOUR

If you don't want to go too far underwater, you'll appreciate an excursion on the Seaworld Explorer semisubmarine, which never fully submerges. Descend into the hull of the boat and observe sea life in air-conditioned comfort from a vantage point 5 ft below the surface. The vessel departs from Port Lucaya and travels to Treasure Reef daily at 9:30, 11:30, and 1:30. The two-hour voyage with transportation and snorkeling costs $39, $25 for children.

➤ CONTACT: **Seaworld Explorer** (✉ Port Lucaya Marina, Port Lucaya, ☎ 242/373–7863).

BREWERY TOUR

A one-hour tour sloshes through the Grand Bahama Brewing Company, the island's only microbrewery, fountainhead of Hammerhead beers, weekdays at 10, 12:30, and 4:40, and Saturday at 10:30 (call ahead on Saturday). Samplings of its four types of beer are available, and the $5 tour price can be credited toward a purchase.

➤ CONTACT: **Grand Bahama Brewing Company** (✉ Logwood Rd., Freeport, ☎ 242/351–5191).

ECO-TOURS

Land-and-sea East End Adventures' guided ecotours include a jeep ride along pristine beaches and through dense pine forests to the site of a now-gone early settlement, and a 6-mi boat trip to Sweeting's Cay and Lightbourne Cay, remote islands off Grand Bahama's eastern extreme. Snorkeling a blue hole, nature and bush medicine lessons, a short wilderness hike, and a home-cooked Bahamian lunch on the beach are all included in this truly worthwhile experience, which is run by native Bahamians. Trips cost $110 per person, begin at 8 AM, and last until 5:30 PM.

Kayak Nature Tours' eco-excursions explore pristine wilderness by kayak (of course), van, snorkel, and foot. The six-hour tour includes 1½ hours of kayaking through Grand Bahama's mangrove environment for a look at bird and marine habitats, a guided nature hike through Lucayan National Park and its caves, swimming on Gold Rock Beach, and lunch. A five-hour excursion combines kayaking and snorkeling at Peterson Cay. Native guides present their information in a most appealing fashion and are extremely knowledgeable about fauna and flora. Air-conditioned transport is provided to and from your hotel. A two-night kayak-camping tour to Water Cay off Grand Bahama's north shore is also available. The tour to Lucayan National Park and to Peterson Cay for snorkeling costs $69.

➤ CONTACTS: **East End Adventures** (✉ Freeport, ☎ 242/373–6662). **Kayak Nature Tours** (✉ Queen's Cove, Freeport, ☎ 242/373–2485, WEB www.bahamasvg.com/kayak.html).

SCOOTER TRAVEL

Grand Bahama's flat terrain and straight, well-paved roads make for good scooter riding. Rentals run about $50 a day (about $15 an hour). Helmets are required and provided. Look for small rental stands in parking lots and along the road in Freeport and Lucaya. Our Lucaya also has scooters for rent. Cruise-ship passengers can rent motor scooters in the Lucayan area.

➤ CONTACT: **Tower at Bahamia** (✉ W. Sunrise Hwy., ☎ 242/352–9661).

TAXIS

Taxi fares are fixed by the government (but generally you are charged a flat fee for routine trips, and these rates can vary slightly) at $3 for the first ¼ mi and 40¢ for each additional ¼ mi, regardless of whether the taxi is a regular-size cab, van, or stretch limo. Additional passengers over two are $3 each. Grand Bahama Taxi Union can provide service for visitors arriving by air. You will find taxis waiting outside the Royal Oasis Golf Resort & Casino and Our Lucaya.

➤ TAXI COMPANIES: **Grand Bahama Taxi Union** (✉ Grand Bahama International Airport, ☎ 242/352–7101).

VISITOR INFORMATION

Grand Bahama Island Tourism Board has its main office and a separate tourist information center at International Bazaar in Freeport. Branch offices are located at the Grand Bahama International Airport and at the southeast entrance to the Port Lucaya Marketplace. Ask about Bahamahosts, specially trained tour guides who will talk to you about island history and culture and pass on their knowledge of Bahamian folklore. Tourist offices are open weekdays 9–5; information centers, Monday–Saturday 9–5. The airport office is also open on Sunday.

➤ TOURIST INFORMATION: **Grand Bahama Island Tourism Board** (☎ 242/352–8044 or 800/448–3386, FAX 242/352–7840, WEB www. grand-bahama.com). **Freeport** (☎ 242/352–6909). **Grand Bahama International Airport** (☎ 242/352–2052). **Port Lucaya** (☎ 242/373–8988).

4 THE OUT ISLANDS

Once mostly the domain of private yacht and plane owners, the Out Islands—at least a dozen or so of them—are now equipped to handle travelers. Here you leave the sophisticated trappings of modern life behind for quiet beaches lined by the shimmering, translucent sea and narrow, winding lanes through tiny, New England–style fishermen's villages, where white clapboard cottages with brightly colored shutters are covered in wild hibiscus.

Updated by
Michael de
Zayas and
JoAnn
Milivojevic

T HE QUIET, SIMPLER WAY OF LIFE of the Bahama Out Islands, sometimes referred to as the Family Islands, is startlingly different from
Nassau's and Freeport's fast-paced glitz and glitter. Outside New
Providence and Grand Bahama, on the dozen or so islands that are
equipped to handle tourists, you leave the sophisticated nightclubs, casinos, and shopping malls behind. If you love the outdoors, however,
you'll be in fine shape: Virtually all the Out Islands have good to excellent fishing, boating, and diving, and you'll often have endless
stretches of beach all to yourself.

For the most part, you won't find hotels that provide the costly creature comforts taken for granted in Nassau and Freeport—with the exception of the Abaco Beach Resort & Boat Harbour in Marsh Harbour,
Abaco, and a megaresort currently under construction on Great Exuma.
Out Islands accommodations are generally modest lodges, rustic cottages, and small inns—many without telephones and TV (inquire when
making reservations if these are important to you). Making a phone
call, or receiving one, will often require a trip to the local BATELCO
(Bahamas Telecommunications Corporation) telephone station.

Along with the utter lack of stress on an Out Islands holiday, you'll
find largely unspoiled environments. Roughing it in Inagua, for example,
is a small price to pay for the glorious spectacle of 60,000 pink flamingos taking off into the sky. And a day of sightseeing can mean little
more than a stroll down narrow, sand-strewn streets in fishing villages,
past small, pastel-color homes where orange, pink, and bright-red
bougainvillea spill over the walls. Meals, even those served in hotels,
almost always incorporate local specialties, from conch and fresh-
caught fish to chicken with peas 'n' rice. Island taverns are tiny and
usually noisy with chatter, and you can make friends with locals over
a beer and a game of pool or darts much more quickly than you would
in the average stateside cocktail lounge. Nightlife may involve listening to a piano player or a small village rake 'n' scrape combo in a clubhouse bar, or joining the crowds at a local disco playing everything from
R&B to calypso.

The Out Islands were once mostly the purview of private plane and
yacht owners. The tourist who discovered a hideaway on Andros,
Eleuthera, or in the Exumas would cherish it and return year after year
to find the same faces as before. But the islands are now becoming more
and more popular, largely because of increased airline activity. Most
islands are served from Nassau or Florida daily. Others may only have
a couple of incoming and outgoing flights a week. If you want to sample an Out Island without feeling completely cut off, choose a slightly
busier spot that is closer to the mainland United States, such as Bimini,
Eleuthera, or Great Abaco Island. If you go farther away from the mainland, to a place like Cat Island or San Salvador, you'll feel much more
like you're getting away from it all.

Pleasures and Pastimes

Dining

For the most part, Out Islands hotels serve a combination of Bahamian, Continental, and American food. Restaurants are often family run and focus on home-style dishes. You'll notice that there is little
variety from one local dining spot to the next. It is each cook's special
flair that creates a loyal following. You'll find fish, especially grouper,
on almost every menu. The Bahamian specialty is boiled fish with tomatoes and spices. You usually can't go wrong with conch or lobster ei-

ther. Side dishes are generally peas 'n' rice, potato salad, and coleslaw—often all three in the same meal.

Because much of the food is imported, eating out in the Bahamas is expensive, even on the less developed islands. Entrées will run anywhere from $10 to $30 per person, and alcoholic beverages aren't cheap. A service charge of 15% is virtually always added to your bill. Lobster, which is found all over the islands, costs the same as an imported New York strip steak.

For general information, *see* Dining *in* Smart Travel Tips A to Z at the front of the book.

CATEGORY	COST*
$$$$	over $40
$$$	$30–$40
$$	$20–$30
$	$10–$20
¢	under $10

per person for a main course at dinner

Lodging

Small hotels on the Out Islands are mostly owner operated, which ensures a personal touch. Some accommodations use an honor-bar system—mix your own and sign for it—so you really feel at home. Many hotels specialize in fishing or diving and offer packages that may include airfare, lodging, meals, and a number of fishing or diving trips. There are also self-contained resorts, which have their own sports facilities. The Romora Bay hotel, an upscale hotel on Harbour Island, splurged on a small negative-edge pool (a buzz word for infinity pools), which seems to run right into the sea. Novel facilities like these are rare in the Out Islands. Find out if the hotel has any special packages. Also, if a hotel doesn't offer certain activities on its property—fishing, snorkeling, diving—it will most likely make such arrangements for you. Be sure to inquire when making reservations.

Although accommodations may be small and out of the way, don't expect your Out Islands vacation to be inexpensive. The islanders have to import almost everything. Produce and other goods coming by mail boat can arrive spoiled or broken. This means $7 hamburgers and gasoline at $3 per gallon—for residents and for you. A pack of cigarettes will run you more than $5. Still, it's hard to put a price on the total escape these resorts offer. What would you pay for a powdery pink beach that stretches for miles with no footprints but your own? Or water so clear that snorkeling makes you feel like you're flying? Or a seafood dinner netted the same day? You might not have an in-room phone, TV, or air-conditioning, but you may find that those conveniences aren't so important in paradise.

The Out Island Promotion Board can also help you find a house to rent. Properties of all sizes and prices are available, and monthly rentals can be as much as one-third less than combined weekly rates. Linens, cookware, and utilities are usually included. Sometimes a part-time cook, fishing or diving trips, and airport pickups are also part of the package.

The peak season is mid-December to mid-April. After that, room rates tend to drop by as much as a third. An 8% tax is added to your hotel bill, representing resort and government levies. Most hotels add a 15% gratuity for maid service, and a 3%–6% surcharge may be added to credit-card payments by some resorts. Ask about taxes, surcharges, and service charges when making your reservation. They can add more than 20% to your bill. An automatic 15% gratuity is usually added to most dining tabs.

For general information, *see* Lodging *in* Smart Travel Tips A to Z at the front of the book.

The prices below are based on high-season (winter) rates, generally in effect from December through March. Expect to pay between 15% and 30% less off-season at most resorts. In general, the best rates are available through packages, which almost every hotel offers. Call the hotel directly or ask your travel agent.

CATEGORY	COST*
$$$$	over $400
$$$	$300–$400
$$	$200–$300
$	$100–$200
¢	under $100

All prices are for a standard double room in high season, excluding 9% tax and 10%–15% service charge. Note that the government hotel tax doesn't apply to guest houses with fewer than four rooms.

THE ABACOS

The Abacos, a boomerang-shape cluster of cays in the northeastern Bahamas, stretch from tiny Walker's Cay in the north to Hole-in-the-Wall, more than 130 mi to the southwest. Many of these cays are very small, providing exquisitely desolate settings for private picnics. The Abacos have their fair share of lagoons, tranquil bays and inlets, and pine forests where wild boar roam, but they also are home to the Bahamas's third-largest community, the commercial center of Marsh Harbour, with all the amenities of a small town, including shops, restaurants, and hotels, and the largest marina in the Bahamas. The two main islands, Great Abaco and Little Abaco, are fringed on their windward shore by an emerald necklace of cays that forms a barrier reef against the broad Atlantic.

The Abacos's calm, naturally protected waters, long admired for their beauty, have helped the area become the Bahamas's sailing capital. The islands' resorts are particularly popular with yachting and fishing enthusiasts because of the fine boating facilities available, among them the Treasure Cay Marina, the Boat Harbour Marina at Marsh Harbour, Hopetown Marina, Sea Spray Marina on Elbow Cay, and Walker's Cay Club Marina. Man-O-War Cay remains the Bahamas's boatbuilding center; its residents turn out traditionally crafted wood dinghies as well as high-tech fiberglass craft. The Abacos play host annually to internationally famous regattas and to a half dozen game-fish tournaments. Outside the resorts, the oceanside villages of Hope Town and New Plymouth also appeal to tourists for their charming New England ambience.

The Abacos's first settlers, New England Loyalists, arrived in 1783. Other families soon followed from Virginia and the Carolinas, bringing with them their plantation lifestyle and slaves. These early arrivals tried to make a living from farming, but the Abacos's land was resistant to growing crops. Next, many settlers turned to the sea for sustenance. Some of them started fishing, whereas others took advantage of the occasional shipwreck.

At the end of the 18th century, Bahamian waters weren't charted, and lighthouses wouldn't be built in the area until 1836. The wreckers of the Abacos worked at night, shining misleading lights to lure ships to destruction onto rocks and shoals—and then seizing the ships' cargo. Of course, not all these wrecks were caused by unscrupulous islanders. Some ships were lost in storms and foundered on hidden reefs as they passed through the Bahamas. Nevertheless, by fair means or foul, wrecking remained a thriving industry in the Abacos until the mid-1800s.

The wreckers' notorious deeds have long faded into history and legend. Today, about 10,000 residents live peacefully in the Abacos. Many of these enterprising, friendly people are seafarers, earning an honest living as boatbuilders, fishermen, and fishing guides. Because the Abacos are one of the Out Islands' most visited destinations, an increasing number of residents work in the tourist industry.

Numbers in the margin correspond to points of interest on the Abacos map.

Great Abaco Island

❶ Most visitors to the Abacos make their first stop on Great Abaco Island's east coast at **Marsh Harbour,** the Bahamas's third-largest city and the Abacos's commercial center. Besides having its own airport, Marsh Harbour is considered by boaters to be one of the easiest harbors to enter. It has several full-service marinas, including the 180-slip Boat Harbour Marina and the 75-slip Conch Inn Marina.

Stock up on groceries and supplies here on the way to other islands. The downtown area has several well-equipped supermarkets and department and hardware stores. Most of the gift shops are on the main street, which has the island's only traffic light. There are also banks, gas stations, and a few good, moderately priced restaurants. For the ultimate in local fare, however, keep an eye out for "Rolling Kitchens," cars from which women sell island-style food. You might nab a huge plate of lamb, conch, pork chops, or other treats for about $5. The kitchens roll through Marsh Harbour and other downtown locations around lunchtime.

On a hilltop overlooking Marsh Harbour stands **Seaview Castle,** built by "Doctor" Evans Cottman (d. 1976), a high-school biology teacher from Madison, Indiana, who became the islands' official "unqualified practitioner" in the 1940s (i.e., he wasn't really a doctor, but he played one in the Bahamas). Cottman wrote of his experiences in a fascinating book, *Out Island Doctor.* The castle is not open to the public, but you can walk around its grounds.

❷ About 30 mi south of Marsh Harbour lies the small, eclectic artist's colony of **Little Harbour.** The centerpiece is **Pete Johnston's Foundry** (☎ 242/367–2720), out of which sculptor Johnston casts magnificent lifelike bronze figures using the age-old lost-wax method. Alas! As in all art, some days the muse is absent. Your visit could be enchanting or downright sleepy. No trip to Little Harbour would be complete without a stop at Gilligan's Islandesque **Pete's Pub** (☎ no phone), which has an Abacos-wide reputation for its laid-back attitude and decor.

About 20 mi south of Marsh Harbour is the little settlement of **Cherokee Sound** (population 165), whose inhabitants mostly make their living crawfishing. The deserted Atlantic beaches and serene salt marshes in this area are breathtaking.

❸ **Sandy Point,** a rustic fishing village with a lovely beach that attracts shell collectors, is slightly more than 50 mi southwest of Marsh Harbour. There are no communities to visit south of Sandy Point, but a major navigational lighthouse stands at **Hole-in-the-Wall,** on Great Abaco's southern tip. It's not open to visitors.

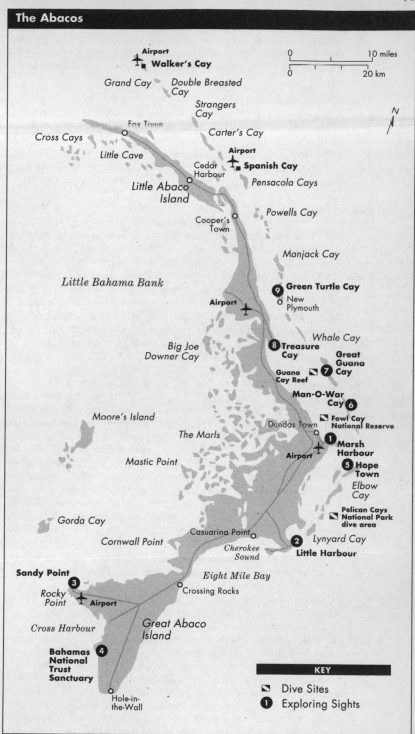

The Abacos

Airport
✈ ■ **Walker's Cay**

Grand Cay   *Double Breasted Cay*

Strangers Cay

Fox Town   *Carter's Cay*

Cross Cays

Little Cave

Airport
✈ ■ **Spanish Cay**

Cedar Harbour   *Pensacola Cays*

Little Abaco Island

Cooper's Town   *Powells Cay*

Manjack Cay

Little Bahama Bank

9 **Green Turtle Cay**
○ *New Plymouth*

Airport ✈

Whale Cay

Big Joe Downer Cay

8 **Treasure Cay**

Great Guana Cay **7**

Guana Cay Reef ◰

Man-O-War Cay
6

Moore's Island

◰ **Fowl Cay National Reserve**

The Marls   *Dundas Town* ○

1 **Marsh Harbour**

Airport ✈

Mastic Point

5 **Hope Town**

Elbow Cay

◰ **Pelican Cays National Park dive area**

Gorda Cay

Cornwall Point   *Casuarina Point*

Cherokee Sound

2 *Lynyard Cay*
Little Harbour

Sandy Point

Eight Mile Bay

3 *Crossing Rocks*

Rocky Point ✈ **Airport**

Cross Harbour   *Great Abaco Island*

Bahamas National Trust Sanctuary **4**

Hole-in-the-Wall

0 ──── 10 miles
0 ──── 20 km

N ↗

KEY	
◰	Dive Sites
1	Exploring Sights

④ A rugged winding road leads off the Great Abaco Highway, about 40 mi south of Marsh Harbour, passing through the dense pine woodlands of the **Bahamas National Trust Sanctuary** (☎ 242/393–1317), a reserve for the endangered Bahamian parrot. Your best chance of seeing that bird is at dawn. More than 100 other species have been sighted in this area.

Dining and Lodging

$–$$ ✕ **Bistro Mezzomare Waterfront Restaurant and Bar.** In the Conch Inn, this waterfront bistro serves breakfast, lunch, and dinner. Entrées include veal marsala, pollo Michelle (boneless chicken breast, breaded and topped with marinara sauce and melted mozzarella), and an array of pasta dishes, including the chef's special fettuccine with marinara sauce, grilled chicken, sun-dried tomatoes, and basil. ⊠ *Queen's Hwy., Marsh Harbour,* ☎ *242/367–4444. AE, MC, V.*

$–$$ ✕ **Flippers.** Coconut grouper and rack of lamb are the heavy hitters at this bistro, but definitely choose owner Marcia Albury's spicy baked mac 'n' cheese as your side dish. A loyal following turns out for the delicious soups, chowders, and curries. ⊠ *Memorial Plaza, Marsh Harbour,* ☎ *242/367–4657. AE, MC, V. No dinner Sun.*

$–$$ ✕ **Sapodilly's.** If the colorful bi-level patios don't grab your eye— Sapodilly's wooden beams are painted lime green, hot pink, and bright yellow—just follow your nose toward savory smells of this restaurant's flavorful dishes, which include conch fritters, a grilled fresh catch-of-the-day, and Marsh Harbour's best burger, topped with blue cheese, bacon, and mushrooms. There is live music Thursday through Saturday nights starting at 7 PM. ⊠ *Queen Elizabeth Dr., Marsh Harbour,* ☎ *242/367–3498. AE, MC, V. Closed Mon.*

$–$$ ✕ **Wally's.** Across the road from the water in a pink two-story build-
★ ing resembling a small mansion, this is one of the Bahamas's best-looking—and most popular—restaurants. Inside are Haitian-style paintings and white wicker chairs on terra-cotta tiles. The menu includes wild Abaco boar, and turtle sautéed in onions and mushrooms, as well as grilled wahoo, tuna, and duck breast—and key lime pie. ⊠ *E. Bay St., Marsh Harbour,* ☎ *242/367–2074. AE, D, MC, V. Closed Sun.–Mon.*

$–$$ ✕ **Jib Room.** Expect casual lunches of hot wings, conch burgers, fish nuggets, and nachos in this harbor-view restaurant and bar. The twice-weekly barbecue nights are especially popular; on Wednesday it's baby-back ribs and Sunday it's grilled steak, featuring New York strip. ⊠ *Pelican Shores, Marsh Harbour,* ☎ *242/367–2700. MC, V. Closed Tues.*

$ ✕ **George-the-Conch-Salad-Man.** Keep your ears pricked for distant megaphone warblings that are mostly unintelligible, save for the two key words: "conch salad." A colorful local character, George stations his pickup truck at the Marsh Harbour Marina and sells what he claims is the "world's-best-conch-salad." Odds are good you'll agree. ⊠ *Queen's Hwy., Marsh Harbour,* ☎ *no phone. No credit cards.*

$–$$$$ ✕🏨 **Abaco Beach Resort & Boat Harbour.** The spacious rooms have
★ natural-stone floors and antique-white wicker furnishings set against salmon or rich blue walls. Bold, artistic textiles, marble wet bars, built-in hair dryers, and in-room satellite TVs round out the accommodations. Dine on island-inspired international cuisine at Angler's Restaurant, which overlooks yachts moored at the Marina. The resort's full-service dive shop will arrange fishing charters and boat rentals. Lounge poolside and serve yourself at the swim-up pool bar or simply order your drinks from the attentive waitstaff that strolls among the sun worshipers. ⊠ *Box AB-20511, Marsh Harbour, Abaco,* ☎ *242/367–2158, 242/367–2736, or 800/468–4799,* FAX *242/367–2819,* WEB *www.greatabacobeach.com. 52 rooms, 6 villas. Restaurant, 2 bars,*

lounge, refrigerators, 2 pools, 2 tennis courts, dive shop, dock, wind-surfing, boating, fishing, mountain bikes, laundry facilities. AE, D, MC, V. FAP, MAP.

$ ▣ **Conch Inn Resort & Marina.** A low-key, one-level marina hotel, this is a good choice for budget travelers. Each simple room has two double beds, white-tile floors, white-rattan furniture, and color-splashed bedspreads. The full-service 75-slip marina is one of Marsh Harbour's busiest and is the Bahamas's headquarters for the Moorings yacht charter service. Small beaches are within walking distance. ✉ *Box AB-20469, Marsh Harbour, Abaco,* ☎ *242/367–4000,* FAX *242/367–4004,* WEB *www.go-abacos.com/conchinn. 10 rooms. Restaurant, bar, refrigerators, pool, dive shop, dock, marina, laundry facilities. MC, V.*

$ ▣ **Lofty Fig Villas.** Owned by the same family for years, this tiny, tidy compound has six spacious villas that overlook the sparkling pool or harbor; restaurants, marinas, bars, and a dive shop are nearby. The villa kitchens are fully equipped, and the supermarket is about a 10-minute walk away. For families or groups on a budget, this is a super option. ✉ *Across from Mangoes Restaurant (Box AB-20437, Marsh Harbour, Abaco),* ☎ FAX *242/367–2681. 6 villas. Air-conditioning, kitchenettes, pool. MC, V.*

$ ▣ **Nettie's Different of Abaco.** Two properties in one, this serene eco-
★ resort embraces the area's natural habitat, alive with wild boars, pea-cocks, herons, and flamingos. The airy, colonial-style rooms at the Seashell Beach Resort have wooden floors, vaulted open-beamed ceilings, and handcrafted furniture. The simpler Heritage Lodge is perched over a lake and has large airy rooms with screened porches. Nettie preserves Bahamian culture with a number of on-site exhibits, including a circa 1500 Lucayan village of 14 *caneyas* (thatched huts). Fishing and birding packages are most popular here. ✉ *Casuarina Point (Box AB-20092, Marsh Harbour, Abaco),* ☎ *242/366–2150 or 242/327–7921,* FAX *242/327–8152,* WEB *www.differentofabaco.com. 28 rooms. Restaurant, bar, some microwaves, refrigerators, lake, pool, outdoor hot tub, beach, snorkeling, boating, fishing, bicycles, billiards, laundry facilities; no room phones, no room TVs. MC, V. EP, FAP.*

Outdoor Activities and Sports

BICYCLING

Rental Wheels of Abaco (☎ 242/367–4643) has no-speed coaster-break style bicycles for $8 day or $30 per week, as well as Suzuki and Yamaha mopeds.

BOATING

Sailboats can be chartered by the week or longer, with or without crew. **Florida Yacht Charters** (☎ 242/367–4853 or 800/537–0050, WEB www.floridayacht.com), at the Boat Harbour Marina, offers air-conditioning and other amenities on its sailboats, power yachts, and catamarans. **The Moorings** (☎ 242/367–4000 or 800/535–7289, WEB www.moorings.com) is based at the Conch Inn Resort & Marina in Marsh Harbour.

In Marsh Harbour, **Boat Harbour Marina** (☎ 242/367–2158) has 180 fully protected slips and a slew of amenities. **Conch Inn Marina** (☎ 242/367–4000) has 75 slips and is the home of The Moorings charters. **Marsh Harbour Marina** (☎ 242/367–2700) has 60 slips.

Renting a boat to tour the Abacos is a must, especially if you're staying on the outer cays. Powerboats, from 18-ft Boston Whalers to 26-ft Paramounts, can be rented on a daily, three-day, or weekly basis. Daily rates run from $85 to $150, three-day rates from $225 to $375, and weekly rates from $440 to $850. Reserving your boat in advance is recommended, and remember that rates don't include fuel. In Marsh Harbor **Rich's Boat Rentals** (☎ 242/367–2742) is the place for 21- to

26-ft Paramount powerboats, all fully equipped for diving and fishing. Reserve at least a month in advance during high season. **Sea Horse Boat Rentals** (☎ 242/367–2513) has a variety of boats, from 26-ft Paramounts to 18-ft Boston Whalers. **Rainbow Rentals** (☎ 242/367–4602) has Twin-Vee catamarans complete with freshwater showers. Catamaran fans should contact **Laysue Rentals** (☎ 242/367–4414).

EVENTS

Several sporting events are held annually in the Abacos. The **Boat Harbour Billfish Championship** is held in June. July brings the weeklong **Regatta Time in Abaco,** a series of five races, accompanied by nightly parties and entertainment. To participate, write to Regatta Time in Abaco (✉ Box 428, Marsh Harbour, Abaco), or contact **David Ralph** (☎ 242/367–2677, FAX 242/367–3677). In September there's a spectator event titled the **All Abaco Regatta** (☎ 242/366–2198 or 242/367–2343), with native Bahamian sloops. For information about Abacos events, call Marsh Harbour's **Abaco Tourist Office** (☎ 242/367–3067). **Out Island Promotion Board** (☎ 877/736–7619 or 800/688–4752) has information on everything from special events to sports to art galleries.

FISHING

You can find bonefish in the flats, yellowtail on the reefs, or marlin in the deeps of the Abacos. The **Heritage Bonefishing Club** (☎ 242/366–2150) lures the fishing crowd to Casuarina Point at Different of Abaco—an angler's paradise. **Capt. Creswell Archer** (☎ 242/367–4000) will seek out marlin and bonefishing spots during a half day or full day of deep-sea fishing. **Pinder's Bone Fishing** (☎ 242/366–2163) offers year-round bonefishing on the Marls, a maze of mangroves and flats on the western side of Abaco.

SCUBA DIVING AND SNORKELING

There's excellent diving throughout the Abacos. Many sites are clustered around Marsh Harbour, including the reef behind **Guana Cay,** which is filled with little cavelike catacombs, and **Fowl Cay National Reserve,** which contains wide tunnels and a variety of fish.

Pelican Cays National Park is a popular dive and snorkeling area south of Marsh Harbour. This shallow, 25-ft dive is filled with sea life; turtles are often sighted, as are spotted eagle rays and tarpons. The park is a 2,000-acre land and marine park protected and maintained by the Bahamas National Trust. Hook up your own boat to one of the three moorings, or check with the local dive shops to see when trips to the park are scheduled. Snorkelers will want to visit Mermaid Beach, just off Pelican Shores Road in Marsh Harbour, where live reefs and green moray eels make for some of the Abacos's best snorkeling. **Dive Abaco** (☎ 242/367–2787 or 800/247–5338, WEB www.diveabaco.com) at the Conch Inn in Marsh Harbour, offers scuba and snorkeling trips on their custom dive boats. Sites explored include reefs, tunnels, caverns, and wreck dives. **Abaco Dive Centre** (☎ 242/367–4646 or 800/838–4189, WEB www.abacodive.com) is run by personable instructor Danny Holcomb, who offers courses ranging from basic snorkeling and reef and wreck dives to certified dive-master instruction. Signing is available for the hearing-impaired. **Rainbow Rentals** (☎ 242/367–4602) rents catamarans and snorkeling gear. **Sea Horse Boat Rentals** (☎ 242/367–2513) rents snorkeling gear.

TENNIS

Abaco Beach Resort (☎ 242/367–2158) opens its two courts to visitors.

WINDSURFING

Windsurfing is offered at the **Abaco Beach Resort** (☎ 242/367–2158).

Shopping

At Marsh Harbour's traffic light, look for the blue-and-white stripe awnings of **Abaco Treasures** (☎ 242/367–3460), purveyors of fine china, crystal, perfumes, and gifts.

Barefoot Gifts (✉ Queen's Hwy., Marsh Harbour, ☎ 242/367–3596) is your best bet for hats, sandals, tropical jewelry, and souvenir-sportswear.

Cultural Illusions (✉ Memorial Plaza, Marsh Harbour, ☎ 242/367–4648) sells memorable Bahamian creations—Androsia clothing and fabric, stained glass, and handmade keepsakes, such as wooden bowls crafted by local artisan Steven Knowles.

John Bull (✉ Queen's Hwy., Marsh Harbour, ☎ 242/367–2473), near the harbor, is a branch of a leading Nassau shop and sells watches and perfumes.

Johnston Studios Art Gallery (✉ Little Harbour, ☎ 242/367–2720), 45 minutes south of Marsh Harbor, displays original bronzes by the Johnstons, as well as prints and gifts.

Juliette Gallery (✉ Queen Elizabeth Dr., Marsh Harbour, ☎ 242/367–4551) showcases Bahamian art, sculpture, stained glass, and handmade furniture.

Little Switzerland (✉ Queen Elizabeth Dr., Marsh Harbour, ☎ 242/367–3191) sells watches, perfumes, and designer cosmetics. It's at the Abaco Beach Resort's entrance.

Elbow Cay

⑤ The charming village of **Hope Town,** where most of the families among its 300-some residents have lived for generations, lies southeast of Marsh Harbour on Elbow Cay. A ferry from Marsh Harbour arrives here several times a day. You'll find few cars and other pesky trappings of modern life here. In fact, most residents remember well the day the island first got telephone service—back in 1988. Before that, everyone called each other the way many still do here and in other Out Islands: by VHF, the party line for boaters.

This laid-back community enthusiastically welcomes visitors. Upon arrival you'll first see a much-photographed Bahamas landmark, a 120-ft-tall, peppermint-stripe lighthouse built in 1838. The light's construction was delayed for several years by acts of vandalism; then residents feared it would end their profitable wrecking practice. Today, the **Hope Town lighthouse** is one of the Bahamas's last three hand-turned, kerosene-fueled beacons. Weekdays 10–4 the lighthouse keeper will welcome you at the top for a superb view of the sea and the nearby cays.

For an interesting walking or bicycle tour of Hope Town, follow the two narrow lanes that circle the village and harbor. The saltbox cottages—painted in brilliant blues, purples, pinks, and yellows—with their white picket fences, flowering gardens, and porches and sills decorated with conch shells, will remind you of a New England seaside community—Bahamian style. You may want to stop at the **Wyannie Malone Historical Museum** (☎ no phone) on Queen's Highway, the main street. It contains Hope Town memorabilia and photographs. Admission is free, but hours vary. Many descendants of Mrs. Malone, who settled here with her children in 1875, still live on Elbow Cay.

Smack in the town's center stands an old, turquoise municipal building with offices clearly labeled "Commissioner," "Post Office," and

"Visitor Information." Forget about the first two—they've long since relocated—but Hope Town's Visitor Information "office" is a cement room with a few well-papered bulletin boards on which everything from current happenings to restaurant menus is posted. Poking around the building's ground floor, you'll also find the quirky and charming **Dolphin Exhibit,** where local schoolchildren and marine-life scholars have cooperatively posted the "Get to Know Your Local Dolphins" key, a dorsal-fin guide to a few favorites of the some 85 bottle-nosed dolphins residing in the Sea of Abaco.

There are several churches in this tiny town. On Sunday morning, you'll hear sermons floating through open windows. Don't be surprised if you come upon an alfresco Catholic service in the dockside park. Residents joke that the priest has to stand in the hot sun while the congregation enjoys the shade of sprawling trees "so he won't talk so long."

Dining and Lodging

$–$$$ ✕ **Club Soleil.** Overlooking the water at the Club Soleil Resort and Marina, this spacious, wood-beamed dining room serves up fresh seafood dishes, home-baked bread, and Bahamian peas 'n' rice. People come from all over for Club Soleil's Champagne Sunday Brunch. You should definitely make dinner reservations. Open for breakfast and dinner. ⊠ *Club Soleil Resort, Hope Town,* ☎ *242/366–0003. MC, V. Closed Mon. No dinner Sun. No lunch.*

$–$$$ ✕ **Hope Town Harbour Lodge.** Creamy lobster fettuccine is one of the lodge's most popular dishes, but grouper spring rolls with mustard-chutney sauce and sizzling fresh-fish fajitas are among the creative Bahamian-style dishes. After your meal, order a drink from the Wrackers Bar and mosey into the lounge, where good local art, checkers, backgammon, and a collection of magazines await. Lunch is served at the Reef Bar and Grill, overlooking the ocean. Sunday brunch is also offered. ⊠ *Upper Rd., Hope Town,* ☎ *242/366–0095. Reservations essential. MC, V. No dinner Mon.*

$–$$$ ✕ **Harbour's Edge.** Hope Town's premier hangout, this bar-restaurant has the island's only pool table. Live bands occasionally play on weekends. Try tender conch burgers, grilled grouper, or lobster salad for lunch and dinner. Authentic Bahamian breakfasts are served on Sunday. Rent bikes here for $8 a day. ⊠ *Lower Rd., Hope Town,* ☎ *242/366–0292. MC, V. Closed Tues.*

$$ ✕ **Rudy's Place.** In a renovated house, Rudy's is a favorite. Rave reviews go to the crawfish baked with Parmesan cheese. Complimentary pickup is available from most anywhere on the island; call ahead to make arrangements. ⊠ *Center Line Rd., Hope Town,* ☎ *242/366–0062. MC, V. Closed Sun.*

$–$ ✕ **Cap'n Jack's.** There are a handful of booths and a small bar, but most of this casual eatery's seating is out on the dock-patio under the large pink-and-white stripe awning. The menu has everything from mac 'n' cheese to turtle burgers to pork chops. Cap'n Jack's serves three meals a day and has live music Wednesday and Friday nights mid-December through August. ⊠ *Hope Town,* ☎ *242/366–0247. MC, V.*

$$$ ⬚ **Turtle Hill Vacation Villas.** Bougainvillea- and hibiscus-lined walkways encircle the central swimming pool of this cluster of four two-bedroom villas, each with its own private patio. Inside, villas have light-wood paneling, tile floors, and rattan furnishings, as well as sleeper sofas. The lovely beach is a two-minute walk away, and each villa comes with a golf cart for jaunts into town. Choose an upper villa for distant views of the sea. ⊠ *Off Queens Hwy. between Hope Town and White Sound, Hope Town,* ☎ *508/540–2519 or 800/339–2124,* ☎ FAX *242/366–0557,* WEB *www.turtlehill.com. 4 villas. Air-conditioning, fans, kitchenettes, microwaves, in-room VCRs, pool. AE, D, MC, V.*

$–$$$ ⊡ **Elbow Cay Properties.** Besides being the most cost-efficient way to stay on Elbow Cay, a private house or villa for a week or more is also likely to be the most comfortable. Many of the rental properties are on the water, with a dock or a sandy beach right out front. Owners Jane Patterson and Carrie Cash will find you a place to match your wishes and budget. They can also arrange boat and bike rentals and set you up with a golf cart—perfect for negotiating Hope Town's very narrow lanes. ⊠ *Western Harborfront, Hope Town,* ☎ FAX *242/366–0035. 34 houses and villas. No credit cards.*

$$ ⊡ **Hope Town Hideaways.** If you seek seclusion, this is an excellent choice,
★ as the only way to get to this collection of rental homes is by boat. The property's 11-acre grounds are planted with wild orchids and other exotic flowers. The modern villas have airy cathedral ceilings; large, well-stocked kitchens; and French doors opening onto decks with harbor views. The patio area in front of the villas has a grill for guests' use and a freshwater pool. Restaurants are just minutes away by boat. The Hideaways will provide you with a dinghy for traversing the harbor. ⊠ *1 Purple Porpoise Pl., Hope Town,* ☎ *242/366–0224,* FAX *242/366–0434,* WEB *www.hopetown.com. 4 villas, 1 1-bedroom cottage. Air-conditioning, fans, kitchenettes, in-room VCRs, pool, dock, marina. AE, MC, V.*

$–$$ ⊡ **Abaco Inn.** Upscale singles and couples favor this beachfront resort. The cozy cottages—seven ocean- and seven harbor-view—have simple, comfortable furnishings and individual hammocks. The luxury villa suites have both sunrise and sunset water views. After your complimentary pickup in Hope Town, consider renting your own boat so you can zoom into town or to one of the smaller islets around Elbow Cay. You can tie up at the resort. Excellent reefs for snorkeling and diving are nearby. The lounge has a satellite TV and live music several nights a week. ⊠ *2 mi south of Hope Town,* ☎ *242/366–0133 or 800/468–8799,* FAX *242/366–0113,* WEB *www.oii.net/AbacoInn. 14 cottages, 8 villa suites. Restaurant, bar, lounge, pool, beach, boating, fishing, bicycles, laundry facilities, airport shuttle; no room phones, no room TVs. AE, D, MC, V. EP, MAP.*

$–$$ ⊡ **Sea Spray Resort and Villas.** Consider this resort if you're planning to catch any waves in Hope Town, as the villas are just off Garbanzo Beach, a favorite with surfers. The villas have full kitchens, outdoor grills, and decks. Each is spacious and clean. Sunfish sailboats are available at no cost, and you can rent motorboats, bikes, and snorkeling gear. The on-site store sells everything from charcoal to surfboard wax. There's also a 60-slip full-service marina, a tiki bar, and a gourmet restaurant, where Grouper Royale is the signature dish. ⊠ *South end of White Sound,* ☎ *242/366–0065,* FAX *242/366–0383,* WEB *www.seasprayresort.com. 7 villas. Restaurant, bar, air-conditioning, kitchenettes, pool, dock, snorkeling, surfing, boating, marina, fishing, bicycles. MC, V. EP, MAP.*

$ ⊡ **Club Soleil Resort and Marina.** Nestled in a grove of coconut palms, bougainvillea, and hibiscus, this Spanish-style resort is just across the harbor from Hope Town and a short walk from secluded beaches on Elbow Cay's ocean side. The modern rooms have cedar closets, tile floors, and private balconies. Using local driftwood and other beach finds, the owner has created tasteful works of art for each room. The pool is steps from **Club Soleil,** where windows overlooking the water give you the feeling of being on a ship. The hosts can arrange boat rentals, diving, fishing, sailing, or touring. ⊠ *Hope Town,* ☎ *242/366–0003,* FAX *242/366–0254,* WEB *www.hopetownmarina.com. 6 rooms. Bar, dining room, in-room VCRs, pool, dock, marina; no room phones. MC, V. EP.*

Outdoor Activities and Sports
BOATING

Sail Abaco (☎ 242/366–0172) offers half- or full-day captained charters on catamaran yachts. **Nalu Charters** (☎ 242/366–0224) offers snorkeling, island hopping, sunset cruises, and island picnics aboard Captain Ron Engle's 50-ft Nalu catamaran. **Club Soleil** (☎ 242/366–0003) has 14 slips. **Sea Spray Resort** (☎ 242/366–0065) has a full-service marina with 60 slips. **Hope Town Hideaways** (☎ 242/366–0224) has 12 slips. **Island Marine** (☎ 242/366–0282) has 17- to 22-ft boats available for rent from $80 to $105 a day. **Sea Horse Boat Rentals** (☎ 242/367–2513) has Bimini-top boats from 18-ft Privateers to 22-ft Boston Whalers at its Hope Town location. **Dave's Dive Shop and Boat Rentals** (☎ 242/366–0029) will deliver your boat to your accommodations.

FISHING

Seagull Charters (☎ 242/366–0266) sets up guided deep-sea excursions with Captain Robert Lowe, who has more than 30 years' experience in the local waters. **Wild Pigeon Charters** (☎ 242/366–0461) offers bonefishing, reef fishing, and bottom fishing with Abaco bonefishing champion "Bonefish Dundee."

SCUBA DIVING AND SNORKELING

Dave's Dive Shop and Boat Rentals (☎ 242/366–0029) offers two-tank dives for $65 and resort dives for beginners. It also rents gear to snorkelers heading out for Sandy Cay. **Froggies Out Island Adventures** (☎ 242/366–0431) has snorkel and dive trips, scuba and resort courses, full-day adventure tours, and dolphin encounters.

WINDSURFING

Sea Spray Resort (☎ 242/366–0065) attracts windsurfers to the choice waters just off Garbanzo Beach.

Shopping

Ebbtide (☎ 242/366–0088) is on the upper path road in a renovated Loyalist home. Come here for such Bahamian gifts as batik clothes, original artwork, and nautical jewelry. Browse through the good Bahamian book collection or pick up a magazine.

Fantasy Boutique (✉ Queen's Hwy., ☎ 242/366–0537) has a nice selection of souvenirs, beach wraps, T-shirts, arts and crafts, and Cuban cigars.

Island Gallery (✉ Queen's Hwy., ☎ 242/366–0354) is the only shop in Hope Town that carries the lovely Abaco ceramics handmade in Treasure Cay. It also sells wind chimes, sandals, resort wear, jewelry, and island music.

Man-O-War Cay

❻ Many residents of **Man-O-War Cay** are descendants of early Loyalist settlers named Albury, who started the tradition of handcrafting boats more than two centuries ago. They remain proud of their heritage and continue to build fiberglass boats today. This shipwrighting center of the Abacos lies south of Green Turtle and Great Guana cays, an easy 45-minute ride from Marsh Harbour by water taxi or aboard a small rented outboard dinghy. Man-O-War Cay also has a 26-slip marina.

A mile north of the island, you can dive to the wreck of the U.S.S. *Adirondack,* which sank after hitting a reef in 1862. It lies among a host of cannons in 20 ft of water. The cay is also a marvelous place to walk. Two main roads, Queen's Highway and Sea Road, are often shaded with arching sea grape trees interspersed with palms and pines. The island is secluded, but it has kept up-to-date with satellite television and full phone service. There are three churches and a one-room schoolhouse. No liquor is sold here, but you're welcome to bring your own. Restaurants post their daily specials on "The Pole" in the town's center.

Dining and Lodging

$-$$ ✕ **Man-O-War Marina Pavillion.** Try the grouper fingers here or, if it's Friday or Saturday, the barbecue steak, chicken, or ribs. ⊠ *Waterfront,* ☎ *242/365–6185. No credit cards. Closed Sun.*

$-$ ✕ **Ena's Place.** Stop in at this tiny spot when you want great conch burgers and coconut or pumpkin pie. ⊠ *Waterfront,* ☎ *242/365– 6187. No credit cards. Closed Sun.*

$$ ⛏ **Schooner's Landing.** Perched on a rocky promontory overlooking a long, isolated beach, this small, Mediterranean-style resort has five two-bedroom town-house condos. Rooms are airy with wicker furniture and ceramic tile floors. There's no restaurant, but within walking distance is almost every establishment, eating or otherwise, on the cay. There's a barbecue and wet bar in the gazebo, and nearby grocery stores deliver. There's no alcohol sold on island, so bring your own. ⊠ *Man-O-War Cay, Abaco,* ☎ *242/365–6072,* FAX *242/365–6285,* WEB *schoonerslanding.com. 5 condominiums. Air-conditioning, in-room VCRs, beach, pool boating, fishing, laundry service. AE, MC, V.*

Outdoor Activities and Sports

BOATING

Man-O-War Marina (☎ 242/365–6008) has 26 slips.

SCUBA DIVING

Man-O-War Dive Shop (⊠ Man-O-War Marina, ☎ 242/365–6013) organizes trips and rents tanks.

Shopping

Albury's Sail Shop (☎ 242/365–6014) is popular with boaters, who stock up on colorful canvas duffle bags, briefcases, jackets, hats, and purses.

Caribbean Closet (☎ 242/365–6384) sells clothing and resort wear.

Island Treasures (☎ 242/365–6072) has a wide selection of T-shirts, souvenirs, and Abaco-made ceramics.

Great Guana Cay

★ ❼ Arriving by private boat rental or ferry from Marsh Harbour, you'll be welcomed to **Great Guana Cay,** a narrow island off Marsh Harbour, by a hand-lettered sign that claims IT'S BETTER IN THE BAHAMAS, BUT . . . IT'S GOODER IN GUANA. If you love beautiful empty beaches and grassy dunes, you'll agree. Great Guana Cay is 7 mi long and has only 100 residents. Roosters' cries are about the loudest sound you'll hear in the drowsy village, and cars are absent from the narrow palm-lined roads that are bordered by clapboard cottages with picket fences.

Dining and Lodging

$-$$$ ✕ **Nipper's Beach Bar & Grill.** With awesome ocean views and a snorkeling reef just 10 yards offshore, this set of brightly striped, split-level gazebos is Great Guana Cay's party-hearty spot. There is a solar-heated double pool, one for children and one with a swim-up pool bar for adults. Lunch is mostly burgers and sandwiches. The Sunday night boar roasts and Wednesday night bonfires and fireworks on the beach are not to be missed. Nurse a "Nipper Tripper"—a concoction of five rums and two juices. ⊠ *Great Guana Cay,* ☎ 242/365–5143. AE, D, MC, V.

$-$$ ✕⛏ **Dolphin Beach Resort.** Upscale and pocket-size, this haven has cozy ★ cottages and a two-story wood-frame main building handcrafted of Abaco pine by Guana Cay shipwrights. Three cottages have two stories with private oceanfront decks—ideal for several couples or families. Each cottage is individually furnished and includes modern kitchen appliances. Outside, secluded showers are surrounded by bougainvillea and sea-grape trees. Boardwalk nature trails winding through the carefully tended 15-acre property lead to uninhabited Guana Cay Beach. ✉ *Great Guana Cay, 800/222–2646 or* ☎ ⨳ *242/365–5137,* ⓌⒺⒷ *www.dolphinbeachresort.com. 7 cottages, 4 rooms. Restaurant, airconditioning, kitchenettes, pool, beach, dive shop, dock, snorkeling, windsurfing, boating, bicycles, shops. AE, MC, V. EP, FAP.*

Treasure Cay

★ ❽ Running through large pine forests that are still home to wild horses and boars, the wide, paved Sherben A. Boothe Highway leads north from Marsh Harbour for 20 mi to **Treasure Cay,** which is technically not an island but a large peninsula connected to Great Abaco by a narrow spit of land. Here you'll find a small community of mostly winter residents, a 3,000-acre farm that grows winter vegetables and fruit for export, and a spectacular 3½-mi-long beach.

Treasure Cay is a large-scale real-estate development project. The centerpiece is the Treasure Cay Hotel Resort and Marina, with its Dick Wilson–designed golf course and 150-slip marina. Unlike the rest of the Abacos, Treasure Cay lacks any sense of history or community. Those seeking local color and an authentic Bahamian experience will find Treasure Cay rather sterile. Fortunately, historic Elbow Cay, Man-O-War Cay, and Green Turtle Cay are all easily accessible by boat.

Treasure Cay's commercial center consists of two rows of shops near the resort with a post office, Laundromat, ice-cream parlor, a couple of grocery stores, and the BATELCO. You'll also find car-, scooter-, or bicycle-rental offices here.

Dining and Lodging

$–$$ ✕ **Touch of Class.** Ten minutes north of Treasure Cay, this favorite serves delicious Bahamian cuisine. Call about the free shuttle bus. ✉ *Queen's Hwy. at Treasure Cay Rd.,* ☎ *242/365–8195. No credit cards.*

$–$ ✕ **Café La Florence.** Stop into this bakery/café for coffee and a cinnamon roll or a slice of quiche. Florence's ice-cream parlor next door is your answer for treats à la mode. ✉ *Treasure Cay,* ☎ *242/367–2570. No credit cards. Closed Sun.*

$–$$$ ✕🏠 **Treasure Cay Hotel Resort and Marina.** Hotel room and town house–style accommodations form a long pastel row facing the resort's 150-slip marina. Rooms come in various configurations, some with minirefrigerators, microwaves, and small dining counters. The bi-level suites have vaulted ceilings, pine headboards and armoires, and full modern kitchens; loft bedrooms have large master baths. The restaurant will prepare the day's fresh catch to order (try it Cajun-style "blackened"). The resort has the Out Islands' only 18-hole championship golf course, rated by *Golf Digest* as the Bahamas's number-one golf course. ✉ *On marina (2301 S. Federal Hwy., Fort Lauderdale, FL 33316),* ☎ *242/365–8535; 954/525–7711; 800/327–1584 for reservations,* ⨳ *954/525–1699,* ⓌⒺⒷ *www.treasurecay.com. 62 rooms, 33 suites, 7 villas. Restaurant, 2 bars, lounge, dining room, air-conditioning, kitchenettes, pool, 18-hole golf course, 4 tennis courts, beach, dive shop, dock, snorkeling, windsurfing, boating, marina, fishing, babysitting. AE, MC, V. FAP, MAP.*

$$–$$$ 🏠 **Treasure Houses.** Around a courtyard of interconnected swimming pools, footbridges, and burbling waterfalls, seven octagon-shape houses perch on stilts for lovely beach views. Each two-bedroom guest house has airy, exposed-beam ceilings, plush carpeting, rattan and bamboo furniture, and muted tropical-print textiles. Bedrooms open onto narrow private patios. Queen-size sleeper sofas, and fully equipped kitchens are standard. Rent a golf cart or ride one of the gratis bicycles that accompany each unit. The Treasure Houses, part of Treasure Cay Hotel Resort and Marina, are 1 mi from the main resort and stores. ⊠ *On marina (2301 S. Federal Hwy., Fort Lauderdale, FL 33316),* ☎ *242/365–8535; 954/525–7711; 800/327–1584 for reservations,* FAX *954/525–1699,* WEB *www.treasurecay.com. 7 2-bedroom houses. Air-conditioning, kitchenettes, pool, beach, snorkeling, bicycles, laundry facilities. AE, MC, V. EP, MAP.*

$–$$ ⊞ **Banyan Beach Club.** Directly on Treasure Cay's breathtaking beach, these one-, two-, and three-bedroom Mediterranean-style condos are attractive and well situated. Units have high, whitewashed-beam ceilings, terra-cotta tile floors, and vast ocean views from private balconies or patios. Handsome pine furnishings and full-size modern kitchens round out the digs. The resort's Tiki Bar is the scene for weekly cocktail parties. On-site golf carts can be rented for exploring the cay. ⊠ *¼ mi from village of Treasure Cay (Box AB-22158),* ☎ *242/365–8111 or 888/625–3060,* FAX *561/625–5301,* WEB *www.banyanbeach.com. 21 condos. Bar, air-conditioning, kitchenettes, pool, wading pool, beach, snorkeling. MC, V.*

Outdoor Activities and Sports

BICYCLING

Wendell's Bicycle Rentals (☎ 242/365–8687) rents bikes for $5 per half day, $7 per day, $42 per week.

BOATING

Rich's Rental (☎ 242/365–8582) rents boats by the day, three days, or week. Daily rents are $120 for 21-ft Paramounts, $140 for 24-ft, and $150 for the 27-ft. You can also rent snorkel gear for $8 per set. **J. I. C. Boat Rentals** (☎ 242/365–8465) rents 24- to 26-ft Anglers from $150 to $170 a day; three-day and weekly rates are also available. Try to reserve your boat at least two to three weeks in advance. **Sidney Hart Sightseeing** (☎ 242/365–8572) offers shelling trips, fishing, and beach picnics—accompanied by a great selection of Bahamian music aboard Sidney's sleek 24-ft boat, the *Big H*. Call ahead for reservations and rates.

EVENTS

The Treasure Cay leg of the **Bahamas Billfish Championship** is held in May, as is the annual **Treasure Cay International Billfish Tournament.** The **CABO Sportfishers Challenge** takes place in June. Call **Treasure Cay Services** (☎ 954/525–7711 or 800/327–1584) for information.

FISHING

Arrange for local deep-sea fishing or bonefishing guides through **Treasure Cay Hotel Resort and Marina** (☎ 242/365–8250).

GOLF

★ A half mile from the **Treasure Cay Hotel Resort and Marina** (☎ 242/365–8535) is the property's par-72, Dick Wilson–designed course, with carts available. There's no need to reserve tee times. A driving range, putting green, and small pro shop are also on-site.

SCUBA DIVING AND SNORKELING

No Name Cay and Whale Cay are popular marine-life sites. The 1865 wreck of the steamship freighter *San Jacinto* also affords scenic diving and chances to feed the resident green moray eel. **Divers Down** (☎ 242/365–8465) rents equipment and takes divers and snorkelers out to a variety of sites. **Rich's Rentals** (☎ 242/365–8582) offers dive trips and a $55 "Snorkel Island" trip, which includes reef snorkeling and a beach cookout.

TENNIS
Treasure Cay Hotel Resort and Marina (☎ 242/365–8535) has six of the best courts in the Abacos, and four are lighted for night play. Fees are $14 per hour for the hard courts and $16 per hour for the clay courts; rackets rent for $4.

WINDSURFING
Windsurfers and a complete line of nonmotorized water craft are available for rent at the **Treasure Cay Hotel Resort and Marina** (☎ 242/365–8250).

Shopping
Adjacent to Treasure Cay resort is **Abaco Ceramics** (☎ 242/365–8489), which offers its signature white clay pottery with blue fish designs. Closed Sat. and Sun.

Green Turtle Cay

❾ A 10-minute ferry ride from a Treasure Cay dock will take you to **Green Turtle Cay.** The tiny island is steeped in Loyalist history and is surrounded by several deep bays, sounds, and a nearly continuous strip of fine ocean beach. An easy way to explore the entire island is by golf cart or small outboard dinghy or Boston Whaler, which can be rented by the hour or the day at most resorts and marinas. Golf carts are essential for getting around Green Turtle Cay and should be reserved well in advance during high season and holiday travel times. Hotels can arrange rentals on request.

New Plymouth, first settled in 1783, is Green Turtle's main community. Most of its approximately 550 residents eke out a living by diving for conch or exporting lobster and fish through the Abaco Seafood Company. Narrow streets flanked by wild-growing flora (such as amaryllis, hibiscus, and poinciana) wind between rows of New England–style white-clapboard cottages with brightly colored shutters. During the Civil War, New Plymouth provided a safe haven for Confederate blockade runners. One Union ship, the U.S.S. *Adirondack,* was pursuing a gunrunner and wrecked on a reef in 1862 at nearby Man-O-War Cay. One of the ship's cannons now sits at the town harbor.

If your accommodations aren't in New Plymouth proper, you'll need transportation into town. Many hotels provide an occasional shuttle, and there is one taxi on the island, but most people travel via golf cart or rental boat.

New Plymouth's most frequently visited attraction is the **Albert Lowe Museum,** on the main thoroughfare, Parliament Street. The Bahamas's oldest historical museum, it's dedicated to a model-ship builder and direct descendant of the island's original European-American settlers. You can learn island history through local memorabilia from the 1700s, Lowe's model schooners, and old photographs, including one of the aftermath of the 1932 hurricane that nearly flattened New Plymouth. Schooners Gallery, in the Lowe Museum's basement, displays paintings by acclaimed artist Alton Lowe, Albert's son. If you are fortunate to drop by on the same day as Mr. Noel Roberts, a survivor of the '32 hurricane and seaman in the days of wooden schooners, he will delight you with his stories of the Bahamas and Green Turtle Cay. ⊠ *Parliament St.,* ☎ *242/365–4094.* ▣ *$3.* ☺ *Mon.–Sat. 9–11:45 and 1–4.*

Just a few blocks from the Albert Lowe Museum, on Victoria Street, is **Miss Emily's Blue Bee Bar** (☎ 242/365–4181), which stands next to the old gaol (jail). Mrs. Emily Cooper, creator of the popular drink Goombay Smash, passed away in 1997, but her daughter Violet continues to serve up the famous rum, pineapple juice, and apricot brandy concoction. Mementos of customers—business cards, expired credit cards, T-shirts—and Junkanoo masks cover the walls.

The past is present in the **Memorial Sculpture Garden,** across the street from the New Plymouth Inn. Note that it is laid out in the pattern of the British flag. Immortalized in busts perched on pedestals are local residents who have made important contributions to the Bahamas. Plaques detail the accomplishments of British Loyalists, who came to the Abacos from New England and the Carolinas; their descendants; and the descendants of those brought as slaves, such as Jeanne I. Thompson, a contemporary playwright and the country's second woman to practice law.

Dining and Lodging

$-$ ✕ **Laura's Kitchen.** A simple, two-room eatery, Laura's is ideal for an inexpensive lunch or dinner. Complimentary transportation is provided to and from your hotel. Call by 5 PM to arrange it. Final score: ambience 2, conch burger 10. There is a 4% surcharge for credit cards. ⊠ *Across from Shellhut, on King St.,* ☎ 242/365–4287. *MC, V.*

$-$ ✕ **The Wrecking Tree.** The casual restaurant's wooden deck was built around the wrecking tree, a place where 19th-century wrecking vessels brought their salvage. Come for hearty breakfasts or lunches of cracked conch or fish-and-chips. Dinners may include curried mutton or (on request) turtle steak. ⊠ *Bay St.,* ☎ 242/365–4263. *No credit cards. No lunch Sun.*

$–$$$$ ✕⌂ **Bluff House Beach Hotel.** Enjoy sweeping views of the sheltered harbor from this romantic hilltop hideaway. Accommodations include split-level rooms, suites, and one-, two-, or three-bedroom villas. Suites are the premier rooms, with tropical-style wicker furniture, parquet-inlay floors, and double doors opening onto balconies with sensational ocean vistas. The open air natural pine cocktail lounge–library overlooks the sparkling Sea of Abaco. Bluff House's Thursday night barbecue and beach bonfire, with live Junkanoo entertainment, is a popular weekly event. ⊠ *Between Abaco Sea and White Sound (Box AB-22886, Green Turtle Cay, Abaco),* ☎ 242/365–4247 *or* 800/745–4911, FAX 242/365–4248, WEB *www.BluffHouse.com. 4 rooms, 10 suites, 1 studio with kitchen, 10 villas. Bar, dining room, lounge, air-conditioning, refrigerators, pool, tennis court, beach, dock, snorkeling, boating, 38-slip marina, fishing, laundry service; no room phones, no room TVs. AE, D, MC, V. EP, MAP.*

$–$$$ ✕⌂ **Green Turtle Club.** The vibe is simultaneously refined and easygoing at this well-known resort. The cheerful yellow cottages are scattered amid lush trees and shrubs. Villa accommodations are available, but choose one of the handsomely appointed poolside rooms, furnished with mahogany Queen Anne–style furniture, gleaming hardwood floors, and Oriental rugs. Breakfasts and lunches are served on a terracotta tile veranda, but it's the lively dinner seating under the harborview dining room's chandeliers—giving the aura of the 1920s—that makes the inn come alive. The resort has a 35-slip marina and a 1920s-designed motor vessel, *Abaco Queen,* available for charters and touring. ⊠ *North end of White Sound (Box AB-22792, Green Turtle Cay, Abaco),* ☎ 242/365–4271 *or* 800/688–4752, FAX 242/365–4272, WEB *www.greenturtleclub.com. 24 rooms, 2 suites, 8 villas. Restaurant, bar, lounge, dining room, air-conditioning, fans, refrigerators, in-room VCRs, pool, beach, dock, snorkeling, boating, marina, fishing, piano, laundry facilities. AE, MC, V. EP, MAP.*

$ ✕⌂ **New Plymouth Club & Inn.** The charming, two-story historic hostelry with white balconies is in New Plymouth's center. Built in 1830, it was a French mercantile exchange, a warehouse, and a private residence before it opened as a hotel in 1946. Present owner Wally Davies built the charming patio pool and expanded the tropical gardens. Cozy rooms have canopy beds and terra-cotta tile baths. The top room upstairs contains a queen-size bed plus two twins and has lovely views of the sea and village rooftops. The restaurant is popular, so make reservations. ⊠ *Parliament St.,* ☎ *242/365–4161 or 800/688–4752,* FAX *242/ 365–4138. 9 rooms. Restaurant, bar, lounge, dining room, air-conditioning, fans, pool. MC, V. MAP.*

$$ ⊡ **Linton's Cottages.** These two snug cottages were built after the Second World War by Winston Churchill's private pilot, Captain Stephen Cliff. On a rise overlooking an isolated beach, the lovely cottages attract families, groups of friends, and couples looking for escape. Each has two comfortable bedrooms, a screened-in porch, a combination living and dining room with built-in settees, a well-stocked library, and a fully equipped kitchen. You can arrange to have someone prepare meals. Rental boats are available. ⊠ *S. Loyalist Rd. (Box 158601, Nashville, TN 37215),* ☎ *615/269–5682 or 242/365–4003,* FAX *242/365–4002. 2 cottages. Fans, kitchenettes, boating, bicycles, library. No credit cards.*

$–$$ ⊡ **Coco Bay Cottages.** Sandwiched between one beach on the Atlantic and another calmer sandy stretch on the bay, these homey cottages (three with two bedrooms and one with three) have water views. Attractively furnished, they come complete with telephones, modern kitchens, and linens. Snorkeling and diving are excellent around the reef that protects the Atlantic beach. The bay, where sunset views are fabulous, is prime territory for shell collecting and bonefishing. ⊠ *North of New Plymouth,* ☎ *242/365–5464 or 800/752–0166,* FAX *242/365– 5465,* WEB *www.cocobaycottages.com. 4 cottages. Kitchenettes, gym, snorkeling, library. MC, V.*

$ ⊡ **Treehouse by the Sea of Abaco.** Surrounded by lush tropical foliage and large fruit trees, three octagonal tree houses perch on pedestals and face the Sea of Abacos's mint-color waters, footsteps away. Each house comfortably accommodates up to six people, has two bedrooms, two baths, a large living area, fully equipped kitchen, and deck overlooking the sparkling bay. The large dock is perfect for sunning. Four-night minimum stay required. ⊠ *Between Abaco Sea and White Sound,* ☎ *800/942–9304 Ext. 20510 or 242/365–4258,* WEB *www.oii.net/treehouse. 3 houses. Air-conditioning, kitchenettes, dock. No credit cards.*

Nightlife

Nightlife on the Out Islands is virtually nonexistent, but the place to go in New Plymouth is the **Rooster's Rest** (☎ 242/365–4066), a pub and restaurant in a bright red building. On weekends, the joint shakes until the wee hours. Try to catch the reggae-calypso sounds of the local band, the **Gully Roosters**—check with the **Green Turtle Club** (☎ 242/ 365–4271) or **Bluff House Beach Hotel** (☎ 242/365–4247) to find out where they're playing. The world famous Goombay Smash cocktail is a favorite at **Miss Emily's Blue Bee Bar** (☎ 242/365–4181), where the much imitated drink was invented.

Outdoor Activities and Sports

BICYCLING

Curtis Bike Rentals (☎ 242/365–4128) is open Monday through Saturday and rents coast-brake bikes for $10 a day. **D&P Rentals** (☎ 242/ 365–4125) rents bikes on Green Turtle Cay.

BOATING

If you're unable to rent a vessel on Green Turtle Cay, try nearby Treasure Cay.

Green Turtle Club (☎ 242/365–4271) has 35 slips. **Bluff House Beach Hotel** (☎ 242/365–4247) has a marina with 38 slips.

Donny's Boat Rentals (☏ 242/365–4119) rents boats ranging from 14-ft Whalers to 23-ft Makos. **Dame's Rentals** (☏ 242/365–4205) has 17- and 22-ft boats. **Reef Rentals** (☏ 242/365–4145) has 19-ft Wellcrafts and 17-ft Boston Whalers.

EVENTS

The **Green Turtle Yacht Club Fishing Tournament** is held in May. In the beginning of July, the **Bahamas Cup** boat race circumnavigates Green Turtle Cay. **All Abaco Regatta,** the work-boat race between Green Turtle and Treasure Cay, is held at the end of October. For information on special events, call the **Abaco Tourist Office** (☏ 242/367–3067). The **Out Island Promotion Board** (☏ 954/359–8099 or 800/688–4752) also has details on island tournaments.

FISHING

Ronnie Sawyer (☏ 242/365–4070) is one of the Bahamas's premier bonefishing guides. Call **Joe Sawyer** (☏ 242/365–4173) for a morning of reef fishing in his 29-ft boat. He's Ronnie Sawyer's father. **Rick Sawyer** (☏ 242/365–4261) offers deep-sea and bonefishing aboard his 27-ft Alben or 17-ft Whaler. He's not related to Ronnie or Joe. All the Sawyers work independently of one another.

SCUBA DIVING AND SNORKELING

Brendal's Dive Shop (☏ 242/365–4411 or 800/780–9941, WEB www.brendal.com) is a longtime favorite with Green Turtle Cay visitors—don't miss the chance to hand-feed stingrays, groupers, and moray eels. Brendal's gourmet seafood beach picnic is a must. **Green Turtle Club Divers** (☏ 242/365–4271) has a full-service dive shop at the hotel and offers a 15% discount to divers and snorkelers staying there.

Rent your snorkel gear at one of the dive shops, and call **Lincoln Jones** (☏ 242/365–4223), known affectionately as "the Daniel Boone of the Bahamas," for an unforgettable snorkeling adventure and lunch of fresh conch or lobster on a deserted beach.

TENNIS

Bluff House Beach Hotel (☏ 242/365–4247) has one court.

Shopping

Annexed to the Plymouth Rock Café, **Ocean Blue Gallery and Liquors** (✉ Parliament St., ☏ 242/365–4234) is a small two-room gallery with framed and unframed paintings, sculptures, and other works by more than 50 local artists.

The **Sand Dollar Shoppe** (☏ 242/365–4221) sells upscale souvenir items and handcrafted Abaco gold jewelry.

Sid's Grocery (☏ 242/365–4055) has books on local Bahamian subjects—great for souvenirs or for replenishing your stock of reading material.

Vert's Model Ship Shop (✉ corner of Bay St. and Gully Alley, ☏ 242/365–4170) has Vert Lowe's handcrafted two-mast schooners and sloops. Model prices range anywhere from $100 to $1,200. If Vert's shop door is locked, knock at the white house with bright pink shutters next door.

Spanish Cay

Only 3-mi-long, this island is owned by a Florida conglomerate, and there are private upscale homes, a resort, and condos available for rent. A marina, full-service dive shop, and some fine beaches are among the attractions here.

Dining and Lodging

$$–$$$ ✕🏠 **Spanish Cay Resort.** The two-room hotel suites here are tucked away on a hill overlooking the marina and the Sea of Abaco. Each room has white tile floors, pretty pastel drapery and bedspreads, private porch, king or double bed, refrigerator, microwave, coffeemaker, and a desk. The resort also manages the "Barefoot Beach" villas, which are right on the Atlantic. An 81-slip marina is on-site. ✉ *Cay Resorts Limited, 110 N.E. 7th Ave., Dania, FL 33004,* ☎ *242/365–0083 or 888/722– 6474,* FAX *242/365–0453,* WEB *www.spanishcay.com. 18 rooms, 5 condos, 12 villas. 2 restaurants, tiki bar, air-conditioning, pool, 4 tennis courts, marina; no room phones. MC, V. EP, MAP.*

Walker's Cay

Fishing enthusiasts have been returning to this privately owned islet for years, and the lone hotel caters to anglers and divers. With few of the wispy casuarina trees that abound on most Out Islands, Walker's Cay, the Bahamas's northernmost island, sprouts more of the gnarled, thick-trunked trees more common in cooler regions. Walker's Cay isn't known for its beaches. Most visitors sail off to sandy shores on neighboring islands.

Dining and Lodging

$–$$$$ ✕🏠 **Walker's Cay Hotel and Marina.** The 100 acres of Walker's Cay is under the auspices of this resort, served by Chalks-Ocean out of Fort Lauderdale. The waters are renowned for their spectacular fishing, and the complex is a favorite with anglers who flock to the annual Bahamas Billfish Tournament held here in early April. Sportsmen gather at the Lobster Trap restaurant to swap fish stories. Rooms are cheerfully decorated with tropical-style rattan furniture and have private patios. Diving options include an exciting shark dive, cavernous coral reefs, and sunken tugboats. ✉ *700 S.W. 34th St., Fort Lauderdale, FL 33315,* ☎ *954/359– 1400 or 800/925–5377,* FAX *954/359–1414,* WEB *www.walkerscay.com. 62 rooms, 3 villas. 2 restaurants, 2 bars, lounge, air-conditioning, pool, saltwater pool, 2 tennis courts, dive shop, dock, boating, marina, fishing, laundry service. AE, DC, MC, V. EP, MAP.*

Outdoor Activities and Sports

BOATING

Walker's Cay Hotel and Marina (☎ 954/359–1400) has a full-service 75-slip marina and some of the Bahamas's best yachting facilities.

EVENTS

Spring brings the **Bahamas Billfish Championship.** Call the Bimini Big Game Hotel (☎ 242/347–3391) for information.

SCUBA DIVING

All the diving off the cay can be booked either through the hotel or through **Neal Watson's Undersea Adventures** (☎ 800/327–8150). The living reefs here grow atop a fossil coral reef that forms a limestone buttress. The Shark Rodeo dive allows you to safely float among 100-plus blacktip and Caribbean reef sharks as they feed.

Abacos A to Z

AIR TRAVEL

There are two airports in the Abacos. Various national and international airlines service both.

CARRIERS

Air Sunshine flies from Fort Lauderdale to both airports. American Eagle has two daily flights to Marsh Harbour from Miami. Bahamasair flies from Nassau to Marsh Harbour three times daily, and from Nassau to Treasure Cay twice daily. Direct international flights depart Palm Beach into Marsh Harbour once daily Thursday through Monday. Cherokee Air is the charter-plane service of choice for island hopping to or from the Abacos. Continental Connection flies into both Marsh Harbour and Treasure Cay from Miami, Fort Lauderdale, and Palm Beach. Twin Air has scheduled flights to Treasure Cay and Marsh Harbour from Fort Lauderdale and flies to other parts of the Abacos by charter. US Airways Express flies into both public airports from Orlando and Palm Beach.

➤ AIRLINES AND CONTACTS: **Air Sunshine** (☎ 242/367–2800 in Marsh Harbour; 242/365–8900 in Treasure Cay; 954/434–8900; 800/327–8900 in the U.S.). **American Eagle** (☎ 242/367–2231 or 800/433–7300). **Bahamasair** (☎ 242/367–2095 in Marsh Harbour; 242/365–8601 in Treasure Cay; 800/222–4262). **Cherokee Air** (☎ 242/367–2089 or 242/367–2613). **Continental Connection** (☎ 242/367–3415 in Marsh Harbour; 242/365–8615 in Treasure Cay; 800/231–0856). **Twin Air** (☎ 954/359–8266). **US Airways Express** (☎ 242/365–8686 or 800/622–1015).

AIRPORTS AND TRANSFERS

The Abacos's two public airports are Treasure Cay (☎ 242/365–0605) and Marsh Harbour on Great Abaco Island (☎ 242/367–3884).

TRANSFERS
Taxi services meet arriving planes at the airports to take you to your hotel or to the dock, where you can take a water taxi to neighboring islands such as Green Turtle Cay or Elbow Cay. Hotels will arrange for taxis to take you on short trips and back to the airport. A combination taxi–water taxi ride from Treasure Cay Airport to Green Turtle Cay costs $13. The ride from Marsh Harbour Airport to Hope Town on Elbow Cay costs $11. Fares are generally $1.50 per mile. A 15% tip is customary.

BOAT AND FERRY TRAVEL

You can reach the Abacos by mail boat. From Potter's Cay, Nassau, the M/V *Mia Dean* sails Tuesday to Green Turtle Cay, Hope Town, Marsh Harbour, and Turtle Cay; it arrives back in Nassau on Thursday. The fare is $45, and the round-trip takes 12 hours. The *Captain Gurth Dean* departs Nassau on Tuesday and calls on Sandy Point and Moore's Island, goes to the Berry Islands on Friday, and returns to Nassau on Sunday. The fare is $45. Trip times vary by location, and schedules are subject to change owing to weather conditions or occasional dry-docking. For details, call the Dockmaster's Office at Potter's Cay.

Every day except Sunday and holidays, Albury's Ferry Service leaves Marsh Harbour for the 20-minute ride to Hope Town at 9, 10:30, 12:15, 2, 4, and 5:30; ferries make the return trip at 8, 9:45, 11:30, 1:30, 3, 4, and 5. If you take the 5:30 PM ferry, you must stay overnight. A same-day round-trip costs $12. One-way costs $8. Albury's also provides service between Marsh Harbour and Man-O-War Cay or Guana Cay.

Green Turtle Cay Ferry leaves the Treasure Cay airport dock at 8:30, 10:30, 11:30, 1:30, 2:30, 3:30, 4:30, and 5 (except Sunday) and returns from Green Turtle Cay at 8, 9, 11, 12:15, 1:30, 3, and 4:30. One-way fares are $8. The ferry also services Guana Cay and can be chartered to Scotland Cay and Man-O-Way Cay.

Because the Abacos are made up of so many islands, many agree that a small boat is the easiest way to get around and allows the freedom to explore uninhabited areas and secluded beaches. When traveling during high season, remember to reserve your boat at least two or three

BOATING IN THE ABACOS

THE ABACOS PROVIDE SUPERB cruising grounds. Marinas and services for yachters range from rugged and rustic to high-tech facilities, but are mostly the latter. Walker's Cay, at the top of the Abacos, is about 55 mi northeast of West End at the tip of Grand Bahama Island, and it's also a 55-mi crossing from Palm Beach. Many yachters coming from the north opt for the 110-mi route from Florida's Fort Pierce–Vero Beach area to Walker's Cay.

Walker's Cay and its neighbor, Grand Cay, represent the contrasts in facilities available. Walker's Cay has a high-class 75-slip, full-service marina; a 2,500-ft paved airstrip; and extravagant hotel comforts. Grand Cay is a ramshackle settlement of about 200 people and four times that many dogs of mixed breed, called Bahamian potcakes. Yachters will find the anchorage off the community dock adequate. Double anchors are advised to handle the harbor's tidal current.

Heading south from Walker's Cay and Grand Cay, you will pass (and maybe want to explore by dinghy) a clutch of tiny cays and islets, such as Double Breasted Cays, Roder Rocks, Barracuda Rocks, Miss Romer Cay, Little Sale Cay, and Great Sale Cay. Great Sale Harbour provides excellent shelter. Snorkeling in the shallows along the mangroves, you might spot manta rays and eagle rays, sand sharks, and perhaps a school of small barracuda. Other small islands in the area are Carter Cay, Moraine Cay, Umbrella Cay, Guineaman Cay, Pensacola and Allen's cays (which are now virtually one island since a hurricane filled in the gap between them), and the Hawksbill Cays. Most offer varying degrees of lee anchorage. Fox Town, due south of Hawksbill Cay on Little Abaco's western

tip, is the first refueling stop for powerboats traveling east from West End.

A narrow causeway joins Little Abaco to Great Abaco, where the largest community at the north end is Cooper's Town. Stock up here on groceries, hardware, marine parts, liquor, and beer. There's also a coin laundry, a telephone station, a few restaurants, bakeries, and a resident doctor. Green Turtle Cay has excellent yachting facilities at White Sound to the north and Black Sound to the south. The Green Turtle Club dominates White Sound's northern end, whereas Bluff House, halfway up the sound, has docks on the inside and a dinghy dock below the club on the bank side.

South of New Plymouth on Great Abaco's mainland stands the Treasure Cay Hotel Resort and Marina, with one of the area's finest and longest beaches. A New England–style charmer lies a little to the south: Man-O-War Cay, a boatbuilding settlement. This island, with the 26-slip Man-O-War Marina, is devoid of cars and liquor.

The Bahamas's most photogenic lighthouse sits atop Elbow Cay, signaling the harbor opening to Hope Town. Boats also make their way to two less-developed neighboring islands: Guana Cay, with a 22-slip marina, and Spanish Cay, with an 81-slip full-service marina.

Back on Great Abaco, you'll find the Abacos's most populous settlement at Marsh Harbour, which has plenty of facilities for boaters. These include the modern (and growing) 180-slip Boat Harbour Marina, a full-service operation on the island's east side. The other side of town has additional marinas, including the 75-slip Conch Inn Marina, Marsh Harbour Marina and its 60 slips, and a couple of smaller facilities.

weeks in advance. It's advisable to check with your hotel, too, before renting a boat. It can either make arrangements for you or recommend the most convenient agent.

In Marsh Harbour, Rich's Boat Rentals has 21- and 26-ft Paramount powerboats. Boats at Rainbow Rentals in Marsh Harbour include 10 Twin-Vee catamarans, 22-ft C.D.M. WhiteCaps, and the 26-ft X-Treme, which can carry up to 12 people. Laysue Rentals in Marsh Harbour has twin-engine, twin-hull rental boats as well as 21- and 25-ft SeaCats. In Treasure Cay, check out J. I. C. Boat Rentals, which rents boats on a daily, three-day, or weekly basis. In Hope Town, HopeTown Sea Sports rents a 17-ft Boston Whaler and a 21-ft Paramount.

➤ BOAT AND FERRY INFORMATION: **Albury's Ferry Service** (☎ 242/367–3147 or 242/365–6010, WEB www.oii.net/alburysferry). **Dockmaster's Office** (☎ 242/393–1064). **Green Turtle Cay Ferry** (☎ 242/365–4032). **HopeTown Sea Sports** (☎ 242/366–0133). **J. I. C. Boat Rentals** (☎ 242/365–8465). **Laysue Rentals** (☎ 242/367–4414). **Rainbow Rentals** (☎ 242/367–4602). **Rich's Boat Rentals** (☎ 242/367–2742).

BUSINESS HOURS

Banks, located in Marsh Harbour and Treasure Cay on Great Abaco Island, in New Plymouth on Green Turtle Cay, in Hope Town on Elbow Cay, and on Man-O-War Cay, are generally open Monday–Thursday 9–1, Friday 9–5.

CAR RENTAL

Although you can explore Marsh Harbour on foot, you will need a car to see the rest of Great Abaco. In Marsh Harbour, you can rent automobiles from H & L Car Rentals. Reliable Car Rentals rents cars in Marsh Harbour. A & P Rentals is another Marsh Harbour car rental establishment. At Treasure Cay Airport, Corniche Car Rentals has a large rental fleet. Rentals are expensive, at about $70 a day and up. Weekly rentals are cheaper. It's easiest to have your hotel make arrangements.

➤ LOCAL AGENCIES: **A & P Rentals** (☎ 242/367–2655). **Corniche Car Rentals** (☎ 242/365–8623). **H & L Car Rentals** (✉ Shell Gas Station, ☎ 242/367–2854). **Reliable Car Rentals** (☎ 242/367–3015).

EMERGENCIES

The Marsh Harbour Clinic has a resident doctor and a nurse. A few areas in the Abacos still do not have direct long-distance dialing, and emergencies have to be reported to the hotel management. BATELCO (the Bahamas Telecommunications Corporation) has a system of microwave relay stations in the Abacos that provides direct-dial international connections.

➤ CONTACTS: **Marsh Harbour Clinic** (☎ 242/367–2510). **Police or Fire Emergencies** (☎ 919).

GOLF CART TRAVEL

In Hope Town, try Hope Town Cart Rentals, which rents gas carts for $45 per day or $270 per week, or electric carts for $40 per day or $240 per week. Island Cart Rentals also rents carts for $40 per day and $240 per week.

On Treasure Cay, you can rent carts from Cash's Resort Carts. Blue Marlin Rentals has cart rentals. Chris Carts rents by the half day, day, week, or month.

In Green Turtle, Bay Street Rentals rents electric carts for $40 daily with a one-day minimum. D & P Rentals is another outlet for carts on Green Turtle Cay.

➤ CONTACTS: **Bay Street Rentals** (☎ 242/365–4070). **Blue Marlin Rentals** (☎ 242/365–8687). **Cash's Resort Carts** (☎ 242/365–8465). **Chris Carts** (☎ 242/365–8053). **D & P Rentals** (☎ 242/365–4125). **Hope Town Cart Rentals** (☎ 242/366–0064). **Island Cart Rentals** (☎ 242/366–0448).

SIGHTSEEING TOURS
Papa-Tango Tours depart daily from Marsh Harbour's Boat Harbour Marina for daylong trips that include touring the islands, shopping, fishing, shelling, and snorkeling. From Green Turtle, Brendal's Dive Center offers glass-bottom-boat excursions, sailboat cruising, and fully catered and captained and sunset "booze cruises."
➤ CONTACTS: **Brendal's Dive Center** (☎ 242/365–4411 or 800/780–9941). **Papa-Tango Tours** (☎ 242/367–3753).

TAXIS
Taxi services meet arriving planes at the airports to take you to your hotel or to the dock, where you can catch a water taxi to neighboring islands such as Green Turtle Cay or Elbow Cay. Hotels will arrange for taxis to take you on short trips and back to the airport. A combination taxi–water taxi ride from Treasure Cay Airport to Green Turtle Cay costs $13. The ride from Marsh Harbour Airport to Hope Town on Elbow Cay costs $11. Fares are generally $1.50 per mile. A 15% tip is customary.

VISITOR INFORMATION
Visit, call, or write Marsh Harbour's Abaco Tourist Office.
➤ TOURIST INFORMATION: **Abaco Tourist Office** (✉ Box AB-20663, Marsh Harbour, Abaco, ☎ 242/367–3067, FAX 242/367–3068).

ANDROS

Andros, the Bahamas's largest island (100 mi long and 40 mi wide), is the least explored of them all, a place serrated by channels and tiny inlets with such names as North Bight, Middle Bight, and South Bight. Although not frequently visited, Andros is popular with sports lovers for its excellent bonefishing and diving. The Spaniards who came here in the 16th century called it *La Isla del Espíritu Santo*—the Island of the Holy Spirit—and it has retained its eerie mystique to this day.

In fact, the descendants of a group of Seminole Indians and runaway slaves who left the Florida Everglades in the mid-19th century settled in Andros and remained hidden until a few decades ago. They continue to live as a tribal society. Their village, near the island's northern tip, is called Red Bay, and they make a living by weaving straw goods. The Seminoles are credited with originating the myth of the island's legendary (and elusive) chickcharnies—red-eyed, bearded, green-feathered creatures with three fingers and three toes that hang upside down by their tails from pine trees. These mythical characters supposedly wait deep in the forests to wish good luck to the friendly trespasser and vent their mischief on the hostile.

Andros's western shore, which lies 30 mi west of Nassau, is utterly barren and not recommended to yachters. The island's lush green interior is covered with wild orchids and dense pine and mahogany forests, fringed on its western edge by miles of mangrove swamps. The forests provide nesting grounds for parrots, partridges, quail, white-crowned pigeons, and whistling ducks, and hunters come to Andros from September through March in search of game. There are only about a dozen settlements and a handful of hotels on the eastern shore.

The Andros Barrier Reef—the world's third-largest reef—is within a mile of the east shore and runs for 140 mi. It has an enchanting variety of marine life and is easily accessible to divers. Sheltered waters within the reef average 6–15 ft, but on the other side of the reef ("over the wall") lie the depths (more than 6,000 ft) of the Tongue of the Ocean, which is used for testing submarines and underwater weapons by the U.S. and British navies. They operate under the acronym AUTEC (Atlantic Underwater Test and Evaluation Center), and their base is near Andros Town.

Numbers in the margin correspond to points of interest on the Andros map.

Nicholl's Town

⑩ **Nicholl's Town,** at Andros's northeastern corner, is the island's largest village, with a population of about 600. This friendly community has stores for supplies and groceries, a few hotels, a public medical clinic, a telephone station, and small restaurants. A few miles north of Nicholl's Town is a crescent beach and a headland known as **Morgan's Bluff,** named after the 17th-century pirate Henry Morgan, who allegedly dropped off some of his stolen loot in the area.

Dining and Lodging

$–$ ✕▥ **Conch Sound Resort Inn.** The inn has six simple and spacious rooms with carpeting, mahogany furniture, handmade quilts, soft-cushioned chairs, and satellite TV. There are also four two-bedroom suites with kitchenettes. Bonefishing and diving can be arranged. The beach is a 10-minute walk away, but the hotel will provide transportation. ✉ *Box 23029, Conch Sound Hwy.,* ☎ *242/329–2060 or 242/329–2341. 6 rooms, 4 suites. Restaurant, bar, air-conditioning, kitchenettes, pool, fishing. No credit cards.*

$ ✕▥ **Green Windows Inn.** Rooms at this inn are right above a restaurant and bar (which means they can be noisy). The beach is a 10-minute walk away, and flats are nearby for bonefishing aficionados (bonefishing guides are easily procured). The restaurant serves seafood and Bahamian fare, such as steamed fish and peas 'n' rice. Fishing packages are available. ✉ *Box 23076, Rawfon St.,* ☎ *242/329–2194,* ℻ *242/329–2016. 10 rooms, 4 with private bath. Restaurant, bar. AE, MC, V.*

Fresh Creek–Andros Town

⑪ Batik fabric called Androsia is made in **Fresh Creek,** a small community about 45 minutes from Nicholl's Town. This brilliantly colored fabric is designed and dyed at the **Androsia Batik Works Factory** (☎ 242/368–2080), a 3-mi drive from Andros Town airport. You can visit the factory and see how the material is made. It's open weekdays 8–4 and Saturday 8–1. The batik fabric is turned into wall hangings and clothing for men and women, which are sold throughout the Bahamas and the Caribbean. Fresh Creek is also home to the Small Hope Bay Lodge, the area's dive resort.

⑫ A 10-minute drive from Fresh Creek (and about 30 mi south of Nicholl's Town on the east coast) is the small hamlet of **Andros Town.** Although the only thing to see here is the airport, 5 mi inland from Andros Town is **Captain Bill's Blue Hole**—one of several on the island— a delightful freshwater spring with ropes for swinging across. Also near Andros Town, you can commune with nature by strolling along forest paths and taking in the wild orchids.

⑬ Andros lures fishing enthusiasts to its fabulous bonefishing flats, and divers can't get enough of the sprawling **Andros Barrier Reef,** just off

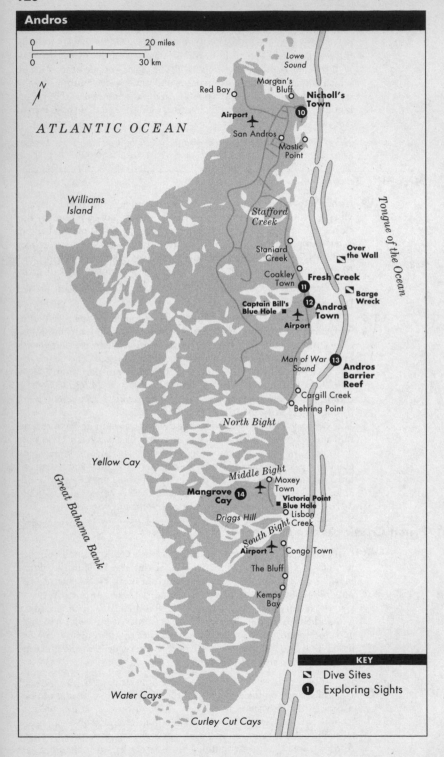

0   20 miles
0   30 km

ATLANTIC OCEAN

Lowe Sound

Red Bay

Morgan's Bluff

Nicholl's Town

10

Airport

San Andros

Mastic Point

Williams Island

Stafford Creek

Tongue of the Ocean

Staniard Creek

Over the Wall

Coakley Town

Fresh Creek

11

Captain Bill's Blue Hole

12

Andros Town

Barge Wreck

Airport

Man of War Sound

13

Andros Barrier Reef

Cargill Creek

Behring Point

North Bight

Yellow Cay

Middle Bight

Moxey Town

Mangrove Cay

14

Victoria Point Blue Hole

Great Bahama Bank

Driggs Hill

Lisbon Creek

South Bight

Airport

Congo Town

The Bluff

Kemps Bay

Water Cays

Curley Cut Cays

KEY

◨ Dive Sites
❶ Exploring Sights

Fresh Creek–Andros Town. Snorkelers can explore such reefs as the Three Sisters, where visibility is clear 15 ft to the sandy floor and jungles of elkhorn coral snake up to the surface. Divers can delve into the 60-ft-deep coral caves of the Petrified Forest, beyond which the wall slopes down to depths of 9,000 ft.

Dining and Lodging

$–$$ ✕⊞ **Small Hope Bay Lodge.** Casual and all-inclusive, this property attracts divers, snorkelers, and anglers. Rooms with local Androsia batik prints and straw work are in beachside cottages made of coral rock and Andros pine. The resort offers bonefishing and specialty diving excursions, such as one-on-one guided explorations of blue holes and tunnels. Rates include all taxes, service charges, and airport transfers. The property is in the process of rebuilding its dock, destroyed by Hurricane Michelle in late 2001. ⊠ *Small Hope Bay, Central Andros (Box 21667, Fort Lauderdale, FL 33335),* ☎ *242/368–2014 or 800/223–6961,* FAX *242/368–2015,* WEB *www.smallhope.com. 20 beachfront cottages, 1 villa. 2 bars, dining room, lounge, hot tub, massage, beach, dive shop, snorkeling, windsurfing, boating, fishing, bicycles, recreation room, library, laundry service; no room phones, no room TVs. AE, D, MC, V. All-inclusive.*

$ ✕⊞ **Andros Lighthouse Yacht Club and Marina.** The yachting crowd favors this spot, so you're sure to meet an ever-changing parade of people in the cocktail lounge and restaurant. The luxurious rooms and villas have tropical fabrics, ceiling fans, phones, TVs, refrigerators, and private patios. Boat rentals and fishing guides can be arranged. ⊠ *Andros Town, Andros,* ☎ *242/368–2305,* FAX *242/368–2300,* WEB *www.androslighthouse.com. 12 rooms, 8 villas. Restaurant, bar, fans, refrigerators, pool, beach, 21-slip marina, dock, boating, fishing, bicycles. AE, D, MC, V. EP, MAP.*

Outdoor Activities and Sports

BOATING AND FISHING

Small Hope Bay Lodge (☎ 242/368–2014 or 800/223–6961) has bonefishing, deep-sea fishing (wahoo, kingfish tuna), fly-fishing, reef fishing, seasonal tarpon fishing, and a "west side overnight"—a two-night camping and bone- and tarpon-fishing trip to the island's uninhabited western end. Rates run $175–$275 for a half day and $300–$480 for a full day (full-day trips include all gear and lunch).

Cargill Creek

Fishing—bonefishing in particular—is this quiet area's principal appeal, with wadeable flats just 100 yards offshore. Consider renting a car if you plan to spend time back in Andros Town and Fresh Creek; the taxi fare is $40 one-way. Bonefishing packages run about $300 a day.

Dining and Lodging

$$$ ✕⊞ **Andros Island Bonefishing Club.** Hardcore bonefishermen are drawn to this down-home, few-frills establishment. Guests have access to 100 square mi of lightly fished flats. Owner Captain Rupert Leadon is a warm, commanding presence with many a story of the elusive bonefish. Accommodations are functional, with two queen-size beds and ceiling fans. The dining room–lounge has satellite TV, a fly-tying table, and a well-stocked bar. Meals are hearty, with Bahamian fare such as seafood and the indigenous boil fish and peas 'n' rice served up at long family-style tables. Rates include boats, guides, and meals. ⊠ *Northeast Cargill Creek (Box 959, Wexford, PA 15090),* ☎ *242/368–5167 or 800/245–1950,* WEB *www.bonefishandros.com. 12 rooms. Bar, dining room, lounge, some refrigerators, fans, boating, fishing. MC, V. All-inclusive.*

UNDERSEA ADVENTURES IN ANDROS

ANDROS PROBABLY HAS THE largest number of dive sites in the country. With the third-longest barrier reef in the world (behind those of Australia and Belize), the island offers about 100 mi of drop-off diving into the Tongue of the Ocean. Uncounted numbers of **blue holes** are forming in the area. In some places, these constitute vast submarine networks that can extend more than 200 ft down into the coral (Fresh Creek, 40–100 ft; North Andros, 40–200+ ft; South Bight, 40–200 ft). Blue holes are named for their inky-blue aura when viewed from above and for the light-blue filtered sunlight that is visible from many feet below. Some of the holes have vast cathedral-like interior chambers with stalactites and stalagmites, offshoot tunnels, and seemingly endless corridors. Others have distinct thermoclines (temperature changes) between layers of water or are subject to tidal flow. The dramatic Fresh Creek site provides an insight into the complex Andros cave system. There isn't much coral growth but there are plenty of midnight parrot fish, big southern stingrays, and some blacktip sharks. Similar blue holes are found all along the barrier reef, including several at Mastic Point in the north and the ones explored and filmed off South Bight.

Undersea adventurers also have the opportunity to investigate wrecks such as the *Potomac*, a steel-hulled freighter that sank in 1952 and lies in 40 ft of water close to the Andros Beach Hotel in Nicholl's Town. And off the waters of Fresh Creek, at 70 ft, lies the 56-ft-long World War II LCM (landing craft mechanized) known only as the **Barge Wreck,** which was sunk in 1963 to create an artificial reef. Now encrusted with coral, it has become home to a group of groupers and a blizzard of tiny silverfish. There is a fish-cleaning station where miniature cleaning shrimp and yellow gobies clean grouper and rockfish by swimming into their mouths and out their gills, picking up food particles. It's excellent subject matter for close-up photography.

The split-level **Over the Wall** dive at Fresh Creek takes novices to the 80-ft ledge and experienced divers to a pre–Ice Age beach at 185 ft. The wall is covered with black coral and a wide variety of tube sponges. **Small Hope Bay Lodge** is the most respected dive resort on Andros. It's a friendly, informal place where the only thing taken seriously is diving. There's a fully equipped dive center with a wide variety of specialty dives, including customized family-dive trips with a private dive boat and dive master. If you're not certified, check out the lodge's morning "resort course" and be ready to explore the depths by afternoon.

Mangrove Cay

⑭ Remote and undeveloped, **Mangrove Cay** attracts anglers, divers, naturalists, and those who really want to get away from it all. Separated from Andros's north and south parts by bights, Mangrove Cay is an 18-mi island unto itself, where electricity and a paved road weren't introduced until 1989. In Little Harbour and Moxey Town, at the cay's northern tip, you'll likely spy porous mounds of sponges—bounty piled up to dry before being shipped to Nassau to be sold. The **Victoria Point Blue Hole** is good for snorkeling and diving, and the island has a number of pristine spots that are sure to please strollers looking for birds or wild orchids. Just across from the government dock, the pink **Traveller's Rest** (☎ 242/369–0044) is the only place in town for weekend nightlife and DJ-dancing. To the south, at Lisbon Creek, a free government ferry (☎ 242/369–0331) makes trips twice daily to South Andros, at 8 and 4. Bonefishing devotees know that Mangrove Cay is a good base for the 15-minute excursion to Bigwood Cay Flat, where the pale turquoise water appears to stretch forever.

Dining and Lodging

$–$$ ✕ **Dianne Cash's Ultimate Delight.** What's on the menu? "Nothing," says Dianne. "What do you want?" Dianne cooks three meals a day to order. Just call a day in advance, to give her enough time to procure the ingredients. Ask for pork chops, lobster, conch salad, or Dianne's specialty—stuffed baked crabs. That's it: just four tables with white rattan chairs, a couple of spots at the counter, and your own personal chef. ⊠ *Queen's Highway,* ☎ *242/369–0430. No credit cards.*

$–$$ ✕🏠 **Mangrove Cay Inn.** Chairs on the narrow front-patio walkway overlook the wild orchid and hibiscus garden. The rooms are done in peach and green with light Andros pine walls. Rent one of the inn's bicycles to explore the cay, take nature walks, or just challenge a friend to one of the parlor's many board games. The restaurant is an inviting spot, with richly stained wooden walls and an attached bar with high captain's-chair stools. There is also a 3-bedroom cottage with full kitchen available for rent. Rates include taxes and gratuity. ⊠ *General Post Office, Mangrove Cay, Andros,* ☎ *242/369–0069,* FAX *242/369–0014,* WEB *www.mangrovecayinn.com. 12 rooms. Restaurant, bar, air-conditioning, bicycles. No credit cards. EP, FAP, MAP.*

$ ✕🏠 **Seascape Inn.** These individual cottages with private decks over-
★ looking the ocean are Mangrove Cay's quaintest accommodations. Owners Mickey and Joan McGowan have decorated each one with handcrafted wooden furniture and original art. The elevated restaurant–dining room is the inn's meeting place. It holds the reading library, hosts locals who drop in for a drink or game of darts, and serves savory fare such as steaks and chicken in white wine sauce. The hearty breakfasts (included in the rate) are also delicious. Joan bakes killer banana bread and an assortment of yummy muffins. ⊠ *Mangrove Cay, Andros,* ☎ FAX *242/369–0342,* WEB *www.seascapeinn.com. 4 1-bedroom cottages, 1 cottage suite. Restaurant, bar, dive shop, snorkeling, fishing, kayaks, bicycles, library. MC, V. BP, FAP.*

Outdoor Activities and Sports

FISHING

Private bonefishing guide **Dennis Leadon** (☎ 242/368–5156) is highly recommended for leading anglers through the flats above Mangrove Cay. Contact **Moxey's** (☎ 242/369–0023) for bonefishing guides for hire.

SCUBA DIVING AND SNORKELING

The dive shop at **Seascape Inn** (☎ 242/369–0342) offers snorkeling and diving excursions, rents dive equipment and kayaks, and organizes a weekly night dive.

South Andros–Driggs Hill

Driggs Hill, on South Andros, is a small settlement of pastel houses, a tiny church, a grocery store, and the Ritz Beach Resort. At the Bluff settlement, near Congo Town, which has the island's third airport, skeletons of Arawak natives were found huddled together. A local resident attests that another skeleton was found—this one of a 4-ft-tall, one-eyed owl, which may have given rise to the legend of the mythical, elflike chickcharnie.

Dining and Lodging

$–$ ✕⊞ **Ritz Beach Resort.** For upscale resort accommodations on Andros, this property, formerly Emerald Palms by the Sea, is your best bet. Rooms have wainscoting, heavy pine furnishings with carved-seashell designs, and four-poster beds with mosquito netting. Satellite TVs in each room are an almost anachronistic touch. Lined with French doors, the airy dining room is particularly handsome, with richly upholstered rattan chairs and a latticework ceiling. Bahamian and international cuisine are served here; you might feast on eggs Benedict for breakfast or grilled lobster for dinner. ⊠ *Box 800, Driggs Hill, Andros,* ☎ *242/369–2661,* FAX *242/369–2667. 20 rooms, 2 suites. Bar, dining room, refrigerators, pool, snorkeling, boating, fishing, car rental. AE, MC, V. EP, MAP.*

Sightseeing Tours

Explore the pristine ecosystem of Andros by taking a walking tour with Gibson McKenzie. He also leads scuba divers on tours of the blue holes, a complex maze of underwater caves that surround Andros.
➤ CONTACT: **GIBCO** (☎ 242/339–1744), for nature walks and blue hole scuba diving tours.

Outdoor Activities and Sports

FISHING
Andros Lighthouse Yacht Club and Marina (☎ 242/368–2305) rents boats and can provide guides for bonefishing, reef fishing, or deep-sea fishing.

Andros A to Z

AIR TRAVEL
There are four airports on Andros, and several small airlines offer flights from Nassau and Freeport, but you can also leave from Fort Lauderdale.

CARRIERS
Bahamasair has two daily flights (except Wednesday) from Nassau to San Andros, Andros Town, and Congo Town. Flights to Mangrove Cay leave once a day, except Tuesday and Wednesday. Lynx Air International flies from Fort Lauderdale to Congo Town three days a week. Major Air has service from Freeport to all four airports. Small Hope Bay Lodge offers flights from Fort Lauderdale to Andros Town for a minimum of two passengers and can arrange charter flights for island hopping.
➤ AIRLINES AND CONTACTS: **Bahamasair** (☎ 242/339–4415 or 800/222–4262). **Lynx Air International** (☎ 888/596–9247). **Major Air** (☎ 242/352–5778). **Small Hope Bay Lodge** (☎ 242/368–2014 or 800/223–6961).

AIRPORTS AND TRANSFERS
The San Andros airport is in North Andros. Andros Town airport is in Central Andros. There's also an airport on Mangrove Cay. South Andros airport is in Congo Town. Check with your hotel for the closest airport.

> ➤ AIRPORT INFORMATION: **Andros Town** (☎ 242/368–2030). **Congo Town** (☎ 242/369–2640). **Mangrove Cay** (☎ 242/369–0083). **San Andros** (☎ 242/329–4224).

Taxis meet incoming planes at the airports, and they can also be arranged through the hotels. Rates are around $1.50 a mile.

BIKE TRAVEL

Bicycles are available at Andros Lighthouse Yacht Club and Marina. You can rent bicycles at Small Hope Bay Lodge. Seascape Inn rents bicycles.
> ➤ BIKE RENTALS: **Andros Lighthouse Yacht Club and Marina** (✉ Andros Town, ☎ 242/368–2305). **Small Hope Bay Lodge** (✉ Fresh Creek, ☎ 242/368–2014).

BOAT AND FERRY TRAVEL

A free government ferry makes the half-hour trip between Mangrove Cay and South Andros twice daily. It departs South Andros at 8 AM and 4 PM and departs Mangrove Cay at 8:30 AM and 4:30 PM. Call the Commissioner's Office for more information.

From Potter's Cay Dock in Nassau, the M/V *Lisa J II* sails to Morgan's Bluff, Mastic Point, and Nicholl's Town in the north of the island every Wednesday, returning to Nassau the following Tuesday. The trip takes five hours and costs $30. The M/V *Lady D* leaves Nassau on Tuesday for Fresh Creek (with stops at Spaniard Creek, Blanket Sound, and Bowne Sound) and returns to Nassau on Sunday. The trip takes 5½ hours, and the fare is $30. The M/V *Mangrove Cay Express* leaves Nassau on Wednesday evening for Lisbon Creek and returns on Monday afternoon; the trip takes 5½ hours and costs $30. The M/V *Captain Moxey* leaves Nassau on Monday and calls at Kemps Bay, Long Bay Cays, and the Bluff on South Andros. It returns to Nassau on Wednesday. The trip takes 7½ hours; the fare is $30. Schedules are subject to change due to weather conditions or occasional dry-docking. For more information, contact the Dockmaster's Office at Potter's Cay.
> ➤ BOAT AND FERRY INFORMATION: **Commissioner's Office** (☎ 242/369–0331). **Dockmaster's Office** (☎ 242/393–1064).

BUSINESS HOURS
The Canadian Imperial Bank of Commerce in San Andros is open Wednesday from 10:30 to 2:30.
> ➤ BANK INFORMATION: **Canadian Imperial Bank of Commerce** (☎ 242/329–2382).

CAR RENTAL

If you need a rental car, your best bet is to have your hotel make arrangements. It's smart to book a week in advance during high season as the number of vehicles is limited.

EMERGENCIES

Telephone service is available only through the front desk at Andros hotels, so emergencies should be reported to the management. A doctor lives in San Andros. Medical clinics are in Mastic Point, Nicholl's Town, and Lowe Sound, each with a resident nurse. A health center at Fresh Creek has both a doctor and a nurse. A clinic at Mangrove Cay has a nurse.
> ➤ CONTACTS: **Police** (☎ 919 North Andros; 242/368–2626 Central Andros; 242/329–4733 South Andros). **Medical Clinics** (☎ 242/329–2239 North Andros; 242/369–0089 Mangrove Cay; 242/369–4620 South Andros).

TRANSPORTATION AROUND SAN ANDROS
Cab drivers will charge around $80–$120 for a half-day tour of the
island. Most visitors opt to get around by bicycle.

THE BERRY ISLANDS

The Berry Islands consist of more than two dozen small cays stretching in a curve like a new moon north of Andros and New Providence
Island. Although a few of the islands are privately owned, most of them
are uninhabited—except by rare birds using the territory as their nesting grounds or by visiting yachters dropping anchor in secluded havens.
The Berry Islands start in the north at Great Stirrup Cay, where a lighthouse guides passing ships, and they end in the south at Chub Cay,
only 35 mi north of Nassau.

Most of the islands' 700 residents live on Great Harbour Cay, which
is 10 mi long and 1½ mi wide. Its main settlement, Bullock's Harbour,
has a couple of small restaurants and a grocery store. The Great Harbour Cay resort, a few miles away from Bullock's Harbour, was developed in the early 1970s. It is geared toward fishing enthusiasts. Both
Chub and Great Harbour cays are close to the Tongue of the Ocean,
where big game fish roam.

The Berry Islands appear just north of Andros Island on the Bahamas
map at the front of the book.

Chub Cay

Dining and Lodging

$–$$$ ✕🏨 **Chub Cay Club.** The resort's huge marina can handle more than
96 oceangoing craft and offers charter boats with guides for big-game
and flat fishing, the main pursuits here. The cay claims to be the "fish
bowl" of the Bahamas. The resort's rooms overlook the ocean or are
clustered next to a freshwater pool; villas are on the horseshoe-shape
beach facing west. The Harbour House Restaurant serves a good va-
riety of Bahamian and Continental dishes. ✉ *Chub Cay Club, Chub
Cay, Berry Islands*, ☎ *242/325–1490 or 800/662–8555*, ℻ *242/322–
5199*, 🌐 *www.chubcay.com. 26 rooms, 9 villas. Restaurant, 3 bars,
dining room, grocery, refrigerators, 2 pools, 2 tennis courts, beach, dock,
boating, marina, fishing, bicycles. AE, MC, V. EP, MAP.*

Outdoor Activities and Sports

BOATING
The clarity of Bahamian waters is particularly evident when you cross
the Great Bahama Bank from the Bimini area along the Berry Islands
on the way to Nassau. The water's depth is seldom more than 20 ft
here. Grass patches and an occasional coral head or flat coral patch
dot the light sand bottom. Starfish abound, and you can often catch
a glimpse of a gliding stingray or eagle ray. You might spot the odd
turtle, and if you care to jump over the boat's side with a mask, you
might also pick up a conch or two in the grass.

Great Harbour Cay

Dining and Lodging

$–$$$$ ✕🏨 **Tropical Diversions Resort.** Formerly the Great Harbour Cay Yacht
Club, the resort rents out privately owned beach villas and town houses
on a daily or weekly basis. The furnishings and layouts differ, but all
units have sundecks. Management meets you at the airport and can
help you find fishing guides. Have a light lunch at the Beach Club; in
the marina, full meals are available at the Wharf Restaurant, or a more

expensive fish-and-seafood buffet is served a couple of nights weekly at the Tamboo Club (☎ 242/367–8203). ⊠ *3512 N. Ocean Dr., Hollywood, FL 33019, ☎ 242/367–8838, 954/921–9084, or 800/343–7256, FAX 242/367–8115 or 954/921–9089. 13 beach villas, 4 town houses. 3 restaurants, beach, dock, snorkeling, boating, fishing; no room phones. AE, MC, V.*

Outdoor Activities and Sports

BOATING

In the upper Berry Islands, the full-service **Great Harbour Cay Marina** (☎ 242/367–8005) has 70-slips that can handle boats up to 150 ft. Accessible through an 80-ft-wide channel from the bank side, the marina has one of the Bahamas's most pristine beaches running along its east side.

Berry Islands A to Z

AIR TRAVEL

Both Great Harbour Cay and Chub Cay resorts provide transportation from the airport for their guests. Tropical Diversions Air flies to Great Harbour Cay from Fort Lauderdale.

➤ AIRLINES AND CONTACTS: **Tropical Diversions Air** (☎ 954/921–9084 or 800/343–7256).

BOAT AND FERRY TRAVEL

Captain Gurth Dean leaves Potter's Cay, Nassau, every Thursday for the Berry Islands. The trip takes about five hours and costs $35 one-way. For schedules and specific destinations, call the Dockmaster's Office at Potter's Cay.

➤ BOAT AND FERRY INFORMATION: **Dockmaster's Office** (☎ 242/393–1064).

EMERGENCIES

Immediately contact the police or a doctor in case of an emergency.

➤ CONTACTS: **Great Harbour Cay Medical Clinic** (☎ 242/367–8400). **Police** (⊠ Bullock's Harbour, Great Harbour Cay, ☎ 242/367–8344).

TRANSPORTATION AROUND THE BERRY ISLANDS

Happy People's has rental bikes, jeeps, and boats available for exploring the island.

➤ CONTACT: **Happy People's** (☎ 242/367–8117).

THE BIMINIS

The Biminis have long been known as the Bahamas's big-game-fishing capital. The nearest of the Bahamian islands to the U.S. mainland, they consist of a handful of islands and cays just 50 mi east of Miami, across the Gulf Stream that sweeps the area's western shores. Most visitors spend their time on North Bimini. Throughout the year, more than a dozen billfish tournaments draw anglers to the Gulf Stream and the Great Bahama Bank from the United States, Canada, Britain, and the rest of Europe. Marinas such as Weech's Bimini Dock, the Bimini Big Game Fishing Club, and Blue Water Marina, all on skinny North Bimini's eastern side, provide more than 150 slips for oceangoing craft, many of them belonging to weekend visitors who make the short trip from Florida ports. South Bimini now has a 35-slip marina complete with a customs and immigration center at the Bimini Sands resort complex. North Bimini's western side, along Queen's Highway, is one long stretch of beautiful beach.

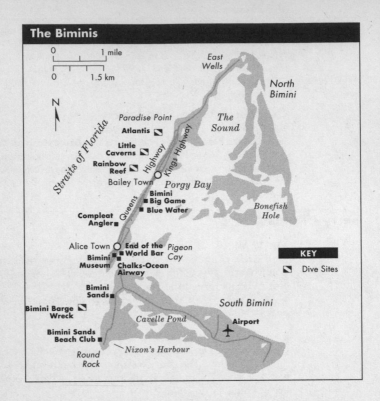

The Biminis

0   1 mile

0   1.5 km

N

East Wells

North Bimini

The Sound

Straits of Florida

Paradise Point

Atlantis

Little Caverns

Rainbow Reef

Bailey Town

Porgy Bay

Kings Highway

Highway

Queens

Bimini Big Game

Blue Water

Compleat Angler

Bonefish Hole

Alice Town

End of the World Bar

Bimini Museum

Pigeon Cay

Chalks-Ocean Airway

Bimini Sands

South Bimini

Bimini Barge Wreck

Cavelle Pond

Airport

Bimini Sands Beach Club

Nixon's Harbour

Round Rock

KEY

Dive Sites

All the hotels, restaurants, churches, and stores in the Biminis are along North Bimini's King's and Queen's highways, which run parallel to each other. Everything on North Bimini, where most of the islands' 1,600 inhabitants reside, is so close together you do not need a car to get around. Sparsely populated South Bimini, separated from its big brother by a narrow ocean passage, is where Juan Ponce de León allegedly looked for the Fountain of Youth in 1513. Tourists have easy access to the Fountain of Youth site, by way of a very good road, close to South Bimini's little airstrip.

Ernest Hemingway did battle with his share of game fish around North Bimini, which he visited for the first time in 1935 from his home in Key West. He made frequent visits here, where he wrote much of *To Have and Have Not* and *Islands in the Stream*. He is remembered in the area as a picaresque hero, not only for his graphic descriptions of his fishing exploits, but for his drinking and brawling, including a fistfight he had with his brother Leicester on the Bimini dock.

Other notables lured to the island have included Howard Hughes and Richard Nixon. The American with the strongest ties to the Biminis was entrepreneur Michael Lerner. He discovered Bimini years before Hemingway and is the man credited with teaching Papa how to catch giant tuna. Lerner was a great friend to the Biminis and established, among other things, the Lerner Marine Research Laboratory, which conducted research on dolphins and sharks from 1947 to 1974.

The Biminis also have a notorious history as a jumping-off place for illicit dealings; first during the Civil War, when it was a refuge for profiteers bringing in war supplies from Europe, and then during Prohibition, when it was a haven for rumrunners. Today things are pretty quiet—rumrunners have been replaced by fishermen and Floridians. Spring break brings lots of students who cruise over from Fort Lauderdale for wild nights at what was Papa Hemingway's favorite watering hole, the Compleat Angler. Unlike the rest of the Out Islands, Bimini experiences its busy season in the summer.

Alice Town

The Biminis' main community, Alice Town, is at North Bimini's southern end. Here, Chalks-Ocean seaplanes splash down in the harbor, lumber up a ramp, and park on the other side of King's Highway. Near the **Chalks-Ocean** seaplane landing area's customs and immigration office are the Art Deco ruins of Bimini's first hotel, the **Bimini Bay Rod and Gun Club,** a resort and casino built in the early 1920s and destroyed by a hurricane in 1926.

The **Compleat Angler Hotel** (⊠ King's Hwy., ☎ 242/347–3122) was Ernest Hemingway's hideaway in the '30s, and the Hemingway legend is perpetuated with a room full of memorabilia related to the writer, including pictures of Hemingway with gigantic fish and framed excerpts from his writings, most of them concerning battles with sharks. A photo of Cuban fisherman and captain of Hemingway's boat *Pilar,* Carlos Fuentes, the supposed model for the hero of *The Old Man and the Sea,* also hangs in the bar. The Angler is where former Colorado senator Gary Hart destroyed his hopes for the 1988 Democratic presidential nomination. He and Donna Rice were photographed in full color whooping it up on the bandstand in the hotel bar. The infamous picture now hangs in a place of honor.

The back door of the small, noisy **End of the World Bar** is always open to the harbor. This place—with a sandy floor and visitors' graffiti, business cards, and other surprises on every inch of wall, ceiling, and bar space—is a good spot to meet some local folk over a beer and a backgammon board. In the late '60s, the bar became a hangout of the late New York congressman Adam Clayton Powell, who retreated to North Bimini while Congress investigated his alleged misdemeanors. Among other guests, Powell entertained American reporters, who knew they could find him here, ready to dispense flowery quotes. A marble plaque in his honor is displayed in the bar. The bar is 100 yards from the Bimini Bay Rod and Gun Club ruins, on your right as you walk north on King's Highway. ⊠ *King's Hwy.,* ☎ *no phone.* ☾ *Daily 9 AM–3 AM.*

Dining and Lodging

$–$$ ✕ **Red Lion.** Venture through twin doors emblazoned with the red Tudor lions for fresh seafood and native dishes in this no-smoking restaurant, which is uncommon in the Bahamas. There's a view out the back sliding-glass doors onto a small bay between the marinas. ⊠ *King's Hwy.,* ☎ *242/347–3259. No credit cards.*

$–$$ ✕ **Opal's Restaurant.** Across from the Bimini Big Game Fishing Club and Hotel, this diminutive, 12-seat dining room delivers huge helpings of ribs and seafood and is noted for its green turtle steaks. ⊠ *Sherman La.,* ☎ *242/347–3082. No credit cards. Closed Sun.*

$–$ ✕ **Big Game Sports Bar.** Part of the Bimini Big Game Fishing Club and Hotel, this is a popular anglers' hangout. On the menu is standard pub fare like burgers and sandwiches along with fritters, chowder, and even conch pizza. It overlooks the marina. ⊠ *King's Hwy.,* ☎ *242/347–3391. AE, MC, V.*

$–$ ✕ **Big John's.** For a hearty breakfast or lunch, this cheerful dining room with bright tablecloths and friendly staff is a favorite. Boiled fish and peas 'n' rice are standard fare. ⊠ *King's Hwy., across from Gateway Gallery,* ☎ *242/347–3117. No credit cards. No dinner.*

$–$$$ ✕⊞ **Bimini Big Game Fishing Club and Hotel.** The club is a favorite among
★ fishing and yachting types who take advantage of the full-service 100-
slip marina. Anglers might prefer the spacious cottages with built-in wet
bar, sink, refrigerator, and outdoor grills. All rooms have tile floors and
two double beds. First-floor rooms have views of the lush gardens or
free-form pool, second-floor rooms have superb bayfront views. The
club's Gulfstream restaurant offers the island's most upscale dining, with
cuisine ranging from escargots to T-bone steaks. If you plan to stay here
during one of the major fishing tournaments, reserve well in advance.
⊠ *King's Hwy., at pink wall (Box 699),* ☎ *242/347–3391 or 800/737–
1007,* ⅎ𝔸𝕏 *242/347–3392,* ⓌⅇⒷ *www.bimini-big-game-club.com. 35 rooms,
2 suites, 12 cottages. 2 restaurants, 3 bars, pool, tennis court, boating,
marina, fishing, shops, baby-sitting, laundry service. AE, MC, V.*

$–$$ ✕⊞ **Bimini Blue Water Resort.** One of Hemingway's Bimini hideaways, this resort belongs to the Browns, who also own the Compleat
Angler Hotel. You can still rent Marlin Cottage, where Hemingway
wrote some of *Islands in the Steam.* Although the hotel's entrance is
on King's Highway, the building and Marlin Cottage sit on top of a
20-ft hill, facing Queen's Highway on the western side. Its smallish rooms
have faded blue-and-white furniture, dark wood-paneled walls, and
private balconies. There's also a 32-slip full-service marina. ⊠ *King's
Hwy. (Box 601),* ☎ *242/347–3166 or 800/688–4752,* ⅎ𝔸𝕏 *242/347–3293.
9 rooms, 1 3-bedroom cottage. Restaurant, bar, pool, beach, marina.
AE, MC, V.*

$–$$ ⊞ **Bimini Sands.** Exquisitely situated near a remote beach that extends
★ to South Bimini's tip and overlooks the Straits of Florida, this luxury
property rents one- or two-bedroom condominiums. The bright, high-
ceiling houses have balconies and patios with views of the tropical surroundings, the marina, or the beach. The Petite Conch restaurant
serves three meals a day, blending Bahamian staples with American favorites. There are a 35-slip marina and a convenient customs office,
so guests with boats can tie up and clear their paperwork without ven-
turing to North Bimini customs. An all-night water taxi shuttles you
to North Bimini to shop, dine, and party. ⊠ *Bimini Sands, South Bimini,* ☎ *242/347–3500,* ⅎ𝔸𝕏 *242/347–3501,* ⓌⅇⒷ *www.biminisands.com.
21 1- or 2-bedroom condominiums. Restaurant, bar, grill, kitchenettes,
2 pools, volleyball, beach, marina. AE, MC, V.*

$–$$ ⊞ **Sea Crest Hotel and Marina.** The yellow, three-story hotel has com-
fortable, simply furnished rooms with tile floors, refrigerators, cable
TV, balconies, and one of the island's friendliest owner/management
teams. Pick a room or suite on the third floor; they have lofty, open-
beam ceilings and lovely views from either side of the building—sea
or marina. The beach is a two-minute walk away. As the name implies,
there is a marina, across the street (King's Highway) from the hotel.
There is a 5% surcharge for credit cards. ⊠ *King's Hwy. (Box 654),*
☎ *242/347–3071,* ⅎ𝔸𝕏 *242/347–3495,* ⓌⅇⒷ *www.seacrestbimini.com.
11 rooms, 1 2-bedroom suite, 1 3-bedroom suite. Refrigerators, marina. MC, V.*

$ ⊞ **Bimini Sands Beach Club.** The ocean- and marina-view rooms have
light-colored interiors and thoughtful touches, like good lighting,
flowers, and throw rugs on gleaming terrazzo tile floors. The beach
club offers a reception-lounge area with large couches placed in front
of a working fireplace, a billiard room, a tiny bar that overlooks the
sparkling pool, and a restaurant with superb Bahamian cuisine and
unparalleled views of the waters surrounding Bimini. ⊠ *Bimini Sands
Beach Club, South Bimini,* ☎ *242/357–3500 or 242/357–9134. 40
rooms. Restaurant, bar, pool, volleyball, beach, billiards. AE, MC, V.
EP, MAP.*

$–$ ⊞ **Compleat Angler Hotel.** The well-worn, informal, wood-sided hotel
★ dates from the early '30s and will forever be associated with Hemingway,
who stayed in Room 1 and often drank here after a day of fishing. It's
far from posh, but these three stories of rich varnished wood paneling
exude an unforgettable sense of place and are Bimini's most charismatic
accommodations. Exterior rooms open onto the wraparound porch,
overlooking the courtyard bar and the street. The bar is the island's
liveliest nightspot, with live music on weekends, a drawback if you're
trying to sleep upstairs. Guests have access to the pool and marina fa
cilities of the Bimini Blue Water Resort. ⊠ *3 blocks from Chalks-Ocean,
King's Hwy. (Box 601),* ☎ *242/347–3122,* ℻ *242/347–3293. 12
rooms. 3 bars, lounge. AE, MC, V.*

Outdoor Activities and Sports

BOATING AND FISHING

Bimini Big Game Fishing Club (☎ 242/347–3391 or 800/737–1007, WEB
www.bimini-big-game-club.com), a full-service 75-slip marina, charges
$800–$900 a day, and $475–$500 for a half day of deep-sea fishing.
Blue Water Marina (☎ 242/347–3166), with 32 modern slips, charges
from $750 a day, and from $450 a half day, with captain, mate, and
gear included. **Bimini Sands Marina** (☎ 242/347–3500), on South Bimini, is a top-notch 35-slip marina offering accommodation to vessels
up to 100 ft. Convenient custom clearance for guests is at the marina.
Rent a 15-ft Whaler for $140 per day or a Wave Runner for $50 per
half hour. Rental fishing gear (flats and blue water) is also available.
Weech's Bimini Dock (☎ 242/347–3028), with 15 slips, has four Boston
Whalers, which it rents for $135 a day or $75 a half day.

EVENTS

The Biminis host a series of fishing tournaments and boating events
throughout the year, including the **Mid-Winter Wahoo Tournament**
(February), the **Annual Bacardi Rum Billfish Tournament** (March), the
Bimini Break and Blue Marlin Tournament (April), the **Bimini Festival
of Champions** (May), **Annual Bimini Native Tournament** (August), the
Bimini Family Fishing Tournament (August), the **Small BOAT—Bimini Open
Angling Tournament** (September), and the **Wahoo Championship Tournament** (November). The island also hosts an annual **Bimini Regatta,**
which takes place in the spring. For information on dates, tournament
regulations, and recommended guides, call the **Bahamas Sports Bureau**
(☎ 800/327–7678).

SCUBA DIVING

The Biminis offer excellent diving opportunities, particularly for watching marine life. The **Bimini Barge Wreck** (a World War II landing craft)
rests in 100 ft of water. **Little Caverns** is a medium-depth dive with scattered coral heads, small tunnels, and swim-throughs. **Rainbow Reef** is
a shallow dive popular for fish gazing. And, of course, there's **Atlantis.**
Dive packages are available through most Bimini hotels.

Bimini Undersea (☎ 242/347–3089 or 800/348–4644, WEB www.
biminiundersea.com) lets you snorkel near a delightful pod of Atlantic
spotted dolphins for $119 per person. You can also rent or buy
snorkel and diving gear. One-, two-, and three-tank dives cost $49,
$89, and $119 per person, respectively.

The **Scuba Bimini Dive Center** (☎ 242/347–4444 or 800/848–4073,
WEB www.scubabimini.com), at the rustic South Bimini Yacht Club, is
a Neal Watson Undersea affiliate offering specialty wreck dives and
a sensational blacktip- and reef shark–feeding one-tank dive experience for $75. (The dive masters feed them while you watch.) Call for
package rates.

Shopping

Upstairs in the Burns House Building, the **Gateway Gallery** (⊠ King's Hwy., ☎ 242/347-3131) sells top-quality Bahamian arts and crafts, original artwork by Biminites, hand-sculpted figures depicting daily Bahamian life, and Bahamian music.

Pritchard's Grocery (⊠ Queen's Hwy., next to Baptist church, ☎ no phone) is known as the home of the sweet Bimini native bread. Consider placing an order to take home.

Elsewhere on North Bimini

The **Bimini Museum**, sheltered in the restored (1920) two-story original post office and jail—a three-minute walk from the seaplane ramp—showcases varied artifacts, including Adam Clayton Powell's domino set, Prohibition photos, rum kegs, Martin Luther King Jr.'s immigration card from 1964, and a fishing log and rare fishing films of Papa Hemingway. The exhibit includes film shot on the island as early as 1922. ⊠ King's Hwy., ☎ 242/347-3038. ☜ $2. ☉ Mon.–Sat. 9–9, Sun. noon–9.

Toward King's Highway's north end, you'll see bars, grocery shops, clothing stores, the pink medical center, and a group of colorful fruit stalls. The island's northwestern part bears the ruins of an unrealized luxury development—Bimini Bay—that was to include a marina, private homes, and a hotel. The original developers ran out of money and abandoned the project.

Atlantis, a curious rock formation under about 20 ft of water, 500 yards offshore at Bimini Bay, is shaped like a backward letter J, some 600 ft long at the longest end. It's the shorter 300-ft extension that piques the interest of scientists and visitors. The precision patchwork of large, curved-edge stones form a perfect rectangle measuring about 30 ft across. A few of the stones are 16 ft square. It is purported to be the "lost city" whose discovery was predicted by Edgar Cayce (1877–1945), a psychic with an interest in prehistoric civilizations. Archaeologists estimate the formation to be between 5,000 and 10,000 years old. Carvings in the rock appear to some scientists to resemble a network of highways. Skeptics have pooh-poohed the theory, conjecturing that they are merely turtle pens built considerably more recently.

Most of the island's residents live in **Bailey Town** in small, pastel-color concrete houses. Bailey Town lies on King's Highway, north of the Bimini Big Game Fishing Club and Hotel.

OFF THE   **HEALING HOLE –** Locals recommend a trip here for curing what ails
BEATEN PATH   you—gout and rheumatism are among the supposedly treatable afflictions. Ask your hotel to arrange a trip out to this natural clearing in North Bimini's mangrove flats. You can take a leap of faith into the water and, if nothing else, enjoy a refreshing dip.

The Biminis A to Z

AIR TRAVEL

The two United States gateways to the Biminis are Fort Lauderdale and Miami. If you've just arrived at Miami International Airport, the taxi ride (about $15) to the Watson Island terminal across from the Port of Miami will take about the same time it takes to get to North Bimini. You can also fly to Bimini from Nassau.

CARRIERS

Island Air offers charter flights from Fort Lauderdale's Jet Center to South Bimini aboard a seven-passenger Islander. Chalks-Ocean Airway has several 25-minute flights daily into Alice Town, North Bimini, from Miami's terminal at Watson Island on the MacArthur Causeway, and from Fort Lauderdale International Airport (40 minutes). North Bimini is also served from Chalks-Ocean Airway base in Nassau–Paradise Island. Chalks-Ocean Airway uses 17-passenger turbo Mallard amphibians, with takeoffs and landings on water. Baggage allowance is 30 pounds per passenger.

➤ AIRLINES AND CONTACTS: **Chalks-Ocean Airway** (☎ 800/424–2557 or 242/363–1687). **Island Air** (☎ 954/359–9942 or 800/444–9904).

TRANSFERS

If you don't have heavy luggage, you might decide to walk to your hotel from the seaplane terminal in Alice Town, North Bimini's main settlement. Sam Brown's Taxi 1 & 2, (no phone) meets planes and takes incoming passengers to Alice Town in 12-passenger vans. The cost is $3. A $5 taxi-and-ferry ride takes visitors from the South Bimini airport to Alice Town.

BIKE TRAVEL

➤ BIKE RENTALS: **Bimini Undersea** (☎ 242/347–3089) rents bikes for $7 per hour or $20 per day.

BOAT AND FERRY TRAVEL

M/V *Bimini Mack* sails from Potter's Cay, Nassau, to Cat Cay and Bimini on a varying schedule. The trip takes 12 hours and costs $45 one-way. For information, call the Dockmaster's Office at Potter's Cay.

➤ BOAT AND FERRY INFORMATION: **Dockmaster's Office** (☎ 242/393–1064).

BUS TRAVEL

Taxi 1 & 2, operated by Sam Brown, has minibuses available for a tour of the island. Arrangements can be made through your hotel.

BUSINESS HOURS

BANKS AND OFFICES

The Royal Bank of Canada is open Monday and Friday from 9 to 3, and Tuesday through Thursday from 9 to 1. Note that most stores are closed Sunday.

➤ BANK INFORMATION: **Royal Bank of Canada** (☎ 242/347–3030).

CAR RENTAL

Visitors do not need a car on North Bimini and usually walk wherever they go; there are no car-rental agencies.

GOLF CART TRAVEL

Rental golf carts are available at the Sea Crest Hotel Marina from Capt. Pat's for $75 a day or $20 for the first hour and $10 for each additional hour.

➤ CONTACT: **Capt. Pat's** (☎ 242/347–3477).

EMERGENCIES

To reach the police and fire department in an emergency, call ☎ 919. North Bimini Medical Clinic has a resident doctor and a nurse.

➤ CONTACT: **North Bimini Medical Clinic** (☎ 242/347–2210).

TELEPHONES

Pay phones, which accept coins only, are scattered along King's Highway. If you have trouble placing your call, the Bimini Big Game Fishing Club and Hotel's office will place a call for you for about $2.50.

VISITOR INFORMATION

The Biminis Tourist Office is open weekdays from 9 to 5:30 and also has a booth at the straw market. The building it occupies was the site of the Lerner Marine Laboratory.

➤ TOURIST INFORMATION: **Biminis Tourist Office** (✉ Government Bldg., Alice Town, ☎ 242/347–3529, FAX 242/347–3530).

CAT ISLAND

Cat Island is 130 mi southeast of Nassau and is a close neighbor of San Salvador, the reputed landing place of Christopher Columbus. Many Cat Islanders maintain, however, that Columbus landed here instead and that Cat Island was once known as San Salvador. Sir Sidney Poitier is a famous native son, who left as a youth before becoming a famed movie actor and director. His daughter Ann lives here and spearheads the annual Rake 'N' Scrape Festival held in June.

The island was named after a frequent notorious visitor, Arthur Catt, a piratical contemporary of Edward "Blackbeard" Teach. Slender Cat Island is about 80 mi long and boot shaped, with high cliffs and dense forest. The Cat is living history with semiruined, vine-covered mansions and crumbling remnants of slave villages that are perfect for exploring. Mrs. Francis Armbrister, the elegant matriarch of the pioneer family that runs Fernandez Bay Village Resort, is the island's unofficial biographer. "Mrs. A," as she is known, has many spellbinding stories about the island, including the practice of obeah, which is a type of voodoo that incorporates bush medicine and witchcraft.

Good roads stretch for miles on end with nary a soul in sight. The Cat's shores are ringed with mile upon mile of exquisite, untrammeled beaches edged with casuarina trees. Some of the original inhabitants' descendants, who migrated long ago to the United States, are slowly returning here. Large new homes have started to appear throughout the island. The population is about 2,000.

Residents fish, farm, and live a peaceful existence. The biggest event of the year is the Annual Cat Island Regatta in August.

Numbers in the margin correspond to points of interest on the Cat Island map.

Arthur's Town and Bennett's Harbour

⑮ The claim to fame of **Arthur's Town** is that it was the boyhood home of actor Sidney Poitier, who has written about growing up here in his autobiography. His parents and relatives were farmers. The village has a BATELCO station, a few stores, and Pat Rolle's **Cookie House Bakery** (☎ 242/354–2027)—a lunch or dinner spot and an island institution. When you drive south from Arthur's Town, which is nearly at the island's northernmost tip, you'll wind along a road that passes through small villages and past bays where fishing boats are tied up.

One of the island's oldest settlements of small, weather-beaten houses,
⑯ **Bennett's Harbour** is some 15 mi south of Arthur's Town.

New Bight

⑰ The settlement of **New Bight,** where you'll find a small grocery store, a bakery, and the Bridge Inn, is near the New Bight (also called "The Bight") airport and is just south of Fernandez Bay Village. The Village is actually a resort on a bay and is where most Cat Island visitors stay.

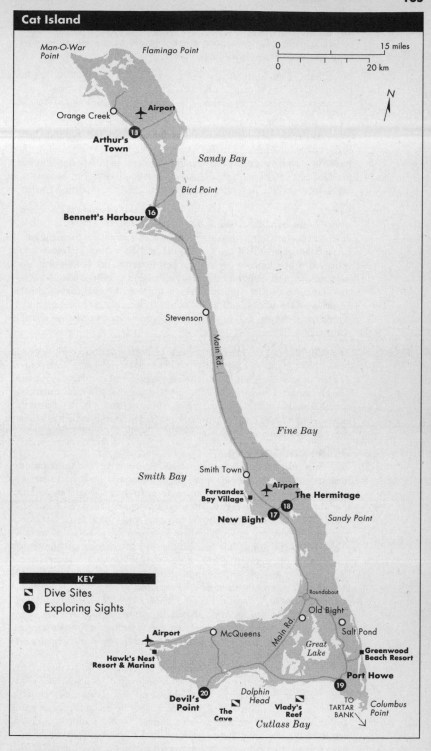

Cat Island

Between the airport and the town is the small blue **First and Last Chance Bar,** run by Iva Thompson. This is a good place to have a beer with the locals, play dominoes, and check out Miss Iva's straw work, which is some of the Bahamas's best.

New Bight is the home of the **Twin Palms** (☎ 242/342–3108), a bar perched right on the ocean, where on Saturday night, you could be fortunate to hear the famous Blind Blake play guitar and rake 'n' scrape.

⑱ At the top of 206-ft Mt. Alvernia, **The Hermitage** is the final resting place of Father Jerome. Above the tomb's entrance, carved in stone, is the epitaph BLESSED ARE THE DEAD WHO DIE IN THE LORD, and inside, past the wooden gate that hangs on its hinges, his body lies interred. He died in 1956 at the age of 80 and was supposedly buried with his arms outstretched, in a pose resembling that of the crucified Christ.

Father Jerome, born John Hawes, traveled the world and eventually settled in the Bahamas. An Anglican who converted to Roman Catholicism, he built two churches, St. Paul's and St. Peter's, on the Bahamas's Long Island, as well as the St. Augustine Monastery in Nassau. He retired to Cat Island to live out his last dozen years as a hermit, and his final, supreme act of religious dedication was to carve the steps up to the top of Mt. Alvernia. Along the way, he also carved the 12 Stations of the Cross, and at the summit, he built a child-size abbey with a small chapel, a conical bell tower, and living quarters comprising three closet-size rooms.

The pilgrimage to the Hermitage begins next to the commissioner's office at New Bight, at a dirt path that leads to the foot of Mt. Alvernia. Try not to miss the slightly laborious experience of climbing to the top. The Hermitage provides a perfect, inspired place to pause for quiet contemplation. It also has glorious views of the ocean on both sides of the island. A caretaker clears the weeds around the tomb, which islanders regard as a shrine, and lights a candle in Father Jerome's memory.

Dining and Lodging

$–$$ ✕▥ **Fernandez Bay Village.** Brick-and-stone villas are spread along
★   a stunning, horseshoe-shape white-sand beach at this resort just north of New Bight. Each accommodates four to six persons and has a kitchen, a terrace facing the sea, and a private garden. Canoes, Sunfish sailboats, and kayaks are free to use, and captained 24-ft boats can be hired by the hour. Nightlife here usually involves conversation around the honor bar or a bonfire—you're in luck if the senior "Mrs. A" is in attendance; her stories are spellbinding. Owners Tony and Pam Armbrister and Donna, the ebullient manager, try to accommodate your every whim. ✉ *1 mi west of airport (1507 S. University Dr., Suite A, Plantation, FL 33324),* ☎ *242/342–3043,* FAX *954/ 474–4864,* WEB *www.fernandezbayvillage.com. 6 villas, 6 1-bedroom cottages. Bar, dining room, grocery, kitchenettes, no room phones, beach, snorkeling, boating, waterskiing, fishing, bicycles, laundry service. AE. EP, MAP.*

$ ✕▥ **Bridge Inn.** Run by Cat Islanders Mr. and Mrs. Russell (with the help of their large family), this motel-style property is about 300 yards from a beach. A more isolated stretch of sand is about a mile down a back road. The wood-paneled, high-ceilinged rooms have private baths and cable TV. Hot breakfasts, from French toast to conch and grits, are served in the hotel's dining room, and picnic lunches can be prepared. Rooms with air-conditioning cost extra. ✉ *New Bight,* ☎ *242/ 342–3013 or 800/688–4752,* FAX *242/342–3041. 12 rooms. Bar, dining room, air-conditioning in some rooms, beach, snorkeling, boating, bicycles, billiards, baby-sitting. MC, V. EP, MAP.*

Port Howe

⑲ At the conch shell–lined traffic roundabout, head east out toward **Port Howe,** believed by many to be Cat Island's oldest settlement. Nearby, you'll see the ruins of the **Deveaux Mansion,** a stark two-story, white-washed building overrun with wild vegetation. Once it was a grand house on a cotton plantation, home of Captain Andrew Deveaux of the British Navy, who was given thousands of acres of Cat Island property as a reward for his daring raid that recaptured Nassau from the Spaniards in 1783. Just beyond the mansion ruin is the entrance road to the Greenwood Beach Resort, which sits on an 8-mi stretch of practically untouched velvet-sand beach.

Dining and Lodging

$ ✕⌂ **Greenwood Beach Resort.** The isolated resort, overlooking a shell-
★ strewn beach, is about 45 minutes from the airport, where a friendly staff member will pick you up. Rooms are bright and cheerfully dec-orated with colorful fish stencils. The large clubhouse, with its purple-and-white walls and vivid tropical paintings, is the center of activity. You can relax at the attractive bar, in the small library and lounge; or on the large stone veranda that overlooks the ocean. Dinner is served family-style: Don't miss the European-Bahamian bread, baked daily. ✉ *Port Howe,* ☎ *242/342–3053 or 800/688–4752,* 𝖥𝖠𝖷 *242/342–3053,* 𝖶𝖤𝖡 *www.greenwoodbeachresort.com. 20 rooms. Bar, dining room, fans, pool, hot tub, beach, dive shop, snorkeling, boating, fishing, bicycles, billiards, laundry service. AE, MC, V. FAP, MAP.*

Outdoor Activities and Sports

SCUBA DIVING AND SNORKELING

Cat Island Dive Centre (✉ Greenwood Beach Resort, Port Howe, ☎ 242/342–3053) is the island's premier dive facility, with a 30-ft dive boat and great snorkeling just a few minutes offshore. Beginners can take the $80 crash course, and seasoned divers will enjoy the spectacular wall-diving opportunities. Snorkelers can rent gear from the dive shop and take half-day specialized snorkeling trips. Bubble watchers may go along for $15.

Devil's Point

⑳ The small village of **Devil's Point,** with its pastel-color, thatch-roof houses, lies about 10 mi west of Columbus Point. Beachcombers will find great shelling on the pristine beach. You'll also come across the ruins of the **Richman Hill–Newfield plantation.**

Lodging

$ ⌂ **Hawk's Nest Resort & Marina.** At Cat Island's southwestern tip, this small waterfront resort, just yards from a long sandy beach, has its own runway and a 28-slip marina. The patios of the guest rooms, the dining room, and the lounge overlook the ocean. With cheerful peach walls and bright bedspreads, rooms have either one king-size or two queen-size beds with baths that have both tubs and showers—a rarity in the Out Islands. A hearty breakfast is included in the daily rate. Families should consider renting the two-bedroom house, which is next to a beach known for its multitude of shells. ✉ *Devil's Point, Cat Island,* ☎ *242/342–7050 or 800/688–4752,* 𝖥𝖠𝖷 *242/342–7051,* 𝖶𝖤𝖡 *www.hawks-nest.com. 10 rooms, 1 2-bedroom house. Bar, dining room, lounge, in-room VCRs, beach, dive shop, snorkeling, boating, marina, fishing, bicycles. MC, V. All-inclusive, BP.*

Outdoor Activities and Sports

SCUBA DIVING

Contact your hotel or the Cat Island Dive Centre for more informa-tion on any of these sites, or to arrange a dive.

Tartar Bank is an offshore site known for its abundant sea life, including sharks, triggerfish, turtles, eagle rays, and barracuda. **The Cave** has a big channel with several exits to deeper ocean. Reef sharks, barracudas, and other tropical fish are frequently seen here. **Vlady's Reef,** also known as "The Chimney," is located near the Guana Cays. Coral heads have created numerous canyons, chimneys, and swim-throughs, and you'll likely catch a glimpse of large stingrays.

Cat Island A to Z

AIR TRAVEL

Air Sunshine flies into New Bight from Fort Lauderdale. From Nassau, Bahamasair flies into Arthur's Town or New Bight Airport in the center of Cat Island twice weekly. Tom Jones Charters offers a six-seat Piper Aztec from Fort Lauderdale into New Bight or Arthur's Town. Lynx Air flies into New Bight from Fort Lauderdale three times a week.

Fernandez Bay Village, Greenwood Beach Resort, and Hawk's Nest Resort & Marina offer charter flights from Nassau.
➤ AIRLINES AND CONTACTS: **Air Sunshine** (☎ 800/327–8900). **Bahamasair** (☎ 800/222–4262). **Fernandez Bay Village** (☎ 800/940–1905). **Greenwood Beach Resort** (☎ 242/342–3053). **Hawk's Nest Resort & Marina** (☎ 800/688–4752). **Lynx Air** (☎ 954/772–9808 or 888/596–9247). **Tom Jones Charters** (☎ 242/335–1353 or 954/359–8099).

AIRPORTS AND TRANSFERS

TRANSFERS
There are no taxis on Cat Island. Resort owners make arrangements with guests beforehand to pick them up at the airport. If you miss your ride, just ask around the parking lot for a lift. Anyone going in your direction (there's only one road) will be happy to drop you off.

BOAT AND FERRY TRAVEL

The *North Cat Island Special* leaves Potter's Cay, Nassau, every Wednesday for Bennett's Harbour and Arthur's Town, returning on Saturday. The trip takes 14 hours and costs $40 one-way. M/V *Sea Hauler* leaves Potter's Cay on Tuesday for Smith Bay and New Bight, returning on Sunday. The trip is seven hours, and the fare is $40. For information, call the Dockmaster's Office at Potter's Cay.
➤ BOAT AND FERRY INFORMATION: **Dockmaster's Office** (☎ 242/393–1064).

CAR RENTAL

The New Bight Service Station rents cars and can pick you up from New Bight airport. You can rent a car from Candy's Market, which also picks up from the airport. Rates depend on the number of days you're renting.
➤ CONTACTS: **Candy's Market** (☎ 242/342–3011). **New Bight Service Station** (☎ 242/342–3014).

EMERGENCIES

Cat Island has three medical clinics—at Smith Town, Old Bight, and Arthur's Town. There are few telephones on the island, but your hotel's front desk will be able to contact the nearest clinic in case of an emergency.

CROOKED AND ACKLINS ISLANDS

Historians of the Bahamas tell us that as Columbus sailed down the lee of Crooked Island and its southern neighbor, Acklins Island (the two are separated by a short water passage), he was riveted by the aroma of native herbs wafting out to his ship. Soon after, Crooked Island, which lies 225 mi southeast of Nassau, became known as one of the "Fragrant Islands." The first known settlers didn't arrive until the late 18th century, when Loyalists brought their slaves from the United States and established cotton plantations. It was a doomed venture because of the island's poor soil, and those who stayed made a living of sorts by farming and fishing. A salt and sponge industry flourished for a while on Fortune Island, south of Crooked Island, but the place is now a ghost town. Today the 400-plus inhabitants who live on Crooked and Acklins islands continue to survive by farming and fishing. The islands are best known for splendid tarpon fishing and bonefishing, but not much else. They are about as remote as populated islands in the Bahamas get. A number of residents rely on generators for electricity. Phone service, where available, often goes out for weeks at a time.

Although the plantations have long crumbled, two relics of those days are preserved by the Bahamas National Trust on Crooked Island's northern part, which overlooks the Crooked Island Passage separating the cay from Long Island. Old Spanish guns have been discovered at one ruin, **Marine Farm,** which may have been used as a fortification. An old structure, **Hope Great House** has orchards and gardens that are still tended by the Bahamas National Trust.

Crooked Island is 30 mi long and surrounded by 45 mi of barrier reefs that are ideal for diving. They slope from 4 ft to 50 ft, then plunge to 3,600 ft in the Crooked Island Passage, once one of the most important sea roads for ships following the southerly route from the West Indies to the Old World. The one-room airport is on **Colonel Hill,** where you get an uninterrupted view of the region all the way to the narrow passage between Crooked Island and Acklins Island. There are two landmark lighthouses. The sparkling-white **Bird Rock Lighthouse** (built in 1872) in the north once guarded the Crooked Island Passage. The rotating flash from its 115-ft tower still welcomes pilots and sailors to the Pittstown Point Landings resort, currently the islands' only suitable lodging.

The **Castle Island** lighthouse (built in 1867), at Acklins Island's southern tip, formerly served as a beacon for pirates who used to retreat there after attacking ships.

Crooked and Acklins islands appear southeast of Andros Island on the Bahamas map at the front of this guide.

Dining and Lodging

$ ✕⛱ **Pittstown Point Landings.** Scenic and completely isolated, this property on Crooked Island's northwestern tip has miles of open beach on its doorstep, coral reefs directly off the beach for excellent snorkeling, and a dramatic 600-fathom plunge beyond the reef for serious scuba diving. Or you can just laze in a hammock, gazing out over the emerald water to Bird Rock Lighthouse island offshore. Conch shells line the path from the main office, a mid-18th-century building that housed the Bahamas's first post office, to the basic guest rooms. Fishing, trips to the lighthouse, and all other activities are arranged by the hotel. Most guests arrive by private plane on the resort's own small landing strip. ✉ *238-A Airport Rd., Statesville, NC 28677,* ☎ *242/344–2507 or 800/ 752–2322,* FAX *704/881–0771,* WEB *www.pittstownpointlandings.com. 12 rooms. Bar, dining room, lounge, air-conditioning in some rooms, shuffleboard, volleyball, beach, snorkeling, fishing, bicycles, library, shop, airstrip. AE, MC, V. EP, FAP.*

Outdoor Activities and Sports

SCUBA DIVING

The Wall starts at around 45 ft deep and goes down thousands more. It's about 50 yards off Crooked Island's coast and follows the shoreline for many miles. For more information, contact the Pittstown Point Landings hotel.

Crooked and Acklins Islands A to Z

AIR TRAVEL

Bahamasair flies from Nassau to Crooked and Acklins islands twice a week. Airports are in Colonel Hill on Crooked Island and at Spring Point on Acklins Island. Pittstown Point Landings can pick up its guests flying into Colonel Hill by prior arrangement.

➤ AIRLINES AND CONTACTS: **Bahamasair** (☎ 800/222–4262).

BOAT AND FERRY TRAVEL

M/V *Lady Mathilda* sails from Potter's Cay in Nassau to Acklins Island, Crooked Island, Inagua, and Mayaguana. The boat leaves Nassau once a week on a varying schedule. Call the Dockmaster's Office in Potter's Cay for schedule information. The fare is $65–$70, depending on your destination. A government ferry service between Crooked Island and Acklins Island operates daily 9–4.

➤ BOAT AND FERRY INFORMATION: **Dockmaster's Office** (☎ 242/393–1064).

EMERGENCIES

The police and commissioner are on Crooked Island. The two government medical clinics on Acklins Island are at Spring Point and Chesters Bay. Crooked Island's clinic is at Landrail Point. The resident doctor and nurse for the area live in Spring Point. Nurses are also available at Colonel Hill on Crooked Island, and Masons Bay on Acklins. You can contact these medical professionals through your hotel.

➤ CONTACTS: **Commissioner** (☎ 242/344–2197). **Police** (☎ 242/344–2599).

ELEUTHERA

Eleuthera is considered by many Out Islands aficionados to be one of the Bahamas's most enjoyable destinations. It's comprised of miles and miles of unspoiled beach, green forests, hills, and rich, red soil in the north that produces pineapples and a variety of vegetables. Eleutheran residents, many of whom live in boldly colored houses adorned with bougainvillea, welcome visitors warmly; most will be happy to let you know where to find bargains at a little tucked-away straw market or recommend the best restaurant on the island for conch chowder. The famous strip of pink-sand beach at Harbour Island gets more attention, but Eleuthera's eastern shore, from remote James Point to Governor's Harbour, is also pink sand.

Shaped like a praying mantis, Eleuthera is 110 mi long and less than 2 mi wide. It lies 200 mi southeast of Florida and 60 mi east of Nassau. The island was named by a group from Britain who came here seeking religious freedom in 1648. Led by William Sayle, a former governor of Bermuda, the group took the name of the island from the Greek word for freedom. The Eleutheran Adventurers, as they called themselves, gave the Bahamas its first written constitution, which called for the establishment of a republic.

The Eleutheran Adventurers landed first on the middle of the island, close to what is now called Governor's Harbour. After quarreling among themselves, the group split up, and Sayle led one faction around the island's northern tip by boat. This group was shipwrecked and took refuge at Preacher's Cave, where an altar-shape rock formation makes it easy to imagine where the castaways held their religious services. The cave, and the crude altar at which they worshiped, is still in existence, close to North Eleuthera.

Later in 1648, Sayle journeyed to the United States to seek help in settling his colony, but the people he left behind began to leave the island. By 1650, most of them had left for New England, leaving only a few of the original Adventurers to trade with passing ships in salt and brasiletto wood. Around 1666, Sayle returned to the Bahamas, this time to what is now called New Providence, which was ideally situated for shipping routes. Eleuthera was "revisited" at the end of the Revolutionary War by Loyalists who fled America with their slaves. The new settlers constructed colonial-style homes that still stand on Harbour Island and started a shipbuilding industry. Today the population of Eleuthera—and of Harbour Island and Spanish Wells, which lie offshore in the north—totals more than 10,500 and consists of descendants of the original Adventurers, Loyalists, and the Loyalists' slaves. It is the Out Islands' second-largest population.

Numbers in the margin correspond to points of interest on the Eleuthera map.

Rock Sound

㉑ One of Eleuthera's largest settlements, the village of **Rock Sound** has a small airport serving the island's southern part. **Front Street,** the main thoroughfare, runs along the seashore, where fishing boats are tied up. If you walk down the street, you'll eventually come to the pretty, whitewashed **St. Luke's Anglican Church,** a contrast to the deep blue and green houses nearby, with their colorful gardens full of poinsettia, hibiscus, and marigolds. If you pass the church on a Sunday, you'll surely hear fervent hymn singing through the open windows. Rock Sound has the island's largest supermarket shopping center, where locals stock up on groceries and supplies. Buy fresh fruit—citrus in the winter and luscious papayas and avocados in the spring and summer—from **Rock Sound Farms** (✉ Queen's Hwy., ☎ no phone) or one of the town's other roadside fruit vendors.

㉒ **Ocean Hole,** a large inland saltwater lake a mile southeast of Rock Sound, is connected by tunnels to the sea. Steps have been cut into the coral on the shore so visitors can climb down to the lake's edge. Bring a piece of bread or some fries and watch the fish emerge for their hors d'oeuvres, swimming their way in from the sea. The hole had been estimated to be more than 100 fathoms (600 ft) deep, but, in fact, its depth was measured by a local diver at about 75 ft. He reports a couple of cars at the bottom, too.

㉓ Ten miles south of Rock Sound, the now defunct **Cotton Bay Club** hotel is where you'll find the well-known Robert Trent Jones golf course (it's only a golf club now), studded with tree groves and nestled against the sea. Cotton Bay was once an exclusive club, the domain of Pan Am's founder, Juan Trippe, who would fly his friends to the island on a 727 Yankee Clipper for a weekend of golf.

㉔ The tiny settlement of **Bannerman Town** (population 40) is at the island's southern tip. From Eleuthera's north end (near Preacher's Cave), it is about a three-hour drive down the Queen's Highway. The beach here is gorgeous, and on a clear day you can see the Bahamas's highest point, Mt. Alvernia (elevation 206 ft), on distant Cat Island. The

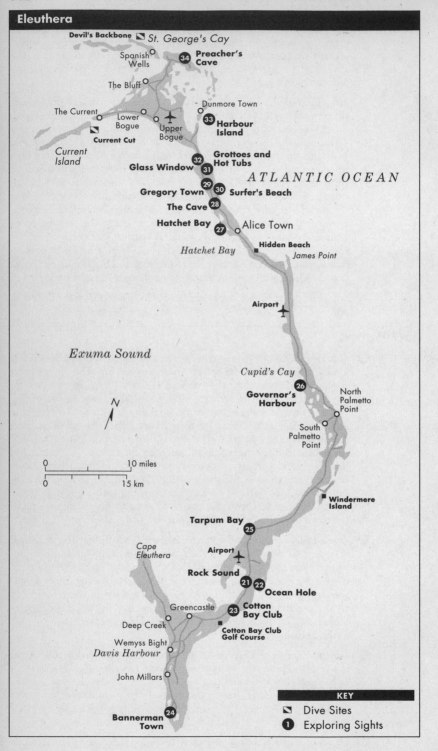

Eleuthera

Devil's Backbone 🏴 St. George's Cay

Spanish Wells ○

34 **Preacher's Cave**

The Bluff ○

Dunmore Town ·

The Current ○   Lower Bogue ○   Upper Bogue   **33** **Harbour Island**

🏴 **Current Cut**

Current Island

✈ Upper Bogue

Grottoes and Hot Tubs

32

31

Glass Window

ATLANTIC OCEAN

Gregory Town **29** **30** **Surfer's Beach**

The Cave **28**

Hatchet Bay **27** ○ **Alice Town**

Hatchet Bay   ■ **Hidden Beach**

James Point

Airport ✈

Exuma Sound

Cupid's Cay

26

Governor's Harbour

North Palmetto Point ○

South Palmetto Point ○

N

■ **Windermere Island**

0 _____ 10 miles
0 _____ 15 km

Tarpum Bay

25

Airport ✈

Rock Sound

Cape Eleuthera

21 **22** **Ocean Hole**

Greencastle ○   **23** **Cotton Bay Club**

Deep Creek ○

■ **Cotton Bay Club Golf Course**

Wemyss Bight ○
Davis Harbour

John Millars ○

24

Bannerman Town

KEY
🏴 Dive Sites
❶ Exploring Sights

town lies about 30 mi from the **Cotton Bay Club,** past the quiet, little fishing villages of **Wemyss Bight** (named after Lord Gordon Wemyss, a 17th-century Scottish slave owner) and **John Millars** (population 15), barely touched over the years.

Dining

$-$$ ✕ **Sammy's Place.** Reasonable and spotless, this stop owned by Sammy Culmer and managed mainly by his personable daughter Margarita, serves conch fritters, fried chicken and fish, and peas 'n' rice. ⊠ *Albury La.,* ☎ *242/334–2121. No credit cards.*

Outdoor Activities and Sports

GOLF

Robert Trent Jones Jr. Course (⊠ Cotton Bay Club, Rock Sound, ☎ 242/334–6156), an 18-hole, 7,068-yard, par-72 course, is Eleuthera's only course, although conditions aren't up to par. You won't find a clubhouse or restaurant, and some fairways are poorly marked. The club has caddies, but no carts. Rates are $70 for 9 holes and $100 for 18 holes. Club rental is $150. Be sure to call ahead for reservations.

Shopping

The **Almond Tree** (⊠ Queen's Hwy., ☎ 242/334–2385) is a blue house with white hibiscus–painted shutters. Inside, the quaint gift shop has a collection of handmade gifts, jewelry, and straw work.

Tarpum Bay

㉕ Waterfront **Tarpum Bay** is one of Eleuthera's loveliest settlements, with hilly roads flanked by weather-beaten homes with colored shutters and goats roaming the streets. Just south of Tarpum Bay is **Flanders Art Studio** (☎ no phone), where Mal Flanders sells watercolors and canvases of local scenes, as well as driftwood paintings. The studio is open Monday through Saturday 9–5.

Dining and Lodging

$-$ ✕▥ **Hilton's Haven.** Not to be confused with the well-known U.S. hotel chain, this Hilton is an unassuming 10-room motel across the road from a beach. This tidy, unpretentious place is run by a matronly local nurse named Mary Hilton. Rooms have private baths and patios. Ms. Hilton serves good home cooking in her small restaurant. The hotel is a two-minute walk from the beach and about 8 mi from the Rock Sound Airport. Room rates are a bargain. ⊠ *Tarpum Bay, Eleuthera,* ☎ *242/334–4231 or 800/688–4752,* ☏ *242/334–4020. 10 rooms, 1 apartment. Bar, dining room, air-conditioning in some rooms. No credit cards. EP, MAP.*

Shopping

You can stock up on groceries, souvenirs, and the like at **Tarpum Bay Shopping Centre** (☎ 242/334–4022).

En Route About halfway between Rock Sound and Governor's Harbour, distinguished **Windermere Island** is the site of vacation homes of the rich and famous, including members of the British royal family. Don't plan on any drive-by ogling of these million-dollar homes. The security gate prevents sightseers from passing.

Governor's Harbour

㉖ **Governor's Harbour** is where the intrepid Eleuthera Adventurers landed. The drive between Governor's Harbour and Rock Sound takes about 35 minutes. If you're here when the mail boats M/V *Bahamas Daybreak III* and M/V *Eleuthera Express* chug in, you'll witness the sight of residents unloading mattresses, lumber, mail, stacks of vegetables, and other household necessities. You might also see the same Eleutherans loading their own vegetables for export to Nassau. While they're here, they'll stop in at their mailboxes at the small post office in the town's pink government building.

If you're cooking during your stay, note that the Governor's Harbour waterfront is a great place to procure fresh fish and conch.

Dining and Lodging

$–$$ ✕ **Mate & Jenny's.** A few miles south of Governor's Harbour, this neighborhood restaurant specializes in pizza. Try one topped with conch. Sandwiches, Bahamian specialties, and ice-cream sundaes are also served. The walls are painted with tropical sunset scenes and decorated with photos, and the jukebox and pool table add to the joint's local color. Pizza pie prices are $10, $15, and $24. ⊠ *S. Palmetto Pt.,* ☎ 242/332–1504. MC, V. Closed Tues. No lunch Sun.

$ ✕⌂ **Buccaneer Club.** On a hillside overlooking the town and the harbor, this mid-19th-century farmhouse has been transformed into a family-run inn. Bougainvillea, hibiscus, and coconut palms flourish on the grounds. The guest rooms, with two double beds and full baths, are decorated with rattan furniture. The spacious third-floor room has a wonderful view of Governor's Harbour and the water. The beach is a leisurely five-minute stroll away, and the harbor, where you can also swim, is within shouting distance. Mal Flanders's paintings grace the walls at the Buccaneer Club, where you can sample such native specialties as grouper, conch, and crawfish. ⊠ *Box 86, Governor's Harbour, Eleuthera,* ☎ *242/332–2000,* ℻ *242/332–2888,* ⓦⓔⓑ *www.buccaneerclub.com. 5 rooms. Restaurant, bar, shop. MC, V.*

$ ✕⌂ **Cocodimama Charming Resort.** If decompressing in a hammock is your thing, you're in luck—you'll find one on the private patios of all 12 rooms at this sedate newcomer, nestled on the Caribbean side of the island, 6 mi north of Governor's Harbour. Rooms are accented with teak furniture imported from Indonesia as well as Italian tiles, which reflects the taste of the married Italian ex-pats who own and manage the property. Their influence also pervades the menu of the restaurant's Italian-Bahamian menu: buffalo mozzarella and other delicacies are flown in to complement the local fare. Snorkeling equipment and catamaran and kayak rentals are included in the rates. ⊠ *Alabaster Bay, Governor's Harbour, Eleuthera,* ☎ *242/332–3150,* ℻ *242/332–3155,* ⓦⓔⓑ *www.cocodimama.com. 12 rooms. Restaurant, Internet. MC, V. Closed Sept.–Nov.*

$ ✕⌂ **Unique Village.** Just south of Governor's Harbour near North Palmetto Point, this resort has large, tile-floor rooms. The round restaurant, with its pagoda-style natural-wood ceiling, wraparound covered deck, and wonderful view of the beach makes this village unique. Try the chateaubriand for two with a Caesar salad, or any of the seafood specialties. The small bar has satellite TV, high captain's chairs, and views from second-story windows. The resort organizes deep sea fishing trips. ⊠ *Box EL-25187, Governor's Harbour, Eleuthera,* ☎ *242/332–1830,* ℻ *242/332–1838,* ⓦⓔⓑ *www.bahamasvg.com/uniquevil.html. 10 rooms, 4 villas. Restaurant, bar, beach, snorkeling, fishing. MC, V. EP, FAP, MAP.*

$$ ⌂ **Cigatoo Resort.** Surrounded by a white picket fence, this resort sits high on a hill overlooking Governor's Harbour. It has crisp white buildings trimmed in vibrant hues with indoor and outdoor tropical gardens. Rooms have bright, sunny decor; modern furnishings; and private patios or balconies. The resort is just minutes from a pink-sand beach. The Cigatoo Room restaurant specializes in Italian and Bahamian cuisine. The guest services department arranges bonefishing or deep-sea fishing trips, day trips to other islands, and car or bike rentals. Note

that the resort is for guests 16 and up. ✉ *Queen's Hwy.*, ☎ *242/332–3060*, FAX *242/332–3061*, WEB *www.cigatooresort.com. 22 rooms. Restaurant, cable TV, pool, 2 tennis courts, recreation room, bar, meeting room, Internet. MC, V. Closed Oct.–Nov.*

$ 🏠 **Duck Inn and Orchid Garden.** Facing west into the sunset, overlooking beautiful Governor's Harbour, two colonial cottages and a home built in the 1850s nestle into a tropical hillside garden surrounded by a world-class orchid collection. John and Kay Duckworth bought the compound from a Canadian timber baron and restyled the houses. With one bedroom each, the cottages are perfect for couples, whereas the four-bedroom house can sleep eight. Each dwelling has a full kitchen (there are two grocery stores just a block away) and a verandah. A full-time gardener tends to tropical fruit trees; guests are welcome to pick and eat—even the apples. ✉ *Queen's Hwy.*, ☎ *242/332–2608*, FAX *242/332–2160*, WEB *www.theduckinn.com. 2 cottages, 1 house. Kitchenettes, fishing. MC, V.*

$–$ 🏠 **Laughing Bird Apartments.** English architect Dan Davies (designer of Windermere Island Club and Jacques Cousteau's villa) and his wife, Jean, own these four tidy apartments on an acre of land at the water's edge. Linens and crockery (including an English teapot and china cups) are furnished. You can stock your kitchen with produce from local stores or dine in any of the four restaurants within walking distance. This is a quiet, on-your-own kind of place, where relaxing and fishing are the name of the game. ✉ *Box EL-25076, Governor's Harbour, Eleuthera*, ☎ *242/332–2012*, FAX *242/332–2358. 4 apartments. Kitchens, beach, fishing, Internet. D, MC, V.*

Outdoor Activities and Sports

SNORKELING

If you have a four-wheel-drive vehicle, take the road east at the settlement of James Cistern to reach James Point, a beautiful beach with snorkeling and 3- to 10-ft waves for surfers. About 4 mi north of James Cistern on the Atlantic side, take the rough-hewn steps down to Hidden Beach, a sandy little hideaway sheltered by a rock-formation canopy, affording maximum privacy and a great spot for novice snorkelers.

Hatchet Bay and Environs

㉗ Hatchet Bay has mid-Eleuthera's only marina. Be sure to notice the names of the town's side roads, which have such colorful designations as Lazy Road, Happy Hill Road, and Smile Lane. Just south of town, the Rainbow Inn and Restaurant is the hub of activity for this stretch of Eleuthera.

㉘ North of Hatchet Bay lies **The Cave,** a subterranean, bat-populated tunnel complete with stalagmites and stalactites. It was supposedly once used by pirates to hide their loot. An underground path leads for more than a mile to the sea, ending in a lofty, cathedral-like cavern. Within its depths fish swim in total darkness. The adventurous may wish to explore this area with a flashlight (follow the length of guide string along the cavern's floor), but it's best to inquire first at one of the local stores or the Rainbow Inn for a guide. To find the cave, drive north from Hatchet Bay and watch for the vine-covered silo on Queen's Highway's north side. Take the left turn soon thereafter, marked by a white stripe down the center of Queen's Highway. En route to the Cave is Sweeting's Pond, the focus of all sorts of local myths. Some claim that there are Loch Ness–like creatures living in it. Others believe that a wrecked plane lies on the bottom.

Dining and Lodging

$ ✗▣ **Rainbow Inn.** Immaculate, generously sized cabins—all with
★   large private porches—dot the waterfront grounds. The restaurant
is one of the island's best, with a classy but no-fuss atmosphere and
exhibition windows that face gorgeous sunsets. Islanders drive great
distances for a meal here, especially when the famed Dr. Seabreeze
strums away, on rib night (Wednesday) and steak night (Friday). The
Nautical Bar, hung with authentic ship's wheels salvaged from wrecks,
drips with local color. Nurse those Goombay Smashes as long as you
like; cantankerous co-owner "Krabby" Ken won't be bashful about
letting you know when it's time to leave. ⊠ *2½ mi south of Hatchet
Bay (Box EL-25053, Governor's Harbour, Eleuthera),* ☎ FAX *242/335–
0294 or* ☎ *800/688–0047,* WEB *www.rainbowinn.com. 4 apartments,
2 2-bedroom villas, 1 3-bedroom villa. Restaurant, bar, kitchenettes,
microwaves, pool, tennis court, fishing, bicycles. MC, V. EP, MAP.
Closed Sept. 1–Nov. 15.*

Gregory Town and Environs

㉙ **Gregory Town** sits on top of a hill, with many of its charming pastel
homes dotting the hillside. The town's annual Pineapple Festival begins on the Thursday evening of the Bahamian Labor Day weekend,
at the beginning of June. With live music, juicy ripe pineapple (served
every possible way), and settlement-wide merriment continuing into
the wee hours, this is Gregory Town's liveliest happening.

Gregory Town's claim to fame lies about 2½ mi south of town, where
㉚ **Surfer's Beach,** a site of the 1960s "Beach Bum" culture, still packs
wave-catchers from December through May. If you don't have a
jeep, you can walk the ¾ mi to this Atlantic-side beach—follow
rough-and-bumpy Ocean Boulevard at Eleuthera Island Shores just
south of town.

If you're too lulled by the ebb and flow of lapping waves and prefer
your shores crashing with dramatic white sprays, perhaps a visit to
㉛ Eleuthera's **Grottoes and Hot Tubs** will revive you. The sun warms these
tidal pools, making them a markedly more temperate soak than the
sometimes-chilly ocean. On most days, refreshing sprays and rivulets
tumble into the tubs, but on some it can turn dangerous; if the waves
are crashing over the top of the cove's centerpiece mesa, pick another
day to stop here. If you're driving from Gregory Town, the entrance
is approximately 5 mi north on the right (Atlantic) side of the Queen's
Highway, across the road from two thin tree stumps. If you reach the
one-lane Glass Window Bridge, you've gone too far.

At a very narrow point of the island a few miles north of Gregory Town,
you'll find a place where a slender concrete bridge, called the Glass Bridge,
links two sea-battered bluffs that separate the Governor's Harbour and
North Eleuthera districts. Sailors going south in the waters between New
㉜ Providence and Eleuthera supposedly named this area the **Glass Window**
because they could see through the narrow cavity to the Atlantic on the
other side. Stop to watch the northeasterly deep-azure Atlantic swirl together under the bridge with the southwesterly turquoise Great Bahama
Bank, producing a brilliant aquamarine froth. Artist Winslow Homer
found the site stunning, too. He painted *Glass Window* in 1885. It's
thought that the bridge was a natural span until the early 1900s, when
rough currents finally washed it away. A 1991 storm lifted up the just-
completed two-lane bridge, setting it down some 7 ft to the south, which
accounts for the now-one-lane scaffold's zig.

Dining and Lodging

$-$ ✕ **Elvina's Bar and Restaurant.** Shoot some pool and enjoy some West Indian specialties like curry chicken at this local favorite that until recently doubled as a laundromat. Walls are covered with license plates and bumper stickers, and the surfboards hanging from the ceiling have been stowed there by surfer-regulars. Elvina's husband, known around these parts as "Chicken Ed," is from Louisiana, and the jambalaya here is the real thing. Be sure to call ahead, as Elvina and Ed don't open every night. ✉ *Queens Hwy., Governor's Harbour,* ☎ *242/335–5032. No credit cards.*

$ ✕▥ **The Cove Eleuthera.** Thirty secluded acres set the tone for this relaxing seaside inn. A rocky promontory separates two coves: one has a small sandy beach with palapas, lounge chairs, and kayaks, the other is rocky and ideal for snorkeling. Guests can easily kayak from the sandy to the rocky cove and other coves nearby. The poolside patio is a good place for breakfast or relaxing cocktails. Clustered rooms have tile floors, high slanted ceilings, and white rattan furnishings. There's also a honeymoon suite built on the promontory with a 180° view of the coves and the sea. The window-lined dining room—popular for sunset viewing—is spacious and bright, serving three meals a day. ✉ *3 mi south of Glass Window Bridge and 1½ mi north of Gregory Town (Box 1548, Gregory Town, Eleuthera),* ☎ *242/335–5142 or 800/552–5960,* ᴆᴬˣ *242/335–5338,* ᵂᴱᴮ *www.thecoveeleuthera.com. 24 rooms, 2 suites. Restaurant, bar, lounge, pool, 2 tennis courts, snorkeling, fishing, bicycles. MC, V. EP, MAP.*

Nightlife

The debonair **Dr. Seabreeze** strums his acoustic guitar while singing native songs that are nothing short of precious oral history. He plays Wednesday and Friday nights at the Rainbow Inn and Thursday night at Unique Village.

Outdoor Activities and Sports

SURFING

In Gregory Town, stop by **Rebecca's** general store and crafts shop (☎ 242/335–5436), where local surf guru "Ponytail Pete" stocks a few supplies and posts a chalkboard listing surf conditions and tidal reports.

Shopping

Island Made Shop (✉ Queen's Hwy., ☎ 242/335–5369), run by Pam and Greg Thompson, is a good place to shop for Bahamian arts and crafts, including Androsia batik (made on Andros Island), driftwood paintings, Abaco ceramics, and prints.

Junkanoo Shack (✉ Queen's Hwy., ☎ no phone) is an interesting Bahamian Heritage stop. Exquisite handmade costumes used in the Junkanoo parade (Boxing Day, or December 26) are created and sometimes sold here. For the shack's hours, ask at one of the local grocery stores.

En Route Snorkelers and divers will want to spend some time at **Gaulding's Cay** beach, 3 mi north of Gregory town. Swim out to the tiny offshore island to witness a concentration of sun anemones—as if someone had laid carpet—so spectacular it dazzled even Jacques Cousteau's biologists. Gaulding's Cay is also a nice 1,500-ft shelling stretch for beachcombers.

Harbour Island

★ ㉝ **Harbour Island** has often been called the Nantucket of the Caribbean and the prettiest of the Out Islands because of its 3 mi of powdery pink-sand beach and its pastel-color clapboard houses with dormer windows, set among white picket fences, narrow lanes, quaint shops, and tropical flowers. The residents have long called it Briland, their faster way of pronouncing "Harbour Island." Although taxis, golf carts, and bikes are available, you can explore the island on foot without too much exertion. Within its 2 square mi are tucked some of the Bahamas's most attractive small hotels, each strikingly distinct. At several that are perched on a bluff above the shore, you can fall asleep with the windows open and listen to the waves lapping the beach. You reach Harbour Island via a five-minute ferry ride from the North Eleuthera dock. Fares are $8 per person, $4 per person in a boat of two or more, plus an extra dollar to be dropped off at the private docks of Valentine's or Romora Bay Club. The ferry also occasionally charges more for nighttime rides.

Old trees line the narrow streets of **Dunmore Town,** named after the 18th-century royal governor of the Bahamas, Lord Dunmore, who built a summer home here and laid out the town. The community was once second in the country to Nassau in terms of its prosperity. It's the only town on Harbour Island, and you can take in all its attractions during a 20-minute stroll. Stop first at the **Harbour Island Tourist Office** (☎ 242/333–2621), in the yellow building opposite the ferry dock. Get a map and ask about current events. Across the street is a row of straw-work stands, including Dorothea's, Pat's, and Sarah's, where you'll find straw bags, hats, accessories, T-shirts, and tourist bric-a-brac. Food stands sell conch and other local fare. On Dunmore Street, you can visit the Bahamas's oldest Anglican church, **St. John's,** built in 1768, and the distinguished 1848 **Wesley Methodist Church.** Both hold services. On Bay Street, **Loyalist Cottage,** one of the original settlers' homes (circa 1797), has also survived. Many other old houses in the area, with gingerbread trim and picket fences, have such amusing names as "Beside the Point," "Up Yonder," and "The Royal Termite." Off the eastern, Atlantic shore lies a long coral reef, which protects the beach and has excellent snorkeling. You can see multicolored fish and a few old wrecks.

Dining and Lodging

Note that most Harbour Island hotels are closed from September through mid- to late November.

$–$$$$ ✕ **Romora Bay Club.** Thomas Chiarelli, probably the Bahamas's only
★ French chef, expertly prepares nightly dinner menus at this enchanting location. The waterfront alfresco bar, Sloppy Joe's, has Fernand Léger drawings and Andy Warhol prints adorning the brightly painted walls. It's also one of the best places to enjoy a cocktail and views of the Harbour Island sunset. Arrive with plenty of time to secure your seat on the deck. Come nightfall, stroll through the gardens to the main hotel complex for fine post-dusk dining in an intimate dining room overlooking the infinity pool. Also make time for a drink in the jungle-hip Parrot Bar. ✉ *South end of Dunmore St., Dunmore Town,* ☎ *242/333– 2325. Reservations essential. AE, MC, V.*

$–$$ ✕ **Harbour Lounge.** The popular former owners of the Picadilly restaurant—a longtime Nassau favorite—now own this pink building with green shutters across from the government dock. Arrive early if you want good seats on the front deck for watching the sunset over cocktails. The lunch and dinner fare might include smoked dolphinfish dip with garlic pita chips or grouper cake salad. ✉ *Bay St., Dunmore Town,* ☎ *242/333–2031. MC, V. Closed Mon.*

$–$ ✕ **Arthur's Bakery and Cafe.** *M*A*S*H* screenwriter Robert Arthur and his Trinidadian wife, Anna, bake sensational bread every morning. Try the four-herb or jalapeño loaf. Anna coordinates and caters weddings as well. ✉ *Corner of Crown St. and Dunmore St., Dunmore Town,* ☎ *242/333–2285. No credit cards. Closed Sun. No dinner.*

$ ✕ **Dunmore Deli.** Under a green-and-white stripe awning shading a wooden deck, this exceptional deli serves alfresco breakfasts and lunches. It stocks a superb variety of international coffee, imported cheese, and other gourmet items you won't find anywhere else on the island. ✉ *King St., Dunmore Town,* ☎ *242/333–2644. MC, V. Closed Sun. No dinner.*

$ ✕ **Queen Conch.** A block and a half from the ferry dock on Bay Street,
★ Lavaughn and Richard Percentie's colorful snack stand overlooking the harbor is renowned for its freshly caught conch salad ($6), which is diced in front of you, mixed with fresh vegetables, and served in deep bowls. Visitors from the world over place large orders to take home. ✉ *Bay St., Dunmore Town,* ☎ *no phone. No credit cards. Closed Sun.*

$$$$ ✕⊞ **Dunmore Beach Club.** The Dunmore is proud of its guest-to-staff
★ ratio (almost one-to-one) and the length of service of its employees (10 years is not considered a long time here). Accommodations are in very private New England–style cottages with exquisite interiors, including gorgeous marble bathrooms with two-person whirlpool tubs, enormous stand-alone showers, and separate sink-vanity areas. Bright bedspreads, white rattan furniture, and tile floors complete the handsome look. In the cozy clubhouse you'll find a Villeroy & Boch–tiled, ocean-view honor bar; comfy settees; a working fireplace; and a well-stocked library. The restaurant serves a four-course international menu at 8 PM. ✉ *Box EL-27122, Harbour Island, Eleuthera,* ☎ *242/333–2200 or 877/ 891–3100,* FAX *242/333–2429,* WEB *www.dunmorebeach.com. 12 units in 6 cottages. Restaurant, bar, refrigerators, tennis court, library, beach, laundry service, Internet. MC, V. FAP.*

$$$$ ✕⊞ **Pink Sands.** Island Records founder Chris Blackwell transformed this old Harbour Island property—on the edge of the famous rosy-hued strands—into a luxury resort. Private, colorful one- or two-bedroom cottages, scattered across the lush, 25-acre property, include such frills as Aveda Spa-Bath toiletries, cordless phone, TV/VCR, CD player, and a king-size bed with dual-controlled heater. The main house has a hand-carved bar and imported Indonesian furniture. The richness extends to the library, which has a working fireplace and plump, comfy couches. Chef Philip Buckingham presides over Euro-Bahamian fare during lunch in the ocean-view Blue Bar, and in the evenings creates four-course "Chef Recommends" menus. ✉ *Box 87, Harbour Island, Eleuthera,* ☎ *242/333–2030 or 800/688–7678,* FAX *242/333–2060,* WEB *www. islandoutpost.com/pinksands. 25 1- and 2-bedroom cottages. 2 restaurants, 2 bars, dining room, in-room safes, minibars, in-room VCRs, pool, 3 tennis courts, gym, beach, snorkeling, library, billiards, shop, babysitting, laundry service, Internet. AE, MC, V. MAP. Closed two weeks in mid-Oct.*

$$ ✕⊞ **Coral Sands Hotel.** Sitting right above the world-famous, 3-mi-long pink beach on 9 hilly acres, this resort has bright, individually decorated guest rooms. Upstairs rooms—reached by attractive, curving steps—have access to expansive rooftop terraces. Some lower rooms have child-size futons and adjoining bedrooms—all have small private balconies overlooking the ocean or gardens through French doors. Breakfast is served on a balcony with open arches framing breathtaking views of the ocean. Cordon Bleu–certified chef Susan Neff prepares ambitious dinner menus. Lunch is served at a beach bar high above the rosy sand. ✉ *Chapel St., Harbour Island, Eleuthera,* ☎ *242/333– 2350, 242/333–2320, or 800/468–2799,* FAX *242/333–2368,* WEB *www. coralsands.com. 39 rooms and suites. Restaurant, pool, tennis court, snorkeling, boating, fishing, billiards, library, 2 bars, beach, laundry service, Internet; no room TVs. AE, MC, V. EP, MAP.*

$$ ✕▦ **The Landing.** Built by uniting two early 19th-century homes, this
★   lovely inn facing the harbor embodies an understated contemporary-rus-
tic chicness. All seven plantation-style bedrooms have harbor views;
pastel walls; Bahamian-made, hand-carved four-poster beds with coor-
dinating Ralph Lauren fabrics; and large, tiled bathrooms. Accommo-
dating co-owners Toby Barry and Brenda Barry (a former Miss Bahamas)
use the large, original parlor with highly polished Abaco pine floors as
an intimate restaurant (closed Wednesday), perhaps the island's finest.
You can also dine on the porch overlooking the harbor, and in a lovely
garden. The small bar is fabulous, offering premium libations you can't
find elsewhere on the island. A hearty breakfast of delicious goodies is
included in the rate. ⊠ *Bay St. (Box 190),* ☎ *242/333–2707 or 242/
333–2740,* ⅧX *242/333–2650,* ﷲ *www.harbourislandlanding.com.
7 rooms. Restaurant, bar, library, business services, Internet; no room
phones, no room TVs. MC, V. CP. Closed Sept. 10–Nov. 1.*

$ ✕▦ **Valentine's Resort and Marina.** Island-hopping yachties like to tie
up at Valentine's modern, fully equipped 39-slip marina. The club hosts
the North Eleuthera Regatta on Columbus Day. Valentine's has a com-
plete dive shop, offering a variety of dives, including trips to Current Cut,
Sink Hole, and Bat Cavern. The resort shuttles guests to the pink-sand
beach and arranges deep-sea and bonefishing excursions. Guests can ex-
pect good Bahamian-American cooking and basic, plainly decorated motel-
style rooms. ⊠ *Northeast Harbour Island, ¼ mi from Dunmore Town
(Box 1, Harbour Island, Eleuthera),* ☎ *242/333–2142 or 800/323–
5655,* ⅧX *242/333–2135,* ﷲ *www.valentinesresort.com. 10 rooms.
Restaurant, bar, pool, tennis court, dive shop, marina, fishing, bicycles,
business services, Internet. AE, MC, V. EP, MAP.*

$–$ ✕▦ **Tingum Village.** The cottages in Ma Percentie's rustic village have
high tongue-and-groove pine ceilings, sea-colored furnishings, netting
above the king-size beds, and two-person whirlpool tubs overlooking
the yard's gardens out of floor-to-ceiling corner windows. In front of
the hotel is Ma Ruby's Restaurant, home of Jimmy Buffet's original
"Cheeseburger in Paradise," where you can sample Bahamian food on
a breezy covered patio three times daily. Leave room for Ma Precen-
tie's home-baked bread, coconut tarts, key lime pie, or native pound
cake. Tingum Village is on the town's south end and a short walk from
Harbour Island's famous pink-sand beach. ⊠ *Next to the Harbour Is-
land Library, Harbour Island, Eleuthera,* ☎ ⅧX *242/333–2161. 12
rooms, 5 1-bedroom and 2 2-bedroom suites, 1 3-bedroom cottage.
Restaurant, bar. MC, V. EP, MAP.*

$$$ ▦ **Romora Bay Club.** Clusters of cottages are scattered about the
★   grounds at this eclectic and artsy resort on Harbour Island's bay side.
Each guest room, suite, or villa is decorated with unique furnishings
(including a custom-made bedspread) and artwork and has a private
patio, TV/VCR, and CD player. While the hotel is not on the famous
pink beach, it's just a short golf-cart ride away. If you'd rather stay on
the property, you won't be bored: Water sports galore are yours for the
taking; the library has hundreds of movies, CDs, and books for you to
borrow; and the lovely pool deck has stunning bay views. ⊠ *South End
of Dunmore St., Dunmore Town,* ☎ *242/333–2325 or 800/688–0425,*
ⅧX *242/333–2500,* ﷲ *www.romorabay.com. 30 rooms, suites, and villas. 2 restaurants, 2 bars, in-room VCRs, pool, tennis court, waterskiing, fishing, library, dock, billiards, Internet. AE, MC, V. MAP.*

$$ ▦ **Runaway Hill Club.** What was once a private seaside mansion is now
★   an enchanting, intimate New England–style inn perched on a bluff above
Harbour Island's fabled beach. Most rooms face the sea; the rest over-
look the gardens. All are individually decorated with antiques, trunks,
original island artwork, lovely bed linens, and coordinating draperies.
The newer hilltop villa building has larger, more uniform rooms with

colorful patchwork quilts and bookshelves with an array of titles. Stairs lead down to the freshwater pool that hovers over the beach. Be sure to make reservations early for the superb dinner. *Box EL-27031, Dunmore Town,* ☎ *242/333–2150,* FAX *242/333–2420,* WEB *www.runawayhill.com. 10 rooms. Restaurant, bar, lounge, pool, beach; no kids. AE, MC, V. EP, MAP. Closed Labor Day–Nov. 15.*

$
★
🖭 **Bahama House Inn.** Harbour Island's only upscale bed-and-breakfast inn was originally deeded in 1796 and built by Thomas W. Johnson, Briland's first justice of the peace. Set in a garden filled with bougainvillea, royal poincianas, and roses, this lovely five-bedroom house thrives thanks to the loving preservation work done by genial owner-hosts John and Joni Hersch. Each guest room has good local artwork, queen- or king-size four-poster beds with decorative netting, a comfy sofa, and gracious Queen Anne–style writing desks. Enjoy Continental breakfast each morning on deck. ⊠ *Dunmore St.,* ☎ *242/333–2201,* FAX *242/ 333–2850,* WEB *www.bahamahouseinn.com. 5 rooms, 1 1-bedroom suite. TV in common area, library; no room TVs. MC, V. CP. Closed Oct.*

Nightlife

Enjoy a brew on the wraparound patio of **Gusty's** (☎ 242/333–2165), on Harbour Island's northern point. This lively hot spot has sand floors, a few tables covered in orange-batiked cloths, and patrons shooting pool or watching sports on satellite TV. On weekends, holidays, and in high season, it is a very crowded and happening dance spot with a DJ.

Enter through the marine life–muraled hallway at **Seagrapes** (⊠ Colebrook and Gibson Sts., ☎ 242/333–2389) to a large nightclub with a raised stage that's home to the local Funk Gang band.

Valentine's Resort and Marina (☎ 242/333–2142) is particularly lively on weekend nights. The waterfront Reach Grill and the second-story Reach Up deck make wonderful vantage points for sunset-watching or imbibing.

Vic-Hum Club (⊠ Barrack St., ☎ 242/333–2161) occasionally hosts live Bahamian bands in a room decorated with classic record album covers; otherwise, you'll find locals playing Ping-Pong and listening and dancing to loud recorded music, from calypso to American pop and R&B.

Outdoor Activities and Sports

BOATING AND FISHING

There are abundant spots around the island to angle for bonefish (at a cost of around $75 a half day), bottom fish ($75 a half day), reef fish ($20 an hour), and deep-sea fish ($250–$600 a full day). And there is great bonefishing right off Dunmore Town at Girl Bay. The Harbour Island Tourist Office can arrange bone- and bottom-fishing trips and excursions, as can all the major hotels.

Valentine's Resort and Marina (☎ 242/333–2142) can arrange various types of fishing and has small boats for rent. **Big Red Rentals** (☎ 242/333–2045) offers Boston Whalers (13 ft–21 ft) and banana-boat rides.

SCUBA DIVING AND SNORKELING

Current Cut, the narrow passage between North Eleuthera and Current Island, is loaded with marine life and provides a roller-coaster ride on the currents. **Devil's Backbone,** in North Eleuthera, offers a tricky reef area with a nearly infinite number of dive sites and a large number of wrecks. **Fox Divers** (☎ 242/333–2323) rents scuba equipment and offers instruction, certification, dive packages, and daily dive trips. **Valentine's Dive Center** (☎ 242/333–2309) rents and sells equipment and provides all levels of instruction, certification, dive packages, and daily group and custom dives. **Big Red Rentals** (☎ 242/333–2045) rents snorkeling equipment and offers snorkeling excursions.

Shopping

Blue Rooster (✉ Dunmore St., ☎ 242/333–2240) has a wonderful selection of Bahama Hand Prints clothing, bags, and elegant gift items from around the world. Closed Sunday.

Briland's Androsia (✉ Bay St., ☎ 242/333–2342) has a good selection of bathing suits, bags, and other items made from the bright batik fabric created on the island of Andros.

Dilly Dally (✉ Dunmore St., ☎ 242/333–3109) sells Bahamian-made jewelry, maps, decorations, and other fun souvenirs.

Harvey Roberts (✉ Bay St., ☎ 242/333–2085) is Briland's native-son politician-artist. Many of his original acrylics and prints may be viewed and purchased in his office–art gallery.

Island Services (✉ Dunmore St., ☎ 242/333–3032) provides E-mail, fax, phone messages, and photocopy service. Closed Saturday and Sunday.

John Bull (✉ Bay St., ☎ 242/333–2950), a duty-free shop near the dock, sells watches, fine jewelry, perfume, cigars, and sun glasses. Closed Sunday.

Princess Street Gallery (✉ Princess St., ☎ 242/333–2788) features original oil and watercolor paintings, hand-loomed throws, painted linens, and wooden bowls by local artists. Closed Sunday.

Sugar Mill (✉ Bay St., ☎ 242/333–2173) sells prints by local artists, Bahamian coin jewelry, picture frames decorated with Eleutheran shells, and wooden puzzles from the nearby island of Spanish Wells. Closed Sunday.

North Eleuthera

㉞ At the island's tip, **Preacher's Cave** is where the Eleutheran Adventurers took refuge and held services when their ship hit a reef more than three centuries ago. Note the original stone altar inside the cave. The last 2 mi of the road to Preacher's Cave is rough, but passable if you go slowly. Across from the cave are a long succession of deserted pink-sand beaches.

Spanish Wells

Off Eleuthera's northern tip lies St. George's Cay, the site of Spanish Wells. The Spaniards used this as a safe harbor during the 17th century while they transferred their riches from the New World to the Old. Supposedly they dug wells from which they drew water during their frequent visits. Today, water comes from the mainland. Residents—the few surnames go back generations—live on the island's eastern end in clapboard houses that look as if they've been transported from a New England fishing village. Tourists have little to do but hang out on the beach, dive, and dine on fresh seafood at **Jack's Out Back** (☎ 242/333–4219). Descendants of the Eleutheran Adventurers continue to sail these waters and bring back to shore fish and lobster (most of the Bahamas's langoustes are caught in these waters), which are prepared and boxed for export in a factory at the dock. So lucrative is the trade in crawfish that the 700 inhabitants may be the most prosperous Out Islanders in the Bahamas. Those who don't fish here grow tomatoes, onions, and pineapples. You reach Spanish Wells by taking a five-minute ferry ride ($5–$9, depending on your stop) from the North Eleuthera dock.

Eleuthera A to Z

AIR TRAVEL

Eleuthera has three airports—Governor's Harbour, North Eleuthera, and Rock Sound. Head for the one closest to your hotel. Fly into Governor's Harbour if you are staying south of Gregory Town, and into North Eleuthera if you are staying in Gregory Town or to the north. Several North American carriers and national airlines fly to each of the airports.

CARRIERS

Bahamasair has daily service from Nassau to all three airports. Cherokee Air is an on-demand charter service based in Marsh Harbour. It flies all over the Bahamas and serves Palm Beach and Fort Lauderdale as well. Continental Connection has daily flights to North Eleuthera from Miami and Fort Lauderdale. GHL Travel Agency charters two inexpensive daily flights from Nassau to North Eleuthera, and depending on demand flights also stop at Governor's Harbour. Major Air has service from Freeport to Governor's Harbour and North Eleuthera. Twin Air flies from Fort Lauderdale four times a week to Governor's Harbour, Rock Sound, and North Eleuthera. US Airways Express flies daily from Miami to Governor's Harbour and North Eleuthera. Tom Jones Air Charters, owned by the former publisher/editor of the *Pilot's Guide to the Bahamas,* flies all over the Bahamas.
➤ AIRLINES AND CONTACTS: **Bahamasair** (☎ 800/222–4262). **Cherokee Air** (☎ 242/367–2089 or 242/367–2613). **Continental Connection** (☎ 800/231–0856). **GHL Travel Agency** (☎ 242/323–7217 in Nassau; 242/335–1574 in North Eleuthera). **Major Air** (☎ 242/352–5778). **Tom Jones Air Charters** (☎ 305/931–6612 or 242/335–1353). **Twin Air** (☎ 954/359–8266). **US Airways Express** (☎ 800/622–1015).

AIRPORTS AND TRANSFERS

Eleuthera has three airports: North Eleuthera; Governor's Harbour, near the center of the island; and Rock Sound, in the southern part of the island.
➤ AIRPORT INFORMATION: **Governor's Harbour** (☎ 242/332–2321). **North Eleuthera** (☎ 242/335–1242). **Rock Sound** (☎ 242/334–2177).

TRANSFERS

Taxis wait for incoming flights at all three airports. Call a taxi prior to departing your resort or hotel; on Eleuthera you should allow a half hour for your cab to arrive; on Harbour Island, taxis come a few minutes after you call. If you land at North Eleuthera and need to get to Harbour Island, off Eleuthera's north coast, take a taxi ($4) to the ferry dock (Three Island Dock) on Eleuthera, a water taxi ($4) to Harbour Island, and, on the other side, another taxi ($3 to Coral Sands, for example). You follow a similar procedure to get to Spanish Wells, which is also off Eleuthera's north shore. Taxi service from Governor's Harbour Airport to the Cove Eleuthera is $42 for two people, though the taxi fare from North Eleuthera to the Cove is only $33 for two people. The fare from Governor's Harbour to Rainbow Inn is $24.
➤ TAXI INFORMATION: **Governor's Harbour Taxi Stand** (☎ 242/332–2568).

BIKE TRAVEL

Bicycles are a popular way to explore Harbour Island. You can rent them at Big Red Rentals or Michael's Cycles.
➤ BIKE RENTALS: **Big Red Rentals** (✉ Harbour Island, ☎ 242/333–2045). **Michael's Cycles** (✉ Harbour Island, ☎ 242/333–2384).

BOAT AND FERRY TRAVEL

The following mail boats leave from Nassau at Potter's Cay; for schedules, contact the Dockmaster's Office at Potter's Cay, Nassau.

M/V *Current Pride* sails to the Current, Lower Bogue, and Upper Bogue, and Hatchet Bay on Thursday, returning Tuesday. M/V *Bahamas Daybreak III* leaves on Monday for South Eleuthera, stopping at Rock Sound, and returns on Tuesday. It then leaves Thursday from Nassau for the Bluff and Harbour Island, returning on Sunday. The *Eleuthera Express* sails for Governor's Harbour and Spanish Wells on Monday and Thursday, returning to Nassau on Tuesday and Sunday, respectively. The fare is $20 for all Eleutheran destinations.

Bahamas Fast Ferries connects Nassau to Harbour Island and North Eleuthera on a sporadic schedule. A round-trip fare costs $100; excursion rates (including a tour, lunch, and a trip to the beach) are somewhat higher. The trip from Fast Ferries terminal on Potter's Cay, Nassau to Harbour Island, with a stop on Spanish Wells, takes two hours. Ferries leave Nassau at 8 AM (and also at 1:30 PM on Fridays and busier weekends) and return at 3:55 (and 6:25 on Fridays on busy weekends). Call to confirm departure times and rates. Make reservations well in advance for trips around Columbus Day, the weekend of the annual North Eleuthera Regatta.

➤ BOAT AND FERRY INFORMATION: **Bahamas Fast Ferry** (☎ 242/323–2166, FAX 242/322–8185, WEB www.bahamasferries.com). **Dockmaster's Office** (☎ 242/393–1064).

BUSINESS HOURS

Most small business on Harbour Island close for a lunch break between 1 and 3, a practice unique in the Bahamas. Banks on Eleuthera and its islands are open Monday through Thursday from 9:30 to 3, Friday until 5. Barclays Bank has a branch in Governor's Harbour. Royal Bank of Canada runs Harbour Island's only bank, in addition to branches in Governor's Harbour and Spanish Wells. Scotia Bank has branches in North Eleuthera and Rock Sound.

➤ CONTACTS: **Barclays Bank** (☎ 242/332–2300). **Royal Bank of Canada** (☎ 242/333–2250 Harbour Island; 242/332–2856 Governor's Harbour; 242/333–2620 Spanish Wells). **Scotia Bank** (North Eleuthera, ☎ 242/335–1400, 242/335–1406, or 242/334–2620; Rock Sound, ☎ 242/335–1400, 242/335–1406, or 242/334–2620).

CAR RENTAL

Your hotel will be the least complicated bet for arranging a car rental and can usually have a vehicle delivered to you at the airport. Request a four-wheel-drive if you plan to visit Preacher's Cave or Surfer's Beach. Johnson's Rentals, Arthur Nixon, Hilton's Car Rentals, and Cecil Cooper all rent cars from Governor's Harbour—call to discuss delivery of your automobile. In Rock Sound, Dingle Motor Service rents cars. Baretta's has cars and minivans. On Harbour Island and Spanish Wells, you're better off renting a golf cart.

➤ LOCAL AGENCIES: **Arthur Nixon** (☎ 242/332–1006 or 242/332–2568). **Baretta's** (✉ Harbour Island, ☎ 242/333–2361). **Cecil Cooper** (☎ 242/359–7007 or 242/332–2568). **Dingle Motor Service** (☎ 242/334–2031). **Hilton's Car Rentals** (☎ 242/335–6241 or 242/332–2568). **Johnson's Rentals** (☎ 242/332–2226).

EMERGENCIES

Governor's Harbour, Harbour Island, Rock Sound, and Spanish Wells each has its own police and medical emergency numbers.

➤ CONTACTS: **Medical Clinics** (☎ 242/332–2001; 242/332–2774 Governor's Harbour; 242/333–2222 Harbour Island; 242/334–2226 Rock

Sound; 242/333–4064 Spanish Wells). **Police** (☎ 242/332–2111 Governor's Harbour; 242/333–2111 Harbour Island; 242/334–2244 Rock Sound; 242/333–4030 Spanish Wells).

GOLF CART TRAVEL

Even if you're a big walker, you'll want a golf cart if you spend more than a couple of days on Harbour Island; there are several golf-cart rental companies there. Cart rates start at $35 for a 2-seater and go up according to size (a six-seater is the largest); definitely negotiate if you'll be renting for longer. On Spanish Wells, you'll be able to rent a cart directly at the dock.

➤ CONTACTS: **Baretta's** (☎ 242/333–2361). **Big Red Rentals** (☎ 242/333–3128). **Dunmore Rentals** (☎ 242/333–2372). **Grant's** (☎ 242/333–2157). **Johnson's Garage** (☎ 242/333–2376). **Ross's Garage** (☎ 242/333–2122). **R&J Golf Carts** (☎ 242/333–2116). **Sunshine Carts** (☎ 242/333–2509).

SIGHTSEEING GUIDES

Arthur Nixon is probably the most knowledgeable authority on Eleuthera. His presentation will make you want to stand up and applaud.

➤ CONTACT: **Arthur Nixon** (☎ 242/332–1006 or 242/332–2568 or cell 242/359–7879).

TAXIS

To explore Eleuthera, you'd best rent a car, which is cheaper than hiring a taxi, unless you consider having a driver who can double as your tour guide worth the expense. Taxis are available through your hotel. On Eleuthera, have your hotel call for a taxi about a half hour before you need it. On Harbour Island, taxis generally arrive a few minutes after being called. Taxis are almost always waiting at the North Eleuthera and Harbour Island water taxi docks.

TRANSPORTATION AROUND ELEUTHERA

Harbour Island is easily explored on foot—it takes only 30 minutes to walk the length of the island—although you'll be wise to rent a golf cart if you're staying for a few days. Visiting Eleuthera's main sights will require renting a car. North to south is about a three-hour drive. Governor's Harbour, which lies approximately at Eleuthera's midpoint, is a 40-minute drive from Glass Window in the north, and a 35-minute drive from Rock Sound in the south. You can also rent a bike or scooter to explore the island.

VISITOR INFORMATION

Contact the Eleuthera Tourist Office in Governor's Harbour or the Harbour Island Tourist Office on Bay St. right off the dock for brochures and information about the islands. Both are open weekdays 9–5.

➤ TOURIST INFORMATION: **Eleuthera Tourist Office** (✉ Governor's Harbour, ☎ 242/332–2142, FAX 242/332–2480). **Harbour Island Tourist Office** (✉ Bay St., ☎ 242/333–2621, FAX 242/333–2622).

THE EXUMAS

On the Exumas, you'll still find wild cotton, leftover from plantations established by Loyalists after the Revolutionary War, and breadfruit trees, which a local preacher bought from Captain William Bligh in the late 18th century. The islands are now known as the Bahamas's onion capital, although many of the 3,600-odd residents earn a living by fishing as well as farming. Your first impression of the people of the Exumas may be that almost all of them have the surname Rolle.

Lord John Rolle, who imported the first cotton seeds to these islands, had more than 300 slaves, to whom he bequeathed not only his name but also the 2,300 acres of land that were bestowed on him by the British government in the late 18th century.

The Exumas begin less than 35 mi southeast of Nassau and stretch south for about 90 mi, flanked by the Great Bahama Bank and Exuma Sound. They are made up largely of some 365 fragmented little cays. The two main islands, Great Exuma and Little Exuma, lie in the south, connected by a bridge. The islands' capital, George Town, on Great Exuma, is the site of one of the Bahamas's most prestigious and popular sailing events, the Out Islands Regatta, in which locally built wooden work boats compete. During the winter, George Town's Elizabeth Harbour is a haven of yachts. The surrounding waters are legendary for their desolate islands, coves, bays, and harbors.

The Exumas certainly offer their share of impressive characters. One of them, Gloria Patience, who is in her eighties and lives south of George Town, is known as the Shark Lady because she used to go out regularly in her 13-ft Boston Whaler and catch sharks with a 150-ft-long hand line. Hundreds of makos, hammerheads, and lemon sharks have met their match with Mrs. Patience, whose family came from Ireland and Scotland. Still making good use of various shark parts, she drills holes in their teeth and vertebrae to create pendants, necklaces, and earrings and turns their jawbones into wall hangings, all of which she sells to visitors from **Patience House,** her home–museum–gift shop in the tiny settlement known as The Ferry. Coming from George Town, she's a few hundred yards beyond the one-lane Ferry bridge. There's a handmade sign—SHARK LADY—on the left, which is at the beginning of a narrow gravel driveway that winds through her lush front yard. Across from the Exuma Market in George Town, "Mom" drives her delectable breads and pastries in daily from Williams Town and couldn't be more gracious. **Mom's Bakery** is the white van parked on the side of the road. Stop to savor a coconut turnover and her company.

Numbers in the margin correspond to points of interest on the Exumas map.

Little Exuma and Great Exuma

③⑤ The old village of **Williams Town** lies at Little Exuma Island's southern tip. Wild cotton still grows out in these parts, along the way to the **Hermitage,** a former plantation house with ruins of slave cottages nearby.

③⑥ Five miles south of George Town lies **Rolle Town,** a typical Exuma village—without the tourist trappings. Residents grow onions, mangoes, bananas, and other crops.

③⑦ Although **George Town** is the island's hive of activity, it's still on the no-need-for-a-traffic-light scale. The most imposing structure here is in the town center—the white-pillared, sandy pink, colonial-style **Government Administration Building,** modeled on Nassau's Government House and containing the commissioner's office, police headquarters, courts, and a jail. Atop a hill across from the government building is the whitewashed **St. Andrew's Anglican Church,** originally built around 1802 and rebuilt in 1991. Behind the church is the small Lake Victoria. A leisurely stroll around town will take you past a straw market and a few shops. You can buy fruit and vegetables and bargain with fishermen for some of the day's catch at the **Government Wharf,** where the mail boat comes in. The wharf is close to **Regatta Point** (☎ 242/336–2206), an attractive guest house named after the annual Out Is-

The Exumas

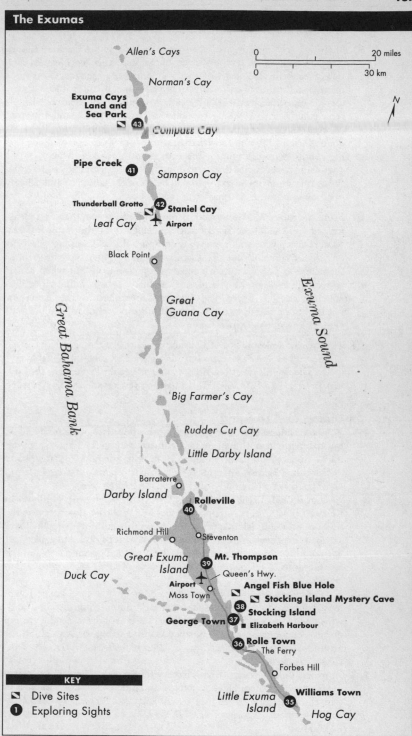

Allen's Cays

Norman's Cay

0   20 miles
0   30 km

N

**Exuma Cays
Land and
Sea Park**

43 *Compass Cay*

Pipe Creek 41

Sampson Cay

Thunderball Grotto 42 **Staniel Cay**

Leaf Cay ✈ **Airport**

Black Point ○

*Great
Guana Cay*

Exuma Sound

Great Bahama Bank

Big Farmer's Cay

Rudder Cut Cay

Little Darby Island

Barraterre ○

Darby Island **Rolleville**
40

Richmond Hill ○

○ **Steventon**

*Great Exuma
Island* 39 **Mt. Thompson**

Duck Cay — Queen's Hwy.

Airport ✈ ○ **Angel Fish Blue Hole**

Moss Town **Stocking Island Mystery Cave**

38 **Stocking Island**

George Town 37 ■ **Elizabeth Harbour**

36 **Rolle Town**
The Ferry

○ **Forbes Hill**

Williams Town

*Little Exuma
Island* 35

Hog Cay

KEY

◨ Dive Sites
❶ Exploring Sights

lands Regatta that curls around Kidd Cove, where the 18th-century pirate Captain Kidd supposedly tied up.

★ ㊳ Slightly more than a mile off George Town's shore lies **Stocking Island.** The 7-mi-long island has only seven inhabitants, a gorgeous white beach rich in seashells, and plenty of good snorkeling sites. Jacques Cousteau's team is said to have traveled a length of some 1,700 ft into **Mystery Cave,** a blue-hole grotto 70 ft beneath the island. Club Peace & Plenty's ferry runs over to Stocking Island twice daily at 10 AM and 1 PM and charges $8 for nonguests. Near the Stocking Island pier, Peace & Plenty Beach Club rents a variety of water-sports gear, provides changing rooms (with plumbing), and operates a lunch spot where Dora's "heavenly burgers and dreamful dogs" are the eats of choice. To enjoy the setting sun from Stocking Island, head for the **Chat & Chill,** a lively open-air restaurant and bar right on the point.

㊴ From the top of **Mt. Thompson,** rising from the beach, there is a pleasing view of the **Three Sisters Rocks** jutting above the water just offshore. During your walks, you may glimpse a flock of roaming peacocks on Great Exuma. Originally, a peacock and a peahen were brought to the island as pets by a man named Shorty Johnson, but when he left to work in Nassau, he abandoned the birds, who gradually proliferated into a colony. Some locals hunt these birds because they eat crops, but they are difficult to catch. Mt. Thompson is about 12 mi north of George Town, past Moss Town.

㊵ The town of **Rolleville** sits on a hill above a harbor, 20 mi north of George Town. Its old slave quarters have been transformed into livable cottages. The town's most prominent citizen, Kermit Rolle, runs the **Hilltop Tavern** (☎ 242/336–6038), a seafood restaurant and bar guarded by an ancient cannon.

Dining and Lodging

$–$$ ✕ **Eddie's Edgewater.** The specialty at this popular spot is turtle steak, but the menu also offers low-fat steamed chicken (call ahead, or wait the 40 minutes' preparation time). Don't miss the rake 'n' scrape band on Monday; rakes and saws serve as instruments. ⊠ *Charlotte St., George Town,* ☎ *242/336–2050. MC, V. Closed Sun.*

$–$ ✕ **Chat & Chill.** Yacht folks, locals, and visitors alike rub shoulders at
★ Kenneth Bowe's very hip and upscale—yet still casual—eatery on the point at Stocking Island. All of the incredible edibles are grilled over an open fire. Awesome conch burgers with secret spices and grilled fish with onions and potatoes are not to be missed. The Sunday pig roasts are fabulous. ⊠ *Stocking Island, George Town,* ☎ *no phone. No credit cards.*

$–$ ✕ **Iva Bowe's Central Highway Inn.** About 10 mi from George Town, close to the airport, this casual lunch and dinner spot has an island-wide reputation for the best native food. Try one of the delectable shrimp dishes—coconut beer shrimp, spicy Cajun shrimp, or scampi, all for around $10. ⊠ *Queen's Hwy.,* ☎ *242/345–7014. No credit cards. Closed weekends.*

$–$ ✕ **Towne Café.** George Town's bakery serves breakfast—consider trying the "stew" fish or chicken souse—and lunch—seafood sandwiches with three sides, or grilled fish. Towne Café is open until 5 PM. ⊠ *Marshall Complex, George Town,* ☎ *242/336–2194. No credit cards. Closed Sun.*

$ ✕ **Jean's Dog House.** A bright-yellow former school bus has been
★ converted into a tiny, spotless kitchen on wheels. Noted for her 'dogs, divine lobster burger, and the "MacJean," a hearty breakfast sandwich with sausage or bacon and sometimes cheese on homemade Bahama bread, Jean cooks them all up in her unique "dry-fry" method (no oil).

The minibus can be found every weekday from 7 to around 3 parked at the bottom of schoolhouse hill (a well-known landmark). Jean has an effervescent personality and is a treasure trove of Exuma history. She is also one of "Shark Lady's" nine children. ⊠ *Queen's Hwy., George Town,* ☎ *no phone. No credit cards. Closed weekends.*

$$$ ✕▥ **Hotel Higgins Landing.** The only resort on undeveloped Stocking
★ Island is this eco hotel, which is 100% solar powered—though everything still works when the weather's overcast. Wood cottages have screen windows with dark-green shutters and private, spacious decks with ocean views. Interiors have antiques, queen-size beds, tile floors, and folksy Americana decor. By day, the bar is an alfresco living room where you can play checkers or darts, or read books from the hotel's library. Colorful blossoms and tropical birds abound. Rates include full breakfasts and gourmet dinners, though be aware that the kitchen cannot accommodate *any* special dietary requests. No children under 16 during the winter season. ⊠ *Box EX-29146, George Town, Exuma,* ☎ *800/ 688–4752 Ext. 457,* ☎ FAX *242/336–2460 or 242/357–0008,* WEB *www.higginslanding.com. 5 cottages. Restaurant, bar, beach, dock, snorkeling, boating, fishing, library. No smoking. MC, V. MAP.*

$ ✕▥ **Club Peace & Plenty.** The granddaddy of Exuma's omnipresent Peace & Plenty empire, this pink, two-story hotel is near the heart of George Town. Rooms have private balconies—most overlooking the pool, with ocean views to the side, although some have have full ocean vistas. In high season, the hotel is known for its Saturday-night parties on the pool patio, where Lermon "Doc" Rolle has been holding court at the bar since the '70s. The indoor bar, which was once a slave kitchen, attracts locals and a yachting crowd, especially during the Out Islands Regatta. The hotel's restaurant serves some of the best breakfasts in town. ⊠ *Box EX 29055, George Town, Exuma,* ☎ *242/336–2551 or 800/525–2210,* FAX *242/336–2093,* WEB *www. peaceandplenty.com. 35 rooms. Restaurant, 2 bars, pool, beach, dock, boating, fishing. AE, MC, V. EP, MAP.*

$ ✕▥ **Coconut Cove Hotel.** The Paradise Suite at this intimate hotel has its own private terrace hot tub, a king-size bed, walk-in closet, and an immense bathroom with a black-marble Jacuzzi. Other rooms have queen-size beds, tile floors, and scenic views from private terraces. Bathrobes and fresh-daily floral arrangements add an elegant touch. The restaurant menu includes Angus beef, fresh pastas, and gourmet pizzas served outside on the deck or inside by the fireplace. ⊠ *Box EX-29299, George Town, Exuma,* ☎ *242/336–2659,* FAX *242/336–2658,* WEB *www.exumabahamas.com. 12 rooms, 1 cottage. Restaurant, bar, air-conditioning, minibars, pool, dive shop, fishing, laundry service. AE, D, MC, V.*

$ ✕▥ **Peace & Plenty Beach Inn.** The 16-room resort on 300 ft of beach is a mile west of its big brother, the Club Peace & Plenty, and a shuttle runs between the two four times daily. The units have white-tile floors, simple tropical-print accents, and French doors opening onto private patios or balconies that overlook the pool and the ocean. Once in the restaurant, marvel at the tiered, stained-pine cathedral ceiling and feast on blackened mahimahi, New York–cut Angus steak, or the delicious chicken breast Alfredo, baked in a crispy puff dough with sun-dried tomatoes. Reservations are required. ⊠ *Box EX 29055, George Town, Exuma,* ☎ *242/336–2250 or 800/525–2210,* FAX *242/336– 2253,* WEB *www.peaceandplenty.com. 16 rooms. Restaurant, 2 bars, refrigerators, pool, beach, fishing. AE, MC, V. EP, MAP.*

$ ✕▥ **Peace & Plenty Bonefish Lodge.** The Out Islands' swankest bone-
★ fishing lodge is on a peninsula 10 mi south of George Town. Dark wood and handsome hunter-green accents lend a gentleman's-club feel to the bar and dining room, where photos of anglers and their catches grace

the walls alongside signed jerseys from Mickey Mantle and Duke Snider. The large rooms have white rattan furnishings, louvered wooden doors, and private balconies overlooking the water. "Reel" adventurers will find contemplative, restful spots on the large deck, upstairs veranda, or in a hammock on the sandy point that juts out beyond the lodge's fish pond. In the dining room, Chef Robert prepares hearty fare—from 16-ounce New York strip steaks to vegetarian dishes. ⊠ *Box EX-29173, George Town, Exuma,* ☎ *242/345–5555 or 800/525–2210,* FAX *242/345–5556,* WEB *www.peaceandplenty.com. 8 rooms. 2 bars, dining room, air-conditioning, fans, snorkeling, boating, fishing, bicycles, library. MC, V. FAP.*

$$–$$$ ⊡ **Bahama Houseboats.** Brightly decorated floating accommodations offer all the comforts of home. There are five houseboats to choose from: three 35-ft boats with one bedroom and two 43-ft boats with two bedrooms. All have water slides that descend from the top deck. No special license or experience is required to rent the houseboats, and you'll be instructed on cruising parameters and safe operation before leaving the dock. The owners are always a radio call away to answer questions and provide peace of mind. Right out your "front door" you can fish, collect shells, snorkel, and cruise Elizabeth Harbour's multihued, incandescent waters. A three-day minimum stay is required. ⊠ *Box EX-29031, Government Dock, George Town, Exuma,* ☎ *242/336–2628,* FAX *242/336–2645,* WEB *www.bahamahouseboats.com. 5 boats. Kitchenettes, water slide. MC, V.*

$–$$ ⊡ **Regatta Point.** Soft pink with hunter-green shutters, this handsome two-story guest house overlooks Kidd Cove from its own petite island. Connected to George Town by a short causeway, the property is only a five-minute walk from town but far enough from the fray to have a secret hideaway's charm. Rooms have picturesque views of Elizabeth Harbour, large vaulted ceiling, and porches. The hotel has no restaurant, but units come with modern kitchens, and maid service is included. Sunfish sailboats and bicycles are available free to guests. ⊠ *Regatta Point across from George Town, Exuma, Box EX 29006,* ☎ *242/336–2206 or 800/688–0309,* FAX *242/336–2046,* WEB *www.exumabahamas.com. 1 1-bedroom unit, 1 2-bedroom unit, 3 suites, 1 cottage. Fans, kitchenettes, beach, dock, boating, fishing, bicycles, laundry service. MC, V.*

Nightlife

On Monday, head to **Eddie's Edgewater** (☎ 242/336–2050) for the rousing rake 'n' scrape music. **Two Turtles Inn** (☎ 242/336–2545) has barbecues in the lively patio courtyard and happy hours at the tables and benches surrounding the central license plate–decorated bar. In season, the poolside bashes at **Club Peace & Plenty** (☎ 242/336–2551), with its resident band, George Willey and the Inn Crowd, keep Bahamians and vacationers on the dance floor Wednesday and Saturday nights.

Outdoor Activities and Sports

BOATING

Renting a boat provides unforgettable explorations of the cays near George Town and beyond. A number of area hotels allow guests to tie up rental boats at their docks. For those who want to take a water jaunt through Stocking Island's hurricane holes, paddleboats and Sunfish sailboats are ideal options. **Exuma Dive Centre** (☎ 242/336–2390) rents 17-ft Polar Craft boats with Bimini tops for $75 a day and $375 a week.

On Stocking Island, **Peace & Plenty Beach Club** (☎ 242/336–2551) rents paddleboats ($15 per half day) and Sunfish sailboats ($20 per half day).

EVENTS

The **Annual New Year's Day Cruising Regatta** is held at the Staniel Cay Yacht Club, with international yachts taking part in a series of races. At the beginning of March, the **Cruiser's Regatta** hosts visiting boats for a week of races, cookouts, and partying in George Town. The **Out Islands Regatta** is the Bahamas's most important yachting event of the year. It takes place in April. Starting the race in Elizabeth Harbour in George Town, island-made wooden sailing boats compete for trophies. Onshore, the town is a three-day riot of Junkanoo parades, Goombay music, arts-and-crafts fairs, and continuous merriment.

FISHING

Most hotels can arrange for local guides, and a list is available from the **Exuma Tourist Office** (☎ 242/336–2430). **Exuma Dive Centre** (☎ 242/336–2390) rents fly and deep-sea fishing rods. **Cooper's Charter Service** (☎ 242/336–2711) will take you out for a day of deep-sea fishing, $300 per half day, $500 per full day. **Reno Rolle** (☎ 242/345–5003) is a highly recommended bonefishing guide. Fisherman and boat owner **Gus Thompson** (☎ 242/345–5062) will help you hook the big game as well as the feisty bonefish. **Peace & Plenty Bonefish Lodge** (☎ 242/345–5555) has excellent bonefishing guides.

SCUBA DIVING

Angel Fish Blue Hole, minutes from George Town, is a popular dive site filled with angel fish, spotted rays, snapper, and the occasional reef shark. **Stocking Island Mystery Cave** is full of mesmerizing schools of colorful fish but is for experienced divers only. **Exuma Dive Centre** (☎ 242/336–2390) offers two-tank dives for $75 with gear; it's $60 if you have your own equipment. **Exuma Scuba Adventures** (☎ 242/336–2893) offers dive instruction, certification courses, and scuba trips. One-tank dives are $45.

SNORKELING

On Stocking Island, **Peace & Plenty Beach Club** (☎ 242/336–2551) rents snorkel gear for $10 a day. **Exuma Dive Centre** (☎ 242/336–2390) has three-hour snorkeling excursions for $35 including mask, fins, and snorkel. **Exuma Scuba Adventures** (☎ 242/336–2893) offers daily snorkeling trips for $15.

TENNIS

Near the airport, **The Palms at Three Sisters Beach Resort** (☎ 242/358–4040) has one court and grants privileges to nonguests for $10 per hour.

WINDSURFING

On Stocking Island, **Peace & Plenty Beach Club** (☎ 242/336–2551) rents Windsurfers for $15 per half day and $30 per full day.

Shopping

In the Exumas, George Town is the place to shop. **Exuma Market** (✉ across from Scotia Bank, George Town, ☎ 242/336–2033) is the island's largest grocery and is considered by many to be the Out Islands' finest. Yachties tie up at the skiff docks in the rear, on Lake Victoria. FedEx, emergency E-mail, and faxes for visitors are accepted here as well.

Exuma Master Tailor Shop (✉ across street from Exuma Market, George Town, ☎ 242/336–2930), with one- to two-day service at very reasonable prices, will duplicate a favorite designer dress or suit while you are out sunning. Bring your own material, buttons, and zippers.

Peace & Plenty Boutique (✉ opposite Club Peace & Plenty, ☎ 242/336–2551) has a good selection of Androsia shirts and dresses.

Sandpiper Boutique (✉ Queen's Hwy., ☎ 242/336–2084) has upscale souvenirs, from high-quality cards and books to batik clothing and art.

Cays of the Exumas

A band of cays—with names like Rudder Cut, Big Farmer's, Great Guana, and Leaf—stretches north from Great Exuma.

④① Boaters will want to explore the waterways known as **Pipe Creek,** a winding passage through the tiny islands between Staniel and Compass cays. There are great spots for shelling, snorkeling, diving, and bonefishing. The **Samson Cay Yacht Club** (☎ 242/355–2034), at the creek's halfway point, is a good place for lunch or dinner.

④② **Staniel Cay** is a favorite destination of yachters and makes the perfect home base for visiting the Exuma Cays Land and Sea Park. The island has an airstrip, two hotels, and one paved road. Virtually everything is within walking distance. Oddly enough, as you stroll past brightly painted houses and sandy shores, you are as likely to see a satellite dish as a woman pulling a bucket of water from a roadside well. At one of three grocery stores, boat owners can replenish their supplies. The friendly village also has a small red-roof church, a post office, and a straw vendor.

Just across the water from the Staniel Cay Yacht Club is one of the Bahamas's most unforgettable attractions: **Thunderball Grotto,** a beautiful marine cave that snorkelers (at low tide) and experienced scuba divers can explore. In the central cavern, shimmering shafts of sunlight pour through holes in the soaring ceiling and illuminate the glass-clear water. You'll see right away why this cave was chosen as an exotic setting for such movies as 007's *Thunderball* and *Never Say Never Again,* and the mermaid tale *Splash.*

Above Staniel Cay, near the Exumas' northern end, lies the 176-square-**④③** mi **Exuma Cays Land and Sea Park,** which spans 22 mi between Conch Cut and Wax Cay Cut. You must charter a small boat or seaplane to reach the park, which has more than 20 mi of petite cays. Hawksbill Cay and Warderick Wells (both with remains of 18th-century Loyalist settlements) have marked hiking trails, as does Hall's Pond. At Shroud Cay, jump into "Camp Driftwood," where the strong current creates a natural whirlpool that whips you around a rocky outcropping to a powdery beach. Part of the Bahamas National Trust, the park appeals to divers, who appreciate the vast underworld of limestone, reefs, drop-offs, blue holes of freshwater springs, caves, and a multitude of exotic marine life, including one of the Bahamas's most impressive stands of rare pillar coral. Strict laws prohibit fishing and removing coral, plants, or even shells as souvenirs. A list of park rules is available at the headquarters on Warderick Wells.

North of the park is **Norman's Cay,** a beautiful island with 10 mi of rarely trod white beaches, which attract an occasional yachter. It was once the private domain of Colombian drug smuggler Carlos Lehder, whose planes left from here for drop-offs in Florida. It's now owned by the Bahamian government. **Allen's Cays** are at the Exumas' northernmost tip and are home to the rare, protected Bahamian iguana.

Dining and Lodging

$–$$ ✕☷ **Staniel Cay Yacht Club.** The club once drew such luminaries as Malcolm Forbes and Robert Mitchum. It's now a low-key getaway for yachties and escapists. The cottages, perched on stilts along a rocky bank, have broad ocean vistas and dramatic sunsets, which you can treasure from the comfort of your bed or from a chaise longue on your spacious private balcony. Matching tab curtains and Berber carpet give these units a modern feel. The "Other Boat" cottage sleeps four and has an upstairs master bedroom with a table and chairs on the unit's large, screened sunporch. Take a tour of the cay in one of the club's golf carts. ⊠ *Staniel Cay (2233 S. Andrews Ave., Fort Lauderdale, FL 33316),* ☎ *242/355–2024 or 954/467–8920,* FAX *954/522–3248 or 242/ 355–2044,* WEB *www.stanielcay.com. 4 1-bedroom cottages, 1 2-bedroom cottage, 1 3-bedroom cottage. Restaurant, bar, fans, boating, fishing, piano, private airstrip. AE, MC, V. MAP.*

$–$ ✕☷ **Happy People Marina.** You may find this casual hotel a bit isolated if you're not interested in yachting. The property is close to Staniel Cay, but it's a long way from the George Town social scene. A local band, however, plays at the Royal Entertainer Lounge, and a small restaurant serves meals. The simple motel-style rooms are on the beach; some have private baths. ⊠ *Staniel Cay,* ☎ *242/355–2008. 8 rooms, 1 2-bedroom apartment. Restaurant, bar, dining room, air-conditioning, beach, dock. No credit cards.*

Nightlife

The **Royal Entertainer Lounge** (⊠ Happy People Marina, ☎ 242/355–2008) has live Bahamian bands perform on special occasions. The **Club Thunderball** (⊠ east of Thunderball Grotto, ☎ 242/355–2012), a sports bar–dance club, is built on a bluff overlooking the water, serves lunch, and has Friday evening barbecues and a mooring. It is run by a local pilot.

Outdoor Activities and Sports

BOATING AND FISHING

Staniel Cay Yacht Club (☎ 242/355–2024) rents 13-ft Whalers and arranges for fishing guides.

SCUBA DIVING AND SNORKELING

Staniel Cay Yacht Club (☎ 242/355–2024) fills tanks from its compressor. Call ahead or plan to bring your own scuba gear. You can rent masks and fins for snorkeling. **Pink Pearl Market** (☎ 242/355–2040) sells snorkel equipment and is open Monday through Saturday. **Exuma Cays Land and Sea Park** and **Thunderball Grotto** are excellent snorkeling sites.

Exumas A to Z

AIR TRAVEL

You can fly one of several airlines from Fort Lauderdale, St. Petersburg, Sarasota, or Miami to the official Exuma International Airport, or to the Staniel Cay airstrip.

CARRIERS

Air Sunshine flies into George Town four days a week, with planes leaving from Fort Lauderdale, St. Petersburg, and Sarasota. American Eagle has daily service from Miami. Call for summer scheduling. Bahamasair has daily flights from Nassau and twice-weekly flights from Fort Lauderdale and Miami to George Town. Executive Air Travel offers charters from Fort Lauderdale Executive Airport to Staniel Cay Yacht Club. Lynx Air International flies from Fort Lauderdale to George Town. Stella Maris is available for charter flights to or from the Exumas.

➤ AIRLINES AND CONTACTS: **Air Sunshine** (☎ 954/435–8900 or 800/ 327–8900). **American Eagle** (☎ 800/433–7300). **Bahamasair** (☎ 800/ 222–4262). **Executive Air Travel** (☎ 954/979–6162 or 954/224– 6022). **Lynx Air International** (☎ 888/596–9247). **Stella Maris** (☎ 954/ 359–8236, 242/336–2106, or 800/426–0466).

AIRPORTS AND TRANSFERS

Exuma International Airport, 9 mi from George Town, is the Exumas' official airport and the official port of entry. It's also one of the Bahamas's tidiest airports. Staniel Cay, near the top of the chain, has a 3,000-ft airstrip that accepts charter flights and private planes, but you must clear customs at the Andros, Nassau, or Exuma airport first.

TRANSFERS

Taxis wait at the airport for incoming flights. The cost of a ride from the airport to George Town is about $22 for two.

BIKE TRAVEL

In George Town's Scotia Bank building, Thompson's Rentals has bicycles. Contact Chamberlain Rentals if you want to pedal around Staniel Cay.

➤ BIKE RENTALS: **Chamberlain Rentals** (☎ 242/355–2020). **Thompson's Rentals** (☎ 242/336–2442).

BOAT AND FERRY TRAVEL

M/V *Grand Master* travels from Nassau to George Town on Tuesday and returns to Nassau on Friday. Travel time is 12 hours, and fares range from $35 to $40 depending on your destination. M/V *Ettienne & Cephas* leaves Nassau on Tuesday for Staniel Cay, Big Farmer's Cay, Black Point, and Barraterre, returning to Nassau on Saturday. The full trip takes 21 hours. Call for fares to specific destinations. For further information, contact the Dockmaster's Office at Potter's Cay, Nassau.

To reach Stocking Island from George Town, the Club Peace & Plenty Ferry leaves from the hotel's dock twice daily at 10 and 1. The ferry departs from the Stocking Island dock at 10:30 and 1:30. The fare is $8 round-trip for non–Peace & Plenty guests.

➤ BOAT AND FERRY INFORMATION: **Club Peace & Plenty Ferry** (☎ 242/336–2551). **Dockmaster's Office** (☎ 242/393–1064).

BUSINESS HOURS

BANKS AND OFFICES

The Bank of Nova Scotia in George Town is open weekdays 9:30–3.

CAR RENTAL

Thompson's Rentals rents cars. Sam Grey Enterprises is a car-rental establishment in George Town. Jeeps can be rented from Two Turtles Inn. Hotels can also arrange car rentals.

➤ LOCAL AGENCIES: **Sam Grey Enterprises** (☎ 242/336–2101). **Thompson's Rentals** (☎ 242/336–2442). **Two Turtles Inn** (☎ 242/336–2545). **Uptown Car Rentals** (☎ 242/245–0112).

EMERGENCIES

➤ CONTACTS: In George Town: **Police** (☎ 242/336–2666 or 919). **Medical Clinic** (☎ 242/336–2220). In Staniel Cay: **Police** (☎ 242/355–2042). **St. Luke's Medical Clinic** (☎ 242/355–2010).

GOLF CART TRAVEL

Staniel Cay Yacht Club rents golf carts for exploring Staniel Cay.

➤ CONTACT: **Staniel Cay Yacht Club** (☎ 242/355–2024).

SCOOTER TRAVEL

In George Town, Exuma Dive Centre rents motor scooters for $40 a day.

➤ CONTACT: **Exuma Dive Centre** (☎ 242/336–2390).

SIGHTSEEING TOURS

From George Town, Captain Cole arranges overnight trips up to the Exuma Cays Land and Sea Park. Kermit Rolle will take you on an informative, enjoyable tour of Little and Great Exuma.

➤ CONTACTS: **Captain Cole** (☎ 242/345–0074). **Kermit Rolle** (☎ 242/345–6038).

TAXIS

Your George Town hotel will arrange for a taxi if you wish to go exploring or need to return to the airport. You can call Kermit Rolle for taxi service. Luther Rolle Taxi Service will take you where you need to go.

➤ CONTACTS: **Kermit Rolle** (☎ 242/345–6038). **Luther Rolle Taxi Service** (☎ 242/345–5003).

TRANSPORTATION AROUND THE EXUMAS

You can stay in George Town proper and enjoy touring Great Exuma by car, but if you want a closer look at any of the hundreds of deserted Exuma cays nearby, you'll appreciate the greater freedom of a boat. If you want to go to Staniel Cay, through Pipe Creek, or to the Exuma Cays Land and Sea Park, water passage via the Exuma Sound or Great Bahama Bank is the only route.

VISITOR INFORMATION

The Exuma Tourist Office is in George Town, across the street from St. Andrew's Anglican Church.

➤ TOURIST INFORMATION: **Exuma Tourist Office** (☎ 242/336–2430, FAX 242/336–2431).

INAGUA

Great Inagua, the Bahamas's third-largest island, is 25 mi wide and 45 mi long. The terrain is mostly flat and covered with scrub. The island's unusual climate of little rainfall and continual trade winds created rich salt ponds, which have brought prosperity to the island over the years. The Morton Salt Company harvests a million tons of salt annually at its Matthew Town factory. About a fourth of the Inaguan population earns its living by working for the company. Inagua is best known for the huge flocks of shy pink flamingos that reside in the island's vast national park and on the property belonging to the salt company. In addition to the famous flamingos, the island is home to one of the largest populations of the rare Bahamian parrot, as well as to herons, egrets, owls, cormorants, and more than a hundred other species of birds.

Although the birds have moved in wholeheartedly, the island remains virtually undiscovered by outsiders. Avid bird-watchers make up the majority of the tourists who undertake the long trip to this most southerly of the Out Islands, about 300 mi southeast of Nassau and 50 mi off the coast of Cuba. Lack of exposure means that people are still friendly and curious about each new face in town. You won't feel like just another tourist. And since crowds and traffic are nonexistent, there's nothing to bother you but the rather persistent mosquito population (be sure to bring strong insect repellent). On the other hand, tourist facilities are very few and far between. The only inhabited settlement on Inagua is Matthew Town, a small, dusty grid of workers' homes and essential services. The four "hotels" are functional at best. There's no official visitor information office (although Great Inagua Tours is very helpful), and if you're a beach lover, Inagua is not for you. Although there are a couple of small swimming areas near Matthew Town and a few longer stretches farther north, no perfect combination of hotel and beach has yet been built. However, the virgin reefs off the island have caused a stir among intrepid divers who bring in their own equipment. The buzz is that Inagua could become a hot dive destination.

Great Inagua Island appears in the southeast corner of the Bahamas map at the front of this guide.

Matthew Town

About 1,000 people live on Inagua, whose capital, Matthew Town, is on the west coast. The "town" is about a block long. There's the large, pink, run-down government building (with the commissioner's office, post office, and customs office); a power plant; a grocery and liquor store; Morton's Main House (a guest house); the After Work Bar; the bank; and the small Kiwanis park that has a bench for sunset-gazing. Most houses here have huge satellite dishes prominently displayed. It is rumored that a lot of the money for these, and the houses they are attached to, came from the heady drug-smuggling days of the 1980s. Today, a U.S. Coast Guard helicopter base at the airport has pretty much put an end to that gold rush.

The **Erickson Museum and Library** is a welcome part of the community, particularly the surprisingly well-stocked and -equipped library. The Morton company built the complex in the former home of the Erickson family, who came to Inagua in 1934 to run the salt giant. The museum displays the island's history, to which the company is inextricably tied. ☒ *Gregory St., on the northern edge of town across from the police station,* ☏ *242/339–1863.* ☐ *Free.* ☉ *Weekdays 9–1 and 3–6, Sat. 9–1.*

The desire to marvel at the salt process lures few visitors to Inagua, but the **Morton Salt Company** (☏ 242/339–1300) is omnipresent on the island: It has more than 2,000 acres of crystallizing ponds and more than 34,000 acres of reservoirs. More than a million tons of salt are produced every year for such industrial uses as salting icy streets. (More is produced when the Northeast has a bad winter.) Even if you decide not to tour the facility, you'll be able to see the mountains of salt glistening in the sun from the plane. In an unusual case of industry assisting its environment, the crystallizers provide a feeding ground for the flamingos. As the water evaporates, the concentration of brine shrimp in the ponds increases, and the flamingos feed on these animals. Tours are available.

Dining and Lodging

$–$ ✕ **Cozy Corner.** Cheerful and loud, this lunch spot has a pool table and a large seating area with a bar. Stop in for a chat with locals over a beer and Bahamian conch burger. ☒ *Matthew Town,* ☏ *242/339–1440. No credit cards.*

$ ✕⊡ **Crystal Beach View.** About ½ mi from the airport, this single-story stone structure is on a coral-stone stretch of coastline, but the grounds are strewn with detritus. It is the town's largest hotel but is in need of some significant sprucing up, although the rooms are adequate. The lobby lounge is a friendly place to watch TV and chat with other guests, as is the bar in the Crystal Ruins restaurant. The restaurant serves breakfast, lunch, and dinner, with a focus on Bahamian cuisine. ☒ *Gregory St.,* ☏ *242/339–1550,* ꜰꜰ *242/339–1670. 13 rooms. Restaurant, bar, lobby lounge, air-conditioning, saltwater pool, hair salon. No credit cards.*

$ ⊡ **Sunset Apartments.** By far your best bet for accommodations on Inagua, these apartments sit right along the water on Matthew Town's southern side. The cement units all have modern Caribbean-style terra-cotta tile floors, rattan furniture, small terraces, a picnic area, and a gas grill. About a five-minute walk away is a small, secluded beach called the Swimming Hole. ⊠ *C/o Ezzard Cartwright, Matthew Town, Inagua,* ☎ *242/339–1362. 2 apartments. Fans, kitchenettes, boating. No credit cards.*

$ ⊞ **Main House.** The Morton Salt Company operates this small, affordable guest house. On the second of two floors, air-conditioned rooms share a sitting area with couches and a telephone. Rooms are spotless and spacious with dark-wood furnishings, Masonite-paneled walls, and floral-print drapes and spreads. The green-and-white hotel is right in Matthew Town, behind the grocery store and directly across the street from the island's noisy power plant. ⊠ *Matthew Town, Inagua,* ☎ *242/ 339–1267. 5 rooms. Cable TV. No credit cards.*

Elsewhere on the Island

Although you'll spot them in salt ponds throughout the island, birds and other wildlife also reside in the **Bahamas National Trust** reserve, which spreads over 287 square mi and occupies most of the island's western half. Nature lovers, ornithologists, and photographers are drawn to the area and to Lake Windsor (a 12-mi-long brackish body of water in the island's center) to view the spectacle of more than 60,000 flamingos feeding, mating, or flying (although you will rarely see all those birds together in the same place). When planning your trip, keep in mind that flamingo mating season is October–February, and the nesting season is March–April. Flamingos live on Inagua year-round, but the greatest concentrations come at these times. If you visit right after hatching, the scrambling flocks of fuzzy, gray baby flamingos are very entertaining. They can't fly until they're older. You don't have to tour the Trust property to see flamingos, but there are camping facilities on the grounds, and wardens will give guided tours. Arrangements can be made through your hotel, or by calling Great Inagua Tours, or the Bahamas National Trust (☎ 242/393–1317).

From **Southwest Point,** a mile or so south of the capital, you can see Cuba's coast on a clear day, slightly more than 50 mi west, from atop the lighthouse (built in 1870 in response to a huge number of ship-wrecks on offshore reefs). This is one of the last four hand-operated kerosene lighthouses in the Bahamas. Be sure to sign the guest book after your climb.

Villa Rental

A four-bedroom cottage in a completely secluded area out toward the island's northwest point rents for about $150 per day (negotiable, depending on the length of stay). The cottage sits right on the beach and has a patio for sunset viewing. There's a fully equipped kitchen, dining area, an outdoor shower in addition to the indoor bath, and a private strip of beach with a section cleared of rocks for swimming. The cottage is not elegant, but it is completely private. Be warned, however: If there has been a recent rain, mosquitoes will be fierce. Be sure to ask about them when booking. Call Larry Ingraham at **Great Inagua Tours** (☎ 242/339–1862) with inquiries.

Inagua A to Z

AIR TRAVEL
Bahamasair has flights on Monday, Wednesday, and Friday from Nassau to Matthew Town Airport.
➤ AIRLINES AND CONTACTS: **Bahamasair** (☎ 242/339–4415 or 800/222–4262).

AIRPORTS AND TRANSFERS

Taxis sometimes meet incoming flights. It's best to make prior arrangements with your hotel to be picked up.

➤ AIRPORT INFORMATION: **Matthew Town Airport** (☎ 242/339–1254).

BOAT AND FERRY TRAVEL

M/V *Lady Mathilda* makes weekly trips from Nassau to Matthew Town, also stopping at Crooked Island, Acklins Island, and Mayaguana. M/V *Abilin* goes to Long Island, and then on to Matthew Town. The boat departs Nassau on Tuesday. For information on specific schedules and fares, contact the Dockmaster's Office at Potter's Cay, Nassau.

➤ BOAT AND FERRY INFORMATION: **Dockmaster's Office** (☎ 242/393–1064).

BIKE TRAVEL

The Pour More Bar rents bikes for exploring. The Crystal Beach View Hotel has rental bikes available for both guests and nonguests.

➤ BIKE RENTALS: **Crystal Beach View Hotel** (☎ 242/339–1550). **Pour More Bar** (☎ 242/339–1232).

BUSINESS HOURS

BANKS AND OFFICES

The Bank of the Bahamas in Matthew Town is open Monday through Thursday 9:30–2 and Friday 9:30–5:30.

➤ CONTACT: **Bank of the Bahamas** (☎ 242/339–1815).

CAR RENTAL

Inagua Trading Ltd. has several cars for rent by the day.

➤ LOCAL AGENCY: **Inagua Trading Ltd.** (☎ 242/339–1330).

EMERGENCIES

There is no general emergency number in Inagua—call the police or hospital directly in case of an emergency.

➤ CONTACTS: **Hospital** (☎ 242/339–1249). **Police** (☎ 242/339–1263).

SIGHTSEEING TOURS

Great Inagua Tours is a full-service information and sightseeing operation run by Larry and Marianne Ingraham. The company specializes in ecotourism and organizes bird-watching and wildlife-viewing excursions, but Larry can arrange anything from a flamingo tour or a bonefishing trip to car rental and accommodations. He is an invaluable source of information and assistance for planning and executing your visit.

➤ CONTACT: **Great Inagua Tours** (☎ 242/339–1232 or 242/339–1862, FAX 242/339–1204).

TAXIS

If you need a taxi for anything, ask your hotel to make arrangements, or call Rocky.

➤ CONTACT: **Rocky** (☎ 242/339–1284).

LONG ISLAND

Never more than 4 mi wide, Long Island, one of Columbus's stopping-off places, lives up to its name. Its Queen's Highway runs for close to 80 mi, through some 35 villages and farming towns where you'll always find a little straw market beckoning. One of the island's 4,500 residents once nicknamed the highway Rhythm Road, a reference perhaps to the many potholes that used to make driving it a syncopated ride. The government has finally completed construction, and Queen's

Highway is now paved and smooth. The scenery on the way changes from shelling beaches and shallow bays on the west coast to rugged headlands that drop suddenly to the sea on the east coast. The island's southern end has sea cliffs unique to the Bahamas.

Numbers in the margin correspond to points of interest on the Long Island map.

Cape Santa Maria and Stella Maris

★ 44 Columbus named the island's northern tip **Cape Santa Maria,** in honor of one of his ships. The area has truly stunning beaches—among the best in the country—and is the home of the elegant Cape Santa Maria Beach Resort.

Take a side trip on the unpaved road out to **Columbus Cove,** 1½ mi north of the Cape Santa Maria resort. The monument and plaque that commemorate Columbus's landing are here, as well as tremendous views of the protected harbor he sailed into. Divers can explore the wreck of a ship, the M/V *Comberbach,* which lies just off the headland. The Stella Maris Resort sunk the leaky 103-ft freighter in 1985 to create an artificial reef and an excellent dive site nearly 100 ft under. The road to the cove is too rough for most vehicles, but it happens to be a fine walk. An easier way to reach the cove is by boat.

45 **Stella Maris** means Star of the Sea, and it's home to the all-encompassing Stella Maris Resort Club, along with its airport. In a world of its own, the resort has a marina, yacht club, and tiny shopping complex, with a bank, a post office, and a general store. If you're interested in aquatic adventures, contact the resort, which runs numerous daily outings, including diving and fishing trips.

At **Shark Reef,** divers can safely watch groups of a dozen sharks at a time being fed fish by a scuba master. Stella Maris lies about 12 mi south of Cape Santa Maria, off Queen's Highway past the ruins of the 19th-century **Adderley's Plantation.** Long Island was another Bahamian island where fleeing Loyalists attempted, with little success, to grow cotton. You can still see parts of the plantation's three buildings up to roof level. The remains of two other plantations, **Dunmore's and Gray's,** are also on the island.

Dining and Lodging

$–$$ ✕ **Barbie's Ice Cream Restaurant and Bar.** Between Stella Maris and Cape Santa Maria, this casual spot serves sandwiches and burgers for lunch and native Bahamian dinner specials—and, of course, ice cream. ✉ *Queen's Hwy., Glintons,* ☎ *242/338–5009. No credit cards.*

$$ ★ ✕🏨 **Cape Santa Maria Beach Resort.** During the 1960s, the Du Ponts, Kelloggs, and Kennedys would hide out here in three lee "fishing cabins." Now, this peaceful luxury resort has expanded to 10 colonial-style cottages spread along a gorgeous, 4-mi stretch of velvety white-sand beach. Spacious one- or two-bedroom units have their own large, fully furnished screened porches. A lovely mahogany staircase leads to the brightly colored dining room, where you can dine on superb broiled lobster and delicious conch salads. The fishing and water-sports activities office arranges Hobie cat sailing, snorkeling, and deep-sea, reef, or bonefishing excursions aboard the resort's many boats. ✉ *Oak Bay Marine Group, 1327 Beach Dr., Victoria, BC V8S 2N4,* ☎ *242/338–5273 or 800/663–7090,* FAX *242/338–6013 or 250/598–1361,* WEB *www.obmg.com. 10 1- to 2-bedroom villas. Restaurant, bar, beach, snorkeling, windsurfing, boating, waterskiing, fishing, bicycles, shops, baby-sitting, laundry facilities; no room TVs, no room phones. AE, D, MC, V. EP, FAP, MAP.*

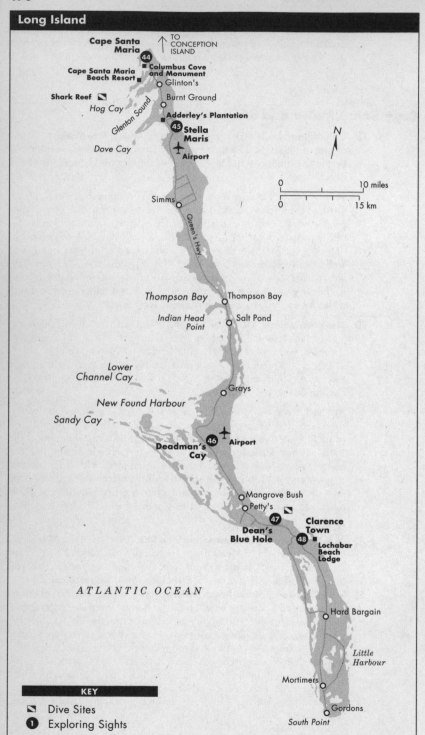

Cape Santa Maria
↑ TO CONCEPTION ISLAND

44

■ Columbus Cove and Monument

Cape Santa Maria Beach Resort
○ Glinton's

Shark Reef ◣
Hog Cay
○ Burnt Ground

Glenton Sound

■ Adderley's Plantation

45 **Stella Maris**
✈ **Airport**

Dove Cay

○ Simms

Queen's Hwy.

N

0 _____ 10 miles
0 _____ 15 km

Thompson Bay   ○ Thompson Bay

Indian Head Point   ○ Salt Pond

Lower Channel Cay

New Found Harbour   ○ Grays

Sandy Cay

46 ✈ **Airport**

Deadman's Cay

○ Mangrove Bush
○ Petty's ◣
47
Dean's Blue Hole   **Clarence Town**
48   ■ **Lochabar Beach Lodge**

ATLANTIC OCEAN

○ Hard Bargain

Little Harbour

○ Mortimers

○ Gordons
South Point

KEY

◣ Dive Sites
① Exploring Sights

$ ✕ᚐ **Stella Maris Resort Club.** Sitting atop a hilly east-coast ridge over-
★ looking the Atlantic, this 3,000-acre resort's range of daily activities
make it a Bahamian classic. You can swim in three freshwater pools,
a series of private beaches, or explore beach coves with excellent
snorkeling; dive, fish, and hike; or take advantage of free morning and
afternoon snorkeling trips, glass-bottom boat cruises, Sunfish sailing,
and bicycling. The resort has rooms, villas, and bungalows, a few with
private pools. The weekly cave party on Monday has buffet barbecue,
music, and dancing set in a cavern on the property. ⊠ *1100 Lee Wa-
gunor Blvd., No. 334, Fort Lauderdale, FL 33315, ☎ 242/338–2051,
800/426–0466, FAX 242/338–2052, WEB www.stellamarisresort.com. 20
rooms, 12 1-bedroom cottages, 7 2-bedroom cottages, 4 beach houses.
Restaurant, grocery, some kitchenettes, refrigerators, 3 pools, dive
shop, snorkeling, boating, waterskiing, marina, fishing, bicycles, Ping-
Pong, billiards, bar, recreation room, shop, complimentary weddings,
laundry service; no room phones, no room TVs. AE, MC, V. EP, MAP.*

Simms and South

Simms is one of Long Island's oldest settlements, 8 mi south of Stella
Maris past little pastel-color houses. Some of these abodes display emblems to ward off evil spirits, an indication of the presence of obeah,
the superstitious voodoolike culture found on many of the Bahamian
islands. There are a few quirky eats to be had roadside on this stretch
of Queen's Highway. On the road's east side, look for a small conch-
salad stand that's intermittently open and prepares the snack right before your eyes. Immediately south of Simms, you may see rising smoke
and tables out in the front yard of **Jeraldine's Jerk Pit** (☎ no phone).
These tasty eats are delectable.

The annual Long Island Regatta, featuring Bahamian-made boats, is
held in **Salt Pond** every June. The regatta is the island's biggest event,
attracting contestants from all over the islands. Salt Pond is 10 mi south
of Simms.

㊻ The town of **Deadman's Cay** is home for most of the island's population. Here you'll find a few shops, churches, and schools. Just east of
Deadman's Cay, **Cartwright's Cave** has stalactites and stalagmites and
eventually leads to the sea. The cave has apparently never been completely explored, although Native American drawings were found on
one wall. For guided cave tours, contact Leonard Cartwright (☎ 242/
337–0235). There are several other caves, supposedly pirate-haunted,
around Simms, Millers, and Salt Pond; a local should be able to point
you in the right direction.

Between Deadman's Cay and Clarence Town, just past the settlement
of Petty's, watch for the pink-and-white pillars that line the turnoff for
㊼ **Dean's Blue Hole.** At 660 ft, it's thought to be the world's second deepest blue hole. Curious divers will want to contact the dive shop at Stella
Maris (☎ 242/338–2050).

㊽ **Clarence Town** has Long Island's most celebrated landmarks, St. Paul's
Church (Anglican) and St. Peter's Church (Catholic). They were both
built by Father Jerome, a priest who is buried in a tomb in the Hermitage atop Cat Island's Mt. Alvernia. As an Anglican named John
Hawes he constructed St. Paul's. Later, after converting to Catholicism,
he built St. Peter's. The architecture of the two churches is similar to
that of the missions established by the Spaniards in California in the
late 18th century. Clarence Town is Long Island's most picturesque settlement, with a harbor and dock and the government headquarters in
addition to the two churches.

Dining and Lodging

$–$$ ✕ **The Forest.** Just south of Clarence Town, this bright pink restaurant serves spicy wings and potato skins, as well as cracked conch, barbecued chicken, and grouper fingers. Enjoy a drink at the bar—which is made of seashells embedded in glossy resin—and a game of pool. On Friday night, enjoy live bands and dancing. ⊠ *Queen's Hwy., Miley's,* ☎ *242/337–3287. No credit cards.*

$–$$ ✕ **Mario's Blue Chip Inn.** Call a day in advance to place your order at this Simms restaurant. You might request the delicious grouper fingers, mutton fish, crawfish, or conch. ⊠ *Queen's Hwy., Simms,* ☎ *242/338–8964. No credit cards.*

¢–$ ✕ **Kooters.** Grab a seat on the deck at this casual, immaculate spot for a lovely view of Mangrove Bush Point and a conch burger or club sandwich with homemade fries. Daily specials range from ribs to seafood. Save room for one of the many flavors of ice cream. ⊠ *Queen's Hwy., Mangrove Bush,* ☎ *242/337–0340. No credit cards. Closed Sun.*

¢–$ ✕ **Max's Conch Grill and Bar.** If you sit all day on a stool at this pink-, green-, and yellow-striped roadside gazebo, nursing beers and nibbling on conch, you'll become a veritable expert on Long Island and the life of its residents. Such is the local draw of this laid-back watering hole. Have a chat with Max while sampling his conch salad ($3.50 or $6), conch dumplings (6 for $1), or daily specials like baked ham and steamed pork. Pink conch shells line the free miniature golf course behind the gazebo; to the side is a general store. ⊠ *Deadman's Cay,* ☎ *242/337–0056. MC, V.*

$ ▥ **Lochabar Beach Lodge.** Mellow and picturesque, this is the best place to stay on southern Long Island. The two thoughtfully constructed 600-square-ft guest studios overlook a dramatic blue hole. Designed to catch the trade winds, double wooden doors open to water views and perpetual breezes. There are dinette islands with stools, although you can also eat alfresco on your deck. The lodge has an inexpensive meal plan with the Forest for lunch and dinner. At low tide, you can stroll the cove's entire beach and round the point into Clarence Town. Your hosts will gladly arrange for a car rental and bonefishing excursions. ⊠ *1 mi south of Clarence Town at Dean's Blue Hole (Box CB-13839, Nassau, Bahamas),* ☎ *242/327–8323,* ℻ *242/327–2567. 2 studios. Fans, kitchenettes, snorkeling, fishing. No credit cards. EP, FAP.*

Nightlife

Just south of Clarence Town, **The Forest** (⊠ Queen's Hwy., Miley's, ☎ 242/337–3287) has dancing Friday night.

Shopping

Wild Tamarind (⊠ about ½ mi east of Queen's Hwy., Petty's, ☎ 242/337–0262) is Denis Knight's ceramics studio. Stop in for a lovely bowl, vase, or sculpture, but call first in case he's out fishing.

Outdoor Activities and Sports

SCUBA DIVING

For more information about these sites, or to arrange a dive, contact the Stella Maris Resort Club.

Dean's Blue Hole is lauded by locals as one of the world's deepest ocean holes. It's surrounded by a powder-beach cove. **Conception Island Wall** is an excellent wall dive, with hard and soft coral, plus interesting sponge formations. **Shark Reef** is the site of the Bahamas's first shark dive. The Stella Maris Resort has been running trips there for more than 25 years.

Long Island A to Z

AIR TRAVEL

Bahamasair flies almost daily from Nassau to Stella Maris and Dead-man's Cay. Flights from Fort Lauderdale are available during the winter season. Stella Maris has charter flights from Exuma and Nassau to Stella Maris. If you're a pilot, the island is a great base for exploring other islands. Stella Maris rents well-maintained planes—a four-seat Piper Seneca and a six-seat Piper Navajo—for about $90 an hour.

➤ AIRLINES AND CONTACTS: Bahamasair (☎ 242/339–4415 or 800/222–4262). Stella Maris (☎ 954/359–8236, 242/338–2051, WEB www. stellamarisresortairservice.com).

AIRPORTS AND TRANSFERS

If you're a guest at Cape Santa Maria or Stella Maris, fly into the Stella Maris airport. Use the Deadman's Cay airport if you're staying in Clarence Town. Landing at the wrong airport will mean a $120 cab ride—in which case, of course, renting a car will save you money.

TRANSFERS

Taxis meet incoming flights. The fare to the resort from the airport is $4.

BOAT AND FERRY TRAVEL

M/V *Abilin* makes a weekly trip from Nassau to Clarence Town, on the island's south end. The boat leaves Nassau on Tuesday; the trip takes 18 hours, and the fare is $45. The M/V *Sherice M* leaves Nassau on a varying schedule with stops in Salt Pond, Deadman's Cay, and Seymour's. The travel time is 15 hours; the fare, $45. For more information, contact the Dockmaster's Office at Potter's Cay, Nassau. Stella Maris Overnight trips can be arranged on Stella Maris's 65-ft dive boat, which sleeps 14.
➤ BOAT AND FERRY INFORMATION: **Dockmaster's Office** (☎ 242/393–1064).

BUSINESS HOURS

BANKS AND OFFICES
At the Stella Maris resort, the Bank of Nova Scotia is open Tuesday and Thursday 9:30–2, Friday 9:30–5. Farther south, the Deadman's Cay branch is open Monday–Thursday 9–1 and Friday 9–5. Royal Bank of Canada has a branch on Deadman's Cay; hours are Monday–Thursday 9–1 and Friday 9–5.
➤ CONTACTS: **Bank of Nova Scotia** (☎ 242/338–2057 Stella Maris; 242/338–2002 Deadman's Cay). **Royal Bank of Canada** (☎ 242/337–1044).

CAR RENTAL

Taylor's Rentals rents high-quality cars for the most reasonable rates on the island. Hotels will also arrange for guests' automobile rental.
➤ LOCAL AGENCY: **Taylor's Rentals** (☎ 242/338–7001).

EMERGENCIES

Clarence Town, Deadman's Cay, and Simms each have their own police departments.
➤ CONTACTS: **Police** (☎ 242/337–0999 Clarence Town; 242/337–0444 Deadman's Cay; 242/338–8555 Simms).

SAN SALVADOR

On October 12, 1492, Christopher Columbus disturbed the lives of the peaceful Lucayan Indians by landing on the island of Guanahani, which he named San Salvador. He knelt on the beach and claimed the land for Spain. (Skeptics have found encouragement: Findings of a computerized study published in a 1986 *National Geographic* article point to Samana Cay, 60 mi southeast, as the exact point of the weary explorer's landing.) Three monuments on the 7- by 12-mi island commemorate Columbus's arrival, and the 500th-anniversary celebration of the event was officially celebrated here.

A 17th-century pirate named George Watling, who frequently sought shelter on the island, changed San Salvador's name to Watling's Island. The Bahamian government switched the name back to San Salvador in 1926.

The island is 12 mi long—roughly the length of Manhattan—and four to five miles wide along its lake-filled interior. Most visitors come for the isolation and the diving; there are about 950 residents over 50 dive sites.

Numbers in the margin correspond to points of interest on the San Salvador map.

Fernandez Bay to Riding Rock Point

In 1492, the inspiring sight that greeted Christopher Columbus by moonlight at 2 AM was a terrain of gleaming beaches and far-reaching forest. The peripatetic traveler and his crews—"men from Heaven," the locals called them—steered the *Niña, Pinta,* and *Santa María* warily
④⑨ among the coral reefs and anchored, so it is recorded, in **Fernandez Bay.** A cross erected in 1956 by Columbus scholar Ruth C. Durlacher Wolper Malvin stands at his approximate landing spot. Ms. Malvin's **New World Museum** (☎ no phone), near North Victoria Hill on the east coast, contains artifacts from the era of the Lucayans. Admission to the museum is free; it's open by appointment (your hotel can make arrangements). An underwater monument marks the place where the *Santa María* anchored. Nearby, another monument commemorates the Olympic flame's passage on its journey from Greece to Mexico City in 1968.

Fernandez Bay is close to what is now the main community of **Cockburn Town,** mid-island on the western shore. Queen's Highway encircles the island from Cockburn Town, where the weekly mail boat docks. This small village's narrow streets contain two churches, a commissioner's office, a police station, a courthouse, a library, a clinic, a drugstore, and a telephone station.

⑤⓪ Columbus first spotted and made a record of **Riding Rock Point.** The area now serves as the home for the Riding Rock Inn, a popular resort for divers. Just north of the point is the island's other resort, the Club Med–Columbus Isle, set at the foot of a gorgeous 2-mi-long beach. Riding Rock Point is about a mile north of Cockburn Town.

Dining and Lodging

$$$–$$$$ ✕🏨 **Club Med–Columbus Isle.** The 80-acre village is billed as one of
★   Club Med's most luxurious resorts, with state-of-the-art dive facilities, including three custom-made 45-ft catamarans and a decompression chamber; elegant rooms; and a long stretch of private beach. The buildings are painted brilliant blues, greens, yellows, pinks, and purples. All rooms have patios or balconies and handcrafted furniture and art. Guided bike tours introduce vacationers to island life beyond the resort. Unlike some Club Meds, this one caters primarily to upscale couples, and the atmosphere is more low-key than at most. ✉ *3 mi north of Riding Rock Point (40 W. 57th St., New York, NY 10019),*

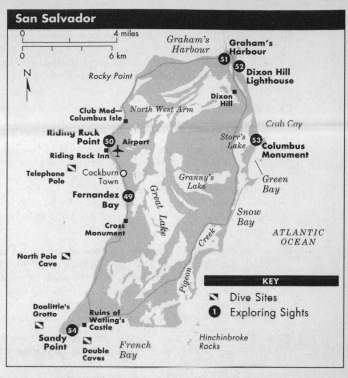

San Salvador

0 ———— 4 miles
0 ———— 6 km

N

Graham's Harbour
Graham's Harbour
51
52 Dixon Hill Lighthouse
Rocky Point
Dixon Hill
Club Med— Columbus Isle
North West Arm
Crab Cay
Riding Rock Point
50 Airport
Storr's Lake
53 Columbus Monument
Riding Rock Inn
Telephone Pole
Cockburn Town
Granny's Lake
Green Bay
Fernandez Bay 49
Great Lake
Snow Bay
Cross Monument
ATLANTIC OCEAN
North Pole Cave
Pigeon Creek
KEY
Doolittle's Grotto
Ruins of Watling's Castle
Sandy Point 54
Double Caves
French Bay
Hinchinbroke Rocks
Dive Sites
1 Exploring Sights

☎ 242/331–2000 or 800/258–2633, ℻ 242/331–2458. 288 rooms. 3 restaurants, lounge, refrigerators, pool, hair salon, massage, 9 tennis courts, gym, beach, dive shop, bicycles, nightclub, theater, laundry service, car rental, Internet. AE, MC, V. All-inclusive.

$ ✕▥ **Riding Rock Resort and Marina.** A diver's paradise, this motel-style resort offers three dives per day to excellent offshore reefs and a drop-off wall teeming with life. It's also the only place to stay on San Salvador where you can avoid the relentless enthusiasm of the Club Med staff. The inn's three buildings house rooms facing either the ocean or the freshwater pool. The oceanside rooms have washed oak furniture, a queen-size bed and sofa bed, sitting area with a table and chairs. Poolside rooms lack refrigerators and queen-size beds. The restaurant serves Bahamian dishes as well as hearty pancake breakfasts. ⊠ *Riding Rock Point (1170 Lee Wagener Blvd., Suite 103, Fort Lauderdale, FL 33315)*, ☎ *954/359–8353 or 800/272–1492*, ℻ *954/359–8254*, ᴡᴇʙ *www.ridingrock.com. 42 rooms, 2 villas. Restaurant, bar, cable TV, some refrigerators, pool, tennis court, dive shop, fishing, bicycles, rental car, Internet. MC, V. EP, FAP.*

Outdoor Activities and Sports

Club Med (☎ 242/331–2000) has dive boats and a decompression chamber. In addition, there are nine tennis courts, sailing, and windsurfing, among other sports.

Riding Rock Inn (☎ 800/272–1492) is affiliated with Guanahani Dive Ltd., which uses mostly buoyed sites to avoid any damage caused to the marine environment by dropping anchor. It also offers resort and certification courses, and a modern underwater photographic facility. It rents all kinds of camera gear and does slide shows of divers' work. Riding Rock also rents bicycles and snorkel gear and will arrange fishing trips ($400 for a half day and $600 for a full day). The waters hold tuna, blue marlin, and, in the winter, wahoo.

Around San Salvador

51 Columbus describes **Graham's Harbour** in his diaries as large enough "to hold all the ships of Christendom." A complex of buildings near the harbor houses the **Bahamian Field Station,** a biological and geological research institution that attracts scientists and students from all over the world.

52 A couple of miles south of Graham's Harbour stands **Dixon Hill Lighthouse.** Built around 1856, it is still hand operated, and the light from its small kerosene lamp beams out to sea every 15 seconds to a maximum distance of 19 mi, depending on visibility. The lighthouse keeper must continuously wind the apparatus that projects the light. A climb to the top of the 160-ft landmark offers a fabulous view of the island, which includes a series of inland lakes. The keeper is present 24 hours a day. Knock on his door, and he'll take you up to the top and explain the machinery. Drop $1 in the box when you sign the guest book on the way out.

53 No road leads to the **Columbus Monument** on Crab Cay; you have to make your way along a bushy path. This initial tribute to the explorer was erected by the *Chicago Herald* newspaper in 1892, far from the presumed site of Columbus's landing. A series of little villages winds south of here for several miles, such as Holiday Track and Polly Hill, which once contained plantations.

54 **Sandy Point** anchors the island's southwestern end, overlooking French Bay. Here, on a hill, you'll find the **ruins of Watling's Castle,** named after the 17th-century pirate. The ruins are more likely the remains of a Loyalist plantation house than a castle from buccaneering days. You can walk from Queen's Highway up the hill to see what is left of the ruins, which are now engulfed in vegetation.

Outdoor Activities and Sports

SCUBA DIVING

For more information about these and other sites, contact the Riding Rock Inn, or visit www.ridingrock.com.

Doolittle's Grotto is a popular site featuring a sandy slope down to 140 ft. There are lots of tunnels and crevices for exploring, and usually a large school of horse-eye jacks to keep you company. **Double Caves,** as the name implies, has two parallel caves leading out to a wall at 115 ft. There's typically quite a lot of fish activity along the top of the wall. **North Pole Cave** has a wall that drops sharply from 40 ft to more than 150 ft. You'll see a lot of coral growth, and possibly a hammerhead or two. **Telephone Pole** is a nice wall dive that provides an opportunity to watch stingrays, grouper, snapper, and turtles in action.

San Salvador A to Z

AIR TRAVEL

Air Sunshine flies from Fort Lauderdale into Cockburn Town. Bahamasair flies into Cockburn Town from Nassau and also offers direct service from Miami three days a week. Riding Rock Inn has charter flights every Saturday from Fort Lauderdale.

➤ AIRLINES AND CONTACTS: **Air Sunshine** (☎ 954/434–8900 or 800/327–8900). **Bahamasair** (☎ 242/339–4415 or 800/222–4262). **Riding Rock Inn** (☎ 800/272–1492 or 954/359–8353).

AIRPORTS AND TRANSFERS
TRANSFERS

Taxis meet arriving planes at Cockburn Town Airport. Club Med meets all guests at the airport (your account is charged $10 for the three-minute transfer). Riding Rock provides complimentary transportation for guests.

BIKE TRAVEL
➤ BIKE RENTALS: **Riding Rock Inn** (☎ 800/272–1492 or 954/359–8353) rents bicycles for $8 a day.

BOAT AND FERRY TRAVEL
M/V *Lady Francis,* out of Nassau, leaves Tuesday for San Salvador and Rum Cay. The trip takes 18 hours, for a fare of about $40. For information on specific schedules and fares, contact the Dockmaster's Office at Potter's Cay, Nassau.
➤ BOAT AND FERRY INFORMATION: **Dockmaster's Office** (☎ 242/393–1064).

CAR RENTAL
➤ CONTACT: **Riding Rock Inn** (☎ 800/272–1492 or 954/359–8353) rents cars for $85 a day.

EMERGENCIES
➤ CONTACTS: **Medical Clinic** (☎ 207). **Police** (☎ 218).

OUT ISLANDS A TO Z

To research prices, get advice from other travelers, and book travel arrangements, visit www.fodors.com.

EMERGENCIES
There are health centers and clinics scattered throughout the islands, but in the event of emergency, illnesses, or accidents requiring fast transportation to the United States, AAPI Air Ambulance Services provides aero-medical services out of Fort Lauderdale Executive Airport. Its three jet aircraft are equipped with sophisticated medical equipment and a trained staff of nurses and flight medics.
➤ CONTACT: **AAPI Air Ambulance Services** (☎ 954/491–0555 or 800/752–4195).

TOURS AND PACKAGES
Florida Yacht Charters, at the high-tech Boat Harbour Marina in Marsh Harbour, offers an endless supply of boats (trawlers, sailboats, and catamarans with inflatable dinghies) and amenities, such as air-conditioning, refrigeration, and GPS. Licensed captains, instruction, and provisioning are also available. For captained yacht charters, contact The Moorings in Marsh Harbour. This is the Bahamas's division of one of the largest yacht-charter agencies in the world, which provides many services needed for yachties—from provisions to professional captains. Swift Yacht Charters also has yacht charters. If you're looking for a guided kayak tour, call Ibis Tours.
➤ TOUR-OPERATOR RECOMMENDATIONS: In United States: **Changes in L'Attitudes** (✉ 3080 East Bay Dr., Largo, FL 33771, ☎ 727/573–3536 or 800/330–8272, WEB www.changes.com). **Florida Yacht Charters** (☎ 305/532–8600 or 800/537–0050, WEB www.floridayacht.com). **Future Vacations** (✉ 110 E. Broward Blvd., Box 1525, Fort Lauderdale, FL 33301, ☎ 954/522–1440 or 800/456–2323, FAX 954/357–4687). **Ibis Tours** (✉ Box 208, Pelham, NY 10803, ☎ 800/525–9411, WEB www.ibistours.com). **The Moorings** (✉ Box AB-20469, Marsh Harbour, Abaco, ☎ 242/367–

4000 or 800/535–7289, WEB www.go-abacos.com/conchinn/moorings).
Swift Yacht Charters (⊠ 209 S. Main St., Sherborn, MA 01770, ☎ 800/
866–8340 or 508/647–1554, WEB www.swiftyachts.com). In Canada:
Americanada (⊠ 139 Sauve O, Montréal, Québec H3L LY4, ☎ 514/
384–6431 or 800/361–8242). **Holiday House** (⊠ 110 Richmond St. E,
Suite 304, Toronto, Ontario M5C 1P1, ☎ 416/364–2433).

VISITOR INFORMATION

The Bahama Out Islands Promotion Board has a fantastic staff that
provides information about lodging, travel, and activities in the islands
and can book reservations at many of the hotels. On request, the
board will send color brochures about island resorts.

The Bahamas Ministry of Tourism's Bahamas Tourist Office can as-
sist with travel plans and information.

The Abacos are way ahead of the other Out Islands when it comes to
offering on-line information on boating conditions, changes in ferry
schedules, and weather reports. Log on to the Abacos's premier Web
site, www.oii.net, or try www.go-abacos.com. For info on Eleuthera,
sign on to www.eleutherainformer.com. The best overall Web site for
information on all the islands are the Ministry of Tourism and the Out
Island Promotion Board's Web sites. Also try www.bahamasvg.com and
www.bahamasnet.com.

➤ TOURIST INFORMATION: **Bahama Out Islands Promotion Board** (⊠
19495 Biscayne Blvd., Suite 809, Aventura, FL 33180, ☎ 305/931–
6612 or 800/688–4752, FAX 305/931–6867, WEB www.bahamaoutis-
lands.com). **Bahamas Tourist Office** (⊠ Box N-3701, Market Plaza,
Bay St., Nassau, Bahamas, ☎ 242/322–7500, WEB www.bahamas.com).

5 TURKS AND CAICOS ISLANDS

"Everything cool, man?" Shadow asks with a laugh as he cuts the speedboat through Crocodile Pass en route to Middle Caicos. A Caribbean renaissance man, Shadow took his nickname from an uncanny ability to sneak up on bonefish. He also bats .500 for the local all-star team, fishes for trophy-size blue marlin in the annual rodeo, plays a mean guitar, and tells a great story. When he reaches the shore, he plans to whip up a batch of seviche using fresh conch, onion, sweet peppers, lime juice, and Tabasco— thus adding "cook" to an impressive, island-style résumé.

Updated by
Kathy Borsuk

S PORTFISHERMEN, SCUBA DIVERS, and beach aficionados have long known about the Turks and Caicos (pronounced *kay*-kos). To them this British Crown colony of more than 40 islands and small cays (only eight of which are inhabited) is a gem that offers dazzling turquoise seas, priceless stretches of sand, and reefs rich in marine life. Whether you're swimming with the fishes or attempting to catch them from the surface, the Turks and Caicos won't disappoint. In an archipelago 575 mi (927 km) southeast of Miami and 90 mi (145 km) north of Haiti, the total landmass of these two groups of islands is 193 square mi (500 square km); the total population is less than 25,000.

The Turks Islands include Grand Turk, which is the capital and seat of government, and Salt Cay. It's claimed that Columbus's first landfall was on Grand Turk. Legend also has it that these islands were named by early settlers who thought the scarlet blossoms on the local cactus resembled the Turkish fez.

Approximately 22 mi (35½ km) west of Grand Turk, across the 7,000-ft-deep (2,141-m-deep) Columbus Passage, is the Caicos group: South, East, West, Middle, and North Caicos and Providenciales (nicknamed Provo). South Caicos, Middle Caicos, North Caicos, and Provo are the only inhabited islands in this group; Pine Cay and Parrot Cay are the only inhabited cays. "Caicos" is derived from *cayos,* the Spanish word for "cay" and is believed to mean, appropriately, "string of islands."

In the mid-1600s, Bermudians began to rake salt from the flats on the Turks Islands, returning to Bermuda to sell their crop. Despite French and Spanish attacks and pirate raids, the Bermudians persisted and established a trade that became the bedrock of the islands' economy. In 1766 Andrew Symmers settled here to hold the islands for England. The American Declaration of Independence left British loyalists from South Carolina and Georgia without a country, causing many to take advantage of British Crown land grants in the Turks and Caicos. Cotton plantations were established and prospered for nearly 25 years until the boll weevil, soil exhaustion, and a terrible hurricane in 1813 devastated the land. Left behind to make their living off the land and sea were the former slaves, who remained to shape the culture.

Today the Turks and Caicos are known as a reputable offshore tax haven whose company formation, banking, trusts, and insurance institutions lure investors from North America and beyond. Provo, in particular, is on its way to becoming a popular Caribbean tourist destination. Mass tourism, however, shouldn't be in the cards; government guidelines promote a quality, not quantity policy, including conservation awareness. And without a port for cruise ships, the islands remain uncrowded and peaceful.

Pleasures and Pastimes

Dining
Like everything else on these islands, dining out is a very laid-back affair, which is not to say it's cheap. Because of the high cost of importing all edibles, the price of a meal is higher than in the United States. Reservations are generally not required, and dress tends to be casual.

CATEGORY	COST*
$$$$	over $30
$$$	$20–$30
$$	$10–$20
$	under $10

*per person for a main course at dinner

Lodging

Throughout the islands accommodations range from small (sometimes non air-conditioned) inns to splashy resorts and hotels that are the ultimate in luxury. Most medium and large hotels offer a choice of EP and MAP. Almost all hotels offer dive packages.

CATEGORY	COST EP/CP*	COST A.I.**
$$$$	over $350	over $375
$$$	$250–$350	$275–$375
$$	$150–$250	$175–$275
$	under $150	under $175

*EP/CP prices are per night for a standard double room in high season, excluding taxes, service charges, and meal plans**A.I. (all-inclusive) prices are per person, per night based on double-occupancy during high season, excluding taxes and service charges

THE TURKS

Grand Turk

Bermudian colonial architecture abounds on this string bean of an island (just 7 mi [11 km] long and 1½ mi [2½ km] wide). Buildings have walled-in courtyards to keep wandering horses from nibbling on the foliage. The island caters to divers, and it's no wonder: the wall, a slice of vertical coral mountain, is less than 300 yards from the beach.

Exploring Grand Turk

Pristine beaches with vistas of turquoise waters, small local settlements, historic ruins, and native flora and fauna are among the sights on Grand Turk. Fewer than 5,000 people live on this 7½-square-mi (19-square-km) island, and it's hard to get lost as there aren't many roads.

Numbers in the margin correspond to points of interest on the Turks and Caicos Islands map.

① **Cockburn Town.** The buildings in the colony's capital and seat of government reflect a 19th-century Bermudian style of architecture. Narrow streets are lined with low stone walls and old street lamps, now powered by electricity. The once-vital salinas have been restored, and covered benches along the sluices offer shady spots for observing wading birds, including flamingos that frequent the shallows. In one of the oldest stone buildings on the islands, the **Turks & Caicos National Museum** (✉ Duke St., Grand Turk, ☎ 649/946–2160) houses the Molasses Reef wreck of 1513, the earliest shipwreck discovered in the Americas. The natural history exhibits include artifacts left by Taíno, African, North American, Bermudian, French, and Latin American settlers. An impressive addition to the museum is the coral-reef and sealife exhibit, faithfully modeled on a popular dive site just off the island. The museum is open Monday–Tuesday and Thursday–Friday 9–4, Wednesday 9–6, and Saturday 9–1. Admission is $5.

Beaches

There are more than 230 mi (370 km) of beaches in the Turks and Caicos Islands, ranging from secluded coves to miles-long stretches, and most beaches are soft coralline sand. Tiny cays offer complete isolation for

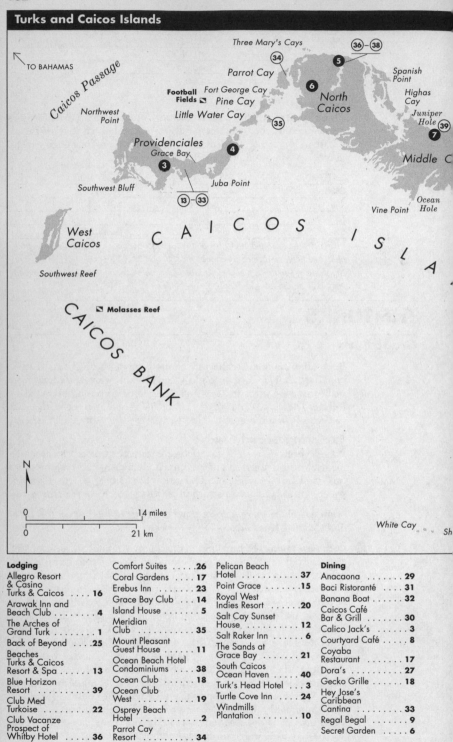

TO BAHAMAS

Caicos Passage

Three Mary's Cays

Parrot Cay

Football Fields

Fort George Cay

Pine Cay

Little Water Cay

Northwest Point

Providenciales

Grace Bay

Southwest Bluff

Juba Point

West Caicos

Southwest Reef

North Caicos

Spanish Point

Highas Cay

Juniper Hole

Middle C

Ocean Hole

Vine Point

C A I C O S   I S L A

CAICOS BANK

Molasses Reef

N

| 0 | | 14 miles |
| 0 | | 21 km |

White Cay

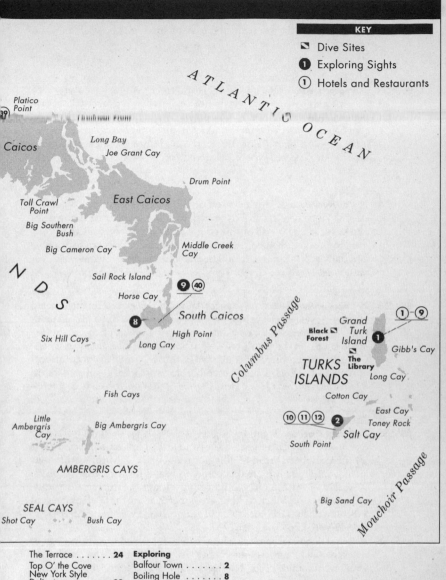

KEY

↘ Dive Sites

❶ Exploring Sights

① Hotels and Restaurants

ATLANTIC OCEAN

Platico Point

Caicos

Long Bay
Joe Grant Cay

Drum Point

East Caicos

Toll Crawl Point

Big Southern Bush

Big Cameron Cay

Middle Creek Cay

N D S

Sail Rock Island

Horse Cay

❾ ㊵

❽

South Caicos

High Point

Six Hill Cays

Long Cay

Columbus Passage

Black Forest ↘

Grand Turk Island

① ⑨

❶

Gibb's Cay

TURKS ISLANDS

↘ The Library

Long Cay

Fish Cays

Cotton Cay

Little Ambergris Cay

Big Ambergris Cay

⑩ ⑪ ⑫ ❷

East Cay
Toney Rock

Salt Cay

AMBERGRIS CAYS

South Point

Mouchoir Passage

SEAL CAYS

Shot Cay   Bush Cay

Big Sand Cay

nude sunbathing and skinny-dipping. Many are accessible only by boat. **Governor's Beach,** a long white strip on the west coast of Grand Turk, is one of the nicest, with plenty of sparkling, powder-soft sand on which to stroll.

Dining

AMERICAN

$$–$$$ ✕ **Water's Edge.** This pleasantly rustic eatery would have to float to be any closer to the ocean. Proprietor Seamus Day is committed to serving conch in any way, shape, or form—conch salad, cracked conch, conch creole, curried conch, and even conch po'boys. Other choices include giant, juicy "Goo Burgers," made-from-scratch pizza, and homemade pies. ⊠ *Duke St., Grand Turk,* ☎ *649/946–1680. MC, V. Closed Sun.*

CAFÉS

$ ✕ **Courtyard Café.** Homemade waffles with fresh fruit and whipped cream? Huge omelets and oversized muffins? Submarine sandwiches and pasta salad? It's all at this casual café, where you can enjoy your meal in the cool shade of the garden courtyard. Prices are reasonable and daily specials range from lasagna and quiche to island-style beef patties. ⊠ *Duke St., Grand Turk,* ☎ *649/946–1453. AE, MC, V.*

ECLECTIC

$$–$$$ ✕ **Calico Jack's.** The menu changes daily at this lively restaurant—touted by many residents as the best on the island—in the Turks Head Hotel. Look for lobster, steaks, chicken curry, lamb shanks, pizza, and homemade soups on the menu, as well as an excellent selection of wines. On Friday nights there's a courtyard barbecue, with live music by local musicians. The English pub is usually abuzz with local gossip and mirthful chatter. ⊠ *Turks Head Hotel, Duke St., Grand Turk,* ☎ *649/946– 2466. MC, V.*

SEAFOOD

$$–$$$ ✕ **Secret Garden.** Menu highlights at the Salt Raker Inn's restaurant include local conch and fish dishes and grilled lobster tail. For dessert try the Caribbean bread pudding or Key Lime pie. Morning offerings include a full English breakfast and an island favorite, fish-and-grits. Wednesday- and Sunday-night sing-alongs, featuring local guitarist/divemaster Mitch Rolling, are popular, as are the Wednesday- and Saturday-night barbecues. ⊠ *Salt Raker Inn, Duke St., Grand Turk,* ☎ *649/946–2260. AE, MC, V.*

$–$$ ✕ **Regal Begal.** Drop by this local eatery for island specialties such as cracked conch, minced lobster, and fish-and-chips. It's a casual place with unmemorable decor, but the portions are large and the prices easy on your wallet. ⊠ *Hospital Rd., Grand Turk,* ☎ *649/946–2274. No credit cards.*

Lodging

$$ 🏠 **The Arches of Grand Turk.** If you're looking for a home away from home, these immaculate vacation town houses offer space, privacy, and a loving touch. Each of the four two-story suites is fully furnished in clean-cut country style. Kitchen/dining areas are on the lower levels, with two huge bedrooms upstairs. Arched balconies front and back promise breathtaking sunrises and sunsets. Atop the ridge northeast of town, steady breezes keep insects away, and there is an eagle's-eye view of the island. ⊠ *Lighthouse Rd., Grand Turk, (Box 226),* ☎ FAX *649/946–2941,* WEB *www.grandturkarches.com. 4 town homes. Kitchens, microwaves, cable TV with movies, bicycles, laundry facilities. D, MC, V. EP.*

$ 🏠 **Arawak Inn and Beach Club.** These newly renovated condo-style accommodations have private bedrooms, full-size baths and kitchens, and living rooms with sofa beds. The complex fronts a fabulous white-sand beach, and there's a seaside freshwater pool and volleyball court. Don't feel like cooking? The restaurant serves delicious Caribbean meals. ✉ *Near White Sands Beach, Grand Turk, (Box 190),* ☎ *649/946–2277,* FAX *649/946–2279. 16 units. Restaurant, bar, kitchens, cable TV with movies, pool, beach, snorkeling, horseback riding, volleyball, laundry service. AE, MC, V. CP, MAP.*

$ 🏠 **Island House.** Perched on a breezy hill overlooking North Creek, this Mediterranean-style all-suites inn offers romantic comfort and panoramic views from large porches. One mile (1½ km) from town, gas-powered golf carts are provided free of charge. Relax on the expansive, palm-shaded pool/patio area with barbecue grill. Fishing from the dock and bird-watching are popular at this peaceful retreat, but dive packages are available for active types. ✉ *Lighthouse Rd., Grand Turk, (Box 36),* ☎ *649/946–1519,* FAX *649/946–2646,* WEB *www.islandhouse-tci.com. 9 suites. Kitchenettes, microwaves, cable TV with movies, pool, dock, fishing, bicycles, laundry facilities, Internet, some pets allowed. AE, MC, V. EP.*

$ 🏠 **Osprey Beach Hotel.** Rooms in this two-story oceanfront building open onto a private veranda overlooking the beach; there are airy cathedral ceilings on the top floors. Deluxe units have brand-new furnishings, king-size beds, and bathrooms; suites include sitting rooms and full kitchens. The pool bar serves drinks and tapas to the sound of breaking waves just steps away. A pleasant touch is the lush foliage lining the walkways. ✉ *Duke St., Grand Turk, (Box 1),* ☎ *649/946–2888,* FAX *649/946–2817,* WEB *www.ospreybeachhotel.com. 28 rooms. Coffee shop, bar, some kitchens, microwaves, cable TV with movies, golf privileges, pool, beach, snorkeling, meeting rooms. AE, MC, V. EP, FAP, MAP.*

$ 🏠 **Salt Raker Inn.** Across a quaint one-way street from the beach, this inn—once the home of a Bermudian shipwright—was built more than 170 years ago. The renovated rooms are clean and comfortable, all with the original red pine floors. Upstairs suites have balconies overlooking the ocean, and lush tropical gardens at back envelop the Secret Garden restaurant. Hotel service is unpretentious and friendly. Dive packages are available through Blue Water Divers. ✉ *Duke St., Grand Turk, (Box 1),* ☎ *649/946–2260,* FAX *649/946–2817,* WEB *www.microplan.com. 10 rooms, 3 suites. Restaurant, bar, no phones in some rooms, refrigerators, no TV in some rooms, dive shop, bicycles. AE, MC, V. EP, FAP, MAP.*

$ 🏠 **Turks Head Hotel.** Although thoroughly modernized, the historical Turks Head Hotel has maintained its romantic charm and tranquil ambience. The two-story structure, filled with antique furnishings, was built in 1840 as the home of a prosperous salt miner, and has also served as the American consulate and governor's guest house. Rooms are a comfortable blend of old and new, with a coffeemaker and mini-bar beside the canopied four-poster bed. The hotel bar and Calico Jack's restaurant bustle at night; the beach is only a few strides away, and dive packages are available. ✉ *Duke St., Grand Turk, (Box 58),* ☎ *649/946–2466,* FAX *649/946–1716,* WEB *www.grand-turk.com. 8 rooms. Restaurant, minibars, cable TV with movies, golf privileges, beach, bicycles, pub. MC, V. EP, CP, FAP, MAP.*

Nightlife

A fun crowd gathers at **Turk's Head Hotel** (✉ Duke St., Grand Turk, ☎ 649/946–2466) almost every night. On weekends and holidays the younger crowd heads over to the **Nookie Hill Club** (✉ Nookie Hill, Grand Turk, ☎ no phone) for late-night wining and dancing. There's folk and pop music at the **Salt Raker Inn** (✉ Duke St., Grand Turk, ☎ 649/946–2260) on Wednesday and Sunday nights.

Outdoor Activities and Sports

CYCLING

The island's flat terrain isn't very taxing, and most roads have hard surfaces. Take water with you: there are few places to stop for refreshment. Most hotels in Cockburn Town have bicycles available, but you can also rent them for $10–$15 a day from **Sea Eye Diving** (☎ FAX 649/946–1407).

SCUBA DIVING AND SNORKELING

In these waters you can find undersea cathedrals, coral gardens, and countless tunnels, but note that you must carry and present a valid certificate card before you'll be allowed to dive. As its name suggests, the **Black Forest** offers staggering black-coral formations as well as the occasional black-tip shark. In the **Library** you can study fish galore, including large numbers of yellowtail snapper. At the Columbus Passage separating South Caicos from Grand Turk, each side of a 22-mi-wide (35-km-wide) channel drops more than 7,000 ft (2,141 m). From January through March, thousands of Atlantic humpback whales swim through en route to their winter breeding grounds.

Dive outfitters can all be found in Cockburn Town. Two-tank boat dives generally cost $60–$75. **Blue Water Divers** (⊠ Salt Raker Inn, Duke St., Grand Turk, ☎ FAX 649/946–1226) has been in operation on Grand Turk since 1983. **Oasis Divers** (⊠ Duke St., Grand Turk, ☎ FAX 649/946–1128) specializes in complete gear handling and pampering treatment. It also supplies NITROX. Besides daily dive trips to the wall, **Sea Eye Diving** (⊠ Duke St., Grand Turk, ☎ FAX 649/946–1407) offers encounters with friendly stingrays.

Salt Cay

Fewer than 100 people live on this 2½-square-mi (6-square-km) dot of land, maintaining an unassuming lifestyle against a backdrop of quaint stucco cottages, stone ruins, and weathered wooden windmills standing sentry in the abandoned salinas. There's not much in the way of development, but there are splendid beaches on the north coast. The most spectacular sights are beneath the waves: 10 dive sites are just minutes from shore.

Exploring Salt Cay

Salt sheds and salinas are silent reminders of the days when the island was a leading producer of salt. Island tours are often conducted by motorized golf cart. From January through March whales pass by on the way to their winter breeding grounds.

❷ **Balfour Town.** What little development there is on Salt Cay is found here. It's home to several small hotels and a few stores that sell hand-woven baskets, T-shirts, convenience foods, and beach items.

Beaches

There are superb beaches on the north coast of **Salt Cay. Big Sand Cay,** 7 mi (11 km) south of Salt Cay, is also known for its long, unspoiled stretches of open sand.

Lodging

For approximate costs, *see* the lodging price chart *in* Grand Turk.

$$$–$$$$ 🏨 **Windmills Plantation.** The attraction here is the lack of distraction.
★ The hotel resembles a romantic's version of a colonial-era plantation. The great house has four suites, each with a sitting area, a four-poster bed, ceiling fans, and a veranda or balcony with a sea view. All are furnished in a mix of antique English and wicker furniture. Four other rooms are housed in adjacent buildings. Managers Jim and Sharon Shafer

bring a sterling reputation as gracious hosts. ⊠ *North Beach Rd., Salt Cay,* ☎ *649/946–6962 or 800/822–7715,* FAX *649/946–6930,* WEB *www.windmillsplantation.com. 4 rooms, 4 suites. Restaurant, bar, no air-conditioning, no room phones, no room TVs, pool, beach, snorkeling, fishing, hiking, horseback riding, library, no kids. AE, MC, V. BP.*

$ 🏨 **Mount Pleasant Guest House.** This simple, somewhat rustic hotel was a former salt-plantation home, now serving as a guest house catering to divers. Rooms are bright, clean, and simply furnished. The premises are filled with memorabilia and artifacts, and the gazebo bar overlooks a cut-stone cistern pit converted into a palm grove for hammocks. Meals are superb, with dinners including whelk soup, grilled fresh fish and lobster, buttery cracked conch, and New York strip steaks. ⊠ *Balfour Town,* ☎ FAX *649/946–6927,* WEB *www.turksandcaicos.tc/mtpleasant. 8 rooms. Restaurant, bar, no air-conditioning in some rooms, no room phones, fans, no room TVs, bicycles, horseback riding, library. MC, V. FAP, MAP.*

$ 🏨 **Salt Cay Sunset House.** Built in 1832, this historic bed-and-breakfast and oceanfront café is housed in the oldest salt-plantation home on Salt Cay, lovingly restored by enthusiastic owners Michele Wells and Paul Dinsmore. All three bedrooms have en suite baths; there's a shared living room. Period furnishings can be found throughout. Michelle serves hearty local and Continental fare for breakfast, lunch, and dinner on the breezy veranda at the Blue Mermaid Café. ⊠ *Balfour Town,* ☎ FAX *649/946–6942,* WEB *www.seaone.org. 3 rooms. Restaurant, no air-conditioning, no room phones, fans, no room TVs, beach, snorkeling, horseback riding, Internet. MC, V. BP, MAP.*

Outdoor Activities and Sports

SCUBA DIVING AND SNORKELING

Scuba divers can explore the **Endymion,** a 140-ft wooden-hull British warship that sank in 1790. It's off the southern point of Salt Cay. **Reef Runners** (☎ 649/946–6901) conducts daily trips and rents all the necessary equipment. It costs around $80 for a two-tank dive.

THE CAICOS

West Caicos

Accessible only by boat, this uninhabited, untamed island has no facilities whatsoever. A glorious white beach stretches for 1 mi (1½ km) along the northwest point, and the offshore diving here is among the most exotic in the islands. The "Wilds of West Caicos" encompass a pristine wall, about ¼ mi (½ km) from shore, which starts at 35–45 ft (11–14 m) and cascades to 7,000 ft (2,141 m). Here, sharks, eagle rays, and turtles are commonly seen on the many dive sites. It's about an hour boat ride from Provo, but well worth the trip. Most dive operators depart from satellite locations on the south side of Provo for the journey.

Providenciales

In the mid-18th century, so the story goes, a French ship was wrecked near here, and the survivors were washed ashore on an island they gratefully christened La Providentielle. Under the Spanish, the name was changed to Providenciales. Today about 20,000 people live on Provo (as everybody calls it); a considerable number are expatriate British, Canadian, and American businesspeople and retirees, or refugees from nearby Haiti. The island's 44 square mi (114 square km) are by far the most developed in the Turks and Caicos.

Along the beach-lined north shore there are no less than a dozen high-end condominium hotels (some currently under construction), three all-inclusive resorts, and the country's first time-share resort. Residential development is also booming, especially in the upscale Leeward and Chalk Sound areas. Although roads are in desperate need of upgrading, power, water, telecommunications and cable TV utilities are modern and well-serviced.

Exploring Providenciales
Numbers in the margin correspond to points of interest on the Turks and Caicos Island map.

❸ **Downtown Providenciales.** Near Providenciales International Airport, downtown Provo is really an extended strip mall that houses a grocery store, car-rental and travel agencies, law offices, banks, and other businesses.

❹ **Caicos Conch Farm.** On the northeast tip of Provo, this is a major mariculture operation where mollusks are farmed commercially (more than 3 million conch are here). Guided tours are available; call to confirm times. The small gift shop sells conch-related souvenirs. ✉ *Leeward-Going-Through, Leeward,* ☎ *649/946–5330.* ☞ *$6.* ◷ *Mon.–Sat. 9–4.*

Beaches
A fine white-sand beach stretches 12 mi (19 km) along Provo's **north coast**, where most of the hotels are. There are also good beaches at **Sapodilla Bay** and **Malcolm Roads**, at North West Point, which is accessible only by four-wheel-drive vehicles.

Dining
There are more than 50 restaurants on Provo, ranging from casual to elegant, with cuisine from Continental to Asian (and everything in between). You can spot the islands' own Caribbean influence no matter where you go, exhibited in fresh seafood specials, colorful presentations, and a tangy dose of spice.

For approximate costs, *see* the dining price chart *in* Grand Turk.

CARIBBEAN

$$–$$$ ✕ **Mango Reef.** Third generation restaurateur Doug Camozzi (of Tiki Hut fame) was determined to spotlight Caribbean ingredients when he created the menu for his newest venture, in the Royal West Indies Resort. The end result is a marvelous medley of flavors, colors, and textures made by marinating meats and seafoods prior to grilling and pairing them with inventive fruit- and vegetable-based chutneys and salsas. Meals are served throughout the day, and the separate bar area is a popular evening spot for residents. ✉ *Royal West Indies Resort, Grace Bay,* ☎ *649/946–8200. AE, MC, V.*

DELI

$ ✕ **Top o' the Cove New York Style Delicatessen.** You can walk to this tiny café on Leeward Highway, just south of Turtle Cove. Order breakfast, deli sandwiches, salads, and enticingly rich desserts and freshly baked goods. From the deli case you can buy the fixings for a picnic; the shop's shelves are stocked with an eclectic selection of fancy foodstuffs. Open from 6:30 AM on weekdays and Saturday, from 8 to 2 on Sunday. ✉ *Leeward Hwy., Turtle Cove,* ☎ FAX *649/946–4694. No credit cards.*

ECLECTIC

$$$–$$$$ ✕ **Anacaona.** At the Grace Bay Club, this *palapa*-style restaurant (with
★   tables clustered under large thatched-roof structures) offers a memorable dining experience minus the tie, the air-conditioning, and the at-

titude. Start with a bottle of fine wine and then enjoy a three- or four-course meal of the chef's light but flavorful cooking, which combines traditional European recipes with Caribbean fare. Oil lamps on the tables, gently circulating ceiling fans, and the murmur of the trade winds add to the Eden-like environment. ⊠ *Grace Bay Club, Grace Bay,* ☎ *649/946–5050. AE, MC, V.*

$$$-$$$$ ✕ **Coyaba Restaurant.** As founding member of the local chapter of the Chaîne des Rôtisseurs, chef Paul Newman lets his talent soar at Coral Gardens' elegantly appointed, terrace-style restaurant. A typical meal (served on Royal Doulton china, no less) might start with truffle mousse, follow with chipotle-glazed maple leaf duck breast, and finish with upside down apple pie, all complemented by wines from the outstanding list. The careful attention to detail makes an evening here live up to its name's translation from the Arawak Indian tongue, "heavenly." ⊠ *Coral Gardens, Penn's Rd., The Bight,* ☎ *649/946–5186. Reservations essential. AE, MC, V. Closed Tues.*

$$-$$$$ ✕ **Gecko Grille.** At this Ocean Club resort restaurant you can eat indoors surrounded by tropical murals or out on the garden patio, where the trees are interwoven with tiny twinkling lights. Creative "Floribbean" fare combines native specialties with exotic fruits and zesty island spices and includes Black Angus steaks grilled to order. There's live music Sunday and Wednesday evenings. ⊠ *Ocean Club, Grace Bay,* ☎ *649/ 946–5885. AE, MC, V. Closed Mon.*

$$$ ✕ **Caicos Café Bar and Grill.** There's a pervasive air of celebration in the tree-shaded outdoor dining terrace of this popular eatery. Choose from fresh grilled seafood, steak, lamb, and chicken served hot off the outdoor barbecue. Owner chef Pierrik Marziou adds a French accent to his appetizers, salads, and homemade desserts. ⊠ *Across from Allegro Resort, Grace Bay,* ☎ *649/946–5278. AE, MC, V.*

$$$ ✕ **The Terrace.** One of the most popular dining spots on Provo, on the grounds of the Turtle Cove Inn, specializes in creative conch dishes, such as conch ravioli and conch fillets encrusted with ground pecans, as well as fresh local fish served with fruit salsas. The house salad, sprinkled with pine nuts and shaved, aged Parmesan, is excellent, as are the hot bread pockets served with your meal. Top it all off with a classic crème brûlée or scoop of homemade ice cream. ⊠ *Turtle Cove Inn, Turtle Cove Marina, Turtle Cove,* ☎ *649/946–4763. AE, MC, V. Closed Sun.*

ITALIAN

$$-$$$ ✕ **Baci Ristoranté.** Aromas redolent of the Mediterranean waft from the open kitchen as you walk into this intimate eatery east of Turtle Cove. Outdoor seating is on a romantic canal-front patio. The menu offers a small, varied selection of Italian delights. Main courses focus on veal, but also include pasta, chicken, and fresh fish dishes. House wines are personally selected by the owners and complement the tasteful wine list. Try the tiramisu for dessert with a flavored coffee drink. ⊠ *Harbour Town, Turtle Cove,* ☎ *649/941–3044. AE, MC, V. Closed Mon.*

SEAFOOD

$$ ✕ **Banana Boat.** Buoys and other sea relics deck the walls of this lively restaurant/bar on the wharf. Grilled grouper, lobster salad sandwiches, conch fritters, and conch salad are among the options. Tropical drinks include the rum-filled Banana Breeze—a house specialty. ⊠ *Turtle Cove Marina, Turtle Cove,* ☎ *649/941–5706. AE, MC, V.*

TEX-MEX

$-$$ ✕ **Hey Jose's Caribbean Cantina.** Frequented by locals, this restaurant, just south of Turtle Cove, claims to serve the island's best margaritas. Customers also return for the tasty Tex-Mex treats: tacos, tostados, nachos, burritos, fajitas, and special-recipe hot chicken wings. Thick, hearty pizzas are another favorite—especially the "Kitchen Sink," with a little bit of everything thrown in! ⊠ *Central Square, Leeward Hwy., Turtle Cove,* ☎ 649/946–4812. *MC, V. Closed Sun.*

Lodging

For approximate costs, *see* the lodging price chart *in* Grand Turk.

A popular option on Provo is renting a self-contained villa or private home. **Elliot Holdings and Management Company** (⊠ Box 235, Providenciales, ☎ 649/946–5355, WEB www.ElliotHoldings.com) offers a wide selection of modest to magnificent villas in the Leeward, Grace Bay, and Turtle Cove areas of Providenciales. **T. C. Safari** (⊠ Box 64, Providenciales, ☎ 649/941–5043, WEB www.tcsafari.tc) has exclusive oceanfront properties in the beautiful and tranquil Sapodilla Bay/Chalk Sound neighborhood on Provo's southwest shores. For the best villa selection, plan to make your reservations three to six months in advance.

$$$$
★ **Grace Bay Club.** Staying at this Swiss-owned, Mediterranean-style resort is a little like being the guest of honor of a very gracious host with unbeatable taste. Suites have breathtaking views of stunning Grace Bay and are furnished with rattan and pickled wood, with Mexican-tile floors and elegant Turkish and Indian throw rugs. Activities range from diving to golf to catered picnics on surrounding islands, but relaxing is the major pastime. Elegant French-Caribbean meals are served in the Anacaona restaurant. ⊠ *Grace Bay (Box 128),* ☎ 649/946–5757 or 800/946–5757, FAX 649/946–5758 or 800/946–5758, WEB www.gracebayclub.com. 21 suites. Restaurant, bar, in-room safes, kitchens, cable TV with movies, in-room VCRs, 2 tennis courts, pool, hot tub, massage, beach, snorkeling, windsurfing, boating, parasailing, bicycles, shop, laundry service, concierge, Internet, no kids under 12. Closed Sept. AE, MC, V. CP, MAP.

$$$$
★ **Point Grace.** This boutique hotel raises the bar for luxury resorts on the islands. Majestically designed in British Colonial style, two oceanfront buildings house magnificent two- and three-bedroom suites. All have expansive terraces overlooking Grace Bay and are furnished with Indonesian hardwood and teak. Hand-painted tiles line the bathrooms and Frette linens cover the king-size, four-poster beds. Two four-bedroom penthouse suites have separate massage rooms and rooftop Jacuzzis. Rolls Royce airport transfers can be requested. ⊠ *Grace Bay (Box 700),* ☎ 888/682–3705 or 649/946–5096, FAX 649/946–5097, WEB www.pointgrace.com. 23 suites, 9 cottages, 2 villas. 2 restaurants, 2 bars, in-room fax, in-room safes, some in-room hot tubs, kitchenettes, microwaves, cable TV with movies, in-room VCRs, pool, massage, beach, snorkeling, windsurfing, boating, parasailing, fishing, bicycles, recreation room, baby-sitting, laundry service, concierge, Internet, business services, car rental. Closed Sept. AE, D, MC, V. CP.

$$$–$$$$
★ ☾ **Beaches Turks & Caicos Resort & Spa.** There's plenty to satisfy families at this member of the Sandals chain, including a children's park complete with a video game center, water slides, a swim-up soda bar, a 1950s-style diner, and a teen disco. Nice rooms, lots of activities, extravagant meals, and many kinds of water sports make this beachfront all-inclusive resort an indulgent experience. Rooms are furnished in rich mahogany and warm tropical tones, with king-size beds; honeymoon villas include a Jacuzzi in the bedroom. The spa offers body wraps, massages, and facials. ⊠ *Lower Bight Rd., Grace Bay,* ☎ 649/946–8000 or 800/726–3257, FAX 649/946–8001, WEB www.beaches.com. 359 rooms, 103 suites. 9 restaurants, 8 bars, nightclub, in-room safes, cable TV with movies, 4 tennis courts, 6 pools, gym, hair salon, hot tub, massage, spa, beach, dive shop, snorkeling, windsurfing, boating,

parasailing, fishing, bicycles, recreation room, theater, video game room, shops, baby-sitting, children's programs (ages 0–5), concierge, meeting rooms, car rental. AE, MC, V. All-inclusive.

$$$–$$$$ ▣ **Royal West Indies Resort.** Distinctive British Colonial architecture and extensive gardens highlight this well-run luxury condominium resort. Private balconies front all units to make the most of the sea view, and interiors are an eclectic blend of wood and fabrics from Central and South America. Although the beach is steps away, the 80-ft-long pool surrounded by tropical fruit trees is a peaceful place to relax and sip a drink from the superb on-site Mango Reef restaurant and bar. ⊠ *Grace Bay (Box 482),* ☎ *649/946–5004,* ☐ *649/946–5008,* ☐ *www. royalwestindies.com. 99 suites. Restaurant, bar, in-room data ports, in-room safes, kitchenettes, microwaves, cable TV with movies, 2 pools, beach, snorkeling, boating, fishing, laundry facilities, baby-sitting, car rental. AE, MC, V. EP.*

$$$–$$$$ ▣ **The Sands at Grace Bay.** "Simply breathtaking" describes the
★ sparkling ocean views from the huge screened patios and floor-to-ceiling windows adorning units at this beach lover's haven. The upscale condominium resort offers units ranging from studios to three bedrooms; larger suites have two TVs, extra sleeper sofas, and washer-dryers. Contemporary furnishings combine Indonesian wood, wrought iron, and wicker with seaside-tone fabrics to emphasize the resort's theme of sophisticated simplicity. Hemingway's, an excellent oceanfront cabana restaurant and bar, is on site. ⊠ *Grace Bay (Box 681),* ☎ *649/941–5199,* ☐ *649/946–5198,* ☐ *www.thesandsresort.com. 116 suites. Restaurant, bar, in-room data ports, in-room safes, kitchens, microwaves, cable TV with movies, tennis court, 3 pools, gym, spa, beach, snorkeling, boating, bicycles, shop, baby-sitting, laundry facilities, concierge, car rental. AE, MC, V. EP.*

$$–$$$$ ▣ **Coral Gardens.** This intimate beachfront resort fronts one of Provo's
★ best snorkeling reefs and is in a tranquil area well west of bustling Grace Bay. The deluxe suites have terraces and floor-to-ceiling walls of sliding glass. Gourmet kitchens open into the dining areas, and bedrooms and baths overlook the luxurious gardens. The beachfront area is accented by two dramatic waterfalls cascading down the face of each building. Fine dining alfresco is offered at Coyaba Restaurant. ⊠ *Penn's Rd., The Bight (Box 281),* ☎ *649/941–3713 or 800/532–8536,* ☐ *649/ 941–5171,* ☐ *www.coralgardens.com. 28 suites. 2 restaurants, 2 bars, room service, in-room data ports, in-room safes, kitchens, microwaves, cable TV with movies, 2 pools, aerobics, massage, beach, snorkeling, boating, fishing, laundry facilities, concierge, Internet, car rental. AE, MC, V. EP.*

$$–$$$$ ▣ **Ocean Club.** These luxury all-suites condominiums are on a 12-mi (19-
★ km) stretch of pristine beach, a short walk from Provo's only golf course. Units range from efficiency studios to three-bedroom suites with living rooms, dining rooms, kitchens, and screened balconies. Management and service are consistently superb. You can take a free shuttle to use the facilities of sister property, Ocean Club West. The on-site Gecko Grille serves creative island dishes. ⊠ *Grace Bay (Box 240),* ☎ *649/946–5880 or 800/ 457–8787,* ☐ *649/946–5845,* ☐ *www.oceanclubresorts.com. 86 suites. 2 restaurants, 2 bars, in-room data ports, in-room safes, some kitchens, kitchenettes, microwaves, cable TV with movies, tennis court, 2 pools, gym, spa, beach, dive shop, snorkeling, boating, shops, laundry facilities, concierge, Internet, meeting room, car rental. AE, MC, V. EP.*

$$–$$$$ ▣ **Ocean Club West.** This sister property to the Ocean Club maintains
★ signature details of the original—breathtaking seascapes, large balconies, and exquisite landscaping—while expanding the oceanfront central courtyard area to include a gazebo-capped island, winding free-form

pool, and a seaside café and swim-up bar. Interiors are decorated in subdued sophistication, utilizing whites, light woods, and wicker. Junior one-bedrooms are an especially good value. ⊠ *Grace Bay (Box 640)*, ☎ *649/946–5880 or 800/457–8787*, FAX *649/946–5845*, WEB *www. oceanclubresorts.com. 90 suites. 1 restaurant, 1 bar, in-room data ports, in-room safes, some kitchens, kitchenettes, microwaves, cable TV with movies, tennis court, 2 pools, gym, spa, beach, dive shop, snorkeling, boating, laundry facilities, concierge, Internet, meeting room, car rental. AE, MC, V. EP.*

$$–$$$ ☒ **Allegro Resort and Casino Turks & Caicos.** This sprawling beach-front property is an all-inclusive resort that caters primarily to adults (though it still welcomes children). The oversize oceanfront rooms have rattan furniture, a rich Caribbean color scheme, and private balcony or terrace. A pool-patio area and a PADI 5-Star dive facility are on site. Meals range from Caribbean fare to Italian specialties, with unlimited beverages. The American Casino, the island's only gaming facility, is here. ⊠ *Grace Bay (Box 205)*, ☎ *649/946–5555 or 800/858–2258*, FAX *649/946–5522*, WEB *www.allegroresorts.com. 186 rooms. 3 restaurants, 3 bars, in-room safes, cable TV with movies, 3 tennis courts, pool, aerobics, gym, hot tub, massage, beach, dive shop, snorkeling, windsurfing, boating, fishing, bicycles, volleyball, casino, theater, shops, baby-sitting, children's programs (ages 4–12), laundry service, concierge, Internet, meeting rooms, travel services, car rental. AE, MC, V. All-inclusive.*

$$ ☒ **Club Med Turkoise.** This village is a major water-sports center, with scuba diving, windsurfing, sailing, and waterskiing on the turquoise waters at the doorstep. Two- and three-story bungalows line a 1-mi (1½-km) beach, and all the usual sybaritic pleasures are here. This all-inclusive (except drinks) club is geared toward couples, singles age 18 and over, and divers. There are also a flying trapeze, nightly entertainment, dive packages, and excursions offered to sites in the Turks and Caicos. ⊠ *Grace Bay*, ☎ *649/946–5491 or 800/258–2633*, FAX *649/ 946–5497*, WEB *www.clubmed.com. 288 rooms. 2 restaurants, 3 bars, cable TV with movies, 8 tennis courts, pool, aerobics, gym, hot tub, massage, beach, dive shop, snorkeling, windsurfing, boating, fishing, bicycles, billiards, soccer, volleyball, dance club, theater, shops, laundry services, no kids. AE, MC, V. All-inclusive.*

$–$$ ☒ **Comfort Suites.** Although Comfort Suites is the island's only "franchise" hotel, the property's exceptional hospitality and superior performance are anything but standard. Suites are housed in two three-story buildings built around an Olympic-size pool and landscaped patio area; frosty drinks are served at the tiki bar. Like the rest of the hotel, rooms are spotless and furnished in bright Caribbean colors. Grace Bay's pearly white beach is just across the street. The hotel flanks the Ports of Call shopping village. ⊠ *Grace Bay (Box 590)*, ☎ *649/946–8888 or 888/678–3483*, FAX *649/946–5444*, WEB *www.comfortsuitestci.com. 100 suites. Bar, in-room data ports, in-room safes, refrigerators, cable TV with movies, pool, shops, travel services. AE, MC, V. CP.*

$ ☒ **Back of Beyond.** As the name suggests, this retreat is set apart from Provo's hustle and bustle on the quiet south shore. A burnished-orange stucco, pueblo-style inn houses the nine rooms, each charmingly decorated by proprietress Coleen Darragh, who with husband Ed designed and built the distinctive building to complement the surrounding cactus-dotted terrain. Rooms and the dining patio overlook the turquoise-green hues of the ocean beyond; a secluded white sand beach is just a stroll away. Coleen's hospitality extends to the on-site restaurant and bar, where she cooks and serves home-style "comfort" fare. ⊠ *Venetian Rd., Discovery Bay*, ☎ *649/941–4555*, WEB *www.backofbeyond.tc.*

9 rooms. Restaurant, bar, no air-conditioning, fans, no room TVs, pool. No credit cards. BP.

$ ▦ **Turtle Cove Inn.** This pleasant, two-story inn offers affordable, comfortable lodging much in favor with scuba, boating, and fishing enthusiasts. All rooms include a private balcony or patio overlooking either the courtyard's lush tropical gardens and pool or Turtle Cove Marina. Dockside is the Tiki Hut Cabana Bar and Grill, a popular local watering hole; in another corner there's the more upscale Terrace restaurant. You can readily stroll to the snorkeling trail at Smith's Reef, and access the remaining miles of north shore beach from there. ⊠ *Turtle Cove Marina, Turtle Cove (Box 131),* ☎ *649/946–4203 or 800/887–0477,* FAX *649/946–4141,* WEB *www.turtlecoveinn.com. 28 rooms, 2 suites. 2 restaurants, 2 bars, in-room safes, refrigerators, cable TV with movies, pool, marina, fishing, bicycles, shops, car rental, no smoking rooms. AE, MC, V. EP.*

Nightlife

Residents and tourists flock to **Lattitudes** (⊠ Ports of Call, Grace Bay, ☎ 649/946–5832) on Friday nights to let their hair down. There are a pool table and satellite sports on five TVs in the bar. On Thursday nights you can find a local band and lively crowd at **Sharkbite Bar & Grill** (⊠ Harbour Town, Turtle Cove, ☎ 649/941–5090). Also known as The Nightclub, the new **Stardust & Ashes** (⊠ Leeward Hwy., Grace Bay, ☎ 649/941–5475) sets the stage for a great night out with music and dancing on a torch lit tropical terrace and luxurious lounge areas for private moments. The sound system and lighting are state of the art and entertainment themes vary nightly.

The only casino on the island is the **American Casino** (⊠ Allegro Resort, Grace Bay, ☎ 649/946–5508). It's open to all and includes 80 slot machines and several table games including blackjack, Caribbean stud poker, and roulette. Drinks are free for all players.

Outdoor Activities and Sports

BICYCLING

Provo has a few steep grades to conquer, but they're short. Unfortunately, traffic on Leeward Highway and rugged road edges make pedaling here a less-than-relaxing experience. Instead, try the less-traveled roads through the native settlements of Blue Hills, the Bight, and Five Cays. Most hotels have bikes available. You can rent mountain bikes at **Provo Fun Cycles** (⊠ Ports of Call, Grace Bay, ☎ 649/946–5868) for $15 a day.

BOATING AND SAILING

Provo's calm, reef-protected turquoise seas combine with constant easterly trade winds for excellent sailing conditions. Several multihulled vessels offer charters with snorkeling stops, food and beverage service, and sunset vistas. Prices range from $39 for group trips to $600 or more for private charters. **Atabeyra** (☎ 649/941–5363) is a retired rum runner and the choice of residents for special events. **Sail Provo** (☎ 649/946–4783) runs 57-ft and 48-ft catamarans on scheduled half-day, full-day, and sunset cruises.

FISHING

The island's fertile waters are great for angling—anything from bottom- and reef fishing (most likely to produce plenty of bites and a large catch) to bonefishing and deep-sea fishing (among the finest in the Caribbean). You're required to purchase a $15 visitor's fishing license; operators generally furnish all equipment, drinks, and snacks. Prices range from $100 to $375, depending on the length of trip and size of boat. You can rent a boat with a captain for a half or full day of bottom- or bonefishing through **J&B Tours** (⊠ Leeward Marina, Leeward, ☎ 649/946–5047). For deep-sea fishing trips in search of marlin, sailfish, wahoo, tuna, barracuda, and shark, look up **Sakitumi** (⊠ Turtle Cove Marina, Turtle Cove, ☎ 649/946–4065). Captain Arthur Dean at **Silver Deep** (⊠ Leeward Marina, Leeward, ☎ 649/946–5612) is said to be among the Caribbean's finest bonefishing guides.

GOLF

Provo Golf and Country Club's (☎ 649/946–5991) par-72, 18-hole championship course, designed by Karl Litten, is a combination of lush greens and fairways, rugged limestone outcroppings and freshwater lakes. Fees are $120 for 18 holes with shared cart.

PARASAILING

A 15-minute parasailing flight over Grace Bay is available for $60 (single) or $110 (tandem) at **Turtle Parasail** (☎ 649/231–0643).

SCUBA DIVING AND SNORKELING

For excellent close-to-shore snorkeling, try the **White House Reef,** off Penn's Road in the Bight, and **Smith's Reef,** over Bridge Road east of Turtle Cove. Both offer marked underwater snorkeling trails.

Scuba diving in the crystalline waters surrounding the islands ranks among the best in the Caribbean. The reef and wall drop-offs thrive with bright, unbroken coral formations and lavish numbers of fish and marine life. Mimicking the idyllic climate, waters are warm all year, averaging 76–78°F in the winter and 82–84°F during the summer. With minimal rainfall and soil runoff, visibility is naturally good and frequently superb, ranging from 60 to 150 ft (18 to 46 m) plus. An extensive system of marine national parks and boat moorings, combined with an ecoconscious mindset among dive operators, contributes to an underwater environment little changed in centuries.

Dive operators in Provo regularly visit sites at **Grace Bay** and **Pine Cay** for spur-and-groove coral formations and bustling reef diving. They make the longer journey to the dramatic walls at **North West Point** and **West Caicos,** depending on weather conditions. Instruction from the major diving agencies is available for all levels and certifications.

Art Pickering's Provo Turtle Divers (☎ 649/946–4232 or 800/833–1341), at the Ocean Club, Ocean Club West, and in Turtle Cove Marina, has been on Provo for more than 30 years. The staff is friendly, knowledgeable, and unpretentious. **Big Blue Unlimited** (⊠ Leeward Marina, Leeward, ☎ 649/946–5034) specializes in eco-diving adventures, with a certified marine biologist on staff. It also offers Nitrox, Trimix, and rebreathers. **Caicos Adventures** (⊠ Caicos Cafe Plaza, Grace Bay, ☎ FAX 649/946–3346) is run by friendly Frenchman Fifi Kuntz, and offers daily West Caicos trips with night dives on the West Caicos wall. **Dive Provo** (⊠ Allegro Resort, Ports of Call, Grace Bay, ☎ 649/946–5040 or 800/234–7768) is a resort-based, PADI 5-Star operation that runs daily one- and two-tank dives to popular Grace Bay sites. **Flamingo Divers** (⊠ Turtle Cove Landing, Turtle Cove, ☎ 649/946–4193 or 800/204–9282) focuses on small groups and personalized service.

TENNIS

The following hotels have courts open to nonguests. Prices vary, so call before you go. **Club Med Turkoise** (☎ 649/946–5491) has eight courts; four of them are lit for night games. **Erebus Inn** (☎ 649/946–4240) has clay courts, both of them lit. **Grace Bay Club** (☎ 649/946–5754) has two lit courts. The **Ocean Club and Ocean Club West** (☎ 649/946–5880) have one and two lit courts, respectively. You can rent equipment at **Provo Golf and Country Club** (☎ 649/946–5991) and play on their two lit courts.

Windsurfers find the calm turquoise water ideal. **Windsurfing Provo** (⊠ Ocean Club, Grace Bay, ☎ 649/946–5649; ⊠ Ocean Club West, Grace Bay, ☎ 649/946–5649) rents windsurfers, kayaks, motorboats, and Hobie Cats and offers windsurfing instruction.

Shopping

Don't expect the variety of goods offered on more developed Caribbean destinations. There are several main shopping areas in Provo: Market Place and Central Square, on the Leeward Highway about ½ mi to 1 mi outside of downtown Providenciales, and the shopping village Ports of Call, in Grace Bay. Delicate woven baskets, polished conch shells, paintings, wood carvings, handmade dolls, and small metalwork are the only crafts native to the area.

The **Bamboo Gallery** (⊠ Market Place, Leeward Hwy., Downtown Providenciales, ☎ FAX 649/946–4748) sells Caribbean art, from vivid Haitian paintings to wood carvings and local metal sculptures. For a large selection of duty-free liquors, visit **Carib West** (⊠ Airport Rd., Downtown Providenciales, ☎ 649/946–4215). **Greensleeves** (⊠ Central Square, Leeward Hwy., Turtle Cove, ☎ FAX 649/946–4147) offers paintings by local artists, island-made rag rugs, baskets, jewelry, and sisal mats and bags. **Marilyn's Craft** (⊠ Ports of Call, Grace Bay, no phone) sells handmade dolls, rag rugs, and wood carvings, plus tropical clothing and knickknacks. **Paradise Gifts** (⊠ Central Square, Leeward Hwy., Turtle Cove, ☎ 649/941–3828) offers a creative selection of decorated T-shirts, handmade jewelry, and paintings by local artists. From outlets at the Provo airport, Allegro Resort, Arch Plaza, Beaches, Club Med, Ocean Club Plaza, and The Sands at Grace Bay, **Royal Jewels** (☎ 649/946–4699) sells gold and jewelry, designer watches, perfumes, fine leather goods and cameras—all duty free.

With more than 20,000 items, including a large fresh produce section, on-site bakery, and extensive meat counter, **IGA Supermarket** (⊠ Leeward Hwy., Grace Bay, ☎ 649/941–5000), Provo's largest, is likely to have what you're looking for. Be prepared: prices are much higher than you would expect at home. If you need to supplement your beach reading stock or are looking for island-specific materials, visit **The Unicorn Bookstore** (⊠ Market Place, Leeward Hwy., Downtown Providenciales, ☎ 649/941–5458) for a wide assortment of books and magazines, including a large children's section.

Termed "the best little watersports shop in Provo," **Seatopia** (⊠ Leeward Hwy., Grace Bay, ☎ 649/941–3355; ⊠ Ports of Call, Grace Bay, no phone) sells reasonably priced scuba and snorkeling equipment, swimwear, beachwear, sandals, hats, and related water gear and swim toys. Besides having a licensed pharmacist on duty, **Super Value Pharmacy** (⊠ South Winds Plaza, Downtown Providenciales, ☎ 649/941–3779), just east of downtown Provo, stocks a super selection of cosmetics, greeting cards, baby care products, souvenirs, household goods, even beer, wine, and liquors.

Little Water Cay

This small, uninhabited cay is a protected area under the National Trust of the Turks and Caicos. On these 150 acres are two trails, small lakes, red mangroves, and an abundance of native plants. Boardwalks protect the ground and interpretive signs explain the habitat. The cay is the habitat of about 2,000 rare, endangered rock iguanas. They say the iguanas are shy, but these creatures actually seem rather curious. They waddle right up to you, as if posing for a picture; you can usually get within a foot of them before they move.

Parrot Cay

Once said to be a hideout for pirate Calico Jack Rackham and his lady cohorts Mary Reid and Anne Bonny, the 1,000-acre cay, between Fort George Cay and North Caicos, is now the site of an ultra-exclusive hideaway resort, a holistic health spa, and upscale homesites. Bordered by a wild stretch of pristine beach to the north and mangrove-lined wetlands to the south, tiny Parrot Cay is a natural wonder.

Lodging

For approximate costs, *see* the lodging price chart *in* Grand Turk.

$$$$ 　 🏨 **Parrot Cay Resort.** Frequented by celebrities and the international
★ 　 ultrachic, this exclusive resort combines natural beauty and elegant simplicity to create a rarefied atmosphere of tranquility. Mediterranean-style hillside structures house one- and two-bedroom suites, all with private terraces overlooking the ocean. Seaside villas include some private pools, butler service, and fully equipped kitchens, complete with chef and waitstaff on request. The on-site Shambhala Spa has been ranked among the top 10 in the world. The resort can only be accessed by private boat from Leeward Marina. ⊠ *Box 164, Providenciales,* ☎ *649/ 946–7788,* 𝔽𝔸𝕏 *649/946–7789,* 𝚆𝙴𝙱 *www.parrot-cay.com. 58 rooms. 2 restaurants, 2 bars, room service, in-room data ports, in-room safes, some kitchens, minibars, cable TV with movies, in-room VCRs, 2 tennis courts, pool, gym, hot tub, Japanese baths, massage, sauna, spa, steam room, beach, snorkeling, windsurfing, boating, waterskiing, fishing, mountain bikes, library, baby-sitting, laundry service. AE, MC, V. BP, FAP.*

Pine Cay

One of a chain of small cays linking North Caicos and Provo, 800-acre Pine Cay is where you'll find the Meridian Club—a retreat for people seeking peaceful seclusion. Its 2½-mi (4-km) beach is among the most beautiful in the archipelago. The island has a 3,800-ft (1,162-m) airstrip and electric golf carts for getting around. Offshore is the **Football Fields** dive site, which has been called the Grand Central Station of the fish world.

Lodging

For approximate costs, *see* the lodging price chart *in* Grand Turk.

$$$$ 　 🏨 **Meridian Club.** Here you can enjoy an unspoiled cay with vast
★ 　 stretches of soft, white sand and a 500-acre nature reserve that lures bird-watchers and botanists. A stay here is truly getting away from it all, as there are no air-conditioners, phones, or TVs. Accommodations are in spacious rooms with king-size beds and patios, as well as cottages that range from rustic to well appointed. Meals and activities are included in the room rate, as is your boat or air-taxi trip from Provo. ⊠ *Pine Cay (456 Glenbrook Rd., Stamford, CT 06906),* ☎ *no direct phone to hotel; 800/331–9154 or 203/602–0300 for reservations only,* 𝔽𝔸𝕏 *649/941–7010 direct to hotel; 203/602–2265 U.S. reservations number,* 𝚆𝙴𝙱 *www.meridianclub.com. 12 rooms, 38 cottages. Restaurant, bar, no air-conditioning, no room phones, fans, no room TVs, tennis court, pool, beach, snorkeling, windsurfing, boating, fishing, bicycles, library, airstrip, no kids under 12. No credit cards. All-inclusive, EP, FAP.*

North Caicos

Thanks to abundant rainfall, this 41-square-mi (106-square-km) island is the lushest of the Turks and Caicos. Bird lovers can see a large flock of flamingos here, and fishermen can find creeks full of bonefish and tarpon. Bring all your own gear; this quiet island has no watersports shops. Although there's no traffic, almost all the roads are paved, so bicycling is an excellent way to sightsee.

Exploring North Caicos

⑤ Flamingo Pond. This is a regular nesting place for the beautiful pink birds. They tend to wander out in the middle of the pond, so bring binoculars.

⑥ Kew. This settlement has a small post office, school, church, and ruins of old plantations—all set among lush tropical trees bearing limes, papayas, and custard apples. Visiting Kew will give you a better understanding of the daily life of many islanders.

Beaches

The beaches of North Caicos are superb for shelling and lolling, and the waters offshore have excellent snorkeling, bonefishing, and scuba diving.

Lodging

For approximate costs, *see* the lodging price chart *in* Grand Turk.

$$$ 🏨 **Prospect of Whitby Hotel.** This secluded, all-inclusive retreat is run
★ by an Italian resort chain, Club Vacanze. Miles of beach are yours for sunbathing, windsurfing, or snorkeling. Spacious rooms have elegant Tuscan floor tiles and pastel pink paneling; in true getaway fashion, rooms lack TVs but include minibars. The restaurant, on a veranda overlooking the sea, is excellent, with a selection of local, Italian, and international dishes served buffet style. Scuba diving and daily excursions to nearby natural wonders are included. ⊠ *Whitby,* ☎ *649/946–7119; 305/235–4780 for reservations only,* FAX *649/946–7114; 305/235–4781 for reservations only,* WEB *www.prospectofwhitby.com. 23 rooms, 4 suites. Restaurant, bar, piano bar, minibars, in-room safes, no room TVs, tennis court, pool, beach, dive shop, snorkeling, windsurfing, boating, fishing, bicycles. AE, MC, V. All-inclusive.*

$-$$ 🏨 **Ocean Beach Hotel Condominiums.** This unpretentious place provides family-style accommodations on a 10-mi (16-km) stretch of sheltered beach. The spacious units, some with kitchenettes, face the ocean and are cooled by the constant tradewinds. You can learn about local plants from the botanical walk encircling the premises. Diving, snorkeling, and exploring trips are arranged through Beach Cruiser Charters, at the hotel. ⊠ *Whitby,* ☎ *649/946–7113 or 800/710–5204; 905/690–3817 in Canada,* FAX *649/946–7386,* WEB *www.turksandcaicos.tc/oceanbeach. 3 rooms, 7 suites. Restaurant, bar, no air-conditioning, fans, some kitchenettes, pool, beach, dive shop, snorkeling, boating, fishing, bicycles, car rental. AE, MC, V. Closed from June to Oct. BP, FAP, MAP.*

$$ 🏨 **Pelican Beach Hotel.** Built and operated by Clifford Gardiner (the Islands' first licensed solo pilot) and his family, this laid-back hotel fronts beautiful expanses of deserted, windswept beach. Large rooms are done in pastels and dark-wood trim; the sound of breaking waves will soothe you in the first-floor beachfront units. Excellent local dishes and homemade bread are served in the airy dining room shaded by a grove of whispering casuarina pines. ⊠ *Whitby,* ☎ *649/946–7112,* FAX *649/946–7139. 14 rooms, 2 suites. Restaurant, bar, no room TVs, beach, fishing. MAP.*

Middle Caicos

At 48 square mi (124 square km) and with fewer than 300 residents, this is the largest and least developed of the inhabited Turks and Caicos. A limestone ridge runs to about 125 ft (38 m) above sea level, creating dramatic cliffs on the north shore and a cave system farther inland. Middle Caicos is best suited to those looking to unwind and who enjoy nature.

Exploring Middle Caicos

7 **Conch Bar Caves.** These limestone caves have eerie underground lakes and milky white stalactites and stalagmites. Archaeologists have discovered Lucayan Indian artifacts in the caves and the surrounding area. It's an easy walk through the main part of the cave, but wear sturdy shoes to avoid slipping. You'll hear, see, and smell some bats, but they don't bother visitors. **J&B Tours** (⊠ Leeward Marina, Leeward, Providenciales, ☎ 649/946–5047, WEB www.jbtours.com) offers boat trips from Provo to the caves.

Lodging

For approximate costs, *see* the lodging price chart *in* Grand Turk.

$$ ⛱ **Blue Horizon Resort.** Breathtaking scenery and sweet seclusion abound in this 50-acre retreat. Cottages (and two villas) come in several different sizes; all have screened-in porches, bleached wood furniture, comfortable beds, and spectacular views of the beachfront cliff, where there's a hillside cave and private ocean swimming cove. Fax a (basic) grocery list ahead of time, and management will stock your refrigerator. Activities by request include spelunking, fishing, and snorkeling with local guides. ⊠ *Mudjin Harbor, Conch Bar,* ☎ *649/946–6141,* FAX *649/946–6139,* WEB *www.bhresort.com. 5 cottages, 2 villas. No air-conditioning in some rooms, no phones in some rooms, fans, some kitchenettes, cable TV with movies in some rooms, no TV in some rooms, beach, snorkeling, fishing, hiking, laundry service. AE, MC, V. EP.*

South Caicos

This 8½-square-mi (21-square-km) island was once an important salt producer; today it's the heart of the fishing industry. Nature prevails, with long, white beaches, jagged bluffs, quiet backwater bays, and salt flats. Diving and snorkeling on the pristine wall and reefs are a treat enjoyed by only a few.

Exploring South Caicos

Spiny lobster and queen conch are found in the shallow Caicos Bank to the west, and are harvested for export by local processing plants. The bonefishing here is some of the best in the West Indies. **Beyond the Blue** (⊠ Cockburn Harbour, ☎ 649/231–1703, WEB www.beyondtheblue.com) offers bonefishing charters on a specialized airboat, which can operate in less than a foot of water. At the northern end of the island are fine white-sand beaches; the south coast is great for scuba diving along the drop-off; and there's excellent snorkeling off the windward (east) coast, where large stands of elkhorn and staghorn coral shelter several varieties of small tropical fish.

8 **Boiling Hole.** Abandoned salinas make up the center of this island—the largest, across from the downtown ball park, receives its water directly from an underground source connected to the ocean through this boiling hole.

9 **Cockburn Harbour.** The best natural harbor in the Caicos chain hosts the South Caicos Regatta, held each year in May.

Beaches

Due south is **Big Ambergris Cay,** an uninhabited cay about 14 mi (23 km) beyond the Fish Cays, with a magnificent beach at Long Bay. To the north, uninhabited **East Caicos** has a beautiful 17-mi (27-km) beach on its north coast. The island was once a cattle range and the site of a major sisal-growing industry. Both these cays are accessible only by boat.

Lodging

For approximate costs, *see* the lodging price chart *in* Grand Turk.

$ ▥ **South Caicos Ocean Haven.** On Cockburn Harbour, a protected marine sanctuary, this hotel operates as the base from which divers can discover a pristine paradise waters minutes from the dock. Comfortable, air-conditioned rooms have ocean and pool or town views; evenings bring spectacular sunsets overlooking the harbor. The restaurant emphasizes local seafood. Instructors on staff offer PADI courses, with economical dive packages available. ⊠ *West St., Cockburn Harbour,* ☎ *649/946–3444,* FAX *649/946–3446,* WEB *www.oceanhaven.tc. 22 rooms. Restaurant, bar, saltwater pool, beach, dive shop, snorkeling, windsurfing, boating, fishing. MC, V. EP, FAP.*

TURKS AND CAICOS A TO Z

To research prices, get advice from other travelers, and book travel arrangements, visit www.fodors.com.

AIR TRAVEL

American Airlines flies three times daily between Miami and Provo, with a fourth flight on Thursdays through Sundays between New York/JFK and Provo. British Airways connects London/Heathrow and Provo on Sundays. Air Canada flies between Toronto and Provo on Saturdays. Bahamasair flies between Nassau and Provo on Tuesdays, Thursdays, and Sundays. Air Jamaica Express travels to Provo from Montego Bay from Friday through Monday. Turks & Caicos Airways, the national flag carrier, offers regularly scheduled flights between Provo, Grand Turk, and the outer Turks and Caicos Islands. SkyKing connects Provo with Grand Turk and South Caicos several times daily and also offers flights to Cuba, the Dominican Republic, and Haiti. Additionally, in season there are weekly charter flights from a number of North American cities, including Boston, Chicago, Detroit, New York, Philadelphia, Montréal, and Toronto.
➤ AIRLINES AND CONTACTS: **Air Canada** (☎ 888/247–2262 or 800/361–8071). **Air Jamaica Express** (☎ 800/523–5585). **American Airlines** (☎ 649/946–4948 in Turks and Caicos; 800/433–7300). **Bahamasair** (☎ 800/222–4262). **British Airways** (☎ 800/247–9297). **SkyKing** (☎ 649/941–5464). **Turks & Caicos Airways** (☎ 649/946–4255).

AIRPORTS

All international flights currently arrive at Providenciales International Airport. Then you use domestic carriers to fly on to airports in Grand Turk and the out islands of North Caicos, Middle Caicos, South Caicos, and Salt Cay. All have paved runways in good condition and small buildings serving as terminals. Grand Turk International Airport serves the nation's capital, bustling in the early morning and late afternoon with government officials and lawyers returning to Provo. Providenciales International Airport has modern, secure arrival and check-in services. You'll find taxis at the airports, and most resorts provide pickup service. A trip between Provo's airport and most major hotels runs about $15. On Grand Turk a trip from the airport to Cockburn Town is about $8; it's $8–$12 to hotels outside town.

➤ Airport Information: **Grand Turk International Airport** (☎ 649/946–2233). **Providenciales International Airport** (☎ 649/941–5670).

BIKE AND MOPED TRAVEL

Although scooters are available for rent, in recent years the option has dwindled in popularity with the deteriorating condition of the roads and increase in auto traffic. If you choose to ride a scooter or bicycle, take extra care around steep shoulder drop-offs. Scooter Bob's in Providenciales rents double seater scooters and bicycles (as well as jeeps, SUVs, vans, and cars). Rates are $40 per day for scooters and $20 per day for bicycles.

Bike and Moped Rentals**Scooter Bob's** (☎ 649/946–4684).

BOAT AND FERRY TRAVEL

Surprisingly, there is no scheduled boat or ferry service between Provo and the other Turks and Caicos Islands. Instead, islanders tend to catch rides leaving from the marina at Leeward-Going-Through. *Sea Dancer* offers live-aboard diving with weekly trips out of Provo. The *Turks and Caicos Aggressor* live-aboard dive boat plies the islands' pristine sites with weekly charters from Turtle Cove Marina.

➤ Boat and Ferry Information: *Sea Dancer* (☎ 800/932–6237). **The *Turks and Caicos Aggressor*** (☎ 800/348–2628).

BUSINESS HOURS

BANKS

Banks are open Monday–Thursday 9:00–3:00, Friday 9:00–5:00.

POST OFFICES

Post offices are open weekdays from 8 to 4.

SHOPS

Shops are generally open weekdays from 8 or 8:30 to 5.

CAR RENTALS

Car and jeep rental rates average $35–$80 per day, plus a $15-per-rental-agreement government tax. Reserve well ahead of time during the peak winter season. Most agencies offer free mileage and airport pick-up service.

➤ Major Agencies: On Grand Turk: **Tony's Car Rental** (☎ 649/946–1879). On Provo: **Avis** (☎ 649/946–4705). **Budget** (☎ 649/946–4079). **Provo Rent-a-Car** (☎ 649/946–4404). **Rent a Buggy** (☎ 649/946–4158). **Tropical Auto Rentals** (☎ 649/946–5300).

CAR TRAVEL

GASOLINE

Because it must be imported, gasoline runs around $3.00 per gallon.

ROAD CONDITIONS

There are paved, two-lane roads connecting the resort areas, airport, and major settlements on Providenciales. However, they're often pocked with potholes and have steep shoulder drop-offs. A major road rehabilitation project is reportedly in the making. Dusty, rutted side roads are in worse condition. Ironically, the little-traveled roads in Grand Turk and the out islands are, in general, smooth and paved.

RULES OF THE ROAD

Driving here is on the left side of the road; when pulling out into traffic, remember to look to your right.

ELECTRICITY

Electricity is fairly stable throughout the islands, and the current is suitable for all U.S. appliances (120/240 volts, 60 Hz).

EMERGENCIES

➤ AMBULANCE AND FIRE: **Ambulance and Fire** (☎ 911).

➤ HOSPITALS: **Associated Medical Practices** (✉ Leeward Hwy., Glass Shack, Providenciales, ☎ 649/946–4242). **Grand Turk Hospital** (✉ Hospital Rd., Grand Turk, ☎ 649/946–2333).

➤ PHARMACIES: **Government Clinic** (✉ Grand Turk Hospital, Grand Turk, ☎ 649/946–2040). **Super Value Pharmacy** (✉ South Winds Plaza, Downtown Providenciales, Providenciales, ☎ 649/941–3779).

➤ POLICE: Police (☎ 649/946–2499 in Grand Turk; 649/946–7116 in North Caicos, 649/946–4259 in Provo; 649/946–3299 in South Caicos).

➤ SCUBA DIVING EMERGENCIES: **Associated Medical Practices** (✉ Leeward Hwy., Glass Shack, Providenciales, ☎ 649/946–4242) has a hyperbaric chamber.

HOLIDAYS

Public holidays are: New Year's Day, Commonwealth Day (second Monday in March), Maundy Thursday, Good Friday, Easter Monday, National Heroes Day (last Monday in May), Queen's Birthday (third Monday in June), Emancipation Day (first Monday in August), National Youth Day (last Monday in September), Columbus Day (second Monday in October), International Human Rights Day (last Monday in October), Christmas Day (Dec. 25), and Boxing Day (Dec. 26).

LANGUAGE

The official language of the Turks and Caicos is English. Native islanders (termed "Belongers") are of African descent, though the population—especially on cosmopolitan Provo—also consists of Canadian, British, American, European, Haitian, and Dominican expats.

MAIL AND SHIPPING

The main branch of the post office is in downtown Provo at the corner of Airport Road. It costs 50¢ to send a postcard to the United States, 60¢ to Canada and the United Kingdom, and $1.25 to Australia and New Zealand; letters, per ounce, cost 60¢ to the United States, 80¢ to Canada and the United Kingdom, and $1.40 to Australia and New Zealand. When writing to the Turks and Caicos Islands, be sure to include the specific island and "Turks and Caicos Islands, BWI" (British West Indies). Delivery service is provided by FedEx, with offices in Provo and Grand Turk.

➤ CONTACTS: **FedEx** on Grand Turk (☎ 649/946–2542); on Provo (☎ 649/946–4682).

MONEY MATTERS

Prices quoted in this chapter are in U.S. dollars. Barclays Bank, Scotiabank, and CIBC have offices on Provo, with branches on Grand Turk. Many larger hotels and the casino can take care of your money requests. Bring small denominations to the less-populated islands.

➤ CONTACTS: **Barclays Bank** (☎ 649/946–4245). **CIBC** (☎ 649/946–5303). **Scotiabank** (☎ 649/946–4750).

ATMS

There are few ATMs on the islands.

CREDIT CARDS

Major credit cards and traveler's checks are accepted at many establishments.

CURRENCY

The unit of currency is the U.S. dollar.

PASSPORTS AND VISAS

U.S. and Canadian citizens need some proof of citizenship, such as a birth certificate (original or certified copy), plus a photo ID or a current passport. All other travelers, including those from the United Kingdom, Australia, and New Zealand, require a current passport. Everyone must have an ongoing or return ticket.

SAFETY

Petty crime does occur here, and you're advised to leave your valuables in the hotel safe-deposit box and lock doors in cars and rooms when unattended. Bring along a can of insect repellent: the mosquitoes and no-see-ums can be vicious after rain.

In some hotels on Grand Turk, Salt Cay, and South Caicos, there are signs that read PLEASE HELP US CONSERVE OUR PRECIOUS WATER. These islands have no water supply other than rainwater collected in cisterns, and rainfall is scant. Drink only from the decanter of fresh water your hotel provides.

SIGHTSEEING TOURS

Whether by taxi, boat, or plane, you should try to voyage beyond the resort grounds and beach to better understand the culture and daily life of the islanders. Global Airways specializes in trips to North Caicos. If you want to island-hop on your own schedule, air charters are available through Inter-Island Airways. Nell's Taxi offers taxi tours of the islands; priced between $25 and $30 for the first hour and $25 for each additional hour. J&B Tours offers sea and land tours, including trips to Middle Caicos, the largest of the islands, for a visit to the caves, or to North Caicos to see flamingos and plantation ruins. Aerial photo safaris are provided by Provo Air Charter.
➤ CONTACTS: **Global Airways** (☎ 649/941–3222). **Inter-Island Airways** (☎ 649/941–5481). **J&B Tours** (☎ 649/946–5047, WEB www.jbtours. com). **Nell's Taxi** (☎ 649/231–0051). **Provo Air Charter** (☎ 649/ 941–0685).

TAXES AND SERVICE CHARGES

DEPARTURE TAX

The departure tax is $23, payable only in cash or traveler's checks.

SALES TAX

Hotels add 10%–15% to your bill for service, and restaurants and hotels add a 10% government tax.

TAXIS

Cabs are now metered, and rates are regulated by the government. In Provo call the Provo Taxi and Bus Group for more information.
➤ CONTACTS: **Provo Taxi and Bus Group** (☎ 649/946–5481).

TELEPHONES

To place credit-card calls, dial 810 (English). Cellular phones can be rented through Cable & Wireless. Internet access is available via hotel room phone connections or Internet kiosks on Provo and Grand Turk. Calls from the islands are expensive, and many hotels add steep surcharges for long-distance. Talk fast.
➤ CONTACTS: **Cable & Wireless** (☎ 649/946–2200, WEB www.tcimall.tc).

AREA CODE

The area code for the Turks and Caicos is 649.

INTERNATIONAL CALLS

To make calls from the Turks and Caicos, dial 0, then 1, the area code, and the number.

LOCAL CALLS
To make local calls, dial the seven-digit number.

TIPPING

At restaurants, tip 15% if service isn't included in the bill. Taxi drivers also expect a token tip, about 10% of your fare.

VISITOR INFORMATION

➤ BEFORE YOU LEAVE: **Turks and Caicos Islands Tourist Board** (☎ 649/946–2321 or 800/241–0824, WEB www.turksandcaicostourism.com); in the U.K. **Morris-Kevan International Ltd.** (✉ Mitre House, 66 Abbey Rd., Bush Hill Park, Enfield, Middlesex EN1 2RQ, ☎ 0181/350–1000).

➤ IN TURKS AND CAICOS ISLANDS: **Government Tourist Office** In Grand Turk: (✉ Front St., Cockburn Town, ☎ 649/946–2321). In Provo: ✉ Stubbs Diamond Plaza, The Bight, ☎ 649/946–4970). **Times Publications** (✉ Caribbean Pl., Box 234, ☎ 649/946–4788, WEB www.timespub.tc).

6 PORTRAITS OF THE BAHAMAS

In the Wake of Columbus:
A Short History of the Bahamas

In Search of Columbus

Cashing In: A Casino Gambling Primer

IN THE WAKE OF COLUMBUS:
A SHORT HISTORY OF THE BAHAMAS

You might call Christopher Columbus the first tourist to hit the Bahamas, although he was actually trying to find a route to the East Indies with his *Niña, Pinta,* and *Santa María.* Columbus is popularly believed to have made his first landfall in the New World on October 12, 1492, at San Salvador, in the southern part of the Bahamas. Researchers of the National Geographic Society, however, have come up with the theory that he may first have set foot ashore Samana Cay, some 60 mi southeast of San Salvador. The Bahamians have taken this new theory under consideration, if not too seriously; tradition dies hard in the islands, and they are hardly likely to tear down the New World landfall monument on San Salvador.

The people who met Columbus on his landing day were Arawak Indians, said to have fled from the Caribbean to the Bahamas to escape the depredations of the murderous Caribs around the turn of the 9th century. The Arawaks were a shy, gentle people who offered Columbus and his men their hospitality. He was impressed with their kindness and more than slightly intrigued by the gold ornaments they wore. But the voracious Spaniards who followed in Columbus's footsteps a few years later repaid the Indians' kindness by forcing them to work in the conquistadors' gold and silver mines in Cuba and Haiti; the Bahamas' indigenous peoples were virtually wiped out in the next 30 years, despite the fact that the Spaniards never settled their land.

In 1513 another well-known seafarer stumbled upon the westernmost Bahamian islands. Juan Ponce de León had been a passenger on Columbus's second voyage, in 1493. He conquered Puerto Rico in 1508 and then began searching thirstily for the Fountain of Youth. He thought he had found it on South Bimini, but he changed his mind and moved on to visit the site of St. Augustine, on the northeast coast of Florida.

In 1629 King Charles I claimed the Bahamas for England, though his edict was not implemented until the arrival of English pilgrims in 1648. Having fled the religious repression and political dissension then rocking their country, they settled on the Bahamian island they christened Eleuthera, the Greek word for freedom. Other English immigrants followed, and in 1656 another group of pilgrims, from Bermuda, took over a Bahamian island to the west and named it New Providence because of their links with Providence, Rhode Island. By the last part of the 17th century, some 1,100 settlers were trying to eke out a living, supplemented by the cargoes they salvaged from Spanish galleons that ran aground on the reefs. Many settlers were inclined to give nature a hand by enticing these ships onto the reefs with lights.

Inevitably, the British settlers were joined by a more nefarious subset of humanity, pirates and buccaneers like Edward Teach (better known as Blackbeard, he was said to have had 14 wives), Henry Morgan, and Calico Jack Rackham. Rackham numbered among his crew two violent, cutlass-wielding female members, Anne Bonney and Mary Read, who are said to have disconcerted enemies by swinging aboard their vessels topless. Bonney and Read escaped hanging in Jamaica by feigning pregnancy.

For some 40 years until 1718, pirates in the Bahamas constantly raided the Spanish galleons that carried booty home from the New World. During this period, the Spanish government, furious at the raids, sent ships and troops to destroy the New Providence city of Charles Town, which was later rebuilt and renamed Nassau, in 1695, in honor of King William III, formerly William of Orange-Nassau.

In 1718 King George I appointed Captain Woodes Rogers the first royal governor of the Bahamas, with orders to clean up the place. Why the king chose Rogers for this particular job is unclear—his thinking may well have been that it takes a pirate to know one, for Woodes Rogers had been a privateer. But he did take control of Nassau, hanging eight pirates from trees on the site of what was to become the British Colonial Hotel. Today, a statue of the former governor stands at the hotel entrance, and the street that runs along the waterfront is named after him. Rogers also inspired the saying *Expulsis piratis, restitua commercia* (Piracy expelled, commerce restored), which remained the country's motto until Prime Minister Lynden O. Pindling replaced it with the more appropriate and optimistic Forward, Upward, Onward Together, on the occasion of independence from Britain in 1973.

Although the Bahamas enjoyed a certain measure of tranquillity, thanks to Rogers and the governors who followed him, the British colonies in America at the same time were seething with a desire for independence. The peace of the islanders' lives was to be shattered during the Revolutionary War by a raid in 1778 on Nassau by the American navy, which purloined the city's arms and ammunition without even firing a shot. Next, in 1782, the Spanish came to occupy the Bahamas until the following year. Under the Treaty of Versailles of 1783, Spain took possession of Florida, and the Bahamas reverted to British rule.

THE BAHAMAS WERE ONCE again overrun, between 1784 and 1789, this time by merchants from New England and plantation owners from Virginia and the Carolinas who had been loyal to the British and were fleeing the wrath of the American revolutionaries. Seeking asylum under the British flag, the Southerners brought their families and slaves with them. Many set up new plantations in the islands, but frustrated by the islands' arid soil, they soon opted for greener pastures in the Caribbean. The slaves they left behind were set free in 1834, but many retained the names of their former masters. That is why you'll find many a Johnson, Saunders, and Thompson in the towns and villages throughout the Bahamas.

The land may have been less than fertile, but New Providence Island's almost perfect climate, marred only by the potential for hurricanes during the fall, attracted other interest. Tourism was foreseen as far back as 1861, when the legislature approved the building of the first hotel, the Royal Victoria. Though it was to reign as the grande dame of the island's hotels for more than a century, its early days saw it involved in an entirely different profit-making venture. During the U.S. Civil War, the North-ern forces blockaded the main Southern ports, and the leaders of the Confederacy turned to Nassau, the closest neutral port to the south. The Royal Victoria became the headquarters of the blockade-running industry, which reaped huge profits for the British colonial government from the duties it imposed on arms supplies. (In October 1990, the Royal Victoria Hotel burned down.)

A similar bonanza, also at the expense of the United States, was to come in the 1920s, after Prohibition was signed into U.S. law in 1919. Booze brought into the Bahamas from Europe was funneled into a thirsty United States by rumrunners operating out of Nassau, Bimini, and West End, the community on Grand Bahama Island east of Palm Beach. Racing against, and often exchanging gunfire with, Coast Guard patrol boats, the rumrunners dropped off their supplies in Miami, the Florida Keys, and other Florida destinations, making their contribution to the era known as the Roaring '20s.

Even then, tourists were beginning to trickle into the Bahamas, many in opulent yachts belonging to the likes of Whitney, Vanderbilt, and Astor. In 1929 a new airline, Pan American, started to make daily flights from Miami to Nassau. The Royal Victoria, shedding its shady past, and two new hotels, the Colonial (now the British Colonial Hilton Nassau) and the Fort Montagu Beach, were all in full operation. Nassau even had instant communication with the outside world: A few miles northwest of the Colonial, a subterranean telegraph cable had been laid linking New Providence with Jupiter, Florida. It took no flash of inspiration to name the area Cable Beach.

One of the most colorful and enigmatic characters of the era, Sir Harry Oakes, came to Nassau in the 1930s from Canada. He built the Bahamas Country Club and the Cable Beach Golf Course; he also built Nassau's first airport in the late '30s to lure the well-heeled and to make commuting easier for the wealthy residents. Oakes Field can still be seen on the ride from Nassau International Airport to Cable Beach.

Oakes was to die in an atmosphere of eerie and mysterious intrigue. Only his good friend, the late Sir Harold Christie, a powerful real-estate tycoon, was in the house at the time that Oakes' body was found, battered and burned. This was a period when all of the news that was fit to print was coming out of the war theaters in Europe and the Far East, but the Miami newspapers and wire services had a field day with the society murder.

Although a gruff, unlikable character, Oakes had no known enemies, but there was speculation that mob hit men from Miami had come over and taken care of him because of his unyielding opposition to the introduction of gambling casinos to the Bahamas. Finally, two detectives brought from Miami pinned the murder on Oakes's son-in-law, Count Alfred de Marigny, for whom the Canadian was known to have a strong dislike. De Marigny was tried and acquitted in an overcrowded Nassau court. Much of the detectives' research and testimony was later discredited. For many years afterward, however, the mysterious and still unsolved crime was a sore point with New Providence residents.

During World War II, New Providence also played host to a noble, if unlikely, couple. In 1936 the Duke of Windsor had forsaken the British throne in favor of "the woman I love," an American divorcée named Wallis Warfield Simpson, and the couple temporarily found a carefree life in Paris and the French Riviera. When the Nazis overran France, they fled to neutral Portugal. Secret papers revealed after the war suggest that the Germans had plans to use the duke and duchess, by kidnapping if necessary, as pawns in the German war against Britain. This would have taken the form of declaring them king and queen in exile, and seating them on the throne when Hitler's assumed victory was accomplished.

Word of the plot might have reached the ears of Britain's wartime prime minister, Winston Churchill, who encouraged King George VI, the duke's younger brother and his successor, to send the couple as far away as possible out of harm's way. In 1939 the duke had briefly returned to England, offering his services to his brother in the war effort. He was given a position of perhaps less import than he had expected, for he and Wallis suddenly found themselves in the Bahamas, with the duke as governor and commander in chief.

CHANGES IN THE Bahamas' political climate had to wait for the war's end. For more than 300 years, the country had been ruled by whites; members of the United Bahamian Party (UBP) were known as the Bay Street Boys, after Nassau's main business thoroughfare, because they controlled the islands' commerce. But the voice of the overwhelmingly black majority was making itself heard. In 1953 a London-educated black barrister named Lynden O. Pindling joined the opposition Progressive Liberal Party (PLP); in 1956 he was elected to Parliament.

Pindling continued to stir the growing resentment most Bahamians now had for the Bay Street Boys, and his parliamentary behavior became more and more defiant. In 1965, during one parliamentary session, he picked up the speaker's mace and threw it out the window. Because this mace has to be present and in sight at all sessions, deliberations had to be suspended; meanwhile, Pindling continued his harangue to an enthusiastic throng in the street below. Two years later, Bahamian voters threw the UBP out, and Pindling led the PLP into power.

Pindling's magnetism kept him in power through independence from Britain in 1973 (though loyalty to the mother country led the Bahamians to choose to remain within the Commonwealth of Nations, recognize Queen Elizabeth II as their sovereign, and retain a governor-general appointed by the queen). For his services to his nation, the prime minister was knighted by the queen in 1983. His deputy prime minister Clement Maynard received the same accolade in 1989.

In August 1992 there came the biggest political upset since Pindling took power in 1967. His Progressive Liberal Party was defeated in a general election by the Free National Movement party, headed by lawyer Hubert Alexander Ingraham. The 45-year-old former chairman of the PLP and Cabinet member under Pindling had been expelled from the party by Pindling in 1986 because of his outspoken comments on alleged corruption inside the government. Ingraham's continued emphasis on this issue during the 1992 campaign did much to lead to Pindling's defeat and Ingraham's taking over as prime minister. Ingraham was reelected for another five-year term in 1996.

Residents, for the most part, are proud of their country and are actively involved in bettering their own lot—the last complete census showed about 27% of the population was attending school at one level or another. And in the spirit of their national motto—Forward, Upward, Onward Together—they graciously welcome the ever-increasing numbers of outsiders who have discovered their little piece of paradise.

— Ian Glass

IN SEARCH OF COLUMBUS

I first heard the singing toward the middle of the night, as the mail boat M.V. *Maxine* plowed southward between Eleuthera and the Exumas. The sound drifted faintly to where I lay doubled up on a bench in the main cabin with my head on a cardboard crate of pears and a copy of the *Bahama Journal* shielding my eyes from a yellow bug light.

It was a two-part chant, almost African in its rhythm. I looked down the dim corridor to the bridge, where the crewman at the wheel was singing softly in harmony with his companion on the midnight-to-four watch. The second man was shuffling back and forth, keeping time. It was a scene out of Conrad, and a reminder that this is still what transportation is like in much of the world: pitching through the waters of a dark archipelago, sleeping with your head on a box of fruit, while guys sing and dance on the bridge.

The *Maxine* was 14 hours out of Potter's Cay, Nassau, the Bahamas, on the 22-hour run to the island of San Salvador. I had long since abandoned my claustrophobic upper bunk in the boat's only passenger compartment and had stayed out on deck until dark, sprawling over a tarp that covered bags of cement, taking shallow breaths to ration the stench of diesel fuel. Finally, half soaked from the waves constantly breaching the port rail, I had retreated to the last remotely habitable place on board—the big common room with its table and benches and its clutter of cargo for the islands. Four dozen eggs, the cartons taped together. An oscillating fan. Gallon jars of mayonnaise, their future owners' names written on the labels. Two galvanized tubs. Homemade sound equipment for the band that plays in the bar on San Salvador. My pillow of pears, consigned to Francita Gardiner of Rum Cay. Bags, boxes, crates—and, secured somehow on the opposite bench, with ears alert and bright, eager eyes, a life-size ceramic German shepherd, soon to be a boon companion to someone in a place where a real German shepherd probably would die of heat prostration. Every time I woke to shift positions during that endless night, I would glance across the cabin, and there

would be the good dog, looking as if he were waiting for a biscuit.

It is altogether possible to fly from Nassau to San Salvador in an hour and a half, but I had cast my lot with the mayonnaise and the galvanized tubs because I wanted to reach the island by water. San Salvador is arguably the most famous landfall in history: In 1992 the New World and the Old celebrated (or lamented, depending on one's politics) the 500th anniversary of the arrival of the *Niña, Pinta,* and *Santa María* at this coral-gilt outcrop. Anticipation of the tourism the quincentennial would inspire is no doubt the reason why the creaking and malodorous *Maxine* was eventually replaced by a new 110-ft mail boat with air-conditioned cabins. Fruit-box pillows are finally going out of style in the Bahamas.

My plan was to retrace, by whatever transportation was available, the route Christopher Columbus followed through Bahamian waters after his landing at San Salvador on October 12, 1492. On the face of it, this seems a simple enough task: The log of the first voyage, lost in the original but substantially transcribed by the near-contemporary chronicler Bartolome de Las Casas, describes the fleet's circuitous route through the archipelago and the series of island landfalls it made. The problem is, the island names given are those that Columbus coined with each new discovery. From San Salvador he sailed to what he called "Santa María de la Concepción," then to "Fernandina," then to "Isabela," then to the southwest and out of the Bahamian archipelago on his way to Cuba. With the exception of San Salvador, which was called Watling Island until 1926, none of these islands bears its Columbus name today. And the distances, directions, and descriptions of terrain given in the surviving version of the log are just ambiguous enough, at crucial junctures, to have inspired nine major theories as to exactly which sequence of island landfalls was followed. Some of the theories are more than a bit tenuous, depending heavily on a blithe disregard of their own weak points and an amplification of everyone else's departures from the log or from common sense. You begin to wonder, after a while, if someone couldn't take the Las Casas translation and use it to prove that Columbus landed on Chincoteague and sailed into the Tidal Basin by way of Annapolis.

But two plausible theories stand out. One, championed by the late historian and Columbus biographer Admiral Samuel Eliot Morison, is based on a first landing at today's San Salvador. The other says the first landing was at Samana Cay, a smaller, uninhabited island on the eastern fringes of the chain. Samana Cay's most recent proponent has been Joseph Judge of the National Geographic Society; in 1986 he published an exhaustive defense of his position, based in part on a computer's estimation of where Columbus should have ended up after the Atlantic crossing. The jury is still out on both major theories, as it is on the less commonly held ones. It probably always will be. For the purposes of my trip, though, I had to choose one version and stick with it. On the basis of my layman's reading of the log, I decided to go with Morison.

In this version, San Salvador is San Salvador, Santa María de la Concepción is today's Rum Cay, Fernandina is Long Island, and Isabela is Crooked Island. This was the sequence I planned to follow as the *Maxine* approached San Salvador's Fernandez Bay at 9 o'clock in the morning.

This island is fairly large and very flat. It is green, with many trees and several bodies of water. There is a very large lagoon in the middle of the island and there are no mountains. It is a pleasure to gaze upon this place because it is all so green, and the weather is delightful. *
— Christopher Columbus's log,
October 13, 1492

We docked at Cockburn Town, the only settlement of any size on San Salvador. Cockburn Town, population several hundred souls, was the type and model of the Bahamian Out Island communities I would see along t he Columbus track over the next few days: three or four streets of cinderblock-and-stucco houses, some brightly painted; a grocery store and a bar—the Harlem Square Club, site of a big dominoes tournament that week; a post office/radiophone station; and a couple of churches. On the facade of the Catholic

church, Holy Savior, there was a peeling relief portrait of Christopher Columbus.

In the late morning heat I walked the half mile of blacktop—scrub brush on one side and ocean views on the other—that separates Cockburn Town from the Riding Rock Inn.

The latter is a handful of cottages, a short block of plain but cheerful motel units, and a restaurant/bar, all right on the water; up at the bar most of the talk you hear has to do with skin diving. Divers are the principal clientele here. When I arrived, the place was securely in the hands of a California club called the Flipperdippers. At the poolside cookout just after I pulled in, the first snippet of conversation I caught was a tyro Flipperdipper asking an old hand if a basket starfish would eat until it exploded. The answer was no, and without waiting around to find out why the questioner suspected such a thing I got up for more rice and crabs. That's when the *maîtresse de barbecue* hove into my path and told me about the dance that night: "If you don't dance, you don't get breakfast."

With the assistance of a Flipperdipper or two, I earned my breakfast. The band was a Cockburn Town outfit of indeterminate numerical strength. Guitarists and conga drummers came and went, and everyone kept commenting that things were really supposed to start jumping when the Kiwanis meeting at the Harlem Square Club let out. Shortly after 10, the band did get a transfusion of new talent, all wearing white cabana shirts patterned with yellow-and-black Kiwanis emblems. They played a couple of good sets, but they did an even better job of exemplifying the phenomenon scholars call the "Columbian Exchange," that cross-pollination of peoples, cultures, flora and fauna, foodstuffs, and microorganisms that followed in the wake of the admiral's fleet and has been transmogrifying the Eastern and Western hemispheres ever since. Here were six descendants of African slaves, wearing the insignia of an American fraternal organization, playing music written by a Jamaican who thought Haile Selassie was God, for a merry throng of skin-diving orthodontists from California on an island discovered by an Italian working for Spain

---

*Excerpted from The Log of Christopher Columbus, by Robert H. Fuson, courtesy of International Marine Publishing, © 1987.

but settled along with the rest of the archipelago by British and American planters who imported the slaves to begin with.

About all that was missing were the Lucayans, the native Bahamians extirpated by the Spaniards—who worked them to death in the mines of Hispaniola—within a generation after Columbus's arrival. It was the Lucayans' island I set off to see the following morning, by motor scooter and on foot.

The people here call this island Guanahani in their language, and their speech is very fluent, although I do not understand any of it. They are friendly and well-dispositioned people who bear no arms except for small spears, and they have no iron. I showed one my sword, and through ignorance he grabbed it by the blade and cut himself.

— October 12

The San Salvador of the Lucayans is but a memory, as they are. When Columbus arrived, there were tall trees on the island, but the planters of the late 18th and early 19th centuries deforested the place so that now virtually the only vegetation is the dense, stickery brush called "haulback." The island's interior, though, still conveys the same sense of impenetrability and desolation that it must have to the first Europeans who came here, and no doubt to the Lucayans themselves. Fishermen as well as cultivators must have stayed close to shore, except to travel from one end of San Salvador to the other by dugout canoe across a system of brackish lakes that covers nearly half of the interior. From a crude concrete-and-wood observation platform on a rise near the airport, you can take in the sprawl of these lakes and the lonely, thicketed hills (the terrain isn't all as flat as Columbus described it) that break them into crazy patterns. No one lives there; it's hard to imagine that anyone ever goes there.

I drove the scooter the length of the island's circuit road, past crescent beaches with white sand so fine it coats your feet like flour, past ruined plantation buildings, past "Ed's First and Last Bar," a homey little joint out in the sticks that would be beerless until the cases made it up from the mail boat dock, past four monuments to Columbus's landing at four different places (a fifth

marker is underwater, where somebody decided his anchor hit bottom), and past the Dixon Hill Lighthouse ("Imperial Lighthouse Service"), billed as one of 10 left in the world that run on kerosene. Past, and then back again—I bullied the scooter up Dixon Hill, because you don't get to climb to the top of a lighthouse every day.

I went looking for the light keeper, but instead I found my ride to Rum Cay, according to Morison the second of Columbus's landfalls on his first voyage. It was a family of blue-water sailors—an American named Kent, his German wife, Britta, and their two-month-old baby, Luke, who had cruised to San Salvador from St. Thomas in their 32-foot sailboat. Having hitchhiked up from Cockburn Town, the baby in a shaded basket, they too were waiting for the light keeper to show up; after she did, and took us to the top, the sailing couple offered to let me hitch with them the next day on the 30-mile run to Rum Cay. I soon learned I would be in good hands: Later that day, Kent asked a local if he knew anything about Rum Cay.

"What do you want to know?" the man responded.

"What's the anchorage like in a southeast wind?"

I'd have asked where to eat, or if the Kiwanis had a band.

I made sail and saw so many islands that I could not decide where to go first . . . Finally, I looked for the largest island and decided to go there.

— October 14

Christopher Columbus left San Salvador on October 11, 1492, and later that day arrived at the island he named Santa María de la Concepción. My adopted family and I weighed anchor at Cockburn Town and sailed out of Fernandez Bay early in the morning of a bright June day, flying fish scudding around our bows and cottony trade clouds riding briskly above. Luke, already a veteran mariner, slept in his basket below. We sighted Rum Cay when we were 10 miles out from San Salvador— Columbus had a much higher mast to climb—but the distant shoreline was to loom for a long time before we could draw very close to it. The east shore and much of the south shore of Rum Cay are girded with lethal reefs, and both the charts and the *Yachtsman's Guide to the Bahamas* go to great pains to point out so precise a route to the anchorage that it might as well have been the directions to a parking space in George Town. Six other boats had negotiated the coral gauntlet that day, including one whose captain gave us half of a blackfin tuna he'd just caught. How Columbus safely pulled it off (his anchorage was at a point west of ours) is beyond imagining.

Rum Cay, which once made a living selling sea salt to Nova Scotia's cod packers, has shriveled in population until barely 60 people today inhabit its sole settlement of Port Nelson. An American, David Melville, opened a small skin-diving resort called the Rum Cay Club a mile from town a few years back: When I arrived, the place was closed for renovations. There were no Flipperdippers here—just Melville, a couple of handymen, and the locals down the road. Rum Cay was, for the moment, almost out of things to do and people to do them.

Almost, but not quite. There's always Kay's Bar, where proprietor Dolores Wilson turns out lovely baked chicken and coconut bread to wash down with the Out Islands' requisite gallons of beer and rum in an atmosphere dominated by a satellite TV, an antique space-age jukebox, turtle shells with colored lightbulbs in them, and a giant poster of Bob Marley wearing a beatific grin and knitted hat that looks like a Rasta halo. People who sailed to the Bahamas years ago have told me that Dolores was once something of a hellraiser, but she seems to have settled into sweet grandmotherliness by now. For ethyl-powered amusement, I had to rely on an expatriate Oklahoman named Billy. Billy, whose personal style ran to the pirate-biker look, was Melville's mechanical factotum at the Rum Cay Club. His avocation, as I discovered when I took a Jeep ride with him to the other side of the island, is nonstop talking. In the space of an hour, Billy went chapter and verse on everything from his archery prowess in Oklahoma, to how he could build an ammonia-powered icehouse like the one in *The Mosquito Coast,* to his deepest feelings about the universe: "You know, I like everything and I hate everything."

"That's called having a lover's quarrel with the world," I told him, remembering Frost.

"Oh, they have a name for it now?"

I decided not to linger very long at Santa María de la Concepción, for I saw that there was no gold there and the wind freshened to a SE crosswind. I departed the island for the ship after a two hours' stay.

— October 16

It was Billy who drove me to catch a plane to Long Island—Columbus's Fernandina, his third landfall—on the following afternoon. Back on San Salvador, I'd been told that the ticket to getting off Rum Cay without waiting for the next mail boat was to "ask for Bobby with the plane." But there was no plane on the island's crushed-coral landing strip. Bobby had flown somewhere, so rather than spend another night I asked Melville to radio the Stella Maris Inn on Long Island for a plane. They sent a Cessna four-seater, which landed just as Billy was pouring me a rum-and-powdered-lemonade at his house—he insisted on this hospitable stopover, since it was a whole mile between Kay's Bar and the airstrip. Besides, his own much-loved blue plastic cup was empty.

Long Island: a day's sail from Rum Cay for the *Niña, Pinta,* and *Santa María* on October 17, 1492; 15 minutes in the Cessna. As we approached the landing strip, I looked down to see territory that looked almost like a manicured suburb compared with the trackless scrub forests of Rum Cay and San Salvador. Here were roads, trees, villas, broad beaches, swimming pools . . . in short, a modest but complete resort, and run by Germans to boot. This last fact is worthy of remark because of the concept known as "Bahamian time," best defined as a devil-may-care approach to the minute hand. Somehow, the Germans and Bahamians had arrived at a compromise: The shuttle to the beach leaves more or less on time, but you don't have to eat breakfast at 7:23 AM.

I wanted to follow Columbus up and down this island. Near its northern tip is a shallow cove outside of which he anchored while several of his men went ashore for water. If local legend can be trusted, they filled their casks at a deep natural well in the coral rock, which a Stella Maris driver showed me. He had drawn water there as a small boy, just 450 years after the Spanish expedition.

A couple of miles from the well was the cove, a harbor with "two entrances," according to the 1492 log, which the admiral sounded in his ships' boats. At least it seemed to me to be the place, and "Where Was Columbus?" is a game that anyone with a copy of the log can play. I explored the cove and, while snorkeling, was reminded of the entry for October 17: "Here the fishes are so unlike ours that it is amazing."

To reach Columbus's final Long Island anchorage, at a place called Little Harbour in a village with the pretty name of Roses, was not such an easy job. I rented a VW bug and drove south for nearly 80 miles to the tip of this 2-mile-wide island. The road passed through one little town after another, each with its neat cinder-block school and tiny Protestant church. At Roses I found a storekeeper who knew the road to Little Harbour. It ended at a dump a mile into the bush. I walked nearly another mile—had I been heading due east I would have been in the water. I wasn't going to find Little Harbour, not in this pounding sun on a trail narrowing to the width of an iguana, any more than Columbus was going to find Japan.

Columbus got farther than I did, though. He wandered southeast from Long Island to Crooked Island, then southwest to the southernmost of the Ragged Islands, where the tiny outpost called Duncan Town now stands. This was his last Bahamas anchorage before he sailed off to Cuba, Hispaniola, and immortality.

The odd thing is, Columbus had an easier time pressing ahead than I would have had. Although it's true that he was not only lost in the Caribbean but stuck in the 15th century, at least his fleet was self-contained, and one island was as good as another. For me, the Cessnas were too expensive, the mail boats too infrequent, the lodgings from Long Island south, on Crooked Island and at Duncan Town, nonexistent. These places are as far away as they ever were. They are, in fact, parts of the New World that haven't really been discovered yet.

— William G. Scheller

A resident of Newbury, Massachusetts, William G. Scheller contributes travel pieces regularly to *National Geographic*, *Condé Nast Traveler*, and the *Washington Post Magazine*.

CASHING IN:
A CASINO GAMBLING PRIMER

For a short-form handbook on the rules, the plays, the odds, and the strategies for the most popular casino games—or to decide on the kind of action that's for you and suits your style—read on. You must be 18 to gamble; Bahamians and permanent residents are not permitted to indulge.

The Good Bets

The first part of any viable casino strategy is to risk the most money on wagers that present the lowest edge for the house. Blackjack, craps, video poker, and baccarat are the most advantageous to the bettor in this regard. The two types of bets at baccarat have a house advantage of a little more than 1%. The basic line bets at craps, if backed up with full odds, can be as low as ½%. Blackjack and video poker, at times, can not only put you even with the house (a true 50–50 proposition), but actually give you a slight long-term advantage.

How can a casino possibly provide you with a 50–50 or even a positive expectation at some of its games? First, because a vast number of suckers make the bad bets (those with a house advantage of 5%–35%, such as roulette, keno, and slots) day in and day out. Second, because the casino knows that very few people are aware of the opportunities to beat the odds. Third, because it takes skill—requiring study and practice—to be in a position to exploit these opportunities the casino presents. However, a mere hour or two spent learning strategies for the beatable games will put you light years ahead of the vast majority of visitors who give the gambling industry an average 12% to 15% profit margin.

Baccarat

The most "glamorous" game in the casino, baccarat (pronounced *bah*-kuh-rah) is a version of *chemin de fer,* popular in European gambling halls, and is a favorite with high rollers, because thousands of dollars are often staked on one hand. The Italian word *baccara* means "zero"; this refers to the point value of 10s and picture cards. The game is run by four pit personnel. Two dealers sit side by side in the middle of the table; they handle the winning and losing bets and keep track of each player's "commission" (explained below). The "caller" stands in the middle of the other side of the table and dictates the action. The ladderman supervises the game and acts as final judge if any disputes arise.

HOW TO PLAY

Baccarat is played with eight decks of cards dealt from a large "shoe" (or cardholder). Each player is offered a turn at handling the shoe and dealing the cards. Two two-card hands are dealt, the "player" and the "bank" hands. The player who deals the cards is called the banker, though the house, of course, banks both hands. The players bet on which hand, player or banker, will come closest to adding up to 9 (a "natural"). The cards are totaled as follows: ace through 9 retain face value, while 10s and picture cards are worth zero. If you have a hand adding up to more than 10, the number 10 is subtracted from the total. For example, if one hand contains a 10 and a 4, the hand adds up to 4. If the other holds an ace and 6, it adds up to 7. If a hand has a 7 and 9, it adds up to 6.

Depending on the two hands, the caller either declares a winner and loser (if either hand actually adds up to 8 or 9), or calls for another card for the player hand (if it totals 1, 2, 3, 4, 5, or 10). The bank hand then either stands pat or draws a card, determined by a complex series of rules depending on what the player's total is and dictated by the caller. When one or the other hand is declared a winner, the dealers go into action to pay off the winning wagers, collect the losing wagers, and add up the commission (usually 5%) that the house collects on the bank hand. Both bets have a house advantage of slightly more than 1%.

The player-dealer (or banker) continues to hold the shoe as long as the bank hand wins. As soon as the player hand wins, the shoe moves counterclockwise around the table. Players are not required to deal; they can refuse the shoe and pass it to the next player. Because the caller dictates the action, the player responsibilities are minimal. It's not necessary to know any of the card-drawing rules, even if you're the banker.

BACCARAT STRATEGY

Making a bet at baccarat is very simple. All you have to do is place your money in either the bank, player, or tie box on the layout, which appears directly in front of where you sit at the table. If you're betting that the bank hand will win, you put your chips in the bank box; bets for the player hand go in the player box. (Only real suckers bet on the tie.) Most players bet on the bank hand when they deal, since they "represent" the bank, and to do otherwise would seem as if they were betting "against" themselves. This isn't really true, but it seems that way. In the end, playing baccarat is a simple matter of guessing whether the player or banker hand will come closest to 9, and deciding how much to bet on the outcome.

Blackjack
HOW TO PLAY

Basically, here's how it works: You play blackjack against a dealer, and whichever of you comes closest to a card total of 21 is the winner. Number cards are worth their face value, picture cards are worth 10, and aces are worth either 1 or 11. (Hands with aces in them are known as "soft" hands. Always count the ace first as an 11; if you also have a 10, your total will be 21, not 11.) If the dealer has a 17 and you have a 16, you lose. If you have an 18 against a dealer's 17, you win (even money). If both you and the dealer have a 17, it's a tie (or "push") and no money changes hands. If you go over a total of 21 (or "bust"), you lose immediately, even if the dealer also busts later in the hand. If your first two cards add up to 21 (a "natural"), you're paid 3 to 2. However, if the dealer also has a natural, it's a push. A natural beats a total of 21 achieved with more than two cards.

You're dealt two cards, either face down or face up, depending on the custom of the particular casino. The dealer also gives herself two cards, one face down and one face up (except in double-exposure blackjack, where both the dealer's cards are visible). Depending on your first two cards and the dealer's up card, you can **stand,** or refuse to take another card. You can **hit,** or take as many cards as you need until you stand or bust. You can **double down,** or double your bet and take one card.

You can **split** a like pair; if you're dealt two 8s, for example, you can double your bet and play the 8s as if they're two hands. You can **buy insurance** if the dealer is showing an ace. Here you're wagering half your initial bet that the dealer *does* have a natural; if so, you lose your initial bet, but are paid 2 to 1 on the insurance (which means the whole thing is a push). You can **surrender** half your initial bet if you're holding a bad hand (known as a "stiff") such as a 15 or 16 against a high-up card like a 9 or 10.

BLACKJACK STRATEGY

Playing blackjack is not only knowing the rules—it's also knowing *how* to play. Many people devote a great deal of time to learning complicated statistical schemes. However, if you don't have the time, energy, or inclination to get that seriously involved, the following basic strategies, which cover more than half the situations you'll face, should allow you to play the game with a modicum of skill and a paucity of humiliation:

- When your hand is a stiff (a total of 12, 13, 14, 15, or 16) and the dealer shows a 2, 3, 4, 5, or 6, always stand.

- When your hand is a stiff and the dealer shows a 7, 8, 9, 10, or ace, always hit.

- When you hold 17, 18, 19, or 20, always stand.

- When you hold a 10 or 11 and the dealer shows a 2, 3, 4, 5, 6, 7, 8, or 9, always double down.

- When you hold a pair of aces or a pair of 8s, always split.

- Never buy insurance.

Craps

Craps is a dice game played at a large rectangular table with rounded corners. Up to 12 players can crowd around the table, all standing. The layout is mounted at the bottom of a surrounding "rail," which prevents the dice from being thrown off the table and provides an opposite wall against which to bounce the dice. It can require up to four pit personnel to run an action-packed, fast-paced game of craps. Two dealers handle the bets made on either side of the layout. A "stickman" wields the long wooden "stick," curved at one end, which is used to move the dice around the table; the stickman also calls the number that's rolled and books the proposition bets made in the middle of the layout. The "boxman" sits between the two dealers and oversees the game; he settles any disputes about rules, payoffs, mistakes, and so on.

HOW TO PLAY

To play, just stand at the table wherever you can find an open space. You can start betting casino chips immediately, but you have to wait your turn to be the shooter. The dice move around the table in a clockwise fashion: The person to your right shoots before you, the one to the left after (the stickman will give you the dice at the appropriate time). It's important, when you're the "shooter," to roll the dice hard enough so they bounce off the end wall of the table; this ensures a random bounce and shows that you're not trying to control the dice with a "soft roll."

CRAPS STRATEGY

Playing craps is fairly straightforward; it's the betting that's complicated. The basic concepts are as follows: If, the first time the shooter rolls the dice, he or she turns up a 7 or 11, that's called a "natural"— an automatic win. If a 2, 3, or 12 comes up on the first throw (called the "come-out roll"), that's termed "craps"—an automatic lose. Each of the numbers 4, 5, 6, 8, 9, or 10 on a first roll is known as a "point": The shooter keeps rolling the dice until the point comes up again. If a 7 turns up before the point does, that's another loser. When either the point or a losing 7 is rolled, this is known as a "decision," which happens on average every 3.3 rolls.

But "winning" and "losing" rolls of the dice are entirely relative in this game, because there are two ways you can bet at craps: "for" the shooter or "against" the shooter. Betting for means that the shooter will "make his point" (win). Betting against means that the shooter will "seven out" (lose). (Either way, you're actually betting against the house, which books all wagers.) If you're betting "for" on the come-out, you'd place your chips on the layout's "pass line." If a 7 or 11 is rolled, you win even money. If a 2, 3, or 12 (craps) is rolled, you lose your bet. If you're betting "against" on the come-out, you place your chips in the "don't pass bar." A 7 or 11 loses, a 2, 3, or 12 wins. A shooter can bet for or against himself or herself, as well as for or against the other players.

There are also roughly two dozen wagers you can make on any single specific roll of the dice. Craps strategy books can give you the details on Come/Don't Come, Odds, Place, Buy, Big Six, Field, and Proposition bets.

Roulette

Roulette is a casino game that utilizes a perfectly balanced wheel with 38 numbers (0, 00, and 1 through 36), a small white ball, a large layout with 11 different betting options, and special "wheel chips." The layout organizes 11 different bets into six "inside bets" (the single numbers, or those closest to the dealer) and five "outside bets" (the grouped bets, or those closest to the players).

The dealer spins the wheel clockwise and the ball counterclockwise. When the ball slows, the dealer announces, "No more bets." The ball drops from the "back track" to the "bottom track," caroming off built-in brass barriers and bouncing in and out of the different cups in the wheel before settling into the cup of the winning number. Then the dealer places a marker on the number and scoops all the losing chips into her corner. Depending on how crowded the game is, the casino can count on roughly 50 spins of the wheel per hour.

HOW TO PLAY

To buy in, place your cash on the layout near the wheel. Inform the dealer of the denomination of the individual unit you intend to play (usually 25¢ or $1, but it can go up as high as $500). Know the table limits (displayed on a sign in the dealer area)—don't ask for a 25¢ denomination if the minimum is $1. The dealer gives you a stack of wheel chips of a different color from those of all the other players, and places a chip marker atop one of your wheel chips on the rim of the wheel to identify its denomination. Note that you must cash in your wheel chips at the roulette table before you leave the game. Only the dealer can verify how much they're worth.

ROULETTE STRATEGY

With **inside bets,** you can lay any number of chips (depending on the table limits) on a single number, 1 through 36 or 0 or 00. If the number hits, your payoff is 35 to 1, for a return of $36. You could, conceivably, place a $1 chip on all 38 numbers, but the return of $36 would leave you $2 short, which divides out to 5.26%, the house advantage. If you place a chip on the line between two numbers and one of those numbers hits, you're paid 17 to 1 for a return of $18 (again, $2 short of the true odds). Betting on three numbers returns 11 to 1, four numbers returns 8 to 1, five numbers pays 6 to 1 (this is the worst bet at roulette, with a 7.89% disadvantage), and six numbers pays 5 to 1.

To place an **outside bet,** lay a chip on one of three "columns" at the lower end of the layout next to numbers 34, 35, and 36; this pays 2 to 1. A bet placed in the first 12, second 12, or third 12 boxes also pays 2 to 1. A bet on red or black, odd or even, and 1 through 18 or 19 through 36 pays off at even money, 1 to 1. If you think you can bet on red *and* black, or odd *and* even, in order to play roulette and drink for free all night, think again. The green 0 or 00, which fall outside these two basic categories, will come up on average once every 19 spins of the wheel.

Slot Machines

Around the turn of the century, Charlie Fey built the first mechanical slot in his San Francisco basement. Slot-machine technology has exploded in the past 20 years, and now there are hundreds of different models, which accept everything from pennies to specially minted $500 tokens. The major advance in the game, however, is the progressive jackpot. Banks of slots within a particular casino are connected by computer, and the jackpot total is displayed on a digital meter above the machines. Generally, the total increases by 5% of the wager. If you're playing a dollar machine, each time you pull the handle (or press the spin button), a nickel is added to the jackpot.

HOW TO PLAY

To play, insert your penny, nickel, quarter, silver dollar, or dollar token into the slot at the far right edge of the machine. Pull the handle or press the spin button, then wait for the reels to spin and stop one by one, and for the machine to determine whether you're a winner (occasionally) or a loser (the rest of the time). It's pretty simple—but because there are so many different types of machines nowadays, be sure you know exactly how the one you're playing operates.

SLOT-MACHINE STRATEGY

The house advantage on slots varies widely from machine to machine, between 3% and 25%. Casinos that advertise a 97% payback are telling you that at least one of their slot machines has a house advantage of 3%. Which one? There's really no way of knowing. Generally, $1 machines pay back at a higher percentage than quarter or nickel machines. On the other hand, machines with smaller jackpots pay back more money more frequently, meaning that you'll be playing with more of your winnings.

One of the all-time great myths about slot machines is that they're "due" for a jackpot. Slots, like roulette, craps, keno, and Big Six, are subject to the Law of Independent Trials, which means the odds are permanently and unalterably fixed. If the odds of lining up three sevens on a 25¢ slot machine have been set by the casino at 1 in 10,000, then those odds remain 1 in 10,000 whether the three 7s have been hit three times in a row or not hit for 90,000 plays. Don't waste a lot of time playing a machine that you suspect is "ready," and don't think if someone hits a jackpot on a particular machine only minutes after you've finished playing on it that it was "yours."

Video Poker

Like blackjack, video poker is a game of strategy and skill, and at select times on select machines, the player actually holds the advantage, however slight, over the house. Unlike slot machines, you can determine the exact edge of video poker machines. Like slots, however, video poker machines are often tied into a progressive meter; when the jackpot total reaches high enough, you can beat the casino at its own game. The variety of video poker machines is already large, and it's growing steadily larger. All of the different machines are played in similar fashion, but the strategies are different. This section deals only with straight-draw video poker.

HOW TO PLAY

The schedule for the payback on winning hands is posted on the machine, usually above the screen. It lists the returns for a high pair (generally jacks or better), two pair, three of a kind, a flush, full house, straight flush, four of a kind, and royal flush, depending on the number of coins played—

usually 1, 2, 3, 4, or 5. Look for machines that pay with a single coin played: one coin for "jacks or better" (meaning a pair of jacks, queens, kings, or aces; any other pair is a stiff), two coins for two pairs, three for three of a kind, six for a flush, nine for a full house, 50 for a straight flush, 100 for four of a kind, and 250 for a royal flush. This is known as a 9/6 machine—one that gives a nine-coin payback for the full house and a six-coin payback for the flush with one coin played. Other machines are known as 8/5 (8 for the full house, 5 for the flush), 7/5, and 6/5.

You want a 9/6 machine because it gives you the best odds: The return from a standard 9/6 straight-draw machine is 99.5%; you give up only a half percent to the house. An 8/5 machine returns 97.3%. On 6/5 machines, the figure drops to 95.1%, slightly less than roulette. Machines with varying paybacks are scattered throughout the casinos. In some you'll see an 8/5 machine right next to a 9/6, and someone will be blithely playing the 8/5 machine!

As with slot machines, it's always optimum to play the maximum number of coins to qualify for the jackpot. You insert five coins into the slot and press the "deal" button. Five cards appear on the screen— say, 5, J, Q, 5, 9. To hold the pair of 5s, you press the hold buttons under the first and fourth cards. The word "hold" appears underneath the two 5s. You then press the "draw" button (often the same button as "deal") and three new cards appear on the screen—say, 10, J, 5. You have three 5s; with five coins bet, the machine will give you 15 credits. Now you can press the "max bet" button: five units will be removed from your number of credits,

and five new cards will appear on the screen. You repeat the hold and draw process; if you hit a winning hand, the proper payback will be added to your credits. Those who want coins rather than credit can hit the "cash out" button at any time. Some machines don't have credit counters and automatically dispense coins for a winning hand.

VIDEO-POKER STRATEGY

Like blackjack, video poker has a basic strategy that's been formulated by the computer simulation of hundreds of millions of hands. The most effective way to learn it is with a video poker computer program that deals the cards on your screen, then tutors you in how to play each hand properly. If you don't want to devote that much time to the study of video poker, memorizing these six rules will help you make the right decision for more than half the hands you'll be dealt:

- If you're dealt a completely "stiff" hand (no like cards and no picture cards), draw five new cards.

- If you're dealt a hand with no like cards but with one jack, queen, king, or ace, always hold on to the picture card; if you're dealt two different picture cards, hold both. But if you're dealt three different picture cards, only hold two (the two of the same suit, if that's an option).

- If you're dealt a pair, always hold it, no matter what the face value.

- Never hold a picture card with a pair of 2s through 10s.

- Never draw two cards to try for a straight or a flush.

- Never draw one card to try for an inside straight.

INDEX

Icons and Symbols

★ Our special recommendations

✕ Restaurant

⌂ Lodging establishment

✕⌂ Lodging establishment whose restaurant warrants a special trip

🐤 Good for kids (rubber duck)

☞ Sends you to another section of the guide for more information

✉ Address

☎ Telephone number

🕐 Opening and closing times

💰 Admission prices

Numbers in white and black circles ③ ❸ that appear on the maps, in the margins, and within the tours correspond to one another.

A

Abaco Beach Resort & Boat Harbour ✕⌂, 13, 100–101
Abaco Inn ⌂, 105
Abacos, 6, 97–118
 business hours, 117
 emergencies, 117
 nightlife, 112
 restaurants and lodging, 100–101, 104–105, 107–109, 111–112, 114
 shopping, 106, 107, 110, 113
 sightseeing tours, 118
 sports and outdoor activities, 101–102, 105–106, 107, 109–110, 112–113, 114, 116
 transportation, 114–115, 117–118
 visitor information, 118
Acklins Island, 7, 138–140. ☞ Also Crooked and Acklins Islands
Adderley's Plantation, 169
Addresses, x
Adelaide Beach, 28
Adelaide Village, 25, 27
Air travel, x–xii
 Abacos, 114–115
 Andros, 124–125
 Berry Islands, 127
 Biminis, 132–133
 Cat Island, 138
 with children, xv
 Crooked and Acklins Islands, 140

Eleuthera, 153
 Exumas, 163
 Grand Bahama Island, 89–90
 Inagua, 167–168
 Long Island, 173
 luggage, xxix
 New Providence Island, 54–55
 San Salvador, 176–177
 Turks and Caicos Islands, 199–200
Airports and transfers, xii
 Abacos, 115
 Andros, 124–125
 Cat Island, 138
 Eleuthera, 153
 Exumas, 164
 Grand Bahama Island, 90
 Inagua, 168
 Long Island, 173
 New Providence Island, 55
 San Salvador, 177
 Turks and Caicos Islands, 199–200
Albert Lowe Museum, 110
Alice Town, 129–132
Allen's Cays, 162
Allegro Resort and Casino Turks & Caicos ⌂, 192
Amusement parks, 83
Anacaona ✕, 188–189
Andros, 118–126
 business hours, 135
 emergencies, 135
 restaurants and lodging, 119, 121, 123, 124
 sports and outdoor activities, 121, 122, 123, 124
 transportation, 124–125, 126
Andros Barrier Reef, 119, 121
Andros Island Bonefishing Club ✕⌂, 121
Andros Lighthouse Yacht Club and Marina ✕⌂, 121
Andros Town, 119–121
Androsia Steak & Seafood Restaurant ✕, 35
Androsia Batik Works Factory, 119
Anthony's Caribbean Grill ✕, 33
Apartment and villa rentals, xxiv–xxv, 167, 190. ☞ Also Lodging
Arawak Cay, 27
Arawak Dining Room ✕, 13, 74
Arawak Inn and Beach Club ⌂, 184–185
Arches of Grand Turk ⌂, 184
Ardastra Gardens and Conservation Centre, 27
Arthur's Bakery and Cafe ✕, 148–149

Arthur's Town, 134
Arts. ☞ See Nightlife and the arts
Athena Café ✕, 33
Atlantis (rock formation), 132
Atlantis, Paradise Island ✕⌂, 23–24, 40
ATMs, xxvii, 201
Australian travelers
 customs and duties, xvii
 passports, xxix
Avery's Restaurant and Bar ✕, 27

B

Bacardi Distillery, 27
Baci Ristoranté ✕, 189
Back of Beyond ⌂, 192–193
Bahama House Inn ⌂, 14, 151
Bahama Houseboats ⌂, 160
Bahama Mama Cruises (nightclub), 82–83
Bahamas Historical Society Museum, 20
Bahamas National Trust, 167
Bahamas National Trust Rand Nature Centre, 65
Bahamas National Trust Sanctuary, 100
Bahamian Club ✕, 34
Bahamian Field Station, 176
Bailey Town, 132
Balcony House, 20
Balfour Town, 186
Banana Boat ✕, 189
Banana boating, 47
Bannerman Town, 141, 143
Banyan Beach Club ⌂, 109
Barbary Beach, 70
Barbie's Ice Cream Restaurant and Bar ✕, 169
Barge Wreck, 122
Bay View Village ⌂, 41
Beaches, 8, 12
 Grand Bahama Island, 70
 Gregory Town, 146
 New Providence Island, 24, 28
 Turks and Caicos Islands, 181, 184, 186, 188, 197, 199
Beaches Turquoise Resort & Spa ⌂, 190–191
Becky's Restaurant & Lounge ✕, 71
Bennett's Harbour, 134
Berry Islands, 7, 126–127
 emergencies, 127
 restaurants and lodging, 126–127
 sports and outdoor activities, 126, 127
 transportation, 127
Best Western Castaways ⌂, 79

NOTES

NOTES

NOTES

NOTES

NOTES

NOTES

NOTES

Fodor's Key to the Guides

America's guidebook leader publishes guides for every kind of traveler. Check out our many series and find your perfect match.

Fodor's Gold Guides
America's favorite travel-guide series offers the most detailed insider reviews of hotels, restaurants, and attractions in all price ranges, plus great background information, smart tips, and useful maps.

Fodor's Road Guide USA
Big guides for a big country—the most comprehensive guides to America's roads, packed with places to stay, eat, and play across the U.S.A. Just right for road warriors, family vacationers, and cross-country trekkers.

COMPASS AMERICAN GUIDES
Stunning guides from top local writers and photographers, with gorgeous photos, literary excerpts, and colorful anecdotes. A must-have for culture mavens, history buffs, and new residents.

Fodor's CITYPACKS
Concise city coverage with a foldout map. The right choice for urban travelers who want everything under one cover.

Fodor's EXPLORING GUIDES
Hundreds of color photos bring your destination to life. Lively stories lend insight into the culture, history, and people.

Fodor's POCKET GUIDES
For travelers who need only the essentials. The best of Fodor's in pocket-size packages for just $9.95.

Fodor's To Go
Credit-card–size, magnetized color microguides that fit in the palm of your hand—perfect for "stealth" travelers or as gifts.

Fodor's FLASHMAPS
Every resident's map guide. 60 easy-to-follow maps of public transit, parks, museums, zip codes, and more.

Fodor's CITYGUIDES
Sourcebooks for living in the city: Thousands of in-the-know listings for restaurants, shops, sports, nightlife, and other city resources.

Fodor's AROUND THE CITY WITH KIDS
68 great ideas for family days, recommended by resident parents. Perfect for exploring in your own backyard or on the road.

Fodor's ESCAPES
Fill your trip with once-in-a-lifetime experiences, from ballooning in Chianti to overnighting in the Moroccan desert. These full-color dream books point the way.

Fodor's FYI
Get tips from the pros on planning the perfect trip. Learn how to pack, fly hassle-free, plan a honeymoon or cruise, stay healthy on the road, and travel with your baby.

Fodor's Languages for Travelers
Practice the local language before hitting the road. Available in phrase books, cassette sets, and CD sets.

Karen Brown's Guides
Engaging guides to the most charming inns and B&Bs in the U.S.A. and Europe, with easy-to-follow inn-to-inn itineraries.

Baedeker's Guides
Comprehensive guides, trusted since 1829, packed with A–Z reviews and star ratings.

At bookstores everywhere.   www.fodors.com/books